**Around Unter
den Linden**
See pp56–71

North of the Centre
See pp100–115

East of the Centre
See pp88–99

North of the
Centre

East of the
Centre

Tiergarten

Around Unter
den Linden

Museum
Island

Kreuzberg

Kreuzberg
See pp140–149

Museum Island
See pp72–87

EYEWITNESS TRAVEL

BERLIN

EYEWITNESS TRAVEL

BERLIN

Main Contributor **Małgorzata Omilanowska**

LONDON, NEW YORK,
MELBOURNE, MUNICH AND DELHI
www.dk.com

Produced by Wydawnictwo Wiedza i Życie, Warsaw

Managing Editor Ewa Szwagrzyk
Series Editor Joanna Egert
DTP Designer Pawel Pasternak
Consultant Nils Meyer
Illustrations Andrzej Wielgosz,
Lena Maminajszwili, Dorota Jarymowicz
Photography Dorota and Mariusz Jarymowicz
Correction Bożena Leszkowicz
Production Anna Kożurno-Królikowska, Ewa Roguska

Dorling Kindersley Limited
Editors Nancy Jones, Esther Labi, Hugh Thompson
Senior Editor Helen Townsend

Contributors
Małgorzata Omilanowska, Jürgen Scheunemann, Christian Tempel

Maps
Maria Wojciechowska, Dariusz Osuch (D. Osuch i spółka)

Printed and bound by South China Co. Ltd., China

First American Edition, 2000
13 14 15 16 10 9 8 7 6 5 4 3 2 1

**Reprinted with revisions 2002, 2003, 2004, 2005, 2006, 2008, 2009,
2011, 2012, 2013**

Copyright 2000, 2013 © Dorling Kindersley Limited, London
A Penguin Company

Published in Great Britain by Dorling Kindersley Limited.

A catalog record for this book is available from the Library of Congress.

ISSN 1542-1554
ISBN 978-1-4654-0047-5

Floors are referred to throughout in accordance with European usage,
ie the "first floor" is the floor above ground level.

MIX
Paper from
responsible sources
FSC   FSC™ C018179
www.fsc.org

Front cover main image: Berliner Dom, Lustgarten

◀ The Brandenburg Gate at night

Contents

How to Use this Guide **6**

A child's drawing of Fernsehturm,
Siegessäule and Funkturm

Introducing Berlin

Bomb-damaged Kaiser-Wilhelm-
Gedächtnis-Kirche *(see pp156–7)*

The Spree river passing by the Nikolaiviertel *(see pp90–91)*

Kasseler Nacken (salted and dried pork)
(see pp228–9)

Modern architecture by the former
Checkpoint Charlie *(see p145)*

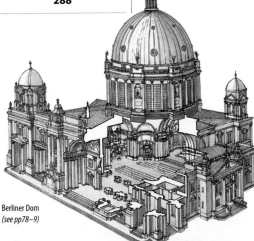

Berliner Dom
(see pp78–9)

HOW TO USE THIS GUIDE

This Dorling Kindersley travel guide helps you to get the most from your visit to Berlin. It provides detailed practical information and expert recommendations. *Introducing Berlin* maps the city and the region, and sets it in its historical and cultural context, and describes events through the entire year. *Berlin at a Glance* is an overview of the city's main attractions. *Berlin Area by Area* starts on page 54. This is the main sightseeing section, which covers all of the important sights, with photographs, maps and illustrations. Greater Berlin covers the nearby historic city of Potsdam, as well as three walking tours. Information about hotels, restaurants, shops and markets, entertainment and sports is found in *Travellers' Needs*. The *Survival Guide* has advice on everything from using Berlin's medical services, telephones and post offices to the public transport system.

Berlin Area by Area

Each of eight sightseeing areas in Berlin is colour-coded for easy reference. Every chapter opens with an introduction to the area of the city it covers, describing its history and character, and has a *Street-by-Street* map illustrating typical parts of that area. Finding your way around the chapter is made simple by the numbering system used throughout. The most important sights are covered in detail in two or more full pages.

Colour-coding Each area has colour-coded tabs.

A locator map shows where you are in relation to other areas in the city centre.

Stars indicate the features that no visitor should miss.

1 Area map
For easy reference, the sights in each area are numbered and plotted on an area map. To help the visitor, this map also shows U- and S-Bahn stations, main bus and tram stops and parking areas. The area's key sights are listed by category, such as museums.

A suggested route takes in some of the most interesting and attractive streets in the area.

2 Street-by-Street map
This gives a bird's-eye view of interesting and important parts of each sightseeing area. The numbering of the sights ties up with the area map and the fuller description of the entries on the pages that follow.

Berlin Area Map

The coloured areas shown on this map *(see inside front cover)* are the eight main sightseeing areas used in this guide. Each is covered in a full chapter in *Berlin Area by Area (see pp54–207)*. They are highlighted on other maps throughout the book. In *Berlin at a Glance*, for example, they help you locate the top sights. They are also used to help you find the position of three walks *(see pp209–215)*.

3 Detailed information on each sight
All the important sights in Berlin are described individually. They are listed in order following the numbering on the area map at the start of the section. Practical information includes a map reference, opening hours and telephone numbers. The key to the symbols is on the back flap.

Practical information provides everything you need to know to visit each sight. Map references pinpoint the sight's location on the *Street Finder* map *(see pp300–323)*.

Numbers refer to each sight's position on the area map and its place in the chapter.

Story boxes provide information about historical or cultural topics relating to the sights.

The Visitors' Checklist gives all the practical information needed to plan your visit.

The star sights recommends the places that no visitor should miss.

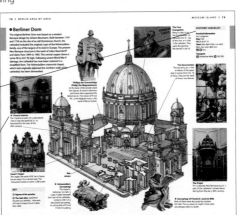

4 Berlin's major sights
Historic buildings are dissected to reveal their interiors; museums and galleries have colour-coded floorplans to help you find the most important exhibits.

INTRODUCING BERLIN

GREAT DAYS IN BERLIN

Berlin is a city packed with treasures and wonderful things to see and do. Whether here for several days, or just wanting a flavour of this great city, you need to make the most of your time so that you can take in as much of the city as possible. Over the following pages, you'll find itineraries for some of the best of the city's attractions, arranged first by theme and then by length of stay. Price guides on pages 10–11 include travel, food and admission for two adults, while family prices are for two adults and two children.

History and Culture

Two adults
allow at least €95

- See Brandenburger Tor
- Walk along Wilhelmstrasse
- Lunch at a brasserie
- Zeughaus/Museum Island
- Checkpoint Charlie

Morning

Start on the Unter den Linden at the city's most famous landmark, **Brandenburger Tor** *(see p69)*, one of the few remaining historic city gates. Walk south from the gate, past or across the Holocaust Memorial, to Wilhelmstrasse. The **Reich's Chancellery** and **Hitler's office** *(see p68)* were to your right at No. 77 Vossstrasse. Another grim reminder of Germany's Nazi

People sitting outside a bar, Kürfurstendamm, Berlin

past is round the corner. **The Topographie des Terrors** *(see p144)*, at the site of the former Gestapo and SS HQ, details crimes at the excavated torture cells. An original section of the Berlin Wall that used to run just behind Neo-Renaissance **Martin-Gropius-Bau** building is nearby *(see p144)*. From here, walk back along Wilhelmstrasse to 39 Unter den Linden for lunch at the brasserie **Dressler** *(see p232)*.

Afternoon

Tour the German history exhibit at the **Zeughaus (Deutsches Historisches Museum)** *(see p60–61)*. Then head north along the canal to **Museum Island** *(see pp73–87)*, a world-class museum complex, and explore the Neues Museum or the Pergamon museum with its famous Pergamon Altar. Detour to Kreuzberg by walking south on Friedrichstrasse to **Checkpoint Charlie**, the former allied border crossing, and visit the museum **Haus am Checkpoint Charlie** *(see p145)*.

The Rotunda gallery of the Altes Museum, Museum Island

A Family Day

Family of four
allow at least €220

- Visit the zoo
- A quick self-service lunch
- Hands-on technology fun
- Studio tour at the Filmpark

Morning

Start at the **Zoo Berlin** *(see p154)*, one of Germany's oldest and biggest zoos. Leave the zoo via the Hardenbergplatz exit and walk east towards the Kaiser-Wilhelm-Gedächtniskirche on bustling Breitscheidplatz. Enjoy the jugglers and street artists on the square, then pop in to see the heavenly blue light in the church's modern section. Lunch at the Marché Mövenpick, set up like a street market on the elegant **Kurfürstendamm** *(see pp151–9)*.

Afternoon

Catch a bus on Kurfürstendamm which will take you to the

◄ Deutscher Dom in the 19th century, Gendarmenmarkt

Deutsches Technikmuseum *(see p148)*, with its planes, vintage cars, trains, boats and hands-on experiments to try. Bus back to Zoologischer Garten and then take the S-Bahn to Potsdam-Babelsberg to its **Filmpark Babelsberg** for a tour of Germany's biggest studio complex *(see p207)*. Grab a simple dinner in Kreuzberg or Neukölln.

A Shopping Day

Two adults
allow at least €50 (cost of lunch and travel only)

- **Shop at KaDeWe**
- **Stroll to Savignyplatz**
- **Snack on the go**
- **Friedrichstadtpassagen chic**

Morning
Begin at **Kaufhaus des Westens**, called KaDeWe by Berliners, Europe's second biggest department store *(see p159)*. Then explore the Tauentzienstrasse, a popular, affordable shopping avenue, and continue on Kurfürstendamm – the further west you go, the more elegant the shops and boutiques. Take detours into even more chic side streets such as **Fasanen-**, **Meineke-**, **Uhland-**, **Bleibtreu-** and **Schlüterstrasse** as you head to **Savignyplatz** *(see p158)* with its many boutiques and eateries.

Afternoon
Take the S-Bahn from Savignyplatz towards the east and exit at

The impressive French department store, Galeries Lafayette

Friedrichstrasse. Walk north; once over Unter den Linden, you'll find the huge complexes of the **Friedrichstadtpassagen** including the French **Galeries Lafayette** and the über-luxurious **Quartier 206**, alongside top designers Gucci, Versace and Donna Karan. If not yet shopped out, walk back north on Friedrichstrasse and then east on Oranienburger Strasse to **Hackescher Markt**. This is a hip area of mostly alternative-style, young fashion, as well as clubs, bars and pubs.

Berlin Outdoors

Two adults
allow at least €90

- **A walk to Grunewald forest**
- **Boat trip to Pfaueninsel**
- **The Tiergarten**
- **Schloss Bellevue**

Morning
From the S-Bahn station Grunewald walk south past interesting villas and museums

Gardens of Sanssouci palace, in Park Sanssouci

(about 60 minutes) to **Jagdschloss Grunewald** *(see p214–15)*, a lovely hunting palace with an art gallery, past fine historic villas. Continue through the forest to **Wannsee lake** *(see p188)* for a swim and a sunbathe or walk back to the S-Bahn and get off at Wannsee station. Take a bus ride to the ferry for a walk on **Pfaueninsel**, a nature reserve *(see p210–11)*. After a walk around the island, take a break at the scenic Wirtshaus Zur Pfaueninsel beer garden at the ferry landing before taking the bus back to Wannsee S-Bahn station.

Afternoon
From Wannsee, take the S-Bahn to the green lung of Berlin, the vast **Tiergarten** *(see pp117–39)*. Follow the Strasse des 17. Juni east and climb the **Siegessäule** *(see p136–7)*, the victory column with a great view of the city. Follow Spreeweg to **Schloss Bellevue** *(see p137)*, the official Presidential seat. To finish, walk southwest to **Neuer See**, a pretty lake in the park. Rent a boat at the Café am Neuen See and return for supper.

2 days in Berlin

- Enjoy a bird's-eye view of the city from the Fernsehturm
- Stroll in leafy Tiergarten
- View a slice of history at Checkpoint Charlie

Day 1

Morning Take a lift to the top of the **Fernsehturm** (p95) for panoramic views of Berlin. Then board bus 100 for a tour of the once-divided city; hop off at Lustgarten for the **Berliner Dom**, Berlin's most lavish church, (pp78–9) and **Museum Island** (pp72–87), where you can see the stunning bust of Egyptian Queen Nefertiti in the **Neues Museum** (p80).

Afternoon Continue by bus along **Unter den Linden** (p62) to Bundestag for the German parliament building, the **Reichstag** (pp138–9) and iconic **Brandenburger Tor** (p69), which once marked the city's western boundary. Nearby is **Tiergarten** (pp136–7), the city's largest central park, and **Kaiser-Wilhelm-Gedächtnis-Kirche** (pp156–7), a monument to victims of World War II.

Day 2

Morning Begin at **Checkpoint Charlie** (p145), the famous border crossing between former East and West Berlin. A section of the Berlin Wall survives on nearby Niederkirchnerstrasse, and a

Twin towers of the Gothic Marienkirche and futuristic Fernsehturm

short walk away is the **Holocaust Denkmal** (p69), a moving memorial to Berlin's Jews. End the morning with some shopping on **Friedrichstrasse** (pp142–3).

Afternoon Cross the Spree over the Schleusenbrücke lock bridge to the **Nikolaiviertel** (p92) to discover the attractive **Nikolaikirche** (p92), the Rococo **Ephraim-Palais** (p93) and Gothic **Marienkirche** (pp96–7). Round off the day at a bar in the old industrial courtyards of **Hackesche Höfe** (p105).

3 days in Berlin

- Time travel through 750 years of Berlin history
- Explore the Kulturforum for some breathtaking art

Day 1

Morning Take a stroll in the **Nikolaiviertel** (p92) on the banks of the Spree, stopping off to see exhibits on Berlin at

the **Ephraim-Palais** (p93) and to visit the city's oldest parish church, the **Nikolaikirche** (p92). Next, head north for **Marienkirche** (pp96–7), with its impressive Neo-Gothic tower. Travel up to the top of the **Fernsehturm** (p95) for an impressive view of Berlin.

Afternoon After lunch, visit Berlin's Protestant cathedral, the **Berliner Dom** (pp78–9), and continue on to Museum Island to see the Pergamon Altar in the **Pergamonmuseum** (pp82–5). Cross Schinkel's beautiful **Schlossbrücke** (p76) and walk the length of famous **Unter den Linden** (p62) to the **Brandenburger Tor** (p69), the city's iconic gateway, and the **Reichstag** (pp138–9) – a potent symbol of reunified Germany. End the day at the **Holocaust Denkmal** (p69), Germany's national Holocaust memorial.

Day 2

Morning Sample the city's two leading cultural centres. In lively **Potsdamer Platz** (pp132–5) visit the entertaining **Filmmuseum Berlin** (p132). There is so much on offer at the **Kulturforum** (pp118–19), but the wonderful **Gemäldegalerie** (pp126–9), Berlin's largest art museum, boasts some of the finest masterpieces of European art. Break for lunch in the **Neue Nationalgalerie** (p130) café.

Afternoon Get some fresh air by exploring the city's green lung, **Tiergarten** (pp136–7). Nearby, the wonderful **Zoo Berlin** (p154) is great for both children and adults alike. End the day with a visit to the church-monument **Kaiser-Wilhelm-Gedächtnis-Kirche** (pp156–7) just south of the zoo.

Day 3

Morning Travel to Kochstrasse for Cold War nostalgia at **Haus am Checkpoint Charlie** (p145). Visit the **Jüdisches Museum** (pp144–5) to learn about the history of Berlin's Jews, or visit the former nerve centre of the Nazi state, the **Topographie des Terrors** (p144).

The exterior of the Neue Nationalgalerie in the Kulturforum

Afternoon Take a trip to **Schloss Charlottenburg** (pp164–5) and tour the state apartments. See decorative arts at the **Bröhan-Museum** (p165) and Picassos at the **Museum Berggruen** (p168) next door. Return to dine on the terraces around **Savignyplatz** (p158) in the evening.

5 days in Berlin

- Discover ancient treasures on Museum Island
- Tread in royalty's steps at Schloss Charlottenburg
- Escape the city on the waterfront at Wannsee

Day 1

Morning Immerse yourself in art and history on **Museum Island** (pp72– 87), selecting from the breathtaking array of galleries and museums here. Head on to **Bebelplatz** (p64), an imposing architectural set piece celebrating Frederick the Great, whose statue stands guard outside. A little further south lies **Gendarmenmarkt** (p66), Berlin's most beautiful square.

Afternoon Stroll down **Unter den Linden** (p62), lined with restaurants and shops. Walk through the central arch of the **Brandenburger Tor** (p69), and to Germany's restored parliament, the **Reichstag** (pp136–7). Its dome was added by Sir Norman Foster in 1999. End with a visit to the **Holocaust Denkmal** (p69), a memorial to Berlin's Jews.

Day 2

Morning Start at **Schloss Charlottenburg** (pp164–5), to the west of the city, and tour the state rooms of King Frederick I and Queen Sophie Charlotte. Art lovers are spoiled for choice with the **Bröhan-Museum** (p165), **Museum Berggruen** (p168) and **Museum Scharf-Gerstenberg** (p168) all nearby.

Afternoon While away a happy hour at the mouthwatering food hall of **KaDeWe** (p159), and once sated, visit the stunning Neo-Romanesque ruins of

The impressive architecture of the Sony Center, Potsdamer Platz

Kaiser-Wilhelm-Gedächtnis-Kirche (pp156–7). Take a stroll down **Kurfürstendamm** (pp152–9), the main artery through Berlin's west end, home to fashionable boutiques.

Day 3

Morning At **Bahnhof Friedrichstrasse** (p71), take in the moving "Border Experiences" exhibition. Visit the famous **Checkpoint Charlie** (p145) border crossing, and watch docu-films on the Cold War era at **Haus am Checkpoint Charlie** (p145). The nearby **Topographie des Terrors** (p144) and **Martin-Gropius-Bau** (p144) were both used by Nazi security services.

Afternoon Walk to the **Jüdisches Museum** (pp144–5), which explores the history of Berlin's Jews, then take a break in the **Tiergarten** park (pp136–7) and **Zoo Berlin** (p154).

Day 4

Morning Take the S-Bahn to **Wannsee** (p188–9) and stroll along the waterfront, or take a boat trip along the Havel. The more adventurous may fancy a dip in the lake. **Glienicker Brücke** (p212), famous for featuring in the spy novels of John Le Carré, offers spectacular views.

Afternoon After lunch take a ferry to **Pfaueninsel's** (p210) ornamental gardens. In the evening head for **Prenzlauer Berg** (pp107–109), and enjoy lunch at one of the cafés on leafy **Kollwitzplatz** (p107).

Day 5

Morning Head to the Gothic **Marienkirche** (pp96–7) to see the medieval fresco, *Dance of Death*. Be sure to view Berlin from above at the city's TV Tower **Fernsehturm** (p95), and wander the **Nikolaiviertel** (p92) area, stopping off to see the exhibition on Berlin's history in the city's oldest sacred building, the **Nikolaikirche** (p92).

Afternoon Take the S-Bahn to **Potsdamer Platz** (pp132–5) to visit the **Filmmuseum Berlin** (p132) for the story of German cinema, and visit one of the museums at the **Kulturforum** (pp118–19). The collection at the **Gemäldegalerie** (pp126–9) includes works by Titian, Vermeer, Holbein and Rubens, and is not to be missed. In the evening, relax in **Kreuzberg** (pp140–49), Berlin's unofficial party quarter.

Statue of the poet Friedrich Schiller in front of the Deutscher Dom, Gendarmenmarkt

Putting Berlin on the Map

Berlin, the capital of the Federal Republic of Germany,
has a population of approximately 3.4 million and covers
889 sq km (343 sq miles). Situated in the eastern part of the
country, in the middle of the Brandenburg region, Berlin
occupies the flatlands on the banks of the Havel and Spree
rivers, which merge in the Spandau district.
The whole city is criss-crossed
with numerous canals.

Berlin and Environs

Oranienburg

Bernau

Hennigsdorf

Nauen

Falkensee

BERLIN

See next page

Potsdam

Werder

Berlin-
Schönefeld

Ludwigsfelde

Königs
Wusterhausen

DENMARK

Stralsund

Greifswald

Rostock

Wismar

Lübeck

Schwerin

Neubrandenburg

Lüneburg

Neustrelitz

Uelzen

Pritzwalk

Schwedt/
Oder

Wittenberge

*See inset map,
right*

Oranienburg

Stendal

BERLIN

Wolfsburg

Potsdam

Braunschweig

Magdeburg

Luckenwalde

POLAND

Schönebeck

Zielona Góra

Goslar

Lübbenau

Lutherstadt
Wittenberg

Żary

Nordhausen

Delitzsch

Cottbus

Glogów

Halle

Leipzig

Hoyerswerda

Legnica

Mühlhausen

Naumburg

Döbeln

Bautzen

Görlitz

Wrocław

Erfurt

Weimar

Zeitz

Dresden

Gotha

Gera

Freiberg

Liberec

Wałbrzych

Ilmenau

Zwickau

Chemnitz

Annaberg-
Buchholz

Ústí nad Labem

Hradec
Králové

Coburg

Hof

Karlovy
Vary

Kladno

Pardubice

Bamberg

Bayreuth

Cheb

Plzeň

Prague

Kolín

CZECH REPUBLIC

Havlíčkův
Brod

Erlangen

Weiden

Nürnberg

Schwandorf

Cham

Klatovy

Tábor

Jihlava

Brno

Ansbach

Regensburg

České
Budějovice

Straubing

Deggendorf

Ingolstadt

Passau

Landshut

Linz

Augsburg

Munich

Wels

Steyr

Kaufbeuren

Rosenheim

Gmunden

Kempten

Salzburg

AUSTRIA

Key

Berlin and Environs

Ferry route

National border

Autobahn (motorway)

Dual carriageway

Major road

Railway

0 kilometres — 100

0 miles — 75

Greater Berlin

Berlin in its present form was created in 1920, through an amalgamation of several towns and villages surrounding the historic centre. It now consists of 12 administrative districts, some of which were formerly separate municipalities, such as Spandau. The city is surrounded by recreational areas, including lakes and woodlands. To the southwest lies the city of Potsdam with its splendid palaces, which can be reached easily by public transport.

Hamburg

Oranienburg

REINICKENDORF

Berlin
Tegel Airport

A111

WEDDING

A100

SPANDAU

Spree

Moabit

Nauen

Westend

CHARLOTTENBURG

Landwehrkanal

215

Zoologischer
Garten

Charlottenburg

Halensee

Teufelsberg ▲

A100

WILMERSDORF

Grunewald

Grunewald

SCHÖNEBERG

BERLINER
FORST
GRUNEWALD

Schmargendorf

Friedenau

A115

Dahlem

STEGLITZ

Leipzig

ZEHLENDORF

Lichterfelde

Schlachtensee

1

Lankv

Potsdam

Teltowkanal

For additional map symbols *see back flap*

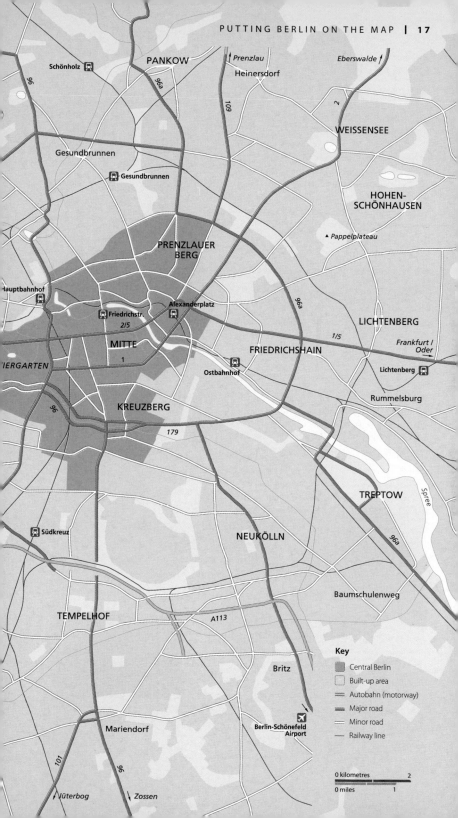

PANKOW

Schönholz

Prenzlau

Heinersdorf

Eberswalde

WEISSENSEE

Gesundbrunnen

Gesundbrunnen

HOHEN-
SCHÖNHAUSEN

Pappelplateau

PRENZLAUER
BERG

Hauptbahnhof

Alexanderplatz

Friedrichstr.
2/5

LICHTENBERG

MITTE

1

FRIEDRICHSHAIN

*Frankfurt /
Oder*

Ostbahnhof

Lichtenberg

1/5

TIERGARTEN

Rummelsburg

KREUZBERG

179

TREPTOW

Spree

Südkreuz

NEUKÖLLN

96a

Baumschulenweg

TEMPELHOF

A113

Britz

Berlin-Schönefeld
Airport

Mariendorf

Key

Central Berlin

Built-up area

Autobahn (motorway)

Major road

Minor road

Railway line

Jüterbog   *Zossen*

0 kilometres   2

0 miles   1

Central Berlin

Central Berlin is divided into eight colour-coded sightseeing areas. The historic core is located along the eastern and northern banks of the Spree river, around the grand boulevard Unter den Linden and on Museum Island. West of the centre is the sprawling green Tiergarten. To the south is Kreuzberg, an area renowned for its alternative lifestyle. Further west is Kurfürstendamm, the centre of former West Berlin. Finally, at the edge of the city centre is the summer residence of the Prussian kings, the Schloss Charlottenburg.

Around Schloss Charlottenburg
The Baroque Charlottenburg Palace, named after Sophie Charlotte (wife of Friedrich III), is one of Berlin's greatest tourist attractions. Its magnificent rooms contain many beautiful objects (see pp160–69).

Kulturforum, Tiergarten
The Kulturforum is a cluster of interesting museums and libraries. It is also the home of the Berlin Philharmonic (see pp116–39).

Around Kurfürstendamm
The Kurfürstendamm, or Ku'damm as it is often called, is the main thoroughfare of western Berlin. This area contains numerous shops, restaurants, bars and cinemas (see pp150–59).

Key

■ Major sight

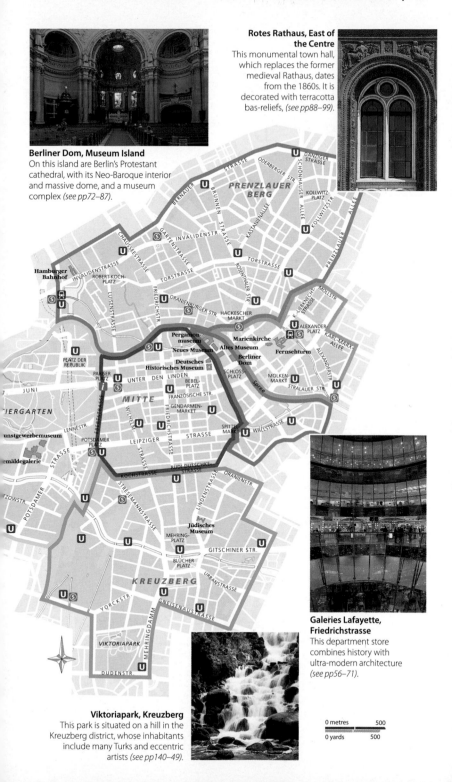

Rotes Rathaus, East of the Centre
This monumental town hall, which replaces the former medieval Rathaus, dates from the 1860s. It is decorated with terracotta bas-reliefs, *(see pp88–99).*

Berliner Dom, Museum Island
On this island are Berlin's Protestant cathedral, with its Neo-Baroque interior and massive dome, and a museum complex *(see pp72–87).*

Galeries Lafayette, Friedrichstrasse
This department store combines history with ultra-modern architecture *(see pp56–71).*

Viktoriapark, Kreuzberg
This park is situated on a hill in the Kreuzberg district, whose inhabitants include many Turks and eccentric artists *(see pp140–49).*

0 metres 500
0 yards 500

THE HISTORY OF BERLIN

Berlin is one of the younger European capitals. The first written reference to the small fishing settlement of Cölln appeared in the year 1237. Together with the equally insignificant settlement of Berlin on the opposite bank of the Spree river, it was to become first a successful trading city under the control of the Margraves of Brandenburg, then capital of Prussia, and finally, the capital of Germany. Following World War II and the 1949 armistice, Berlin became a central arena for the Cold War. In 1991, after the fall of the Berlin Wall, the city became the capital of the newly-united Federal Republic of Germany.

Early Settlements

During the first centuries AD the banks of the Spree and Havel rivers were inhabited by various tribes, most notably the Germanic Semnones. By the end of the 6th century the Semnones were competing for land with Slavic tribes, who built forts at what are now the Berlin suburbs of Köpenick (see p183) and Spandau (see p177). Five hundred years later the Slavic tribes were finally defeated following the arrival of the warlike Saxon, Albrecht the Bear of the House of the Ascanians, who became the first *Markgraf* (Margrave, or Count) of Brandenburg. The banks of the Spree river were now resettled with immigrants from areas to the west including the Harz mountains, the Rhine valley and Franconia.

Beginnings of the Modern City

Berlin's written history began in the early 13th century, when the twin settlements of Berlin and Cölln grew up on opposite banks of the Spree river, around what is now the Nikolaiviertel (see p92). Trading in fish, rye and timber, the towns formed an alliance in 1307, becoming Berlin-Cölln, a deal celebrated by the construction of a joint town hall.

Following the death of the last Ascanian ruler in 1319, Brandenburg became the object of a long and bloody feud between the houses of Luxemburg and Wittelsbach, with devastating effects for the area's inhabitants. In 1411 the desperate townspeople appealed to the Holy Roman Emperor for help, receiving in response Friedrich von Hohenzollern as the town's special protector. Then in 1415 Rome duly rewarded Friedrich by naming him Elector of Brandenburg, a fateful appointment that marked the beginning of the 500-year rule of the House of Hohenzollern.

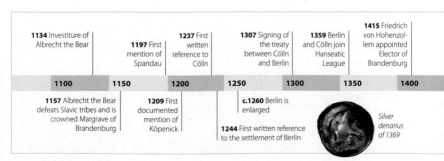

1134 Investiture of Albrecht the Bear		**1237** First written reference to Cölln	**1307** Signing of the treaty between Cölln and Berlin	**1359** Berlin and Cölln join Hanseatic League	**1415** Friedrich von Hohenzollern appointed Elector of Brandenburg
	1197 First mention of Spandau				

1100	1150	1200	1250	1300	1350	1400

1157 Albrecht the Bear defeats Slavic tribes and is crowned Margrave of Brandenburg	**1209** First documented mention of Köpenick	**c.1260** Berlin is enlarged	*Silver denarius of 1369*

1244 First written reference to the settlement of Berlin

◄ Adolf von Menzel's symbolic painting *Borussia*, or *Prussia* (1868), at the Ephraim-Palais

Deposition from the Cross (c.1520), a pane of a Gothic polyptych from the time of the Reformation

The Early Hohenzollerns

In 1432 Berlin and Cölln were formally unified. By 1443 Elector Friedrich II, son of Friedrich I, had begun construction of the town's first castle, the future Stadtschloss *(see p73)*. This was part of his plan to make Berlin-Cölln the capital of Brandenburg and to reduce the powers and privileges of its citizens. Despite fierce opposition from the local population, the castle was built. By 1448 all opposition had been violently crushed, and in 1451 the castle became the Elector's official residence. To symbolize the consolidation of Hohenzollern power, he added an iron chain and padlock around the neck of the city's heraldic bear. By the time Friedrich's nephew Johann Cicero became Elector in 1486, Berlin-Cölln

was formally established as the capital of the March of Brandenburg.

Reformation and the Thirty Years' War

During the first half of the 16th century, the radical religious ideas of Martin Luther (1483–1546) spread quickly throughout the whole of Brandenburg. In 1539 the new Protestantism was adopted by the Elector, Joachim II Hector, and most of the town's aldermen.

For a time the city grew fast, boosted by the arrival of religious refugees from the Netherlands, as well as Italian artists invited by the subsequent elector, Joachim Georg. However, successive epidemics of the bubonic plague occurred in 1576, 1598 and 1600, checking the town's growth. The effect was compounded by the advent of the Thirty Years' War which raged from 1618 to 1648, turning the whole of the Holy Roman Empire into a bloody battlefield. In 1627 the Elector of Brandenburg had fled, relocating his court to the less exposed town of Königsberg. By 1648 the population of Berlin-Cölln had fallen to just 6,000, its population being decimated by famine and disease.

Berlin Under the Great Elector

The fortunes of Berlin were turned by the arrival of Friedrich Wilhelm von Hohenzollern, who ascended the Brandenburg throne in 1640. Under the rule of this man, later known as the Great Elector, Berlin experienced a period of an unprecedented growth. The city's population rose to 20,000 by 1688 at the end of Friedrich Wilhelm's long reign.

1432 Unification of Cölln and Berlin

1486 Elector Johann Cicero makes Berlin his permanent residence

1539 Elector Joachim II converts to the Protestant faith

1415　　　　**1465**　　　　**1515**　　　　**1565**

1447–8 Berlin rebellion against the Elector

1442 Construction begins on the royal castle in Cölln

Tankard in the shape of Berlin's heraldic bear (1562)

1594 Building of the Spandau citadel completed

The former Stadtschloss (Berlin Castle), with Lange Brücke in the foreground, c.1685

The Capital of Prussia

The successor to the Great Elector, Friedrich III inherited the title in 1688. Thirteen years later he raised Brandenburg's status to that of a kingdom, and was crowned King Friedrich I of Prussia. Ambitious and with a taste for luxury, Friedrich became a powerful patron of the arts. Under his rule Berlin acquired its Academies of Fine Arts and Science. Artists transformed the castle into a Baroque palace. The Zeughaus (see p60–61) and the summer palace or Schloss in Lietzenburg, later renamed Charlottenburg (see p164–5), were built at this time.

In 1648 work started on the modern fortification of the city. The Lustgarten (see p76) was established opposite the Stadtschloss and the road later to become known as Unter den Linden (see p62) was planted with lime trees. The city's economic power increased following the building of the canal linking the Spree and Oder rivers, which turned Berlin into the hub of all Brandenburg trade.

Berlin began to expand in all directions with the creation of new satellite towns – first Friedrichswerder, then Dorotheenstadt and Friedrichstadt, all between 1650 and 1690. They would all be absorbed into a unified city of Berlin in 1709.

In 1671 several wealthy Jewish families expelled from Vienna settled in Berlin, while following the 1685 Edict of Potsdam, large numbers of French Huguenots flocked to Brandenburg, forced out of their homeland after Louis XIV repealed the Edict of Nantes. Both these events came to play a major role in the future development of the city.

The next ruler of Prussia, Friedrich Wilhelm I (1713–40), was unlike his father and soon became known as the "Soldier-King". His initiatives were practical: Berlin was further expanded and encircled with a new wall, not for defence but as a measure against the desertion of conscripted citizens. Pariser Platz (see p69), Leipziger Platz (see p130) and Mehringplatz (see p148) were all built at that time, and the population reached 90,000.

The next king was Friedrich II (1740–1786), otherwise known as Frederick the Great or "Alter Fritz" (Old Fritz). An educated man who appreciated art, he oversaw the city's transformation into a sophisticated cultural centre. He was also an aggressive empire builder, sparking the Seven Years' War of 1756–63 with his invasion of Silesia, during which Berlin was briefly occupied by Austrian and Russian troops. The city's development continued, however, and at the time of Friedrich II's death in 1786, its population numbered 150,000.

Friedrich II
(1740–86)

1618–48 Thirty Years' War	**1688** Establishment of the new town of Friedrichstadt	**1751–2** Friedrich II introduces conscription	
1668 Opening of the Spree-Oder canal	**1701** Coronation of Friedrich III as the first king of Prussia	**1756–63** Seven Years' War	

1615	**1665**	**1715**	**1765**
	1685 Edict of Potsdam allows large numbers of French Huguenot refugees to settle in Berlin	**1709** Unification of Berlin	**1740** Coronation of Frederick the Great
		1696 Opening of the Academy of Fine Arts (Akademie der Künste)	

Silver chalice (1695)

The Baroque Period

Berlin's Baroque Period lasted from the second half of the 17th century to the end of the 18th, and saw the expansion of Berlin-Cölln from a small town, devas-tated by successive epidemics of bubonic plague and the ravages of the Thirty Years' War, into a rich and cosmopolitan metropolis. Population growth was rapid, aided by the official amalgamation of Berlin-Cölln with the previously independent communities of Dorotheenstadt, Friedrichstadt and Friedrichswerder. New city walls were built, as were many substantial buildings, including the Akademie der Künste, the Charité and Schloss Charlottenburg.

Extent of the City
☐ 1734   ▨ Today

Flute Concert
This painting by Adolf von Menzel shows the arts-loving King Friedrich II (1740–86) giving a flute recital for his guests in the music room of the Schloss Sanssouci.

Nikolaikirche

Frederick the Great
The famous French-born portrait painter, Antoine Pesne, created this portrait of Friedrich II of Prussia, heir to the Prussian throne, in 1739.

Rococo Tureen
This elaborate silver tureen, decorated with a gilded lemon, was made in the Berlin workshop of Georg Wilhelm Marggraf und Müller in 1765.

Stadtschloss (Royal Palace)

***Love in the Italian Theatre* (1714)**
French painter Jean-Antoine Watteau
(1684–1721) was a favourite with King
Friedrich II, and as a result many of his
works can still be seen in Berlin.

Zeughaus (Former Arsenal)
The splendid Baroque Zeughaus was completed in
1730. Used to store weapons until 1875, it will house
the Deutsches Historisches Museum. This view of it
was painted in 1786 by Carl Traugott Fechhelm.

Rondell (now
Mehringplatz)

Oktogon (now
Leipziger Platz)

King Friedrich I
This medallion bears
the likeness of the
first King of Prussia
(1688–1713). The
work of sculptor
and architect
Andreas Schlüter
(1660–1714), it
adorns the
king's tomb.

Quarré (now
Pariser Platz)

Berlin in 1740

*This map shows the layout of the city's
18th-century fortifications, with various
landmark buildings. Contrary to today's
convention, this map was drawn with the
north pointing down, rather than up.*

Unter den
Linden

Baroque Architecture in Berlin

Many of Berlin's Baroque buildings
have been destroyed, but in the city
centre some fine examples still exist.
Don't miss the Zeughaus *(see p60–61)*,
two fine churches in Gendarmenmarkt –
the Deutscher Dom and the Französischer
Dom *(see p66–7)* – the Parochialkirche
(see p99) and Sophienkirche *(see p106)*.
Another Baroque highlight, even though
it is largely a reconstruction, is Schloss
Charlottenburg *(see p162–3)* with its
delightful park.

Schloss Charlottenburg

Antique scroll depicting the grand boulevard of Unter den Linden, 1821

Beginnings of the Modern Era

By the time Friedrich Wilhelm II (1786–97) ascended the throne of Prussia, the country's era of absolute rulers was nearing an end. New trends associated with Romanticism were gaining popularity, and there was an explosion of ideas from outstanding personalities such as writers Gotthold Ephraim Lessing (1729–81) and Friedrich and August-Wilhelm von Schlegel.

Throughout Europe, French Emperor Napoleon Bonaparte (1769–1821) was waging war, defeating the Prussians in 1806 at the battles of Jena and Austerlitz. As French troops moved in to occupy Berlin, Friedrich Wilhelm took his court to Königsberg, while Berlin's pride, the horse-drawn chariot (Quadriga) crowning the Brandenburg Gate, was dismantled and taken to Paris.

By the end of 1809 the royal court had returned to Berlin, and, having received huge reparations, Napoleon and his troops finally left the city. In 1814 the Quadriga was returned to Berlin, and a year later Napoleon was defeated at Waterloo. Granted the mineral-rich lands of the Rhineland and Westphalia at the subsequent Congress of Vienna, Prussia enjoyed rapid industrialization during the next 30 years, particularly in Berlin. By 1837 August Borsig had opened his locomotive factory in the city, and in 1838 the first train ran on the Berlin–Potsdam railway.

Many outstanding buildings were designed at this time by Karl Friedrich Schinkel (see p181), including the Neue Wache (see p62) and the Schauspielhaus, renamed the Konzerthaus (see p66). Berlin University (now Humboldt Universität) was established in 1810 and became a major seat of learning, attracting famous lecturers such as philosophers Georg Hegel (1770–1831) and Arthur Schopenhauer (1788–1860).

In 1844, however, recession hit Europe, leaving a quarter of all Prussians in poverty. Hunger riots rocked the city in April 1847 and by 1848 Berlin saw a people's uprising in which over 250 demonstrators were shot dead by the Prussian army.

Building an Empire

In 1861 Friedrich Wilhelm IV (1840–1861) was forced by madness to cede the throne to his brother, Wilhelm (1861–1888).

Portrait of Friedrich Wilhelm IV

1791 Building of the Brandenburg Gate completed

1799 Foundation of the Bauakademie

1810 Berlin University established

1831 Cholera epidemic breaks out

1844 Opening of the Berlin zoo (Zoologischer Garten)

1785	1800	1815	1830	1845

Enamelled box, mid-18th century

1806 Beginning of the 2-year French occupation of Berlin

1830 Opening of the Altes Museum

1838 Opening of the Berlin–Potsdam railway line

Otto von Bismarck was soon appointed Chancellor, with a foreign policy to install Prussia in Austria's place at the head of all German-speaking states. In 1864 Prussia declared war on Denmark, and successfully acquired Schleswig-Holstein. In 1866, following war with Austria, Prussia established dominance over the North German Confederation, an association of 22 states and free towns. In 1870 Prussia went to war with France, annexing the provinces of Alsace and Lorraine. Bismarck's next move was the proclamation of a German Empire on 18 January 1871, with Berlin as its capital and King Wilhelm I as Kaiser (Emperor). Thanks to the colossal reparations paid by France and the abolition of trade barriers, Berlin now entered another period of rapid industrial growth, accompanied by a population explosion. By 1877 Berlin's population had grown to one million; by 1905 it was two million.

Poster advertising the Berlin Secession Exhibition of 1990, by Wilhelm Schulz

Triumph and Disaster

The late 19th century saw an explosion of scientific and cultural achievement, including the completion of a new sewage system in 1876, dramatically improving public health. By 1879 electric lamps lit the streets and in 1881 the first telephones were installed. A year later the first urban train line, the S-Bahn, was opened. Berlin's cultural and scientific life flourished, headed by such outstanding personalities as writer Theodor Fontane, painter Adolf von Menzel and bacteriologist Robert Koch. In 1898 Max Liebermann *(see p69)* founded the hugely influential Berlin Secessionist movement, with members including Käthe Kollwitz and Max Slevogt.

As the city prospered, political developments in Germany and throughout Europe were moving towards the stalemate of 1914. Initially, the outbreak of World War I had little effect on the life of Berlin, but the subsequent famine, strikes and total German defeat led to the November Revolution in 1918, and the abdication of Kaiser Wilhelm II.

The Berlin Congress of 1878 by Anton von Werner

1871 Berlin becomes the capital of the German Empire

1878 Berlin Congress takes place

1888 Year of three Kaisers

1902 Operation of the first underground train (U-Bahn)

1914 Outbreak of World War I

| 1860 | 1875 | 1890 | 1905 | 1920 |

1879 Technische Universität established

1882 Opening of the S-Bahn, the first urban train line

Mosaic by Martin-Gropius-Bau

1907 Completion of the Kaufhaus des Westens (KaDeWe)

1918 Abdication of Kaiser Wilhelm II

Capital of the German Empire

On 18 January 1871, Berlin became the capital of the newly-established German Empire, fulfilling the expansionist ambitions of the Prussian Chancellor Otto von Bismarck. Bringing together many previously independent German-speaking regions, the new Empire stretched beyond the borders of present-day Germany, into what are now France, Poland, Russia and Denmark. Massive reparations paid by France after her defeat in the Franco-German war of 1870 stimulated the rapid growth of a fast-industrializing Berlin, accompanied by an explosion of scientific and artistic invention. Standing at just 300,000 in 1850, by 1900 the city's population had reached 1.9 million.

Extent of the City
☐ 1800   ▢ Today

House of Hohenzollern
Mosaics depicting the Hohenzollern rulers decorate the bombed remains of the Kaiser-Wilhelm-Gedächtnis-kirche *(see p156–7)*, completed in 1895.

The Stadtschloss
The Stadtschloss was the royal residence at the declaration of the Prussian Empire in 1871. Decorating the Rathausbrücke, in the foreground, was the magnificent statue of the Great Elector, now in the courtyard of Schloss Charlottenburg *(see p164–5).*

Prussian nobles

Riehmers Hofgarten
In the late 19th century a huge number of buildings were erected, from tenement blocks to grand buildings like this one.

Members of Parliament

Neptunbrunnen
This exuberant fountain *(see p94)* created by sculptor Reinhold Begas in 1891 was a present to Wilhelm II from the Berlin town council.

Hackescher Markt Station
Formerly called Bahnhof Börse, this is one of Berlin's first S-Bahn stations, built to a design by Johannes Vollmer and opened in 1902.

Vase with Portrait of Wilhelm II
Designed by Alexander Kips and bearing a portrait of Kaiser Wilhelm II, this vase was mass-produced at the Berlin Königliche-Porzellan-Manufaktur. Pieces were often presented to visiting heads of state.

Empress Augusta Victoria

Heir to the throne, Wilhelm

Black mourning clothes for women and black armbands for men were obligatory after the deaths of the two Kaisers, Wilhelm I and Friedrich III, in 1888.

Diplomatic corps

Prussian Chancellor Otto von Bismarck

Kaiser Wilhelm II

Opening of the Reichstag
This enormous canvas, painted by Anton von Werner in 1893, portrays Kaiser Wilhelm II giving a speech to the Members of Parliament, nobles and other dignitaries at the official opening of the Reichstag. This important event took place only 11 days after the coronation of the new Kaiser.

Charlotte Berend
The arts flourished in the years before World War I. This 1902 portrait of an actress is by Berlin artist Lovis Corinth.

The burning of one of the thousands of buildings belonging to Jews on *Kristallnacht*, November 1938

The Weimar Republic

On 9 November 1918 two politicians simultaneously proclaimed the birth of two German Republics. Social democrat Philipp Scheidemann announced the founding of a Democratic Republic, while hours later Karl Liebknecht, founder of the German communist movement, declared the Free Socialist Republic of Germany. Rivalries between the two groups erupted in January 1919 in a week of rioting, crushed by the Freikorps army who also brutally murdered communist leaders Karl Liebknecht and Rosa Luxemburg.

In February 1919 the National Assembly elected Social Democrat Friedrich Ebert President of the German Republic. In 1920 urban reform dramatically increased the size of Berlin, causing the population to swell to 3.8 million. Berlin, like the rest of the country, fell on hard times, with rising unemployment and rampant hyper-inflation.

At the same time, the city became the centre of a lively cultural life. Leading figures in theatre included Max Reinhardt and Bertolt Brecht, while from the UFA film studio came such classics as *The Cabinet of Dr Cagliari* and *Metropolis*. Jazz was popular, and the Berlin Philharmonic gained worldwide fame. Architecture flourished with Walter Gropius and Bruno Taut, while Berlin scientists Albert Einstein, Carl Bosch and Werner Heisenberg were all awarded the Nobel Prize.

The Third Reich

The world stock-market crash of October 1929 and the ensuing Depression put the fragile German democracy under great pressure, paving the way for extremist politicians. On 30 January 1933 Adolf Hitler was appointed Chancellor. The Reichstag fire in February was used as a pretext to arrest communist and liberal opponents, and by March 1933 Hitler's Nazi (National Socialist German Workers) Party was in control of the Reichstag. Books by "un-German" authors were burned, and works of art deemed as "degenerate" removed from museums.

The 1936 Olympic Games in Berlin were meant as a showcase for Aryan supremacy. Although Germany won 33 gold medals, the real hero was the black US athlete Jesse Owens. The effects of the Nazi regime were felt particularly by Jews and intellectuals, many of whom were forced to emigrate. On the night of 9–10 November 1938, known as *Kristallnacht* (Night of the Broken Glass), thousands of

Nazi propaganda poster of Hitler, printed in 1938

Historic buildings at the Gendarmenmarkt destroyed by British and American bombs, 1945–6

synagogues, cemeteries, Jewish homes and shops were looted and burned.

World War II

Hitler's invasion of Poland on 1 September 1939 signalled the start of World War II. For the citizens of Berlin, food shortages were followed in August 1940 by British air raids. By 1941 the government policy of the mass deportation of Jews to concentration camps had begun. Other groups targeted included homosexuals, priests and Romany gypsies. In January 1942, following a conference at Wannsee *(see p188)* the systematic extermination of all European Jews began. The unsuccessful attempt to assassinate Hitler in 1944 led to Nazis murdering many members of the German resistance.

After nearly four years of bitter warfare, the tide began to turn against the Germans. In April 1945 more than 1.5 million Soviet soldiers invaded Berlin. On 30 April Hitler committed suicide, and Germany conceded defeat.

Berlin Divided

The Potsdam Conference of 1945 *(see p201)* divided Berlin into four sectors, occupied respectively by Soviet, US, British and French troops, putting the city at the centre

of the Cold War. On 24 June 1948 the Soviet authorities, in their attempt to annex the whole city, introduced a blockade of its Western sectors. The Allies responded with the Berlin Airlift, which thwarted the Soviet plans. On 12 May 1949 the blockade was lifted. The same year saw the birth of the Federal Republic of Germany, with its capital in Bonn, and the German Democratic Republic (GDR), with the capital in East Berlin. West Berlin remained as a separate enclave. On 17 June 1953 workers' strikes in the GDR and East Berlin turned into an uprising which was bloodily crushed. In 1961, the GDR authorities surrounded West Berlin with a wall, and shot at any refugees attempting to cross it.

Reunification

The political changes which occurred all over Eastern Europe in 1989 led to the fall of the Berlin Wall. On 3 October 1990, Germany was officially reunified and Berlin once again became the capital. The government moved here in 1991.

Today, Berlin's cutting-edge cultural scene in art, design, fashion, theatre, music and nightlife attracts visitors from all over the world to this buzzing capital city.

Celebrations as the Berlin Wall falls, 9 November 1989

1987 Celebration of Berlin's 750th anniversary

1990 Official reunification of Germany, 3 October

1991 Berlin becomes the German capital, 20 June

1994 Allies leave Berlin

2008 Opening of new US embassy on Pariser Platz marks complete restoration of the square

| 1980 | 1990 | 2000 | 2010 | 2020 |

Trabant – the most popular car in the GDR

1989 Fall of the Berlin Wall, 9 November

1999 The Federal German Parliament assembles at the rebuilt Reichstag in April

2006 Berlin hosted the World Cup

2004 Re-opening of the Olympiastadion Berlin

2009 Celebrated the 20th anniversary of the fall of the Berlin Wall

BERLIN AT A GLANCE

More than 150 places of interest are described in the Area by Area section of this book. These include a range of sights from historic monuments, such as the Nikolaikirche *(see p92)*, to modern landmarks like the ambitious showcase architecture of the Potsdamer Platz district *(see p130)*; from the peace of the Botanical Garden *(see p186)* to the noisier charms of Berlin's long-established zoo *(see p154)*. To help you make the most of your stay, the following 16 pages provide a time-saving guide to the very best that Berlin has to offer. Museums and galleries, historic buildings, parks and gardens, modern architecture, the legacy of the divided city and famous Berliners all feature in this section. Below is a top ten selection of attractions that no visitor should miss.

Berlin's Top Ten Attractions

Pergamonmuseum
See pp82–5.

Schloss Charlottenburg
See pp164–5.

Kunstgewerbe-museum
See pp122–5.

Gemäldegalerie
See pp126–9.

Nikolaiviertel
See pp90–91.

Zoo Berlin
See p154.

Fernsehturm
See p95.

Brandenburger Tor
See p69.

Reichstag
See p138.

Kaiser-Wilhelm-Gedächtnis-Kirche
See pp156–7.

◀ Old masters paintings at Gemaldegalerie at Kulturforum

Berlin's Best: Museums and Galleries

Berlin boasts some of the finest museum
collections in the world. Since 1990 most
of the collections previously split between
East and West Berlin have been brought
together in new venues. One example is
the Gemäldegalerie collection, a magnificent
collection of Old Master paintings. Berlin's
major museum complexes are located on
Museum Island, around Schloss Charlottenburg,
at the Kulturforum and at Dahlem.

Kunstgewerbemuseum
The arts and crafts
collection at the Kunst-
gewerbemuseum
(*see pp122–5*) is among
the most interesting
in Europe. One of its
many treasures is
this 17th-century
gold elephant-
shaped vessel.

**Around Schloss
Charlottenburg**

Tiergarten

**Around
Kurfürstendamm**

Gemäldegalerie
This world-famous collection illustrates the history of
European painting from the 13th to the 18th
centuries. Originally part of a triptych, *The Adoration
of the Magi* (1470) was painted by Hugo van der
Goes (*see pp126–9*).

| 0 metres | 750 |
| 0 yards | 750 |

Museen Dahlem
This huge complex houses
several museums devoted
to ethnography, Asian art
and European folk art and
culture (*see p185*).

Hamburger Bahnhof
Featuring artists such as Joseph Beuys and Andy Warhol, as well as the renowned Friedrich Christian Flick Collection, this art museum is housed in the former Hamburger railway station *(see pp114–15)*.

Pergamonmuseum
This museum owes its name to the reconstructed Pergamon Zeus altar, which stands in its main hall *(see pp82–3)*.

Altes Museum
The ground floor of Karl Friedrich Schinkel's Neo-Classical building has been used since 1998 to exhibit a collection of Greek and Roman antiquities *(see p77)*.

North of the Centre

East of the Centre

Around Unter den Linden

Museum Island

Kreuzberg

Deutsches Historisches Museum
The Baroque Zeughaus contains the Museum of German History. Everyday objects as well as works of art are used to illustrate historical events *(see pp60–61)*.

Deutsches Technikmuseum
The development of a range of industrial technologies, from locomotive-building to brewing, is illustrated in this entertaining museum *(see pp148)*.

Jüdisches Museum
Berlin's Jewish museum was designed by Daniel Libeskind, an American architect of Jewish descent. The form of the building is based on the Star of David *(see p146–7)*.

Exploring Berlin's Museums

Despite being damaged during World War II, Berlin's numerous museums are still among the finest, and the most heavily subsidized, in the world. Many collections were split up when the city was partitioned in 1946, and although the process of bringing them together again is almost complete, a few collections are still scattered around different sites, and many of the older museums are being refurbished.

Picasso's *Head of the Faun* (1937) in the Museum Berggruen

Ancient Art

The art of ancient Egypt is shown at the **Ägyptisches Museum** (Egyptian Museum). The jewel of this museum, which is housed in the **Neues Museum**, is the bust of Queen Nefertiti. The 19th-century **Altes Museum** contains a large Greek and Roman antiquities collection, as does the **Pergamon-museum**, where visitors can see several reconstructed architectural wonders, including the Pergamon Zeus altar and the Market Gate from Miletus. The museum also holds an impressive collection of Middle Eastern art, including a reconstruction of the Babylonian Ishtar Gate.

The famous bust of Nefertiti, Neues Museum

and Italian sculpture is housed in the **Bode-Museum**, while the **Alte Nationalgalerie** (Old National Gallery) displays 18th- and 19th-century art, including paintings by the German Romantics, amongst which are famous landscapes by Caspar David Friedrich.

A collection of sculpture from the late 16th to the mid-19th centuries can be seen in the **Schinkel-Museum**. The **Neue Nationalgalerie** (New National Gallery) is filled with late 19th- and early 20th-century paintings and sculpture. Art Nouveau and Art Deco works are featured at the **Bröhan-Museum**, while works by modern greats, such as Pablo Picasso, Paul Klee and Georges Braque, are on show at the **Museum Berggruen**

(Berggruen Museum).

The **Brücke-Museum** displays the works of German Expressionists, and contemporary art is exhibited in the **Hamburger Bahnhof**.

Arts and crafts, from the Middle Ages to the present, are displayed at the **Kunstge-werbemuseum** (Museum of Applied Arts). The **Bauhaus-Archiv** displays applied arts from the influential inter-war Bauhaus movement.

Other museums include the **Newton-Sammlung**, which contains the life's work of 20th-century photographer Helmut Newton, while the reopened **Berlinische Galerie** shows the city's collection of modern art and architecture.

Fine Art and Design

Berlin's largest collection of 13th- to 18th-century European painting is displayed in the **Gemäldegalerie** (Picture Gallery). Here are works by old masters including Dürer, Rembrandt, Titian, Botticelli and Caravaggio. In the same museum complex is the **Kupferstichkabinett**, with drawings and prints from the Middle Ages to the present.

Old masters can also be seen in the **Jagdschloss Grunewald**, a Renaissance palace home to German and Dutch paintings from the 14th to 19th centuries. A large collection of predominantly 17th-century paintings is housed in the **Bildergalerie** (Gallery of Paintings) in Potsdam. German

Étienne Chevalier with St Stephen by Jean Fouquet, Gemäldegalerie

Non-European Art

Those interested in Asian art should visit the **Museen Dahlem**. This complex houses three large collections: the Museum für Asiatische Kunst (Museum of Asian Art), the Ethnologisches Museum (Museum of Ethnography), which explores the heritage of non-European nations, and the Museum Europäischer Kulturen (Museum for European Cultures). The **Museum für Islamische Kunst** (Museum of Islamic Art) is located in the same building as the Pergamonmuseum.

Totem pole, Ethnologisches Museum

History

The collection of the **Deutsches Historisches Museum** (Museum of German History) traces German history from the Middle Ages to the present. The **Hugenottenmuseum** (Huguenot Museum), located in the twower of the Französischer Dom, charts the history of the city's Huguenots.

The **Centrum Judaicum** (Jewish Centre) in the Neue Synagogue (New Synagogue), and the **Jüdisches Museum** (Jewish Museum), in a striking building by Daniel Libeskind, are devoted to Jewish history and cultural heritage.

Berlin has several museums associated with World War II. The **Topographie des Terrors** (Topography of Terror) exhibition is displayed at the site of the former Gestapo and SS headquarters. A deeply shocking collection of documents concerning the Holocaust is kept at the **Haus der Wannsee-Konferenz**. The tools of terror used on the citizens of the German Democratic Republic can be seen at the **Stasi-Museum**, while the **Haus am Checkpoint Charlie** (House at Checkpoint Charlie) museum tells the stories of those who crossed the Berlin Wall. The **Alliiertenmuseum** focuses on life during the Cold War.

Technology and Natural History

The **Museum für Naturkunde** (Museum of Natural History) contains the world's biggest dinosaur skeleton. Also popular with visitors is the **Deutsches Technik-museum** (German Technology Museum), which is situated in a large site around a former railway station. German movie history (including props, clips and original costumes worn by divas such as Marlene Dietrich) is presented at the **Filmmuseum Berlin**. Those interested in technology should also visit the **Museum für Kommunikation** (Museum of Communications).

Specialist Subjects

Berlin is not short of specialist museums. There are museums devoted to laundry, sugar and even hemp. Lovers of theatre and literature can visit the one-time home of Bertolt Brecht (1898–1956), now the **Brecht-Weigel Gedenkstätte** (Brecht-Weigel Memorial). Worth a visit to see the magnificent Wurlitzer organ alone is the **Musikinstrumenten-Museum** (Musical Instruments Museum). The outdoor **Domäne Dahlem** (Dahlem Farm Museum) shows 300 years of local farm life and exhibits old-fashioned tools.

Finding the Museums

A wide array of exhibits in the Musikinstrumenten-Museum

Berlin's Best: Historic Architecture

Berlin is a relatively new city. It expanded slowly until the first half of the 19th century, and then grew with increasing rapidity from around 1850 onwards. Although many of the city's finest architectural treasures were destroyed by World War II bombing, it is still possible to discover many interesting historic buildings (for more information, *see pp40–41*). In nearby Potsdam (*see pp192–207*) you can visit the splendid Schloss Sanssouci. Set in magnificent parkland, the palace was built for Friedrich II (1740–1786) and extended by subsequent rulers.

Schloss Charlottenburg
The construction of this Baroque royal palace at Charlottenburg was begun in 1695. Subsequent extension works took place throughout the 18th century (*see pp164–5*).

Around Schloss Charlottenburg

Tiergarten

Around Kurfürstendamm

| 0 metres | 750 |
| 0 yards | 750 |

Schloss Bellevue
This Rococo palace by Michael Philipp Boumann is now the official residence of the President of the Federal Republic of Germany.

Schloss Sanssouci
This small palace was the favourite residence of Friedrich II.

PARADIES-GARTEN
Neues Palais
PARK SANSSOUCI
Schloss Sanssouci
PARK CHARLOTTENHOF
Schloss Charlottenhof

Neues Palais
The Neues Palais combines elements of Baroque and Neo-Classical style.

Potsdam Palaces
The summer palace of Schloss Sanssouci gives its name to Potsdam's Park Sanssouci, a royal complex with highlights including the grand 18th-century Neues Palais and the small but charming Schloss Charlottenhof.

The Reichstag
This massive Neo-Renaissance building was designed in 1884 by Paul Wallot. Its elegant dome is the work of British architect Norman Foster (*see p138*).

Zeughaus
This Baroque arsenal houses the Deutsches Historisches Museum *(see pp60–61)*. Its courtyard contains masks of dying warriors by sculptor Andreas Schlüter (1660–1714).

Marienkirche
This Gothic church, founded in the 13th century, contains a striking 15th-century mural. It is one of the city's oldest buildings *(see pp96–7)*.

North of the Centre

East of the Centre

Around Unter den Linden

Museum Island

Kreuzberg

Rotes Rathaus
Berlin's main Town Hall is named "red" after the colour of its brick exterior, not the political persuasion of the Mayor *(see p92)*.

Berliner Dom
This enormous cathedral, built between 1894 and 1905, is an example of the Neo-Renaissance style in Berlin *(see pp78–9)*.

Brandenburger Tor
This Neo-Classical gate stands at the end of Unter den Linden. Crowned by a Quadriga (chariot) driven by the Goddess of Victory, it is the symbol of Berlin *(see p69)*.

Konzerthaus
Built in 1820 to replace a theatre destroyed by fire, this beautiful building on the Gendarmenmarkt was designed by Karl Friedrich Schinkel *(see pp67)*.

Exploring Berlin's Historic Architecture

Until the industrial revolution of the late 19th century, Berlin was little more than a small town surrounded by villages. As a result, the city's oldest buildings are concentrated in the central core around Unter den Linden and along the Spree river, an area which suffered heavy damage during World War II. Older country residences, however, as well as some important more recent buildings, can be seen in former villages such as Wedding and Charlottenburg, which now form part of Greater Berlin.

14th-century Gothic doorway of the Nikolaikirche in the Nikolaiviertel

Middle Ages and Renaissance

The **Nikolaikirche** is the oldest building in central Berlin. The base of its massive front tower is Romanesque and dates back to about 1230, although the church itself is Gothic and was built between 1380 and 1450. The second Gothic church in the city centre is the **Marienkirche**. Nearby are the ruins of a **Franciscan friary** and the **Heiliggeistkapelle**. Many medieval churches outside the city centre have survived the war. Among the most beautiful is the late Gothic **Nikolaikirche** in Spandau, dating from the early

15th century. A further ten village churches, most dating from the 13th century, can be found hidden among high-rise apartment buildings. **St Annen-Kirche** in Dahlem, however, still enjoys an almost rural setting.

The few surviving secular structures include fragments of the **city walls** in the city centre, and the **Juliusturm** in Spandau, a huge, early 13th-century tower which stands in the grounds of the Spandau Citadel. Berlin's only surviving Renaissance buildings are the **Ribbeckhaus** with its four picturesque gables, the **Jagdschloss-Grunewald**, a modest hunting lodge designed by Casper Theyss in 1542, and the **Spandau Citadel** (or fortress), a well-preserved example of Italian-style military defence architecture. Finished in 1592, the construction of the Citadel was begun in 1560 by Christoph Römer using plans by Italian architect Francesco Chiaramella da Gandino. It was brought to completion by Rochus Guerrini Graf zu Lynar (the Count of Lynar).

Detail of the Zeughaus

Baroque Expansion

The Thirty Years' War (1618–48) put a temporary stop to the town's development, and it was not until the Peace of 1648 that new building work in the Baroque style began. One of the first of the city's Baroque buildings is the late 17th-century **Schloss Köpenick**. More buildings followed, many of which survive today. They include the **Parochialkirche**, the **Deutscher Dom** and the **Französischer Dom**, as well as the magnificent **Zeughaus**, built between 1695 and 1730. During this period Andreas Schlüter (1664–1714) designed the now-demolished Stadt-schloss (Royal Palace), while Johann Arnold Nering (1659–95) designed **Schloss Charlottenburg**. Other surviving Baroque palaces include **Palais Podewils** and **Schloss Schönhausen**. One of the few buildings dating from the reign of Friedrich Wilhelm I (1713–40) is the **Kollegienhaus** at Lindenstrasse No. 14, designed by Philipp Gerlach and built in 1733. During the reign of Friedrich II (1740–86), many buildings were erected in the late Baroque and Rococo styles. These include **Schloss Sanssouci** in Potsdam and the **Alte Bibliothek** building on Unter den Linden, which completed the Forum Fridericianum project, now better known as Bebelplatz (see pp58–9).

Neo-Classicism and Romanticism

The Neo-Classical architecture of the late 18th and early 19th centuries has given Berlin much of its basic form. One dominant figure of this period was Carl Gotthard Langhans (1732–1808), creator of the **Brandenburg Gate** and of **Schloss Bellevue**. Even more influential, however, was Karl Friedrich Schinkel (see p181). His

Renaissance-style defence, the Citadel building at Spandau

work includes some of Berlin's most important public buildings, including the **Neue Wache**, the **Altes Museum** and the **Konzerthaus**. Many of Schinkel's residential commissions are also still standing, with some such as **Schloss Klein Glienicke** and **Schloss Tegel** open to the public. Schinkel's Neo-Gothic work includes **Schloss Babelsberg** and the **Friedrichswerdersche Kirche**.

Elegant Neo-Classicism at Karl Friedrich Schinkel's Schloss Klein Glienicke

Industrialization and the Modern Age

The second half of the 19th century was a time of rapid development for Berlin. After Schinkel's death, his work was continued by his students, Ludwig Persius (1803–45) and Friedrich August Stüler (1800–65). Stüler designed the Neo-Classical **Alte Nationalgalerie** between 1866 and 1876. Some splendid Neo-Romanesque and Neo-Gothic churches and several notable public buildings in various styles were also produced at this time. The spirit of the Italian Neo-Renaissance is seen in the **Rotes Rathaus** designed by Hermann Friedrich Waesemann, and in the **Martin-Gropius-Bau**, by Martin Gropius in 1877. Late Neo-Renaissance features are used in Paul Wallot's **Reichstag**

Decorative frieze on the Martin-Gropius-Bau

20th-century Neo-Renaissance detail of the massive Berliner Dom

building and in Ernst von Ihne's **Statsbibliothek** building. Julius Raschdorff's **Berliner Dom** shows Neo-Baroque influences. Much of the religious architecture of the period continued in the Neo-Gothic style, while Franz Schwechten designed the **Kaiser-Wilhelm-Gedächtnis-Kirche** in the Neo-Romanesque style. Many structures of this period are built in the modernist style inspired by the industrial revolution, the textbook example being the huge power station, **AEG-Turbinenhalle**, designed by Peter Behrens in the 1890s.

Between the Two World Wars

The greatest architectural achievements of this period include a number of splendid housing estates, such as the **Hufeisensiedlung** designed by Bruno Taut and Martin Wagner in 1924, and **Onkel-Toms-Hütte** in Zehlendorf. An interesting example of the Expressionist style is Erich Mendelsohn's **Einsteinturm** in Potsdam. Art Deco is represented by Hans Poelzig's **Haus des Rundfunks**, the country's first Broadcasting House. Hitler's rise to power in the 1930s marked a return to the classical forms which dominated German architecture of the Fascist period. Representatives of this period include the **Tempelhof Airport** Terminal building and the **Olympia-Stadion**, built for the 1936 Olympic Games.

Historic Buildings

Reminders of the Divided City

In 1945, as part of the post-war peace, Berlin was divided into four zones of occupation: Soviet, American, British and French. Hostilities erupted in June 1948, when the Soviets blockaded West Berlin in an attempt to bring the area under their control. The ensuing year-long standoff marked the start of the Cold War. By the 1950s, economic problems in the East had led to bloodily-suppressed riots and a mass exodus to the West. In 1961 the East German government constructed the infamous Berlin Wall *(die Mauer)* to contain its citizens. Between this time and reunification at the end of 1989, more than 180 people were shot trying to cross the Wall.

Berlin Wall
Protected to the east by land mines, the Wall, known by the East German authorities as the "Anti-Fascist Protection Wall", surrounded West Berlin and was 155 km (95 miles) long *(see p113).*

Memorial to Soviet Soldiers
Part of West Berlin, the area around this monument to Red Army troops killed in the 1945 Battle of Berlin was closed for many years due to attacks on its Soviet guards *(see p139).*

Around Schloss Charlottenburg

Tiergarten

0 km 1
0 miles 0.5

Key
— Berlin Wall

Around Kurfürstendamm

Berlin Before Reunification

The Wall cut the city in half, severing its main transport arteries, the S-Bahn and U-Bahn lines. West Berliners were excluded from the centre of the city. Running along the Wall was a no-man's-land.

Key
— Berlin Wall
— Sector boundaries
✈ Airport

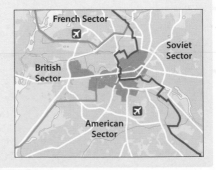

French Sector

British Sector

Soviet Sector

American Sector

Tränenpalast (Palace of Tears)
Until 1989 the Tränenpalast, next to the final S-Bahn station in East Berlin, was a border checkpoint for S-Bahn passengers heading west.

Checkpoint Charlie
This border crossing between the American and Soviet sectors was used by foreign citizens and diplomats. It was the location of many dramatic events during the years of the Cold War (see p145).

East Side Gallery
The longest remaining section of the Berlin Wall became an open-air gallery in 1990, covered with an eclectic mixture of paintings by 118 artists (see p175).

North of the Centre

East of the Centre

Around Unter den Linden

Museum Island

Kreuzberg

Luftbrücke
This striking memorial commemorates those who died during the Berlin Airlift of 1948–9. Allied planes delivered 2.3 million tons of supplies to West Berlin in the face of the year-long Soviet blockade (see p149).

Haus am Checkpoint Charlie
This museum holds photos and other Wall memorabilia, including a selection of escape vehicles (see p145).

Berlin's Best: Modern Architecture

Following Berlin's devastation in World War II, intense post-war reconstruction turned the city into a giant building site. With the help of architects from several countries the city acquired many modern structures and estates, ranked among the best in the world. The city's reunification in 1990 and the reinstatement of Berlin as the main seat of government gave rise to a second wave of building activity, carried out on a scale unprecedented in Europe. The architectural elite are participating in the design of the new Berlin, and the sites in the city centre that stood empty until 1990 are being filled with buildings at an incredible rate.

Bauhaus-Archiv
This cubist structure was completed in 1978 to house the Bauhaus museum. It was designed much earlier by Walter Gropius (1883–1969), director of the Bauhaus art school from 1919 to 1928.

Kammermusiksaal

Around Schloss Charlottenburg

Tiergarten

Around Kurfürstendamm

Gemäldegalerie

Kant-Dreieck
This building, with its pure forms and the eccentric sail-like structure mounted on the roof, is the work of Josef Paul Kleihues.

Nordische Botschaften
Built between 1997 and 1999, the five interconnected embassies of the Scandinavian countries are an example of daring architectural design. The building's green shutters adjust to the intensity and direction of available sunlight.

Kammermusiksaal
Both the Berliner Philharmonie building (1961) and the adjacent Kammermusiksaal, or chamber music hall (1987), were designed by Hans Scharoun. The latter was built posthumously by Edgar Wisniewski, Scharoun's pupil.

Galeries Lafayette
This elegant department store in Friedrichstrasse, designed by Jean Nouvel, brings Parisian chic to the heart of Berlin.

Quartier Schützenstrasse
This part of the city features the work of Italian architect Aldo Rossi. With high-rise blocks and bold colour schemes, the area shows modernity and classical forms standing side by side.

North of the Centre

East of the Centre

Around Unter den Linden

Museum Island

Kreuzberg

| 0 metres | 750 |
| 0 yards | 750 |

Gemäldegalerie
The Gemäldegalerie, designed by the Hilmer and Sattler Partnership, opened in June 1998. The main hall is particularly elegant.

Sony Center
This ultra-modern steel-and-glass building was designed by German-American architect Helmut Jahn. It houses offices, entertainment venues, the Kaisersaal and Sony's European headquarters.

Exploring Berlin's Modern Architecture

Around the world architects are forever designing buildings with innovative and interesting structures, but in Berlin this creative process is happening on an unprecedented scale. The city is a vast melting pot of trends and styles, where the world's greatest architects scramble for commissions and where the buildings compete with each other in the originality of their form and in their use of the latest technology.

Haus der Kulturen der Welt in the Tiergarten

From 1945 to 1970

World War II exacted a heavy price from Berlin. The centre was reduced to rubble and the partitioning of the city made it impossible to carry out any co-ordinated reconstruction. In 1952, East Berlin decided to develop **Karl-Marx-Allee** in the Socialist-Realist style. In reply, West Berlin employed the world's greatest architects to create the **Hansaviertel** estate. Le Corbusier built one of his *unités d'habitation*, while the American architect, Hugh A Stubbins, built the Kongresshalle (now the **Haus der Kulturen der Welt**). The West's response to the cultural venues inherited by the East Berliners, including the opera, the library and the museums, was the **Kulturforum** complex. The complex included such magnificent buildings as the **Philharmonie**, designed by Hans Scharoun, and the **Neue Nationalgalerie**, designed by Mies van der Rohe. While West Berlin acquired its huge "trade temple"– the **Europa-Center**,

constructed in 1965, East Berlin boasted its **Fernsehturm** (television tower), built in 1969.

From 1970 to 1990

The continuing rivalry, as each part of the city tried to outdo the other, resulted in the construction of East Berlin's now demolished **Palast der Republic** in 1976. The West replied with the ultramodern **Internationales Congress Centrum** in 1979. The Kulturforum complex was further extended with designs by Scharoun, including the **Kammermusiksaal** and the **Staatsbibliothek** (library). The impressive **Bauhaus-Archiv** was developed from a design by Walter Gropius. In 1987 Berlin celebrated its 750th anniversary, which in the East saw the completion of the huge **Nikolaiviertel** development, with its pre-war allusions. In the West, the IBA's 1987 scheme gave the town its enormous post-modernist housing estates in Kreuzberg and also in the **Tegel** area.

Post-Reunification Architecture

The government district was constructed within the bend of the Spree river. Its designers include Charlotte Frank and Axel Schultes. The **Reichstag** building has been famously remodelled by Norman Foster. **Pariser Platz** has been filled with designs by Günther Behnisch, Frank O Gehry, Josef Paul Kleihues and others. The magnificent **Friedrichstadt-passagen** complex became the scene of rivalry between Jean Nouvel and Oswald M Ungers. Many interesting office buildings have sprung up around town, including **Ludwig-Erhard-Haus** by Nicholas Grimshaw and the nearby **Kant-Dreieck** by Josef Paul Kleihues. Housing has also been transformed, with perhaps the most original example being Aldo Rossi's **Quartier Schützen-strasse**. The city has also acquired some fine museums, including the **Gemäl-degalerie** designed by the Hilmer and Sattler Partnership, and the Deconstructivist style **Jüdisches Museum**, designed by Daniel Libeskind.

Neue Nationalgalerie at Kulturforum designed by Mies van der Rohe

Potsdamer Platz

Between 1993 and 1998, a financial, business and entertainment district was erected on the once vast and empty wasteland around Potsdamer Platz. It boasts splendid constructions designed by Renzo Piano, Arata Isozaki and Helmut Jahn. As well as office blocks, the area has many public buildings, including cinemas and a theatre, as well as a huge shopping centre – the Arkaden, plus luxury hotels, restaurants and several bars.

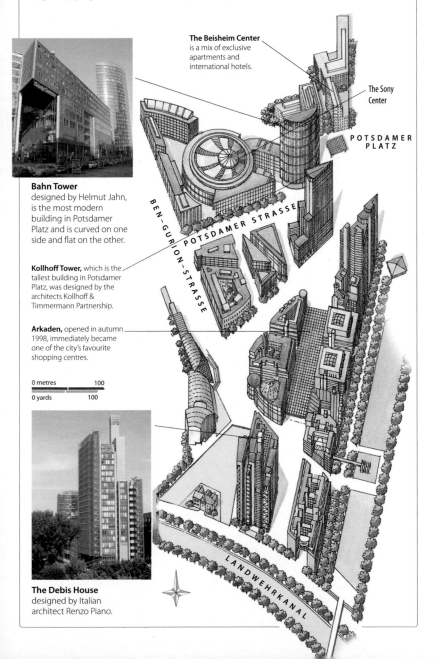

The Beisheim Center is a mix of exclusive apartments and international hotels.

The Sony Center

POTSDAMER PLATZ

BEN-GURION-STRASSE

POTSDAMER STRASSE

LANDWEHRKANAL

Bahn Tower designed by Helmut Jahn, is the most modern building in Potsdamer Platz and is curved on one side and flat on the other.

Kollhoff Tower, which is the tallest building in Potsdamer Platz, was designed by the architects Kollhoff & Timmermann Partnership.

Arkaden, opened in autumn 1998, immediately became one of the city's favourite shopping centres.

0 metres 100
0 yards 100

The Debis House designed by Italian architect Renzo Piano.

Berlin's Best: Parks and Gardens

Berlin is undoubtedly one of Europe's greenest
capital cities, with the sprawling Tiergarten at its
centre. However, most of Berlin's districts have their
own smaller parks and gardens, too, some of them
with children's play areas and nature trails. To the
west of the city is the vast Grunewald, a beautiful
area of forest which contains mountain bike trails
and scenic paths for walkers and cyclists. In summer,
numerous lakes, rivers and canals provide excellent
facilities for water sports.

Schloss Charlottenburg
The well-maintained grounds
of this royal palace were
designed in the French
Baroque style *(see pp164–5)*.

Zoologischer Garten
Popular with children, Berlin's zoo has
some 14,000 animals, representing
1,400 different species. It is the oldest
zoo in Germany *(see p154)*.

**Around Schloss
Charlottenburg**

**Around
Kurfürstendamm**

| 0 metres | 1000 |
| 0 yards | 1000 |

Gutspark Britz
The landscaped park with its
beautiful lime-tree avenue,
surrounds the early
18th-century Schloss Britz
(see p183).

Botanischer Garten
Established from
1899 to 1910 in
Dahlem, this
botanical garden is
one of the biggest in
the world *(see p186)*.

Park Babelsberg
This vast landscaped park was
designed by Peter Joseph
Lenné, and now lies within the
Potsdam city limits. It surrounds
the picturesque Schloss
Babelsberg *(see pp212–13)*.

Tiergarten
Once a hunting reserve, this was converted
into a park after 1818 by landscape designer
Peter Joseph Lenné (see p136).

Monbijoupark
The park once surrounded
Monbijou Palace, which
was destroyed during
World War II (see p105).

North of the
Centre

East of the
Centre

Around Unter
den Linden

Museum
Island

Tiergarten

Kreuzberg

Tierpark Friedrichsfelde
In 1954 the park at Schloss
Friedrichsfelde was
converted into the East
Berlin Zoological Garden
(see p182–3).

Viktoriapark
This large park winds around a hill with good views of Kreuzberg.
At its peak stands a memorial to the wars of liberation fought
against Napoleon (see p149).

BERLIN THROUGH THE YEAR

Like all major European capitals, Berlin offers a wide range of activities throughout the year. The best seasons for cultural and sporting events are spring and autumn, when the city hosts many spectacular fairs and exhibitions. During summer the city's population shrinks, as many locals head for their holiday destinations. But the weather is often pleasant, and rarely very hot, so this is a good time for serious sightseeing. In winter, although it can get quite cold, it is possible to spend time visiting museums or simply walking around the city. The streets teem with shoppers during the run up to Christmas. A more detailed programme of events can be obtained from tourist information offices *(see p278)* or on the Internet at www.visitberlin.de.

The Karneval der Kulturen in the streets of Kreuzberg

Spring

In springtime, Berlin holds many interesting fairs and cultural events in its squares, parks and gardens, allowing the visitor to appreciate fully the beauty of the city as the trees and flowers burst into life. With the arrival of the warmer weather, another natural resource springs to life as cruise and rowing boats start operating on the Spree river and the city's canals.

March

ITB-Internationale Tourismus-Börse *(mid-Mar)*. The biggest European fair devoted to tourism where representatives from around the world try to attract visitors to their countries.
März Musik *(mid-Mar)* is a music festival featuring works by contemporary composers, including both German and world premieres.
Berlin Motorrad Tage *(end Mar)*. Motorcyclists from all over Germany converge on Berlin for this specialist event.

April

Festtage *(Apr)*. A series of popular concerts and operas performed by world-class musicians in the Philharmonie and at the Staatsoper.
Easter *(exact date varies)*. Markets open around the Kaiser-Wilhelm-Gedächtnis-kirche, Alexanderplatz and other central locations.
Britzer Baumblüte *(all of Apr)* is a month-long spring festival organized in Britz, a suburb in the south of the city famous for its gardens.
Neuköllner Maientage *(Apr–May)*, Hasenheide. Traditional springtime festival celebrating the new season.
Köpenicker Winzerfest *(end of Apr)*. Sample top wines and gourmet food in the charming old town square of Köpenick, a district in southeast Berlin.

May

1 Mai *(1 May)*. The traditional May Day celebrations are especially significant in Berlin. They have become a day of widespread demonstrations featuring activists, workers and curious tourists. Most of the daytime demonstrations are peaceful, but Kreuzberg should be avoided at night.
Theatertreffen Berlin *(May)*. This important Berlin theatre festival has been running since 1963, and provides a platform for theatre productions from German-speaking regions around the world.
Berliner Frauenlauf *(late May)* is a popular 5 km fun-run through Tiergarten – but it is reserved for women only.
Big 25 Berlin *(early May)*, formerly known as the Franzosenlauf (French run), starts at the Olympiastadion and winds through the city. All runners can participate.

Street recitation of poetry during the Theatertreffen Berlin in May

Average Daily Hours of Sunshine

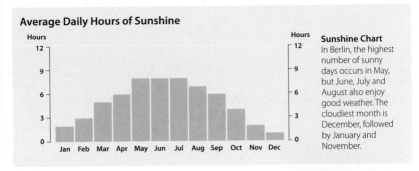

Hours

12 — 9 — 6 — 3 — 0

Jan Feb Mar Apr May Jun Jul Aug Sep Oct Nov Dec

Hours

12 — 9 — 6 — 3 — 0

Sunshine Chart
In Berlin, the highest number of sunny days occurs in May, but June, July and August also enjoy good weather. The cloudiest month is December, followed by January and November.

Summer

Summertime in Berlin is marked by many open-air events. There are concerts of classical music and opera performances, jazz festivals and sports events, an annual air show, a series of open-air concerts and festivals for the young. It is also possible to take advantage of the good weather by taking a walk or bicycle ride in the Grunewald, or swimming in the lakes of Wannsee or Müggelsee.

An outdoor artist at work in the Potsdamer Platz

June
Deutsch-Französisches Volksfest (early Jun–mid-Jul). German-French folk festival near Kurt-Schumacher-Damm.
Internationales Tango Festival Berlin (mid-Jun) brings a bit of South American culture to various venues.
Karneval der Kulturen (mid-Jun). For three days, the streets of Kreuzberg district are brought to life by singing and dancing in this display celebrating multicultural Berlin.
Luft- und Raumfahrtaus-stellung Berlin-Brandenburg (Jun/Sep, check in advance).

This biannual festival and air show of civil, military and space craft fills the skies above Berlin Brandenburg airport.
Christopher Street Day (end Jun) features a gay and lesbian parade with revellers in extravagant outfits, held around Ku'damm. At night, the party continues until late in the city's many gay clubs and kneipen.

July
Classic Open Air (mid-Jul). Concerts and operas on Gendarmenmarkt, complemented by events in Waldbühne.
Konzertsommer im Englischen Garten (early Jul– end Aug). Open-air concerts.
Berliner Gauklerfest (late Jul–early Aug). Stalls on Unter den Linden sell speciality foods, while crowds are entertained by acrobats and musicians.

August
Deutsch-Amerikanisches Volksfest (late Jul–mid-Aug). A programme of entertainment

Ku'damm full of revellers on Christopher Street Day

with an American theme that always draws the crowds.
Kreuzberger Festliche Tage (end Aug–early Sep). This is a large multi-event festival of art and music held in Kreuzberg.
Jüdische Kulturtage (end Aug–early Sep). A festival devoted to Jewish arts and culture with films, plays, concerts and lectures.

Prokofiev's *The Love of Three Oranges* performed in the Komische Oper

Average Monthly Rainfall

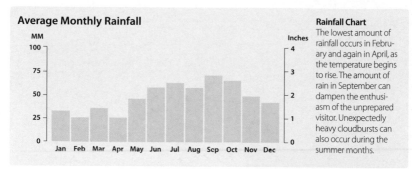

Rainfall Chart
The lowest amount of rainfall occurs in February and again in April, as the temperature begins to rise. The amount of rain in September can dampen the enthusiasm of the unprepared visitor. Unexpectedly heavy cloudbursts can also occur during the summer months.

Autumn

Autumn in Berlin is marked by major cultural events. In September the city's hotels fill with visitors arriving for the Berliner Festwochen, to hear concerts given by some of the world's top artists and to make the most of the wide range of culture on offer. Autumn is also a time for major sports events, including the Berlin Marathon, the third biggest in the world after New York and London.

September

Internationale Funkausstellung *(early Sep, every two years)*. High-tech media and computer fair at the Internationales Congress Centrum *(see p179)*.
Bach Tage Potsdam *(early Sep)* features around 30 concerts of Johann Sebastian Bach's music, performed in concert halls in Potsdam. The festival lasts nine days.

Internationales Literaturfestival *(mid-Sep)*. Readings, lectures and special events featuring old and new writing from around the world.
Popkomm *(mid-Sep)*. This is Europe's biggest pop music fair, which also has a very lively club and dance programme/festival.
Musikfest Berlin *(mid-Sep)*. Orchestras and ensembles from across the world come to Berlin to take part in this impressive classical music event, held mostly at the Philharmonie.
Berlin-Marathon *(3rd Sun in Sep)*. This international running event attracts thousands of runners and brings the city's traffic to a halt for several hours.

Participants in the September Berlin-Marathon

October

Tag der Deutschen Einheit *(3 Oct)*. Berlin celebrates the reunification of Germany with street festivals.
International Salsa Festival *(early Oct)*. Salsa shows and more.
Festival of Lights *(mid-Oct)*. Dozens of modern and historical buildings are illuminated. There's a spectacular opening ceremony.
Haupstadt Turnier *(late Oct)*. International horse-jumping.

November

Jazz Fest Berlin *(early Nov)*. Held annually since 1964, this respected jazz festival kicks off in the Haus der Kulturen der Welt *(see p138)*.
Treffen Junge Musik-Szene *(early Nov)*. Music for the younger generation.
Spielzeit Europa *(Oct–Dec)*. A festival of unusual and high-quality theatre and dance, held at the Haus der Berliner Festspiele.

Marching through the Brandenburg Gate on Tag der Deutschen Einheit

Average Monthly Temperature

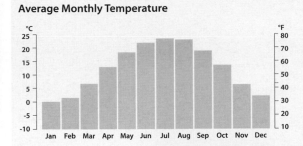

Temperature Chart
Average maximum and minimum temperatures are shown here. The warmest months are June, July and August when the temperature exceeds 20°C. Winters are cold and temperatures can drop below −5°C in January, with the chance of heavy snowfalls or extreme frost.

Winter

Berlin's winters are usually cold and the temperature can sometimes drop to below zero, with a carpet of snow lining the streets. During December, the city prepares for Christmas with many traditional markets. January brings numerous Carnival balls, while the major event in February is the great cinema gala – the Berlin International Film Festival, Berlinale.

December

Weihnachstmärkte (throughout Dec). In the month before Christmas the city is dotted with picturesque fairs and festive stalls selling Christmas gifts and regional culinary specialities.
Christmas (Weihnachten) (25–26 Dec). As in many other European cities, Berlin's traditional celebrations include Christmas trees, present-giving, family gatherings and communal feasts.
New Year's Eve (Silvester) (31 Dec) is celebrated across Berlin, in hotels, restaurants, clubs and in private homes; another traditional activity is the popping of champagne corks at the Brandenburg Gate while watching the fireworks.

January

Berliner Neujahrslauf (1 Jan). For those unaffected by the previous night's revelry, this 4-km (2.4-mile) run along the city streets starts off at the Brandenburg Gate.
Lange Nacht der Museen (end of Jan, also held in Aug). A series of events organized by Berlin's

Berlinale – the grand festival of world cinema

museums which stay open until midnight or later.
Internationale Grüne Woche (last week of Jan). This giant fair is devoted to agriculture and food; it provides an ideal opportunity to sample delicacies from all over the world.
Transmediale (Jan and Feb) is a busy festival of experimental and electronic music.

Christmas shopping in the KaDeWe department store

February

Sechs-Tage-Rennen (early Feb). This meeting in the Velodrome features a six-day bicycle race and other events.
Berlinale – Internationale Filmfestspiele (2nd and 3rd week in Feb). This gala of cinematography attracts movie stars and the best films of the season. It is held in tandem with the **Internationales Forum des Jungen Films** which features low-budget movies (see p99).

Public Holidays

Neujahr New Year (1 Jan)
Karfreitag Good Friday
Ostermontag Easter Mon
Tag der Arbeit Labour Day (1 May)
Christi Himmelfahrt Ascension Day
Pfingsten Whitsun
Tag der Deutschen Einheit (3 Oct)
Weihnachten Christmas (25–26 Dec)

The Reichstag dome from the inside ▶

BERLIN AREA BY AREA

AROUND UNTER DEN LINDEN

The area around the grand avenue Unter den Linden is among the most attractive in Berlin. Its development started during the Baroque period with the establishment of Dorotheenstadt to the north and Friedrichstadt to the south. From the early 18th century, prestigious buildings began to appear here, and work started on the Forum Friedericianum (later Bebelplatz). Over the following two centuries Unter den Linden became one of the city's most imposing avenues. World War II bombing took a heavy toll, but despite only partial reconstruction by the East German government, the area is still home to the highest concentration of historic buildings in Berlin.

Sights at a Glance

Churches
⓫ St-Hedwigs-Kathedrale
⓮ Friedrichswerdersche Kirche
⓰ Französischer Dom
⓲ Deutscher Dom

Museums and Galleries
❶ Zeughaus (Deutsches Historisches Museum) (pp60–61)
❼ Deutsche Bank KunstHalle
㉒ Museum für Kommunikation

Streets and Squares
❷ Unter den Linden
❿ Bebelplatz
⓯ Gendarmenmarkt
㉔ Pariser Platz

Theatres
⓬ Staatsoper Unter den Linden
⓱ Konzerthaus
㉙ Komische Oper
㉛ Admiralspalast
㉜ Maxim Gorki Theater

Historic Buildings and Sites
❸ Neue Wache
❹ Humboldt Universität
❺ Reiterdenkmal Friedrichs des Grossen
❻ Staatsbibliothek
❽ Altes Palais
❾ Alte Bibliothek
⓭ Kronprinzenpalais
⓴ Mohrenkolonnaden
㉑ Spittelkolonnaden
㉕ Brandenburger Tor
㉖ Holocaust Denkmal
㉝ Palais am Festungsgraben

Others
⓳ Friedrichstadtpassagen
㉓ Ehemaliges Regierungsviertel
㉗ Hotel Adlon
㉘ Russische Botschaft
㉚ Bahnhof Friedrichstrasse

▢ Restaurants
see pp 232–3

1 Augustiner am Gemdarmenmarkt
2 Bocca di Bacco
3 Borchardt
4 Cookies Cream
5 Chipps
6 Dressler
7 Einstein Cafe
8 Fischers Fritz
9 Lorenz Adlon Esszimmer
10 Margeaux
11 Nante-Eck
12 Quarré
13 Samadhi
14 Vau
15 Zwolf Apostel

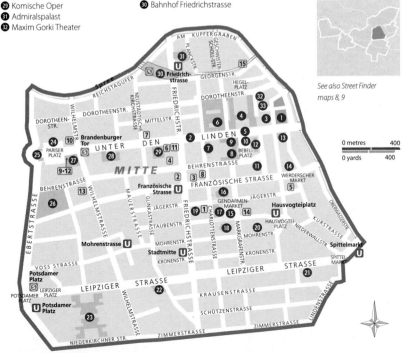

See also Street Finder maps 8, 9

0 metres 400
0 yards 400

Street-by-Street: Around Bebelplatz

The section of Unter Den Linden between Schlossbrücke and Friedrichstrasse is one of the most attractive places in central Berlin. There are some magnificent Baroque and Neo-Classical buildings, many of them designed by famous architects. There are also some restored palaces that are now used as public buildings. Of particular interest is the beautiful Baroque building of the Zeughaus (the former Arsenal), which now houses the German History Museum.

6 Staatsbibliothek
This Neo-Baroque building, designed by Ernst von Ihne, was built between 1903 and 1914. It houses a collection that dates from the 17th century.

4 Humboldt Universität
The entrance to the courtyard is framed by two guardroom pavilions and is crowned with the allegorical figures of Dawn and Dusk.

5 Equestrian Statue of Frederick the Great
The impressive statue dates from 1851 and is the work of Christian Daniel Rauch.

7 Deutsche Bank KunstHalle
Formerly known as Deutsche Guggenheim, this building provides a space for contemporary art exhibitions.

8 Altes Palais
This Neo-Classical palace was built between 1834 and 1837 for the future Kaiser Wilhelm I. It was reconstructed after World War II.

9 Alte Bibliothek
The west side of Bebelplatz features a Baroque building with an unusual concave façade. Locals have nicknamed it the "chest of drawers".

UNIVERSITÄTSSTRASSE

CHARLOTTENSTRASSE

UNTER DEN LINDEN

BEHRENSTRASSE

3 Neue Wache
Since 1993, this monument has served as a memorial to all victims of war and dictatorship.

1 ★ Zeughaus (Deutsches Historisches Museum)
A wing designed by I M Pei has been added to this beautiful Baroque building. The Zeughaus pediment shows the Roman goddess of wisdom.

NORTH OF THE CENTRE

MUSEUM ISLAND

AROUND UNTER DEN LINDEN

KREUZBERG

Locator Map
See Street Finder maps 8, 9

0 metres	100
0 yards	100

2 Unter den Linden
This magnificent avenue was replanted with four rows of lime trees in 1946.

Key

— Suggested route

UNTER DEN LINDEN

13 Kronprinzenpalais
The rear elevation of the palace pavilion features a magnificent portal from the dismantled Bauakademie building.

HINTER DER KATH. KIRCHE

BEBELPLATZ

12 Staatsoper Unter den Linden
Unter den Linden's opera house is Germany's oldest theatre building not attached to a palace residence.

14 ★ Friedrichswerdersche Kirche
In this Neo-Gothic church, designed by Karl Friedrich Schinkel, is a museum devoted to this great architect.

10 Bebelplatz
Designed in the 18th century as the Forum Friedericianum, this square was renamed in 1947 in honour of social activist, August Bebel. The Nazis burned books here in 1933.

11 St-Hedwigs-Kathedrale
Bas-reliefs (1837) by Theodore Wilhelm Achtermann adorn the cathedral's supports.

❶ Zeughaus (Deutsches Historisches Museum)

This former arsenal was built in the Baroque style in 1706 under the guidance of Johann Arnold Nering, Martin Grünberg, Andreas Schlüter and Jean de Bodt. It is a magnificent structure; its wings surrounding an inner courtyard, its exterior decorated with Schlüter's sculptures, including masks of dying warriors in the courtyard. Since 1952 it has housed the German History Museum. Zeughaus is home to a permanent exhibition that contains more than 8,000 objects about German history in a European context. In the adjacent exhibition hall, designed by the famous architect I M Pei, are the museum's temporary exhibitions about significant historical events.

★ Martin Luther
This portrait, painted by Lucas Cranach the Elder in 1529, is the focal point of the exhibition devoted to the Reformation.

★ Gloria Victis
The death of a friend in the final days of the Franco-Prussian War (1870–71) inspired French artist Antonin Mercié to create this moving allegory.

Prisoner's Jacket
This jacket, which once belonged to a concentration camp prisoner, is used to illustrate the horrors of the Nazi regime.

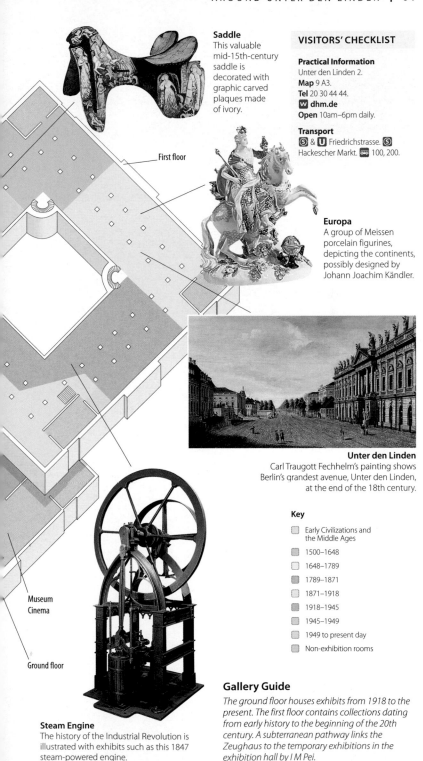

Saddle
This valuable mid-15th-century saddle is decorated with graphic carved plaques made of ivory.

First floor

VISITORS' CHECKLIST

Practical Information
Unter den Linden 2.
Map 9 A3.
Tel 20 30 44 44.
w dhm.de
Open 10am–6pm daily.

Transport
S & **U** Friedrichstrasse. **S** Hackescher Markt. 🚌 100, 200.

Europa
A group of Meissen porcelain figurines, depicting the continents, possibly designed by Johann Joachim Kändler.

Unter den Linden
Carl Traugott Fechhelm's painting shows Berlin's grandest avenue, Unter den Linden, at the end of the 18th century.

Key

- Early Civilizations and the Middle Ages
- 1500–1648
- 1648–1789
- 1789–1871
- 1871–1918
- 1918–1945
- 1945–1949
- 1949 to present day
- Non-exhibition rooms

Museum Cinema

Ground floor

Steam Engine
The history of the Industrial Revolution is illustrated with exhibits such as this 1847 steam-powered engine.

Gallery Guide

The ground floor houses exhibits from 1918 to the present. The first floor contains collections dating from early history to the beginning of the 20th century. A subterranean pathway links the Zeughaus to the temporary exhibitions in the exhibition hall by I M Pei.

Unter den Linden as depicted in Franz Krüger's *Opernplatz Parade* (1824–30)

❷ Unter den Linden

Map 8 E3, 8 F3. Ⓢ & Ⓤ
Brandenburger Tor. 🚌 100, 200, TXL.

One of the most famous streets in Berlin, Unter den Linden starts at Schlossplatz and runs down to Pariser Platz and the Brandenburg Gate. It was once the route to the royal hunting grounds that were later transformed into the Tiergarten. In the 17th century the street was planted with lime trees, to which it owes its name. Although removed around 1658, they were replanted in four rows in 1820.

During the 18th century, Unter den Linden became the main street of the westward-growing city. It was gradually filled with prestigious buildings that were restored after World War II. Following the reunification of Germany, Unter den Linden has acquired several cafés and restaurants, as well as many smart new shops. This street is also the venue for many interesting outdoor events; it is usually crowded with tourists and students browsing the bookstalls around the Humboldt Universität and the Staatsbibliothek.

❸ Neue Wache

Unter den Linden 4. **Map** 9 A3. Ⓢ
Hackescher Markt. 🚌 100, 200, TXL.
Open 10am–6pm daily.

This war memorial, designed by Karl Friedrich Schinkel and built between 1816 and 1818, is considered to be one of the

finest examples of Neo-Classical architecture in Berlin. The front of the monument is dominated by a huge Doric portico with a frieze made up of bas-reliefs depicting goddesses of victory. The triangular tympanum above the pediment shows allegorical representations of Battle, Victory, Flight and Defeat.

The building was originally used as a royal guardhouse, but during 1930 and 1931 it was turned into a monument to the soldiers killed in World War I. In 1960, following its restoration, Neue Wache became the Memorial to the Victims of Fascism and Militarism. Then, in 1993 it was rededicated once again, this time to the memory of all victims of war and dictatorship.

Inside the building is a granite slab over the ashes of an unknown soldier, a resistance fighter and a concentration camp prisoner. Under the circular opening in the roof is a copy of the 20th century sculpture *Mother with her Dead Son*, by Berlin artist Käthe Kollwitz, who lost her own son in World War I.

❹ Humboldt Universität
Humboldt University

Unter den Linden 6. **Map** 9 A3.
Tel 20930. Ⓢ & Ⓤ Friedrichstrasse.
🚌 100, 200, TXL.

The university building was constructed in 1753, for Prince Heinrich of Prussia, the brother of Frederick the Great. The university was founded in 1810 on the initiative of Wilhelm von Humboldt. It became the Berlin University but was renamed in von Humboldt's honour in 1949.

The overall design of the palace, with its main block and the courtyard enclosed within a pair of wings, has been extended many times. Two marble statues (1883) by Paul Otto stand at the entrance gate and represent Wilhelm von Humboldt (holding a book) and his brother Alexander

Wilhelm and Alexander von Humboldt

The Humboldt brothers rank among the most distinguished Berlin citizens. Wilhelm (1767–1835) was a lawyer and politician, occupying various government posts. It was on his initiative that the Berlin University (later renamed Humboldt University) was founded, and he conducted studies in comparative and historical linguistics there. Alexander (1769–1859), a professor at the University, researched natural science, including meteorology, oceanography and agricultural science.

Statue of Alexander von Humboldt

(sitting on a globe), who was a famous explorer. The entrance gate leads to the courtyard, which was designed by Reinhold Begas.

Many famous scholars have worked at the University, including philosophers Fichte and Hegel, physicians Rudolf Virchow and Robert Koch and physicists Max Planck and Albert Einstein. Among its graduates are Heinrich Heine, Karl Marx and Friedrich Engels.

After World War II, the University was in the Russian sector of the divided city and the difficulties encountered by the students of the western zone led to the establishment of a new university in 1948 – the Freie Universität (see p186).

Humboldt University courtyard with statue of Hermann von Helmholtz

❺ Reiterdenkmal Friedrichs des Grossen

Equestrian statue of Frederick the Great

Unter den Linden. **Map** 9 A3. Ⓢ & Ⓤ Friedrichstrasse. 🚌 100, 200.

This is one of the most famous monuments in Berlin, featuring a massive bronze statue 5.6 m (18.5 ft) in height and standing on the centre lane of Unter den Linden. It was designed by Christian Daniel Rauch and created between 1839 and 1851. It depicts Frederick the Great on horseback, wearing a uniform and a royal cloak. The base of the high plinth is surrounded by statues of famous military leaders,

politicians, scientists and artists. The top tier of the plinth is decorated with bas-reliefs depicting scenes from the life of Frederick the Great. Out of line with GDR ideology, the monument was removed to Potsdam, where until 1980 it stood by the Hippodrome in Park Sanssouci.

❻ Staatsbibliothek

State Library

Unter den Linden 8. **Map** 9 A3. **Tel** 2660. Ⓢ & Ⓤ Friedrichstrasse. 🚌 100, 200, TXL. **Open** 9am–9pm Mon–Fri, 9am–5pm Sat.

The nucleus of the State Library collection was the library belonging to the Great Elector – Friedrich Wilhelm – founded in 1661 and situated in the Stadtschloss. At the end of the 18th century it was moved to the Alte Bibliothek building. Its current home was designed by Ernst von Ihne and constructed between 1903 and 1914 on the site of the Academy of Science and the Academy of Fine Arts. This impressive building was severely damaged during World

War II and underwent extensive restoration. The collection, numbering 3 million books and periodicals, was scattered during the war, including a collection of priceless music manuscripts, which ended up in the Jagiellonian Library in Cracow, Poland.

After the war only part of the collection was returned to the building in Unter den Linden, and the rest was held in West Berlin. Since reunification, both collections are once again under the same administration.

❼ Deutsche Bank KunstHalle

Unter den Linden 13–15. **Map** 9 A3. **Tel** 202 09 30. **Open** 10am–8pm daily. Ⓢ & Ⓤ Friedrichstrasse. 🚌 100, 200, TXL. 🎨 free on Mon.

After completing its successful collaboration with the Guggenheim Foundation, Deutsche Bank has opened its own gallery that showcases its private 56,000-piece collection, called "Art Works". The collection comprises valuable works of German modernism.

The ivy-clad Staatsbibliothek building on Unter den Linden

A window with a heraldic shield on the Altes Palais

❽ Altes Palais
The Old Palace

Unter den Linden 9. **Map** 9 A3. Ⓢ & Ⓤ Friedrichstrasse. 🚌 100, 200, TXL. **Closed** to the public.

This Neo-Classical palace, near the former Opernplatz (Bebelplatz), was built for the heir to the throne – Prince Wilhelm (later Kaiser Wilhelm I). The Kaiser lived here all his life. He was able to watch the changing of the guards every day from the ground-floor window on the far left.

The palace, built from 1834 to 1837, was designed by Carl Ferdinand Langhans but its splendid furnishings were destroyed during World War II. The palace was subsequently restored and is now used by Humboldt Universität.

❾ Alte Bibliothek
The Old Library

Bebelplatz. **Map** 9 A3. **Tel** 20 930. Ⓢ & Ⓤ Friedrichstrasse. 🚌 100, 200, TXL.

The Old Library, known by locals as the *Kommode* or "chest of drawers" after its curved façade, is actually one of the city's most beautiful Baroque buildings. It was designed by Georg Christian Unger and built around 1775 to house the royal library collection. In fact, Unger based his design on an unrealized plan for an extension to the Hofburg complex in Vienna by Josef Emanuel Fischer von Erlach some 50 years earlier. The concave façade of the building is accentuated by the insertion of three breaks, surrounded at the top by a row of massive Corinthian pilasters. The building now houses the law faculty of Humboldt University.

❿ Bebelplatz

Map 9 A3. Ⓢ & Ⓤ Friedrichstrasse. 🚌 100, 200, TXL.

Once named Opernplatz (Opera Square), Bebelplatz was to be the focal point of the intended Forum Fridericianum, an area designed by Georg Wenzeslaus von Knobelsdorff to mirror the grandeur of ancient Rome. Although the initial plans were only partly implemented, many important buildings rose around the square with the passage of time.

On 10 May 1933 Opernplatz was the scene of the infamous book burning act organized by the Nazi propaganda machine. Some 25,000 books written by authors considered to be enemies of the Third Reich were burned. These included works by Thomas and Heinrich Mann, Robert Musil and Lion Feuchtwanger.

Today, a monument at the centre of the square, designed by Micha Ullman, commemorates this dramatic event. A translucent panel inserted into the road surface provides a glimpse of a room filled with empty bookshelves. Next to it is a plaque bearing the tragically prophetic words of the poet Heinrich Heine, written in 1820: "Where books are burned, in the end people will burn."

⓫ St-Hedwigs-Kathedrale
St Hedwig's Cathedral

Bebelplatz. **Map** 9 A4. **Tel** 203 48 10. Ⓢ & Ⓤ Hausvogteiplatz. 🚌 100, 200, TXL. **Open** 10am–5pm Mon–Sat, 1–5pm Sun.

This huge church, set back from the road and crowned with a dome, is the Catholic Cathedral of the Roman Archdiocese of Berlin. It was built to serve the Catholics of Silesia (part of present-day Poland), which became part of the Kingdom of Prussia in 1742 following defeat in the Silesian Wars of 1740–63.

The initial design, by Georg Wenzeslaus von Knobelsdorff, was similar to the Roman Pantheon. Construction began in 1747 and the cathedral was consecrated in 1773, although work continued on and off until 1778. Its design was modified

The façade of St-Hedwigs-Kathedrale featuring beautiful bas-relief sculptures

repeatedly. Later, additional work was carried out from 1886 to 1887. The cathedral was damaged during World War II, and rebuilt between 1952 and 1963.

The crypt holds the tombs of many bishops of Berlin, a 16th-century Madonna and a Pietà dating from 1420. It is also the resting place of Bernhard Lichtenberg, a priest killed in a concentration camp and beatified as a martyr by Pope John Paul II.

The imposing façade of the Kronprinzenpalais

Bas-relief of Apollo and Mars on the façade of the Staatsoper

⓬ Staatsoper Unter den Linden
State Opera House

Unter den Linden 7. **Map** 9 A3. **Tel** 20 35 45 55. Ⓢ & Ⓤ Friedrichstrasse. 🚌 100, 200, TXL. **Closed** for restoration until October 2015. Performances at Schiller Theater, Bismarckstrasse 110.

The early Neo-Classical façade of the State Opera House is one of the most beautiful sights along Unter den Linden. It was built by Georg Wenzeslaus von Knobelsdorff in 1741–3 as the first building of the intended Forum Fridericianum. After a fire, the opera house was restored from 1843 to 1844 under the direction of Carl Ferdinand Langhans, who altered only its interior.

Following wartime destruction, the opera house was rebuilt from 1952 to 1955 and is currently being restored. It has played host to famous singers, musicians and artists; one of its directors and conductors was Richard Strauss.

⓭ Kronprinzen-palais
Crown Prince's Palace

Unter den Linden 3. **Map** 9 A3. Ⓢ & Ⓤ Friedrichstrasse. 🚌 100, 200, TXL. **Closed** to the public.

This striking late Neo-Classical palace takes its name from its original inhabitants – the heirs to the royal, and later to the imperial, throne. Its form is the outcome of numerous changes made to what was originally a modest house dating from 1663–9. The first extensions, designed in the late-Baroque style, were conducted by Philipp Gerlach in 1732 and 1733. Between 1856 and 1857 Johann Heinrich Strack added the second floor. These extensions were rebuilt following World War II.

The palace served the royal family until the abolition of the monarchy. From 1919 to 1937, it was used by the Nationalgalerie. Under Communist rule it was renamed Palais Unter den Linden and reserved for official government guests. It was here, on 31 August 1990, that the pact was signed paving the way for reunification.

Next to the palace, with the prestigious address of Unter den Linden 1, is where the Kommandantur, the official quarters of the city's garrison commander, once stood. Totally destroyed in the last days of World War II, the original façade was rebuilt in 2003 by the German media

company Bertelsmann, as part of their Berlin headquarters.

Joined to the main palace by an overhanging passageway is the smaller Prinzessinnenpalais (Princesses' Palace), built for the daughters of Friedrich Wilhelm III. The café is an excellent place for a coffee and pastry break.

⓮ Friedrichswerd-ersche Kirche (Schinkel-Museum)

Werderscher Markt. **Map** 9 B4. **Tel** 208 1323. Ⓢ & Ⓤ Friedrichstrasse. 🚌 100, 147, 200, TXL. **Open** 10am–6pm daily. 🚫 ♿

This picturesque church, designed by Karl Friedrich Schinkel and constructed between 1824 and 1830, was the first Neo-Gothic church to be built in Berlin. The small single-nave structure, with its twin-tower façade, resembles an English college chapel. Schinkel's original interior of the church was largely destroyed in World War II.

Following its reconstruction, the church was converted to a museum. It is now used by the Nationalgalerie to house its permanent exhibition of sculptures from the late 16th to the mid-19th century.

Princesses Luise and Friederike in the Schinkel-Museum

Highlights include a model of the famous group sculpture by Johann Gottfried Schadow, depicting the princesses Friederike and Luise (later Queen of Prussia).

⓯ Gendarmenmarkt

This is one of Berlin's most beautiful squares, created at the end of 17th century as a market square for the newly established Friedrichstadt. It is named after the Regiment Gens d'Armes who had their stables here. In 1950 it was renamed Platz der Akademie; after reunification the square reverted to its original name.

Französischer Dom

JÄGERSTRASSE

GENDARMENMARKT

TAUBENSTRASSE

CHARLOTTENSTRASSE

Galeries Lafayette

Quartier 206

Deutscher Dom

Quartier 205

Schiller's Monument
The poet's monument stands in the centre of the square, in front of the Konzerthaus.

| 0 metres | 85 |
| 0 yards | 80 |

⓰ Französischer Dom

French Cathedral

Gendarmenmarkt 6. **Map** 9 A4.
Tel 20 64 99 22. Ⓤ Stadtmitte or Französische Strasse. Museum: **Open** noon–5pm Tue–Sun. 🎨 Church: **Open** noon–5pm Tue–Sun (from 11am Sun). ✝ 9:30am & 11am Sun.

Although the two churches on the opposite sides of Schauspielhaus seem identical, they differ from each other quite considerably. Their only common feature is the front towers. The French cathedral was built for the Huguenot community, who found refuge in protestant Berlin following their expulsion from France after the revocation of the Edict of Nantes. The modest church, built between 1701 and 1705 by Louis Cayart and Abraham

Side elevation of the Französischer Dom, built for Huguenot refugees

Quesnay, was modelled on the Huguenot church in Charenton, France, which was destroyed in 1688. The main entrance, on the west elevation (facing Charlottenstrasse), leads to an uncomplicated interior with a

rectangular nave and semi-circular sections on both sides. It features a late Baroque organ from 1754.

The structure is dominated by a massive, cylindrical tower which is encircled by Corinthian porticoes at its base. The restored tower and porticoes were designed by Carl von Gontard and added around 1785, some 80 years after the church was built. It houses the Huguenot Museum, which details the history of the Huguenots in France and Brandenburg. Well-educated and highly skilled, they played a crucial part in Berlin's rise as a city of science, craft and commerce. The French language they brought with them survives to this day in many words used in the Berlin dialect.

The interior of the Konzerthaus, formerly the Schauspielhaus

⑰ Konzerthaus
Concert Hall

Gendarmenmarkt 2. **Map** 9 A4.
Tel 20 30 921 01. Ⓤ Stadtmitte or Französische Strasse.

A late Neo-Classical jewel, this magnificent theatre building, formerly known as the Schauspielhaus, is one of the greatest achievements of Berlin's best-known architect, Karl Friedrich Schinkel. It was built between 1818 and 1821 around the ruins of Langhan's National Theatre, destroyed by fire in 1817. The original portico columns were retained. Schinkel was responsible for the architectural structure and for the interior design,down to the door handles. Following bomb damage in World War II, it was reconstructed as a concert hall with a different interior layout. The exterior was restored to its former glory. The Konzerthaus is home to the Konzerthaus-orchestra (formerly the Berlin Symphony Orchestra).

The theatre façade includes a huge Ionic portico with a set of stairs that was only used by the middle classes (the upper classes entered via a separate entrance where they could leave their horse-drawn carriages). The whole building is richly decorated with sculptures

alluding to drama and music: statues of musical geniuses mounted on lions and panthers, as well as figures representing the Muses and a Bacchanal procession. The façade is crowned with the sculpture of Apollo riding a chariot pulled by griffins.

In front of the theatre stands a shining, white marble statue of Friedrich Schiller. It was sculpted by Reinhold Begas, and erected in 1869. Removed by the Nazis during the 1930s, the monument was finally returned to its rightful place in 1988. Schiller's head was copied by the sculptor from a bust of the poet created in 1794 by Johann Heinrich Dannecker. The statue is mounted on a high pedestal surrounded by allegorical figures representing Lyric Poetry, Drama, Philosophy and History.

⑱ Deutscher Dom
German Cathedral

Gendarmenmarkt 1. **Map** 9 A4.
Ⓤ Stadtmitte or Französische Strasse. **Tel** 22 73 04 31. Exhibition: **Open** May–Sep: 10am–7pm Tue–Sun; Oct–Apr: 10am–6pm Tue–Sun.

The Cathedral at the southern end of the square, to the left of Konzerthaus, is an old German Protestant-Reformed church. It was designed by Martin Grünberg and built in 1708 by Giovanni Simonetti. The design was based on a five-petal shape, and in 1785 it acquired a dome-covered tower identical to that of the French cathedral. Burned down in 1945, the church was finally rebuilt in 1993. Its exterior was painstakingly reconstructed, including its sculpted decorations. The interior is now modern and has been adapted as an exhibition space. On display is *"Wege, Irrwege, Umwege"* ("Paths, Confusions, Detours"), an exhibition about Germany's parliamentary democracy.

Sculpture from the Deutscher Dom

⑲ Friedrichstadt-passagen
Friedrichstadt Passages

Friedrichstrasse Quartiere 205, 206, 207. **Map** 8 F4. Ⓤ Französische Strasse or Stadtmitte.

This group of passages is part of a huge development of luxury shops, offices, restaurants and apartments built along Friedrichstrasse.

Quartier 207 is the famous Galeries Lafayette, a branch of the French department store occupying a charming building designed by Jean Nouvel and constructed almost entirely of glass. The building's axis is formed by an inner courtyard, which is defined by two glass cones with their bases facing each other. The highly reflective glass panes, together with the multicoloured stands that are clustered around the structure, make an extraordinary impression on the visitor.

The next passage, Quartier 206, has offices and smart luxury boutiques, and is the work of the American design team Pei, Cobb, Freed & Partners. The building owes its alluring, but somewhat nouveau-riche appearance to the use of forms inspired by Art Deco architecture, including sophisticated details and expensive stone cladding.

The southernmost building in the complex, and the largest passage, is Quartier 205, now called "The Q", which is the work of Oswald Mathias Ungers.

The exterior and main entrance of Quartier 206

⑳ Mohren-kolonnaden

Mohrenstrasse 37b and 40/41.
Map 8 F5. Ⓤ Stadtmitte or Hausvogteiplatz.

Designed by Carl Gotthard Langhans, these Neo-Classical arcades resting on twin columns were constructed in 1787. They originally surrounded a bridge that spanned the moat around the city of Berlin. The bridge has since been demolished, and the arcades have been incorporated into buildings of a much later architectural style located on Mohrenstrasse.

One of the original arcades known as the Mohrenkolonnaden

㉑ Spittel-kolonnaden

Leipziger Strasse. **Map** 9 B5.
Ⓤ Spittelmarkt.

In the vicinity of Spittelmarkt is a picturesque Baroque-Neo-Classical colonnade squeezed between several 20-storey tower blocks. These tower blocks were erected to obscure the view of the Axel Springer Publishers' building, which stood on the opposite side of the Berlin Wall.

A pair of such semicircular colonnades, designed by Carl von Gontard and built in 1776, originally surrounded Spittelmarkt. The southern one was demolished in 1929, and the

A copy of one of the original Spittelkolonnaden in Leipziger Strasse

northern one was destroyed during World War II. In 1979, a copy of one of the colonnades was erected in Leipziger Strasse, using elements from the original.

㉒ Museum für Kommunikation

Museum of Telecommunications

Leipziger Strasse 16. **Map** 8 F5.
Ⓤ Stadtmitte or Mohrenstrasse.
🚌 200, 265, M48. **Tel** 20 29 40.
Open 9am–8pm Tue, 9am–5pm Wed–Fri, 10am–6pm Sat & Sun.
Closed Mon, 24–25 & 31 Dec. 🐾

Founded in 1872 as the Post Office museum, this is the world's oldest establishment of its kind. A dozen or so years after it was founded, it moved into the corner of the huge building constructed for the main post office. The office wings, with their modest Neo-Renaissance elevations, contrast with the museum premises, which has a grand Neo-Baroque façade. The museum houses exhibits that illustrate the history of postal and telecommunication services, including contemporary digital communications.

㉓ Ehemaliges Regierungsviertel

Wilhelmstrasse, Leipziger Strasse, Voss Strasse. **Map** 8 E5. Ⓤ Potsdamer Platz, Mohrenstrasse.

Wilhelmstrasse, and the area situated to the west of it up to Leipziger Platz, was the former

German government district, where the main departments had offices from the mid-19th century until 1945. The building at Voss Strasse No. 77 was once the Reich's Chancellery and Otto von Bismarck's office. From 1933, it served as the office of Adolf Hitler, for whom the building was specially extended by Albert Speer.

In the spring of 1945 the square was the scene of fierce fighting, and after World War II most of the buildings had to be demolished. Among those that survived are the former Prussian Landtag offices – the huge complex occupying the site between Leipziger and Niederkirchner Strasse. This building in the Italian Renaissance-style was designed by Friedrich Schulz, and constructed from 1892 to 1904. It consists of two segments: the one on the side of Leipziger Strasse (No. 3–4) once housed the upper chamber of the National Assembly (the Herrenhaus) and is now used by the Bundesrat. The building on the side of Niederkirchner Strasse (No. 5) was once the seat of the Landtag's lower chamber, and is now the Berliner Abgeordnetenhaus (House of Representatives).

The second surviving complex is the former Ministry of Aviation (Reichsluftfahrtministerium), at Leipziger Strasse No. 5, built for Hermann Göring in 1936 by Ernst Sagebiel. This awesome building is typical of architecture of the Third Reich.

㉔ Pariser Platz

Map 8 E3. ⑤ & Ⓤ Brandenburger Tor. 🚌 100, 200.

This square, at the end of Unter den Linden, was created in 1734. Originally called Quarrée, it was renamed Pariser Platz after 1814, when the *Quadriga* sculpture from the Brandenburg Gate was returned to Berlin from Paris.

The square, enclosed on the west by the Brandenburg Gate, saw most of its buildings, including the house of painter Max Liebermann, destroyed in 1945. Following reunification, the square was redeveloped.

Twin houses designed by Josef Paul Kleihues now flank the Brandenburg Gate. On the north side of the square are the Dresdner Bank building and the French Embassy. On the south are the US Embassy, the DZ Bank head office and the Akademie der Künste (Academy of Fine Arts). To the east is the Adlon Hotel.

㉕ Brandenburger Tor

Brandenburg Gate

Pariser Platz. **Map** 8 E3. ⑤ & Ⓤ Brandenburger Tor. 🚌 100, 200.

The Brandenburg Gate is the quintessential symbol of Berlin. This magnificent Neo-Classical structure, completed in 1795, was designed by Carl Gotthard Langhans and modelled on the entrance to the Acropolis in Athens. A pair of pavilions, once used by guards and customs officers, frames its powerful Doric colonnade. The bas-reliefs depict scenes from Greek mythology, and the whole structure is crowned by the sculpture *Quadriga*, designed by Johann Gottfried Schadow. The *Quadriga* was originally regarded as a symbol of peace. In 1806, during the French occupation, it was dismantled on Napoleon's orders and taken to Paris. On its return in 1814, it was declared a symbol of victory, and the goddess received the staff bearing the Prussian eagle and the iron cross adorned with a laurel wreath. The Brandenburg Gate has borne witness to many of Berlin's important events, from military parades to celebrations marking the birth of the Third Reich and Hitler's ascent to power. It was here, too, that the Russian flag was raised in May 1945, and on 17 June 1953 that 25 workers demonstrating for better conditions were killed.

The gate, in East Berlin, was restored from 1956–8, when the damaged *Quadriga* was rebuilt in West Berlin. Until 1989 it stood watch over the divided city. It was restored between 2000 and 2002.

㉖ Holocaust Denkmal

Holocaust Memorial

Ebertstrasse. **Map** 8 E3. **Tel** 28 04 59 60. ⑤ & Ⓤ Brandenburger Tor. 🚌 100, 200. **Open** Information Centre: Apr–Sep: 10am–8pm; Oct–Mar: 10am–7pm. **Closed** Mon.

The memorial for the Jews killed by the Nazis between 1933 and 1945 was inaugurated in 2005. It covers 19,000 sq m (205,000 sq ft) next to the Brandenburg Gate. Above ground, visitors can walk through an undulating field of concrete slabs; beneath lies an information centre on the history of the genocide.

Max Liebermann (1849–1935)

One of the greatest German painters, Max Liebermann was also one of the most interesting and controversial figures of Berlin's élite circles at the start of the 20th century. A sensitive observer as well as an outstanding portraitist, Liebermann was famously stubborn – he could stand up even to the Kaiser himself. From 1920 he was president of the Akademie der Künste (Academy of Fine Arts), but in view of his Jewish origin he was removed from office in 1933. He died just two years later, alone, and his wife committed suicide to escape being sent to a concentration camp.

A frieze from the Brandenburg Gate

Oskar Kokoschka's *Pariser Platz in Berlin* (1925–6), Nationalgalerie

The luxurious interior of the Adlon Hotel

㉗ Hotel Adlon

Unter den Linden 77. **Map** 8 E3, 8 E4.
Tel 226 10. Ⓢ & Ⓤ Brandenburger
Tor. 🚌 100, 200.

Considered the most important
society venue in Berlin, the
original Hotel Adlon opened its
doors in 1907. Its luxurious
suites were once used by the
world's celebrities, including
Greta Garbo, Enrico Caruso and
Charlie Chaplin. The hotel
suffered bomb damage in
World War II, and was demolished in 1945. A building
bearing the same name opened
in a blaze of publicity on 23
August 1997 and was later
bought and branded Hotel
Adlon Kempinski.
　Today, it is once again the
best address in town. Comfort,
discretion and interiors
featuring exotic timber, marble
and heavy silk tempt visitors
despite high prices. Those who
cannot afford to stay should at
least drop in for a cup of coffee:
in the main hall stands the only
authentic remnant of the former
Adlon Hotel, an elegant black
marble fountain decorated with
elephants, which once stood in
the orangery.

㉘ Russische Botschaft

Russian Embassy

Unter den Linden 63/65. **Map** 8 F3.
Ⓢ & Ⓤ Brandenburger Tor.
🚌 100, 200.

The monumental, white
Russian Embassy building is
an example of the Stalinist
"wedding cake" style, or
Zuckerbäckerstil. Built between
1948 and 1953, it was the first
postwar building erected on
Unter den Linden. It is built
on the site of a former
palace that had housed
the Russian (originally
Tsarist) embassy
from 1837.
　The work of
Russian architect
Anatoli Strizhevsky,
this structure, with
its strictly sym-
metrical layout,
resembles the old
Berlin palaces of the
Neo-Classical period.
The sculptures that
adorn it, however, belong
to an altogether different
era: the gods of
ancient Greece and
Rome have been
replaced by working-
class heroes.

Statue of a worker
on the Russian
Embassy building

㉙ Komische Oper

Comic Opera

Behrenstr. 55/57. **Map** 8 F4. **Tel** 47 99
74 00. Ⓤ Französische Strasse.
Ⓢ & Ⓤ Brandenburger Tor. 🚌 100,
147, 200.

Looking at the modern façade
of this theatre it is hard to
believe that it hides one of
Berlin's most impressive
interiors. Originally called the
Theater Unter den Linden, the
theatre was built in 1892 by the
internationally famous Viennese
architectural practice of
Ferdinand Fellner and Hermann
Helmer. It has served as a variety
theatre and as the German
National Theatre in the past, and
has only housed the Komische
Oper since World War II. The
postwar reconstruction
deprived the building of its
former façades but the
beautiful Viennese
Neo-Baroque interior
remained, full of
stuccoes and gilded
ornaments. Particu-
larly interesting are
the expressive and
dynamically posed
statues on the pilasters
of the top balcony – the
work of Theodor Friedel.
The Komische Oper is
one of Berlin's three
leading opera
companies. Its
repertoire consists
mainly of light opera.

Crowded balconies and the plush interior of the Komische Oper

⏰ Bahnhof Friedrichstrasse

Map 8 F2, 8 F3.

One of the city's most famous urban railway stations, Bahnhof Friedrichstrasse used to be the border station between East and West Berlin. It was built in 1882 to a design by Johannes Vollmer. In 1925 a roof was added, covering the hall and the platforms.

The original labyrinth of passages, staircases and checkpoints no longer exists but it is possible to see a model of the station at the Stasi-Museum *(see p175)*. Now a museum, the only remaining structure from the original station is the special pavilion once used as a waiting room by those waiting for emigration clearance. It earned the nickname Tränenpalast, the "Palace of Tears", as it is here that Berliners from different sides of the city would say goodbye to each other after a visit.

⏰ Admiralspalast

Friedrichstr. 101–102. **Map** 8 F2.
Tel 479 97 74 99. Ⓤ &
Ⓢ Friedrichstrasse.

The Admiralspalast, built in 1911, was one of the Roaring Twenties' premier entertainment complexes in Berlin, and one of the many variety and vaudeville theatres once lining Friedrichstrasse. Originally designed as an indoor swimming pool above a natural hot spring, it was later transformed into an ice-skating rink and, after heavy damage in World War II, an Operettenthater that staged light musical entertainment.

In 2006, the theatre reopened with a much discussed production of Bertolt Brecht's *Dreigroschenoper (The Threepenny Opera)*, and now once again serves as a vibrant entertainment complex, with a large stage, a café and a nightclub. Designed by Heinrich Schweitzer, the beautifully restored façade is punctuated by Doric half-columns and inlaid with slabs of Istrian

A window of the Admiralspalast decorated with marble slabs

marble. The restored façade on Planckstrasse, designed by Ernst Westphal, features exotic overlapping motifs.

⏰ Maxim Gorki Theater

Am Festungsgraben 2. **Map** 9 A3.
Tel 20 22 11 15. Ⓤ & Ⓢ Friedrichstrasse. 🚌 100, 200. 🚊 M1.

The Maxim Gorki theatre was once a singing school or *Sing-Akademie*. Berlin's oldest concert hall, it was built in 1827 by Karl Theodor Ottmer, who based his design on drawings by Karl Friedrich Schinkel. This modest Neo-Classical building, with its attractive façade resembling a Greco-Roman temple, was well known for the excellent acoustic qualities of its concert hall.

Many famous composer-musicians performed here, including violinist Niccolò Paganini and pianist Franz Liszt. In 1829, Felix Mendelssohn-Bartholdy conducted a

Maxim Gorki Theater occupying the oldest concert hall in Berlin

performance of the *St Matthew Passion* by Johann Sebastian Bach, the first since the composer's death in 1750. Following reconstruction after World War II, the building is now used as a theatre.

⏰ Palais am Festungsgraben

Festungsgraben Palace

Am Festungsgraben 1. **Map** 9 A3.
Tel 618 14 60. Ⓢ Friedrichstrasse. 🚌 100, 200. 🚊 M1.

The Palace in Festungsgraben is one of the few structures in this part of town that has maintained its original interior decor. Built as a small Baroque palace in 1753, it owes its present form to major extension work, carried out in 1864 in the style of Karl Friedrich Schinkel, by Heinrich Bürde and Hermann von der Hude.

The late Neo-Classical style of the building is reminiscent of Schinkel's later designs. The interior includes a magnificent double-height marble hall in the Neo-Renaissance style and modelled on the White Room in the former Stadtschloss *(see p73)*. In 1934 one of the ground-floor rooms was turned into a music salon, and many musical instruments were brought here from the 19th century house (now demolished) of wealthy merchant and manufacturer Johann Weydinger (1773–1837).

Until 2009 the Palace in Festungsgraben housed the Museum Mitte. It is now used for private events.

MUSEUM ISLAND

The long island that nestles in the tributaries of the Spree river is the cradle of Berlin's history. It was here that the first settlements appeared at the beginning of the 13th century – Cölln is mentioned in documents dating back to 1237 and its twin settlement, Berlin, is mentioned a few years later (1244). Not a trace of Gothic and Renaissance Cölln is left now: the island's character was transformed by the construction of the Brandenburg Electors'

palace, which served as their residence from 1470. Over the following centuries, the palace was converted first into a royal and later into an imperial palace – the huge Stadtschloss. Although it was razed to the ground in 1950, some interesting buildings on the island's north side have survived, including the huge Berliner Dom (cathedral) and the impressive collection of museums that give the island its name – Museumsinsel.

Sights at a Glance

Museums and Galleries

⑥ Altes Museum *p77*
⑦ Alte Nationalgalerie
⑧ Neues Museum
⑨ Pergamonmuseum *pp82–5*
⑩ Bode-Museum
⑬ Historischer Hafen Berlin
⑭ Märkisches Museum
⑲ Galgenhaus

Streets, Squares and Parks

① Schlossplatz
⑤ Lustgarten
⑮ Märkisches Ufer

Historic Buildings

③ Schlossbrücke
④ Berliner Dom *pp78–9*
⑪ Marstall
⑫ Ribbeckhaus
⑯ Ermeler-Haus
⑰ Gertraudenbrücke
⑱ Nicolai-Haus

Other Buildings

② Staatsratsgebäude

☐ **Restaurants**
  see p233
  1 Café im Bodermuseum
  2 Ming Dynastie

See also Street Finder maps 9, 10

0 metres 400
0 yards 400

Street-by-Street: Museum Island

On this island are the pretty Lustgarten and the Berliner Dom (Berlin Cathedral). It is also where you will find some of the most important museums in the east of the city. These include the Bode-Museum, the Altes Museum, the Alte Nationalgalerie and the splendid Pergamonmuseum, famous for its collection of antiquities and visited by crowds of art-lovers from around the world.

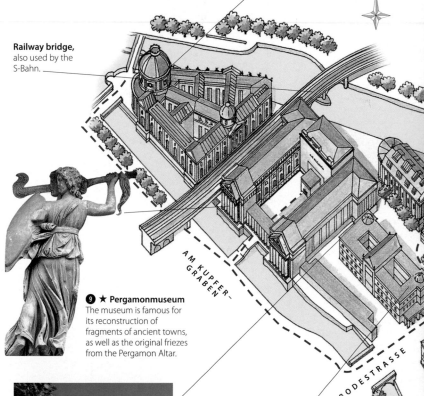

⑩ Bode-Museum
The dome-covered rounded corner of the building provides a prominent landmark at the tip of the island.

Railway bridge, also used by the S-Bahn.

⑨ ★ Pergamonmuseum
The museum is famous for its reconstruction of fragments of ancient towns, as well as the original friezes from the Pergamon Altar.

AM KUPFER-GRABEN

BODESTRASSE

⑧ Neues Museum
This museum houses the Egyptian Museum plus parts of the Museum of Pre- and Early History, as well as items from the Collection of Classical Antiquities.

| 0 metres | 100 |
| 0 yards | 100 |

⑦ Alte Nationalgalerie
The equestrian statue of King Friedrich Wilhelm IV in front of the building is the work of Alexander Calandrelli.

Key

— Suggested route

❻ ★ Altes Museum
The corners of the central building feature figures of Castor and Pollux, heroes of Greek myth also known as the Dioscuri.

Locator Map
See Street Finder map 9

❺ Lustgarten
The 70-ton granite bowl was the biggest in the world when it was placed in the garden in 1828.

❹ ★ Berliner Dom
The Neo-Baroque interior of the Berlin Cathedral features some extravagant late 19th-century furnishings.

❸ Schlossbrücke
Under the GDR regime this unusual bridge was called Marx-Engels-Brücke. It features statues made of stunning white Carrara marble.

❶ Schlossplatz
Excavations conducted here have unearthed the cellars of the demolished Stadtschloss.

LUSTGARTEN

BODESTRASSE

KARL–LIEBKNECHT

SSBRÜCKE

SCHLOSSPLATZ

❶ Schlossplatz

Map 9 B3. Ⓢ Hackescher Markt.
🚌 100, 200.

This square was once the site of a gigantic residential complex known as Stadtschloss (City Palace). Built in 1451, it served as the main residence of the Brandenburg Electors. It was transformed from a castle to a palace in the mid-16th century when Elector Friedrich III (later King Friedrich I) ordered its reconstruction in the Baroque style. The building works (1698–1716) were overseen initially by Andreas Schlüter and then by Johann von Göthe and Martin Heinrich Böhme.

The three-storey residence, designed around two courtyards, was the main seat of the Hohenzollern family *(see pp21–2)* for almost 500 years until the end of the monarchy. The palace was partly burned during World War II, but after 1945 it was provisionally restored and used as a museum. In 1950–51, despite protests, the palace was demolished and the square was renamed Marx-Engels-Platz under the GDR.

Now all that remains of the palace is the triumphal-arch portal that once adorned the façade on the Lustgarten side. This is now incorporated into the wall of the government building, the Staatsratsgebäude.

In 1989 the square reverted to its original name. In 1993 a full-scale model of the palace was built out of cloth stretched over scaffolding. After a lengthy debate and an architectural competition won by Franco Stella, it was decided to rebuild the palace as a museum complex that will have three reconstructed historical façades and a modern one. This Humboldt-Forum will house the Dahlem museums' overseas collections. Completion is due in 2018. Until then, the temporary Humboldt Box will serve as an information centre.

The surviving Stadtschloss portal fronting a government building

❷ Staatsratsgebäude

Map 9 B3. Ⓢ & Ⓤ Alexanderplatz.
🚌 100, 147, 200, M48, TXL.

The former Staatsratsgebäude, once the seat of the highest state government council of East Germany, was built in 1964. It now stands alone on the southern side of the square, as all the other former Socialist state buildings that once formed the government centre in this area have long been demolished. The Staatsratsgebäude features the remaining original sculptures, including the magnificent atlantes by the famous Dresden sculptor Balthasar Permoser. Their inclusion, however, was not due to their artistic merit, but rather to their propaganda value: it was from the balcony of the portal that Karl Liebknecht proclaimed the birth of the Socialist Republic *(see p30)*.

❸ Schlossbrücke

Map 9 B3. Ⓢ Hackescher Markt.
🚌 100, 200.

This is one of the town's most beautiful bridges, connecting Schlossplatz with Unter den Linden. It was built in 1824 to a design by Karl Friedrich Schinkel, who was one of Germany's most influential architects *(see p181)*. Statues were added to the top of the bridge's sparkling granite

Sculptures on the Schlossbrücke

pillars in 1853. These figures were also created by Schinkel and made of stunning white Carrara marble. The statues depict tableaux taken from Greek mythology, for instance Iris, Nike and Athena training and looking after their favourite young warriors. The wrought-iron balustrade is decorated with intertwined sea creatures.

❹ Berliner Dom

Berlin Cathedral

See pp78–9.

❺ Lustgarten

Map 9 B3. Ⓢ Hackescher Markt.
🚌 100, 200.

The enchanting garden in front of the Altes Museum looks as though it has always been here, but in its present form it was established from 1998 to 1999.

Used to grow vegetables and herbs for the Stadtschloss until the late 16th century, it became a real *Lustgarten* (pleasure garden) in the reign of the Great Elector (1620–88). However, its statues, grottoes, fountains and exotic vegetation were removed when Friedrich Wilhelm I (1688–1740), known for his love of military pursuits, turned the garden into an army drill ground.

Following the construction of the Altes Museum, the ground became a park, designed by Peter Joseph Lenné. In 1831 it was adorned with a monolithic granite bowl by Christian Gottlieb Cantian, to a design by Schinkel. The 70-ton bowl, measuring nearly 7 m (23 ft) in diameter, was intended for the museum rotunda, but was too heavy to carry inside.

After 1933, the Lustgarten was paved over and turned into a parade ground, remaining as such until 1989. Its current restoration is based on Lenné's designs.

❻ Altes Museum

The museum building, designed by Karl Friedrich Schinkel, is undoubtedly one of the world's most beautiful Neo-Classical structures, with an impressive 87-m (285-ft) high portico supported by 18 Ionic columns. Officially opened in 1830, it was built to house the royal collection of paintings and antiquities. It now houses part of Berlin's Collection of Classical Antiquities, with an exhibition focused on the art and culture of ancient Greece. The first floor houses a permanent exhibition of Roman and Etruscan art and sculptures and the second floor is used for temporary exhibitions.

VISITORS' CHECKLIST

Practical Information
Am Lustgarten (Bodestrasse 1–3).
Map 9 B3.
Open 10am–6pm daily (to 10pm Thu). 🅿 🏧 📷

Transport
Ⓢ Hackescher Markt. 🚌 100, 200, TXL.

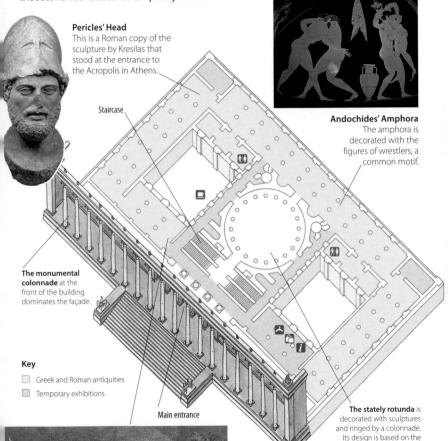

Pericles' Head
This is a Roman copy of the sculpture by Kresilas that stood at the entrance to the Acropolis in Athens.

Staircase

Andochides' Amphora
The amphora is decorated with the figures of wrestlers, a common motif.

The monumental colonnade at the front of the building dominates the façade.

Key

☐ Greek and Roman antiquities

☐ Temporary exhibitions

Main entrance

The stately rotunda is decorated with sculptures and ringed by a colonnade. Its design is based on the ancient Pantheon.

Mosaic from Hadrian's Villa
(c.117–138)
This colourful mosaic depicts a battle scene between centaurs and a tiger and lion. The mosaic comes from a floor of Hadrian's Villa, near Tivoli on the outskirts of Rome.

Gallery Guide
The ground floor galleries house Greek and Roman antiquities; the first floor is used for temporary exhibitions.

❹ Berliner Dom

The original Berliner Dom was based on a modest Baroque design by Johann Boumann. Built between 1747 and 1750 on the site of an old Dominican church, the cathedral included the original crypt of the Hohenzollern family, one of the largest of its kind in Europe. The present Neo-Baroque structure is the work of Julius Raschdorff and dates from 1894 to 1905. The central copper dome is some 98 m (321 ft) high. Following severe World War II damage, the cathedral has now been restored in a simplified form. The Hohenzollern memorial chapel, which had originally adjoined the northern walls of the cathedral, has been dismantled.

Phil.d.Grossm.

Philipp der Grossmütige (Philip the Magnanimous)
At the base of the arcade stand the statues of church reformers and those who supported the Reformation. The statue of Prince Philip the Magnanimous is the work of Walter Schott.

★ **Church Interior**
The impressive and richly-decorated interior was designed by Julius Raschdorff at the start of the 20th century.

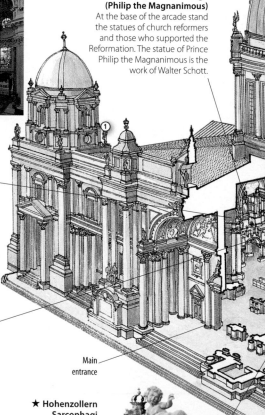

①

Sauer's Organ
The organ, the work of Wilhelm Sauer, has an exquisitely carved case. The instrument contains some 7,200 pipes.

Main entrance

KEY

① **Figures of the apostles**

② **The main altar**, saved from the previous cathedral, is the work of Friedrich August Stüler. It dates from 1820.

★ **Hohenzollern Sarcophagi**
The Imperial Hohenzollern family crypt, hidden beneath the floor of the cathedral, contains 100 richly decorated sarcophagi, including that of Prince Friedrich Ludwig.

The Four Evangelists
Mosaics depicting the Four Evangelists decorate the ceilings of the smaller niches in the cathedral. They were designed by Woldemar Friedrich.

The Resurrection
The stained glass in the windows of the apses depict scenes from the life of Jesus. They are the work of Anton von Werner.

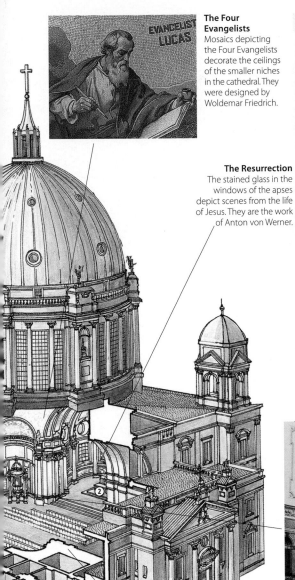

The Pulpit
This elaborate Neo-Baroque pulpit is part of the cathedral's ornate decor dating from the early 20th century.

★ **Sarcophagi of Friedrich I and his Wife**
Both of these were designed by Andreas Schlüter. The sculpture on Sophie Charlotte's sarcophagus depicts death.

Arnold Böcklin's *The Island of the Dead*, 1883, Alte Nationalgalerie

❼ Alte Nationalgalerie
Old National Gallery

Bodestrasse 1–3. **Map** 9 B2.
Tel 20 90 58 01. Ⓢ Hackescher Markt, Friedrichstrasse. 🚌 100, 200. 🚊 12, M1, M4, M5. **Open** 10am–6pm Tue–Sun (to 10pm Thu).

The Nationalgalerie building was erected between 1866 and 1876 and designed by Friedrich August Stüler, who took into account the sketches made by Friedrich Wilhelm IV. The building is situated on a high platform reached via a double staircase. On the top stands an equestrian statue of Friedrich Wilhelm IV, the work of Alexander Calandrelli in 1886. The façade of the building is preceded by a magnificent colonnade, which becomes a row of half-columns higher up. The decorations are in keeping with the purpose of the building – the tympanum features Germania as patroness of art, while the top is crowned with the personification of the arts.

The museum was originally meant to house the collection of modern art that had been on display since 1861 in the Akademie der Künste *(see p69)*. The current collection includes works of masters such as Adolph von Menzel, Wilhelm Leibl, Max Liebermann and Arnold Böcklin. Other works include paintings by the Nazarene Brotherhood and the French Impressionists. There is also no shortage of sculptures, including works by Christian Daniel Rauch, Johann Gottfried Schadow, Antonio Canova and Reinhold Begas. Two additional exhibition halls now present paintings (formerly shown at the Schloss Charlottenburg) from the German Romantic era, as well as works by Caspar David Friedrich, Karl Friedrich Schinkel and Karl Blechen.

❽ Neues Museum
New Museum

Bodestrasse 1–3. **Map** 9 B2.
Tel 26 64 24 242. Ⓢ Hackescher Markt or Friedrichstrasse. 🚌 100, 200. 🚊 12, M1, M4, M5. **Open** 10am–6pm Sun–Wed, 10am–8pm Thu–Sat.

The Neues Museum was built on Museum Island in order to relieve the Altes Museum, which was already very crowded. The building was erected between 1841 and 1855 to a design by Friedrich August Stüler. Until World War II it housed a collection of antiquities, mainly ancient Egyptian art. The monumental building's beautiful rooms were decorated to complement the exhibitions they contained. Wall paintings by Wilhelm von Kaulbach depicted key events in world history.

In 1945 the building was badly damaged and it took a long time to decide if it would be feasible to rebuild it. But the reconstruction effort under British architect David Chipperfield, a skilful blend of conservation, restoration and creating new spaces, was highly successful. History remains palpable in every room. The resurrected museum again houses the collection of Egyptian art (with the bust of Queen Nefertiti as its star exhibit), the Collection of Classical Antiquities and the Museum for Pre– and Early History. The latter portrays the evolution of mankind from prehistoric to medieval times, including a magnificent collection from the ancient city of Troy and gold jewellery belonging to the "Treasure of Priam".

Façade statue, Neues Museum

❾ Pergamon-museum

See pp82–3.

❿ Bode-Museum

Monbijoubrücke. (Bodestrasse 1–3). **Map** 9 A2. **Tel** 20 90 55 77. Ⓢ Hackescher Markt or Friedrichstrasse. 🚌 100, 147, 200. 🚃 12, M1, M4, M5, M6. **Open** 10am–6pm daily (to 10pm Thu). 📷

The fourth museum building on the island was erected between 1897 and 1904. It was designed by Ernst von Ihne to fit the wedge-shaped end of the island. The interior was designed with the help of an art historian, Wilhelm von Bode, who was the director of the Berlin state museums at the time. The museum displayed a rather mixed collection that included some Old Masters. Its original name, Kaiser Friedrich Museum, was changed after World War II. Following the reassembling of the Berlin collections, all of the paintings were put in the Kulturforum *(see pp126–7)*. The Egyptian art and the papyrus collection were moved to the Ägyptisches Museum (Egyptian Museum) at Charlottenburg. They are now housed at the Neues Museum *(see p80)*.

All the collections are back on display following renovation work. Highlights include an outstanding coin collection of some of the world's oldest coins, from Athens in the 6th century BC, as well as Roman, medieval and 20th-century coins. There are also sculptures by Tilman Riemenschneider, Donatello, Gianlorenzo Bernini and Antonio Canova.

⓫ Marstall
The Royal Stables

Schlossplatz/Breite Strasse 36–37. **Map** 9 B3, C3, C4. Ⓤ Spittelmarkt. 🚌 147, 248, M48.

This huge complex, occupying the area between the Spree and Breitestrasse, south of Schlossplatz, is the old Royal Stables block. The wing on the side of Breite Strasse is a fragment of the old structure built in 1669. It was designed by Michael Matthias Smids and is the only surviving early Baroque building in Berlin. The wings running along Schlossplatz and the Spree river were built much later, between 1898 and 1901. Although they were designed by Ernst von Ihne, these buildings are reminiscent of the Berlin Baroque style – probably because von Ihne modelled them on designs by Jean de Bodt from 1700.

⓬ Ribbeckhaus
Ribbeck's House

Breite Strasse 35. **Map** 9 C4. Ⓤ Spittelmarkt. 🚌 147, 248, M48.

Four identical, picturesque gables crown central Berlin's only surviving Renaissance building. The house was built c.1624 for Hans Georg von Ribbeck, a court counsellor, who sold it shortly afterwards to Anna Sophie of Brunswick. The architect Balthasar Benzelt converted the house for her in 1629. After her death in 1659, the house passed to her

The Ribbeckhaus, central Berlin's only surviving Renaissance building

nephew Elector Friedrich Wilhelm. As crown property, the building later housed various state administrative offices. When another storey was added, the row of gables was retained by royal decree.

The house also has an interesting late Renaissance portal, ornamented with the date and coat of arms of the first owners – von Ribbeck and Katharina von Brösicke his wife. This was replaced in 1960 with a copy. Original features of interest include the beautiful wrought-iron grilles on the ground-floor windows.

⓭ Historischer Hafen Berlin
Historic Port of Berlin

Märkisches Ufer. **Map** 10 D4. **Tel** 0172 315 2049. Ⓤ Märkisches Ufer. Ⓢ Jannowitzbrücke. 🚌 147, 248, 265. **Open** 11am–5pm Tue–Sun. 📷

Moored on the south shore of Museum Island, in an area called Fischerinsel, and opposite the Märkisches Ufer are several examples of boats, barges and tug-boats operated on the Spree river at the end of the 19th century. These craft constitute an open-air museum which was once located in the Humboldt Port. One of the boats is now used as a summer café, while another, the *Renate Angelika*, houses a small exhibition illustrating the history of inland waterway transport on the Spree and Havel.

The Bode-Museum designed by Ernst von Ihne

Pergamonmuseum

Built between 1910 and 1930 to a design by Alfred Messels and Ludwig Hoffmann, this museum houses one of Europe's most famous collections of antiquities. It is named for the famous Pergamon Altar displayed in the main hall. The three independent collections – the Museum of Classical Antiquities (Greek and Roman), the Museum of the Ancient Near East and the Museum of Islamic Art – are the result of intensive archaeological excavations by late 19th- and early 20th-century German expeditions to the Near and Middle East. Some displays may be closed or relocated during the major renovation scheduled to end in 2020.

★ **Pergamon Altar** (170 BC)
This scene, featuring the goddess Athena, appears on the large frieze illustrating a battle between the gods and the giants.

Roman Mosaic
(3rd or 4th century AD)
This ancient mosaic was found at Jerash, Jordan. A second part of it was sold to an unknown collector.

First floor

The Goddesss Athena
This enchanting Hellenistic sculpture of the goddess Athena is one of many displayed in the museum.

Ground floor

Main entrance

Assyrian Palace
Parts of this beautifully reconstructed palace interior, from the ancient kingdom of Assyria, date from the 9th and 13th centuries BC.

Aleppo Zimmer
(c.1601–3)
This magnificent panelled room comes from a merchant's house in the Syrian city of Aleppo.

VISITORS' CHECKLIST

Practical Information
Am Kupfergraben 5.
Map 9 A2, B2.
Tel 266 424 242.
w smb-spk-berlin.de
Open 10am–6pm daily (to 8pm Thu).

Transport
S Hackescher Markt or Friedrichstrasse. 🚌 100, 200. 🚋 12, M1.

Key

- ☐ Collection of Classical Antiquities
- ☐ Museum of the Ancient Near East (Vorderasiatisches Museum)
- ☐ Museum of Islamic Art (Museum für Islamische Kunst)
- ☐ Special exhibition rooms

Façade of the Mshatta Palace (744 AD)
This fragment is from the southern façade of the Jordanian Mshatta Palace, presented to Wilhelm II by Sultan Abdul Hamid of Ottoman in 1903.

★ **Market Gate from Miletus** (c.120 AD)
This gate, measuring over 16 m (52 ft) in height, opened on to the southern market of Miletus, a Roman town in Asia Minor.

★ **Ishtar Gate from Babylon**
(6th century BC)
Original glazed bricks decorate both the huge Ishtar Gate and the impressive Processional Way that leads up to it.

Gallery Guide

The central section of the ground floor houses reconstructions of ancient monumental structures, and the left wing is devoted to the Antiquities of Greece and Rome. The right wing houses the Museum of the Ancient Near East; the first floor of the right wing houses the Museum of Islamic Art.

Exploring the Pergamonmuseum

Opened in 1930, the Pergamonmuseum is the newest museum in the Museum Island complex and is one of Berlin's major attractions. The building was one of the first in Europe designed specifically to house big architectural exhibits. The richness of its collections is the result of large-scale excavations by German archaeologists at the beginning of the 20th century. Currently, the museum is at the heart of a significant redevelopment programme, due for completion in 2020, that will considerably increase the range of large-scale exhibits on display.

The Greek goddess Persephone, from Tarentum, 5th century BC

Restored entrance hall of the Athena temple from Pergamon, 2nd century BC

Collection of Classical Antiquities

Berlin's collection of Greek and Roman antiquities (Antikensammlung) came into existence during the 17th century. Growing steadily in size, the collection was opened for public viewing in 1830, initially in the Altes Museum (see p77), and from 1930 in the new, purpose-built Pergamonmuseum. The highlight of the collection is the huge

Pergamon Altar from the acropolis of the ancient city of Pergamon in Asia Minor (now Bergama, Turkey). It formed part of a larger architectural complex, a model of which is also on display in the museum. The magnificently restored altar is thought to have been built to celebrate victory in war and to have been commissioned by King Eumenes in 170 BC. Probably dedicated to the god Zeus and the goddess Athena, this artistic masterpiece was discovered in a decrepit state by German archaeologist Carl Humann who, after long negotiations, was allowed to transport the surviving portions of the altar to Berlin. The front section of the building was restored at the museum, together with the so-called small frieze, which once adorned the inside of the building, and fragments of the large frieze, which originally encircled the base of the colonnade. The large frieze has now been reconstructed around the interior walls of the museum and its theme is the Gigantomachy (the battle of the gods against the

giants). The small frieze tells the story of Telephos, supposed founder of the city and son of the hero Heracles. The frieze is an attempt to claim an illustrious ancestry for Pergamon's rulers.

The collection also contains fragments of other Pergamon structures from the same period, including part of the Athena temple. Also featured here are some excellent examples of Greek sculpture, both originals and Roman copies, as well as many statues of the Greek gods unearthed at Miletus, Samos and Nakosos, and various examples of Greek ceramic art.

Roman architecture is represented by the striking market gate from the Roman city of Miletus, on the west coast of Asia Minor. The gate dates from the 2nd century AD, and shows strong Hellenistic influences. Discovered by a German archaeological expedition, it was transported to Berlin where it was restored in 1903. Also on display are a number of magnificent Roman mosaics.

Roman marble sarcophagus depicting the story of Medea, 2nd century AD

A huge and impressive marble sarcophagus dates from the 2nd century AD and is decorated with delicate bas-relief carvings depicting the story of the Greek heroine Medea.

Glazed-brick wall cladding from the palace of Darius I in Susa, capital of the Persian Empire

Museum of the Ancient Near East

The collection now on display in the Museum of Near Eastern Antiquities (Vorderasiatisches Museum) was made up initially of donations from individual collectors. However, hugely successful excavations, begun during the 1880s, formed the basis of a royal collection that is one of the richest in the world. It features architecture, sculpture and jewellery from Babylon, Iran and Assyria.

One striking exhibit is the magnificent Ishtar Gate and the Processional Way that leads to it. They were built during the reign of Nebuchadnezzar II (604–562 BC) in the ancient city of Babylon. The original avenue was about 180 m (590 ft) long. Many of the bricks used in its recon-struction are new, but the lions – sacred animals of the goddess Ishtar (mistress of the sky, goddess of love and patron of the army) – are all originals. Although impressive in size, the Ishtar Gate has in fact not been reconstructed in full and a model of the whole structure shows the scale of the original complex. Only the inner gate is

on display, framed by two towers. Dragons and bulls decorate the gate, emblems of the Babylonian gods Marduk, patron of the city, and Adad, god of storms.

The collection also includes pieces from the neighbouring regions of Persia, Syria and Palestine including a gigantic basalt sculpture of a bird from Tell Halaf and a glazed wall relief of a spear bearer from Darius I's palace in Susa. Other Mesopotamian peoples, including the Assyrians and the Cassians, are represented here too, as are the inhabitants of Sumer in the southern part of the Babylonian Empire with pieces dating from the 4th century BC.

Museum of Islamic Art

The history of the Museum of Islamic Art (Museum für Islamische Kunst) begins in 1904 when Wilhelm von Bode launched the collection by donating his own extensive selection of carpets. He also brought to Berlin a 45-m (150-ft) long section of the façade of a Jordanian desert palace. The façade, covered with exquisitely carved limestone cladding, was presented to Kaiser Wilhelm II in 1903 by Sultan Abdul Hamid of Ottoman. The palace was part of a group of defence fortresses and residential buildings dating from the Omayyad period (AD 661–750). These were probably built for the Caliph al-Walid II.

Another fascinating exhibit is a beautiful 13th-century *mihrab*, the niche in a mosque that shows the direction of Mecca.

Brilliantly-glazed *mihrab* from a Kashan mosque built in 1226

Made in the Iranian town of Kashan renowned for its ceramics, the *mihrab* is covered in lustrous metallic glazes that make it sparkle as if studded with sapphires and gold.

The collection's many vivid carpets come from as far afield as Iran, Asia Minor, Egypt and the Caucasus. High- lights include an early 15th-century carpet from Anatolia decorated with an unusual dragon and phoenix motif and, dating from the 14th century, one of the earliest Turkish carpets in existence.

Other rooms hold collections of miniature paintings and various objects for daily use. An interesting example of provincial Ottoman archi-tecture is an exquisitely-panelled early 17th-century reception room, known as t he Aleppo Zimmer, which was once part of a Christian merchant's house in the Syrian city of Aleppo.

17th-century carpet with flower motif from western Anatolia

The exterior of the Märkisches Museum, echoing a medieval monastery

⓮ Märkisches Museum

Am Köllnischen Park 5. **Map** 10 D4. **Tel** 24 00 21 62. Ⓤ Jannowitzbrücke, Märkisches Museum. Ⓢ Jannowitzbrücke. 🚌 147, 248, 265, M48. **Open** 10am–6pm Tue, Thu–Sun; noon–8pm Wed. 🎵 Presentation of mechanical musical instruments 3pm Sun.

This architectural pastiche is a complex of red brick buildings that most resembles a medieval monastery. It was built between 1901 and 1908 to house a collection relating to the history of Berlin and the Brandenburg region, from the time of the earliest settlers to the present. Inspired by the brick-Gothic style popular in the Brandenburg region, architect Ludwig Hoffmann included references to Wittstock Castle and to St Catherine's Church in the city of Brandenburg. In the entrance hall, a statue of the hero Roland stands guard, a copy of the 15th-century monument in the city of Brandenburg. The main hall features the original Gothic portal from the Berlin residence of the Margraves of Brandenburg (see pp19–21), demolished in 1931. Also featured is a horse's head from the Schadow *Quadriga*, which once crowned the Brandenburg Gate (see p69). A further collection in the same building is devoted to the Berlin theatre during the period 1730 to 1933, including many posters, old programmes and stage sets. One of the galleries houses some charming old-time mechanical musical instruments, which can be heard playing during special shows.

The Märkisches Museum is a branch of the Stadtmuseum Berlin organization, and those who wish to find out more about the history of the city can visit other affiliated museums and monuments such as the Nikolaikirche (see pp92–3) and the Ephraim-Palais (see p93). Surrounding the museum is the Köllnischer Park, home to three brown bears, the official city mascots, and an unusual statue of Berlin artist Heinrich Zille.

⓯ Märkisches Ufer

Map 10 D4. Ⓤ Märkisches Museum. Ⓢ Jannowitzbrücke. 🚌 147, 248, 265, M48.

Once called Neukölln am Wasser, this street, which runs along the Spree river, is one of the few corners of Berlin where it is still possible to see the town much as it must have looked in the 18th and 19th centuries. Eight picturesque houses have been meticulously conserved here.

Two Neo-Baroque houses at No. 16 and No. 18, known as Otto-Nagel Haus, used to contain a small museum displaying paintings by Otto Nagel, a great favourite with the communist authorities. The building now houses the photographic archives for the state museums of Berlin. A number of picturesque garden cafés and fashionable restaurants make this attractive area very popular with tourists.

The Neo-Classical exterior of the Ermeler-Haus

⓰ Ermeler-Haus

Ermeler House

Märkisches Ufer 10. **Map** 9 C4. Ⓤ Märkisches Museum. Ⓢ Jannowitzbrücke. 🚌 147, 248, 265, M48.

With its harmonious Neo-Classical façade, Märkisches Ufer No. 12 stands out as one of the most handsome villas in Berlin. This house was once the town residence of Wilhelm Ferdinand Ermeler, a wealthy merchant and shop-keeper, who made his money trading in tobacco. It originally stood on Fischerinsel on the opposite bank of the river, at Breite Strasse No. 11, but in 1968 the house was dismantled and reconstructed on this new site. The house was remodelled in 1825 to Ermeler's specifications, with a decor that

Barges moored alongside Märkisches Ufer

includes a frieze alluding to aspects of the tobacco business. Restorers have recreated much of the original façade. The Rococo furniture dates from about 1760 and the notable 18th-century staircase has also been rebuilt.

A modern hotel has been built to the rear of the house facing Wallstrasse, using Ermeler-Haus as its kitchens while the first-floor rooms are used for special events.

⑰ Gertrauden-brücke
St Gertrude's Bridge

Map 9 B4. Ⓤ Spittelmarkt.
265, M48.

One of Berlin's more interesting bridges, this connects Fischer Island with Spittelmarkt at the point where St Gertrude's Hospital once stood. The Gertraudenbrücke was designed by Otto Stahn and built in 1894.

Standing in the middle of the bridge is a bronze statue of the hospital's patron saint, St Gertrude, by Rudolf Siemering. A 13th-century Christian mystic, St Gertrude is shown here as a Benedictine abbess. Leaning over a poor youth she hands him a lily (symbol of virginity), a distaff (care for the poor) and a vessel filled with wine (love). The pedestal is surrounded by mice, a reference to the fact that Gertrude is patron saint of farmland and graves – both popular environments for mice.

Statue of St Gertrude

⑱ Nicolai-Haus

Brüderstr. 13. **Map** 9 B4. **Tel** 24 00 21 62. Ⓤ Spittelmarkt. 147, 265, M48. **Open** by appointment only.

Built around 1670, the Nicolai-Haus is a fine example of Baroque architecture with the original, magnificent oak staircase still in place. The house owes its fame, however, to its time as the home and bookshop of the publisher, writer and critic Christoph Friedrich Nicolai (1733–1811). Nicolai acquired the house around 1788 when he had it rebuilt to a Neo-Classical design by Karl Friedrich Zelter to become a bookshop and major German cultural centre.

One of the outstanding personalities of the Berlin Enlightenment, Nicolai was a great supporter of such talents as the Jewish philosopher Moses Mendelssohn (*see p104*) and the playwright Gotthold Ephraim Lessing (1729–81). Other regular literary visitors to the Nicolai-Haus at this period included Johann Gottfried Schadow, Karl Wilhelm Ramler and Daniel Chodowiecki, all of whom are commemorated with a wall plaque.

Between 1905 and 1935 the building housed a museum devoted to Gotthold Ephraim Lessing. Today the rear wing features a fine staircase from the Weydinger-Haus, demolished in 1935. Installed in the Nicolai-Haus in the late 1970s, the staircase previously stood in the nearby Ermeler Haus (*see p86*).

East German fashion now on show in the Märkisches Museum (*see p86*)

⑲ Galgenhaus
Gallows House

Brüderstrasse 10. **Map** 9 B4.
Tel 206 13 29 13. Ⓤ Spittelmarkt.
147, 265, M48. **Open** only during special events.

Local legend has it that an innocent girl was once hanged in front of this building, which dates from 1700. It was originally built as the presbytery of the now vanished church of St Peter. Redesigned in the Neo-Classical style around 1805, the front portal and one of the rooms on the ground floor are all that remain of the original Baroque structure.

Today the Galgenhaus houses an archive of historic photographs. These reveal the ways in which Berlin has developed over the years through changes in its buildings and monuments.

Cölln

An ancient settlement in the area called Fischerinsel at the southern end of Museum Island, the village of Cölln has now been razed almost to the ground. Not even a trace remains of the medieval St Peter's parish church. Until 1939, however, this working-class area with its tangle of narrow streets maintained a historic character and unique identity of its own. This vanished completely in the 1960s when most of the buildings were demo-lished, to be replaced with prefab-ricated tower blocks. A few historic houses, including Ermeler-Haus (*see p86*), were reconstructed else-where, but the atmosphere of this part of town has changed forever.

An engraving of old Cölln

EAST OF THE CENTRE

This part of Berlin, belonging to the Mitte district, is the historic centre. A settlement called Berlin was first established on the eastern bank of the Spree river in the 13th century. Together with its twin settlement, Cölln, it grew into a town. This district contains traces of Berlin's earliest history, including the oldest surviving church (Marienkirche). In later centuries, it became a trade and residential district, but the Old Town (around today's Nikolaiviertel)

survived until World War II. The GDR regime replaced the huge apartment buildings and department stores just to the north with a square, Marx-Engels- Forum, and built the Fernsehturm (television tower). Their redevelopment of the Nikolaiviertel was controversial – buildings were faithfully rebuilt but were grouped rather than being placed in their original locations. The area still offers cosy mews and alleys, which are surrounded by postwar high-rise blocks.

Sights at a Glance

Churches
❸ Nikolaikirche
❿ Heiliggeistkapelle
⓬ Marienkirche
⓰ Franziskaner Klosterkirche
⓲ Parochialkirche

Historic Buildings
❶ Rotes Rathaus
❹ Knoblauchhaus
❺ Palais Schwerin and Münze
❻ Ephraim-Palais
❼ Gerichtslaube
⓯ Stadtgericht
⓱ Palais Podewils
⓳ Gaststätte "Zur letzten Instanz"
⓴ Stadtmauer

Others
❷ Nikolaiviertel
❽ Martx-Engels-Forum
❾ DDR Museum
⓫ Neptunbrunnen
⓭ *Fernsehturm p95*
⓮ Alexanderplatz

☐ Restaurants
see p233
1 Domklause
2 Fernsehturm Telecafe
3 Reinhard's
4 Típica
5 Zur Letzten Instanz
6 Zum Nussbaum

See also Street Finder maps 9, 10

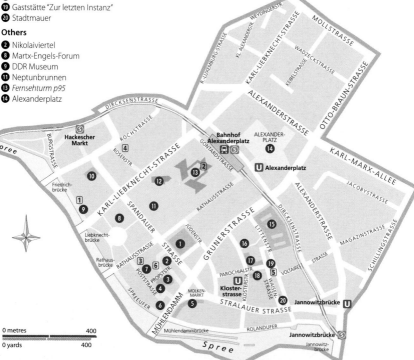

| 0 metres | 400 |
| 0 yards | 400 |

◀ **Detail from the Neptunbrunnen (Neptune Fountain)**

For map symbols *see back flap*

Street-by-Street: Nikolaiviertel

St Nicholas' Quarter, or the Nikolaiviertel, owes its name to the parish church whose spires rise above the small buildings in this part of town. The Nikolaiviertel is full of narrow alleys crammed with popular restaurants, tiny souvenir shops and small museums. The district retains the old features of long-destroyed Old Berlin and is usually filled with tourists looking for a place to rest after an exhausting day of sightseeing – particularly in the summer. Almost every other house is occupied by a restaurant, inn, pub or café, so the area is quite lively until late at night.

❸ Nikolaikirche
The church is now a museum, with its original furnishings incorporated into the exhibition.

❼ Gerichtslaube
The replica arcades and medieval courthouse now contain restaurants.

St George Slaying the Dragon
This statue once graced a courtyard of the Stadtschloss.

❹ Knoblauchhaus
This Biedermeirer-style room is on the first floor of the building, which is one of the few to survive World War II damage.

❻ Ephraim-Palais
A feature of this palace is the elegant façade. Inside there is also an impressive spiral staircase and balustrade.

❶ ★ Rotes Rathaus
This monumental town hall, which once stood in a densely built-up area, now rises from an empty square.

Locator Map
See Street Finder maps 9 & 10

The Stadthaus, built in 1911 by Ludwig Hoffmann, now houses some of the departments of the Town Hall.

❷ ★ Nikolaiviertel
The narrow alleys of this district were a source of inspiration for Gotthold Ephraim Lessing, who lived here from 1752 to 1755.

The Hemp Museum (Hanfmuseum) is a small museum that specializes in all aspects of the hemp plant.

SPANDAUER STRASSE

MÜHLENDAMM

JÜDENSTRASSE

MOLKEN MARKT

STRALAUER STRASSE

ROLANDUFER

Key

— Suggested route

0 metres   75
0 yards   75

Canal locks on the Spree

❺ Palais Schwerin and Münze
The palace façade is decorated with a Neo-Classical frieze by Johann Gottfried Schadow, depicting the development of metal processing and coin minting.

Red-brick walls giving the Red Town Hall its name

❶ Rotes Rathaus

Red Town Hall

Rathausstr. 15. **Map** 9 C3. **Tel** 90 26 0. **U** & **S** Alexanderplatz. **U** Klosterstrasse. 🚌 100, 200, 248, M48, TXL. **Open** 9am–6pm Mon–Fri.

This impressive structure is Berlin's main town hall. Its predecessor was a much more modest structure and by the end of the 19th century, it was insufficient to the needs of the growing metropolis.

The present building was designed by Hermann Friedrich Waesemann, and the construction went on from 1861 until 1869. The architect took his main inspiration from Italian Renaissance municipal buildings, but the tower is reminiscent of Laon cathedral in France. The walls are made from red brick and it was this, rather than the political orientation of the mayors, that gave the town hall its name. The building has a continuous frieze known as the "stone chronicle", which was added in 1879. It features scenes and figures from the city's history and the development of its economy and science.

The Rotes Rathaus was badly damaged during World War II and, following its reconstruction (1951–8), it became the seat of the East Berlin authorities. The West Berlin magistrate was housed in the Schöneberg town hall *(see p187)*. After the reunification of Germany, the Rotes Rathaus became the centre of authority, housing the

offices of the mayor, the magistrates' offices and state rooms. The forecourt sculptures were added in 1958. These are by Fritz Cremer and depict Berliners helping to rebuild the city.

❷ Nikolaiviertel

Map 9 C3, C4. **U** & **S** Alexanderplatz. **U** Klosterstrasse. 🚌 100, 200, 248, M48, TXL.

This small area on the bank of the Spree, known as the Nikolaiviertel (St Nicholas Quarter), is a favourite place for strolling, for both Berliners and tourists. Some of Berlin's oldest houses stood here until they were destroyed in World War II. The redevelopment of the whole area, carried out by the GDR government between 1979 and 1987, was an interesting, if somewhat controversial, attempt at recreating a medieval village. With the exception of one or two restored buildings, the Nikolaiviertel consists of replicas of historic buildings.

The narrow streets of the Nikolaiviertel tempt the visitor with their small shops, as well as many cafés, bars and restaurants. One of the most popular is Zum Nussbaum, a historical inn that was once located on Fischer Island. The original building, dating from 1507, was destroyed but was subsequently reconstructed at the junction of Am Nussbaum and Propststrasse.

The interior of the Nikolaikirche, one of Berlin's oldest churches

❸ Nikolaikirche

Nikolaikirchplatz. **Map** 9 C3. **Tel** 24 00 21 62. **U** & **S** Alexanderplatz. **U** Klosterstrasse. 🚌 100, 147, 200, 248, M48, TXL. **Open** 10am–6pm daily. ♿

The Nikolaikirche is the oldest sacred building of historic Berlin. The original structure erected on this site was started probably around 1230, when the town was granted its municipal rights. What remains now of this stone building is the massive base of the two-tower façade of the present church, which dates from c.1300. The presbytery was completed around 1402, but the construction of the main building went on until the mid-15th century. The result was a magnificent Gothic brick hall-church, featuring a chancel with an ambulatory and a row of low chapels. In 1877 Hermann

Riverside buildings of the Nikolaiviertel

Blankenstein, who conducted the church restoration works, removed most of its Baroque modifications and reconstructed the front towers.

Destroyed by bombing in 1945, the Nikolaikirche was eventually rebuilt in 1987 and shows a permanent exhibit on Berlin's history. The west wall of the southern nave contains Andreas Schlüter's monument to the goldsmith Daniel Männlich and his wife, which features a gilded relief portrait of the couple above a mock doorway.

❹ Knoblauchhaus

Poststr. 23. **Map** 9 C3. **Tel** 24 00 21 62. Ⓤ & Ⓢ Alexanderplatz. Ⓤ Klosterstrasse. 🚌 248, M48. **Open** 10am–6pm Tue & Thu–Sun, noon–8pm Wed. 🖼

This small townhouse in Poststrasse is the only Baroque building in Nikolaiviertel that escaped damage during World War II. It was built in 1759 for the Knoblauch family which includes the famous architect, Eduard Knoblauch. His works include, among others, the Neue Synagoge *(see p104)*.

The current appearance of the building is the result of work carried out in 1835, when the façade was given a Neo-Classical look. The ground floor houses a popular wine bar, while the upper floors belong to a museum. On the first floor it is possible to see the interior of an early 19th-century middle-class home, including a beautiful Biedermeier-style room.

❺ Palais Schwerin and Münze

Molkenmarkt 1–3. **Map** 9 C4. Ⓤ & Ⓢ Alexanderplatz. Ⓤ Klosterstrasse. 🚌 248, M48.

These two adjoining houses have quite different histories. The older one, at Molkenmarkt No. 2, is Palais Schwerin, which was built by Jean de Bodt in 1704 for a government minister, Otto von Schwerin. Despite subsequent remodelling, the

A fine example of German Baroque architecture, the Ephraim-Palais

palace kept its beautiful sculptured window cornices, the interior wooden staircase, and the magnificent cartouche featuring the von Schwerin family crest.

The adjoining house is the mint which was built in 1936. Its façade is decorated with a copy of the frieze that once adorned the previous Neo-Classical mint building in Werderscher Markt. The antique style of the frieze was designed by Friedrich Gilly and produced in the workshop of JG Schadow.

❻ Ephraim-Palais

Poststr. 16. **Map** 9 C3. **Tel** 24 00 21 62. Ⓤ & Ⓢ Alexanderplatz. Ⓤ Klosterstrasse. 🚌 248, M48. **Open** 10am–6pm Tue & Thu–Sun, noon–8pm Wed. 🖼

The corner entrance of the Ephraim-Palais, standing at the junction of Poststrasse and Mühlendamm, used to be called "die schönste Ecke Berlins", meaning "Berlin's most beautiful corner". This Baroque palace was

built by Friedrich Wilhelm Diterichs in 1766 for Nathan Veitel Heinrich Ephraim, Frederick the Great's mint master and court jeweller.

During the widening of the Mühlendamm bridge in 1935 the palace was demolished, which may have been due in some part to the Jewish origin of its owner. Parts of the façade, saved from demolition, were stored in a warehouse in the western part of the city. In 1983 they were sent to East Berlin and used in the reconstruction of the palace, which was erected a few metres from its original site. One of the first floor rooms features a restored Baroque ceiling, designed by Andreas Schlüter. The ceiling previously adorned Palais Wartenberg, which was dismantled in 1889.

Currently Ephraim-Palais houses a branch of the Stadtmuseum Berlin (Berlin City Museum). It shows a series of temporary exhibitions on Berlin's local artistic and cultural history.

Frieze from the façade of the Münze (the Mint)

❼ Gerichtslaube

Poststrasse. 28. **Map** 9 C3. **Tel** 241 56 97. Ⓤ & Ⓢ Alexanderplatz. Ⓤ Klosterstrasse. 🚌 100, 200, 248, M48, TXL.

This small building, with its sharply angled arcades, has had a turbulent history. It was built around 1280 as part of Berlin's old town hall in Spandauer Strasse. The original building was a single storey arcaded construction with vaults supported by a central pillar. It was open on three sides and adjoined the shorter wall of the town hall. A further storey was added in 1485 to provide a hall to which the magnificent lattice vaults were added a few decades later, in 1555.

In 1692, Johann Arnold Nering refurbished the town hall in a Baroque style but left the arcades unaltered. Then, in 1868, the whole structure was dismantled to provide space for the new town hall, the Rotes Rathaus (*see p92*). The Baroque part was lost forever, but the Gothic arcades and the first floor hall were moved to the palace gardens in Babelsberg, where they were reassembled as a building in their own right (*see pp212–13*). When the Nikolaiviertel was undergoing restoration it was decided to restore the court of justice as well. The present building in Poststrasse is a copy of a part of the former town hall, erected on a different site from the original one. Inside is a restaurant serving local cuisine.

❽ Marx-Engels-Forum

Map 9 C3. Ⓢ Hackescher Markt or Alexanderplatz. 🚌 100, 200, 248, M48, TXL.

This vast, eerily empty square, stretching from the Neptune river to the Spree river in the west, was given the inappropriate name Marx-Engels-Forum (it is not really a forum). Devoid of any surroundings, the only features in this square are the statues of Karl Marx and Friedrich Engels.

Statue of Karl Marx and Friedrich Engels in Marx-Engels-Forum

The statues, added in 1986, are by Ludwig Engelhart. Due to the extension of an underground line which started in 2010, the statues were moved into a corner and the square will be inaccessible for several years. Berlin plans to build up the area after completing the underground works, rather than restore the uninspiring square.

❾ DDR Museum

Karl-Liebknecht-Strasse 1. **Map** 9 B3. **Tel** 847 12 37 31. Ⓢ Hackescher Markt. 🚌 100, 200. **Open** 10am–8pm daily (to 10pm Sat). 🅆 ddr-museum.de

This hands-on museum on the Spree embankment opposite the Berlin cathedral, gives an insight into the daily lives of East Germans and demonstrates how the secret police kept a watchful eye on the city's people. Exhibits include the replica of a typical living room and a shiny Trabant car.

❿ Heiliggeistkapelle
Chapel of the Holy Spirit

Spandauer Strasse 1. **Map** 9 B2. Ⓢ Hackescher Markt. 🚌 100, 200, 248, M48, TXL. 🚊 M4, M5, M6.

This modest Gothic structure is the only surviving hospital chapel in Berlin. It was built as part of a hospital complex in the second half of the 13th century, but was subsequently rebuilt in the 15th century. The hospital was demolished in 1825, but the chapel was retained. In 1906, it was made into a newly erected College of Trade, designed by Cremer and Wolffenstein.

The chapel is a fine example of Gothic brick construction. Its modest interior features a 15th-century star-shaped vault. The supports under the vault are decorated with half-statues of prophets and saints.

⓫ Neptunbrunnen
Neptune Fountain

Spandauer Str. (Rathausvorplatz). **Map** 9 C3. Ⓢ & Ⓤ Alexanderplatz. Ⓢ Hackescher Markt. 🚌 100, 200, 248, M48, TXL.

This magnificent, Neo-Baroque style fountain, sparkling with cascades of running water, provides a splendid feature on the main axis of the town hall building. It was created in 1886 by Reinhold Begas, to stand in front of the southern wall of the former Stadtschloss (Berlin Castle). It was moved to its present site in 1969.

The statue of Neptune, in a dynamic pose and in the centre of the fountain, is surrounded by four figures representing Germany's greatest rivers of the time: the Rhine, the Vistula, the Oder and the Elbe. The naturalism of the composition and the attention to detail, such as the beautiful bronze fish, crayfish, snails and fishing nets, are noteworthy.

Neptune surrounded by goddesses personifying Germany's rivers

⓬ Marienkirche

See pp96–7.

⓭ Fernsehturm

The television tower, called by the locals *Telespargel,* or toothpick, remains to this day the city's tallest structure at 368 m (1,207 ft), and one of the tallest structures in Europe. The tower was built in 1969 to a design by a team of architects including Fritz Dieter and Günter Franke, with the help of Swedish engineering experts. However, the idea for such a colossal tower in Berlin originated much earlier from Hermann Henselmann (creator of the Karl-Marx-Allee development) in the Socialist-Realist style. The interior was given a facelift in 2012.

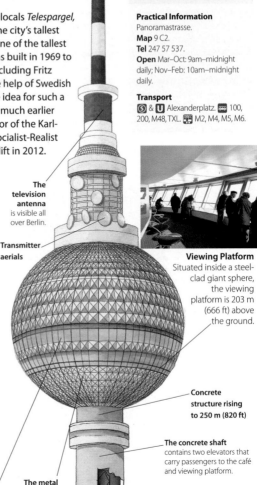

The
**television
antenna**
is visible all
over Berlin.

**Transmitter
aerials**

Viewing Platform
Situated inside a steel-clad giant sphere, the viewing platform is 203 m (666 ft) above the ground.

**Concrete
structure rising
to 250 m (820 ft)**

The concrete shaft
contains two elevators that carry passengers to the café and viewing platform.

**The metal
sphere**
is covered
with steel
cladding.

The elevators are small, resulting in long queues at the base of the tower.

Television Tower
The slim silhouette of the Fernsehturm is visible from almost any point in Berlin. The ticket office and elevator entrance are located at the base of the tower.

Sphere Restaurant
One of the attractions of the tower is the revolving restaurant. A full rotation takes about half an hour, so it is possible to get a bird's-eye-view of the whole city while sipping a cup of coffee.

View from the Tower
On a clear day the viewing platform offers a full view of Berlin. Visibility can reach up to 40 km (25 miles).

⑫ Marienkirche

St Mary's Church, or the Marienkirche, was first established as a parish church in the second half of the 13th century. Construction started around 1280 and was completed early in the 14th century. During reconstruction works in 1380, following a fire, the church was altered slightly but its overall shape changed only in the 15th century when it acquired the front tower. In 1790, the tower was crowned with a dome designed by Carl Gotthard Langhans. The church was once hemmed in by buildings, but today it stands alone in the shadow of the Fernsehturm (Television Tower). The early-Gothic hall design and the lavish decor-ative touches make this church one of the most interesting in Berlin.

Crucifixion (1562)
This image of Christ, flanked by Moses and St John the Baptist, was painted in the Mannerist style by Michael Rihestein.

Retable
The central part of the Gothic altar, dating from 1510, features figures of three unknown monks.

KEY

① **Totentanz,** meaning "dance of death", is the name of a 22-m (72-ft) long Gothic wall fresco, dating from 1485.

② **The dome** that crowns the tower includes both Baroque and Neo-Gothic elements.

Main entrance

★ Pulpit

Carved from alabaster, this masterpiece by Andreas Schlüter, completed in 1703, is placed by the fourth pillar. The pulpit is decorated with bas-reliefs of St John the Baptist and the personifications of the Virtues.

Von Röbel Family Tomb

This richly decorated Mannerist-Baroque tomb of Ehrentreich and Anna von Röbel was probably built after 1630.

Main Altar

The Baroque altar was designed by Andreas Krüger c.1762. The paintings, including *Deposition from the Cross* in the centre; *Christ on the Mount of Olives* and *Doubting Thomas* on the sides, are the works of Christian Bernhard Rode.

★ Baptismal Font

This Gothic font dating from 1437 is supported by three black dragons and decorated with the figures of Jesus Christ, Mary and the Apostles.

The magnificent interior of the Stadtgericht

⑭ Alexanderplatz

Map 10 D2. 🚇 & Ⓢ Alexanderplatz.
🚌 100, 200, 248, M48, TXL.
🚊 M5, M6, M8.

Alexanderplatz, or "Alex" as it is locally called, has a long history, although it would be difficult now to find any visible traces of the past. Once called Ochsenmarkt (oxen market), it was the site of a cattle and wool market. It was later renamed after Tsar Alexander I, who visited Berlin in 1805. At the time, the square boasted a magnificent monumental colonnade designed by Carl von Gontard (see p187).

With the passage of time, many houses and shops sprang up around the square, and a market hall and an urban train line were built nearby. "Alex" had become one of the town's busiest spots. Its frenzied atmosphere was captured by Alfred Döblin (1878–1957) in his novel, Berlin Alexanderplatz.

In 1929, attempts were made to develop the square, though only two office buildings were added – the Alexanderhaus and the Berolinahaus. These two, both by Peter Behrens, are still standing today. World War II erased most of the square's buildings. It is now surrounded by characterless 1960s edifices, including the Park Inn (formerly Hotel Stadt Berlin) and the Fernsehturm (see p95).

Alexanderplatz awaits its next transformation, which might happen soon: a winning design has been chosen from a competition for the square's redevelopment.

⑮ Stadtgericht
Courts of Justice

Littenstrasse 13–17. **Map** 10 D3.
🚇 & Ⓢ Alexanderplatz or
🚇 Klosterstrasse. 🚌 248.

This gigantic building, situated on a long stretch of Littenstrasse, does not seem particularly inviting, but its interior hides a true masterpiece of the Viennese Secession style of architecture.

At the time of its construction, the building was the largest in Berlin after the Stadtschloss (see p76). The Neo-Baroque structure, built between 1896 and 1905, was designed by Paul Thomer and Rudolf Mönnich, but its final shape is the work of Otto Schmalz. This maze-like complex, with its 11 inner courtyards, was partly demolished in 1969. What remains, however, is still worth seeing, especially the magnificent staircase in the form of overlying ellipses. The staircase is an example of Secession architecture at its boldest. The slim Neo-Gothic pillars and the Neo-Baroque balustrades further enhance the fairytale interior.

⑯ Franziskaner Klosterkirche
Franciscan Friary Church

Klosterstrasse 74. **Map** 10 D3.
🚇 Klosterstrasse. 🚌 248.

These picturesque ruins surrounded by greenery are the remains of an early Gothic Franciscan church. The Franciscan friars settled in Berlin in the early 13th century. Between 1250 and 1265 they built a church and a friary, which survived almost unchanged until 1945. The church was a triple-nave basilica with an elongated presbytery, widening into a heptagonal section that was added to the structure in c.1300. Protestants took over the church after the Reformation and the friary became a famous grammar school, whose graduates included Otto von Bismarck.

The friary was so damaged in World War II that it was subsequently demolished, while the church was partially reconstructed in 2003/4 and is now a venue for concerts and exhibitions. The giant Corinthian capitals, emerging

Ruins of the Franziskaner Klosterkirche
(Franciscan Friary Church)

from the grass near the church ruins, are from a portal from the Stadtschloss (Berlin Castle) *(see p76)*.

Façade of the twice-restored Palais Podewils

⓱ Palais Podewils
Podewils Palace

Klosterstrasse 68–70. **Map** 10 D3. Ⓤ Klosterstrasse. 🚌 248.

This charming Baroque palace, set back from the street, was built between 1701 and 1704 for the Royal Court's counsellor, Caspar Jean de Bodt. Its owes its present name to its subsequent owner, a minister of state called von Podewils, who bought the palace in 1732.

After World War II, the palace was restored twice: in 1954 and then again in 1966 after it had been damaged by fire. The carefully reconstructed building did not lose much of its austere beauty, but the interior completely changed to suit its current needs. It is now a performance space used by several arts companies and a number of dance groups, who conduct classes on the site.

⓲ Parochialkirche
Parish Church

Klosterstr. 67. **Map** 10 D3. **Tel** 247 59 510. Ⓤ Klosterstrasse. 🚌 248. **Open** 9am–5pm Mon–Fri.

This building was, at one time, one of most beautiful Baroque churches in Berlin. Johann Arnold Nering prepared the initial design, with four chapels

framing a central tower. Unfortunately, Nering died as construction started in 1695. The work was continued by Martin Grünberg, but the collapse of the nearly completed vaults forced a change in the design. Instead of the intended tower over the main structure, a vestibule with a front tower was built. The church was completed in 1703, but then, in 1714, its tower was enlarged by Jean de Bodt in order to accommodate a carillon.

World War II had a devastating effect on the Parochialkirche. The interior was completely destroyed, and the tower collapsed. Following stabilization of the main structure, the façade has been restored, with some reproduced historic elements set within a plain interior. During the summer, mass is held in the church.

Medallion from a headstone in the Parochialkirche

⓳ Gaststätte Zur letzten Instanz
Inn of the Last Instance

Waisenstrasse 14–16. **Map** 10 D3. Ⓤ Klosterstrasse. 🚌 248.

The small street at the rear of the Parochialkirche leads directly to one of the oldest inns in Berlin, Zur letzten Instanz, which translates as the Inn of the Last Instance. The inn occupies one of the four picturesque houses on Waisenstrasse – the only survivors of the whole row of houses that once adjoined the

town wall. Their history goes back to medieval times, but their present form dates from the 18th century. The houses are actually the result of an almost total reconstruction carried out after World War II. This was when one of the houses acquired its spiral Rococo staircase, which came from a dismantled house on the Fischerinsel.

The Zur letzten Instanz was first established in 1621 and initially specialized in serving alcoholic beverages. Interestingly, it was frequently patronized by lawyers. Today, however, the Zur letzten Instanz is one of Berlin's finest historic pub-restaurants frequented by all types of people, not just lawyers *(see p233)*. Its interior is full of old memorabilia.

⓴ Stadtmauer
Town Wall

Waisenstrasse. **Map** 10 D3. Ⓤ & Ⓢ Alexanderplatz or Ⓤ Klosterstrasse. 🚌 248.

The town wall that once surrounded the settlements of Berlin and Cölln was erected in the second half of the 13th century. The ring of fortifications, built from fieldstone and brick, was made taller in the 14th century. Having finally lost its military significance by the 17th century, the wall was almost entirely dismantled. Today, some small sections survive around Waisenstrasse, because they were incorporated into other buildings.

Remains of the Berlin's Stadtmauer (old town wall)

NORTH OF THE CENTRE

The area northwest of Alexanderplatz, formerly called Spandauer Vorstadt, is a historic district that has developed into a lively neighbourhood, buzzing with bars, cafés and designer shops. The southeastern part of the area is known as Scheunenviertel (Barn Quarter). In 1672, the Great Elector moved the hay barns – a fire hazard – out of the city limits. From that time it became a refuge for Jews fleeing Russia and Eastern Europe. To the north is Prenzlauer Berg, a bohemian hub in the 1990s and now, after gentrification, a beautiful and pleasant place to live and visit.

Sights at a Glance

Streets and Parks
- ❸ Oranienburger Strasse
- ❹ Monbijoupark
- ❾ Sophienstrasse
- ❿ Alte and Neue Schönhauser Strasse
- ⓬ Torstrasse
- ⓭ Kollwitzplatz

Churches and Synagogues
- ❶ Neue Synagoge
- ❽ Sophienkirche
- ⓮ Synagogue Rykestrasse
- ⓳ Zionskirche

Theatres
- ⓫ Volksbühne
- ⓴ Friedrichstadtpalast
- ㉑ Berliner Ensemble
- ㉓ Deutsches Theater

Museums
- ❷ Centrum Judaicum
- ㉖ Brecht-Weigel-Gedenkstätte
- ㉘ Museum für Naturkunde
- ㉙ *Hamburger Bahnhof pp114–15*

Cemeteries
- ❼ Alter Jüdischer Friedhof
- ⓰ Jüdischer Friedhof
- ㉕ *Dorotheenstädtischer Friedhof pp110–11*

Others
- ❺ Hackesche Höfe
- ❻ Gedenkstätte Grosse Hamburger Strasse
- ⓯ Wasserturm
- ⓱ Kulturbrauerei
- ⓲ Prater
- ㉒ Sammlung Boros
- ㉔ Charité
- ㉗ Gedenkstätte Berliner Mauer

```
0 metres    600
0 yards     600
```

See also Streetfinder maps 1, 2, 8 & 9

◀ **The golden Neue Synagoge**

For map symbols *see back flap*

Street-by-Street: Scheunenviertel

Until World War II Scheunenviertel lay at the heart of Berlin's large Jewish district. During the 19th century the community flourished, its prosperity reflected in grand buildings such as the Neue Synagoge, which opened in 1866 in the presence of Chancellor Otto von Bismarck. Left to crumble for nearly 50 years after the double devastations of the Nazis and Allied bombing, the district has enjoyed a huge revival since the fall of the Wall. Cafés and bars have opened and visitors can expect to find some of the liveliest nightlife in East Berlin.

❶ ★ Neue Synagoge
Sparkling with gold, the restored New Synagogue is now used again for services.

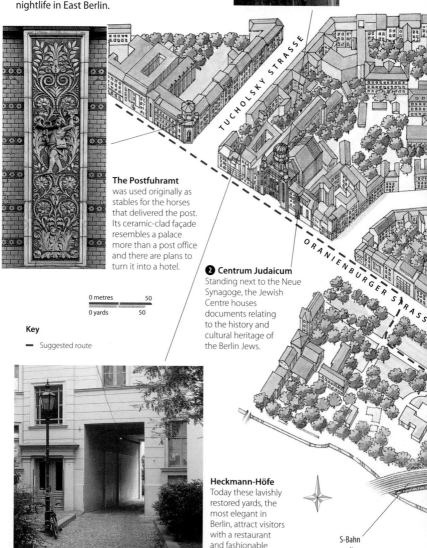

The Postfuhramt
was used originally as stables for the horses that delivered the post. Its ceramic-clad façade resembles a palace more than a post office and there are plans to turn it into a hotel.

❷ Centrum Judaicum
Standing next to the Neue Synagoge, the Jewish Centre houses documents relating to the history and cultural heritage of the Berlin Jews.

0 metres 50
0 yards 50

Key
— Suggested route

Heckmann-Höfe
Today these lavishly restored yards, the most elegant in Berlin, attract visitors with a restaurant and fashionable clothes shops.

S-Bahn line

8 **Sophienkirche**
This small Protestant church was founded in 1712 by Queen Sophie Luisa.

An dieser Stelle befand sich das erste Altenheim der Jüdischen Gemeinde Berlin. 1942 verwandelte die Gestapo es in ein Sammellager für jüdische Bürger. 55000 Berliner Juden vom Säugling bis zum Greis wurden in die KZ-Lager Auschwitz und Theresienstadt verschleppt und bestialisch ermordet.

VERGESST DAS NIE
WEHRET DEM KRIEG
HÜTET DEN FRIEDEN

Locator Map
See Street Finder map 9

NORTH OF THE CENTRE

AROUND UNTER DEN LINDEN

EAST OF THE CENTRE

6 **Gedenkstätte Grosse Hamburger Strasse**
This modest memorial to the Berlin Jews stands on the site of the city's first Jewish old people's home.

Dorotheenstädtischer Friedhof

GROSSE HAMBURGER STRASSE

HACKESCHER MARKT

5 ★ **Hackesche Höfe**
This attractive series of interconnected courtyards is home to many popular entertainment venues.

7 **Alter Jüdischer Friedhof**
Now a tree-filled park, the city's oldest Jewish cemetery was systematically destroyed by the Gestapo in 1943.

Fernsehturm
(television tower)

4 **Monbijoupark**
Once the grounds of a royal palace, this small park contains a marble bust of the poet Adelbert von Chamisso.

❶ Neue Synagoge
New Synagogue

Oranienburger Strasse 30. **Map** 9 A1. **Tel** 880 28 316. Ⓢ Oranienburger Strasse. 🚋 M1, M6. **Open** Mar–Oct: 10am–8pm Sun & Mon, 10am–6pm Tue–Thu, 10am–2pm Fri (to 5pm Fri from Apr–Sep); Nov–Feb: 10am–6pm daily (to 2pm Fri). 🚫 **Closed** Jewish festivals. 🖼

The building of the New Synagogue was started in 1859 by architect Eduard Knoblauch, and completed in 1866. The design, a highly sophisticated response to the asymmetrical shape of the plot of land, used a narrow façade flanked by a pair of towers and crowned with a dome containing a round vestibule. Small rooms opened off the vestibule, including an anteroom and two prayer rooms – one large and one small. The two towers opened onto a staircase leading to the galleries, and the main hall had space for around 3,000 worshippers. An innovative use of iron in the construction of the roof and galleries put the synagogue at the forefront of 19th-century civil engineering.

This fascinating structure was Berlin's largest synagogue, until 9 November 1938, when it was partially destroyed during the infamous *"Kristallnacht" (see pp30–1)*. The building was damaged further by Allied bombing in 1943 and was finally demolished in 1958 by government authorities.

Reconstruction began in 1988 and was completed with due ceremony in 1995. The building is used for public exhibitions by the Centrum Judaicum and includes a small prayer room.

The Centrum Judaicum, centre for research into Jewish heritage

❷ Centrum Judaicum
Jewish Centre

Oranienburger Strasse 28–30. **Map** 9 A1. **Tel** 880 28 316. Ⓢ Oranienburger Strasse. 🚋 M1, M6. **Open** Mar–Oct: 10am–8pm Sun & Mon, 10am–6pm Tue–Thu, 10am–2pm Fri (to 5pm Fri from Apr–Sep); Nov–Feb: 10am–6pm daily (to 2pm Fri). 🚫 **Closed** Jewish festivals. 🖼

The entrance to the Jewish Centre is easy to recognize thanks to the policemen permanently stationed here. All visitors must undergo a strict security check involving the use of a metal detector: the guards are polite but firm. The Centrum Judaicum occupies the former premises of the Jewish community council, and contains a library, archives and a research centre devoted to the history and cultural heritage of the Berlin Jews. Next door to the Centrum, the restored rooms of the Neue Synagoge are used to exhibit material relating to the local Jewish community, including one of the greatest of all Jewish thinkers and social activists, Moses Mendelssohn.

❸ Oranienburger Strasse

Map 8 F1, 9 A1, 9 B2. Ⓢ Oranienburger Strasse or Hackescher Markt. Ⓤ Oranienburger Tor. 🚋 12, M1, M4, M5, M6.

Oranienburger Strasse is home to many of Berlin's most popular nightspots. People of all ages flock here, spending pleasant hours in the area's numerous cafés, restaurants and bars. The district has traditionally been a centre for alternative culture, home to the famous state-sponsored Tacheles centre for the arts, previously occupied by artist squatters. The Tacheles centre has closed, but many good art galleries remain in this area. As you stroll around the district it is worth looking out for a number of interesting buildings, such as the one at Oranienburger Strasse No. 71–2, which was built by Christian

The Neue Synagoge with its splendidly reconstructed dome

Moses Mendelssohn (1729–1786)

One of the greatest German philosophers of the 18th century, Moses Mendelssohn arrived in Berlin in 1743 and was a central figure in the Jewish struggle for citizenship rights. About 50 years later the first Jewish family was granted full civic rights, however it wasn't until the Emancipation Edict of 1812 that Jewish men finally became full citizens. The grandfather of composer Felix Mendelssohn-Bartholdy, he is immortalized in the drama *Nathan der Weise* (Nathan the Wise) by his friend Gotthold Ephraim Lessing.

Friedrich Becherer in 1789 for the Great National Masonic Lodge of Germany.

Note that there is a seedy red-light edge to the area at night.

④ Monbijoupark

Monbijou Park

Oranienburger Strasse. **Map** 9 B2. Ⓢ Oranienburger Strasse or Hackescher Markt. 🚋 M1, M4, M5, M6.

This small park, situated between Oranienburger Strasse and the Spree river, was once the grounds of the Monbijou Palace. Damaged by bombing during World War II, the ruined palace was dismantled in 1960. A rare green space in this part of the city, the well-kept park is a pleasant place to spend time relaxing. It features a marble bust of the poet Adelbert von Chamisso, and there is also an open-air swimming pool for children.

⑤ Hackesche Höfe

Rosenthaler Strasse 40–41. **Map** 9 B1, 9 B2. Ⓢ Hackescher Markt. Ⓤ Weinmeisterstrasse 🚋 M1, M4, M5, M6.

Running from Oranienburger Strasse and Rosenthaler up as far as Sophienstrasse, the Hackesche Höfe (*Höfe* means yards) is a huge, early 20th-century complex. It is made up of an intricate series of nine interconnecting courtyards surrounded by tall and beautifully proportioned

One of the striking inner courtyards at the Hackesche Höfe

buildings. The development dates from 1906, and was designed by Kurt Berendt and August Endell, both of whom were outstanding exponents of the German Secession style.

Damaged during World War II, Hackesche Höfe has been restored to its original splendour. The first courtyard is especially attractive, featuring glazed facings with geometric designs decorated in fabulous colours. A whole range of restaurants, bars, art galleries, shops and restaurants can be found here, as well as offices and apartments on the upper floors. The complex also has its own theatre, the Hackesche Hoftheater, specializing in mime. For many Berliners the Hackesche Höfe has became something of a cult spot, and for visitors it is definitely a sight not to be missed.

⑥ Gedenkstätte Grosse Hamburger Strasse

Grosse Hamburger Strasse Memorial

Grosse Hamburger Strasse. **Map** 9 B1. Ⓢ Hackescher Markt. 🚋 12, M1, M4, M5, M6.

Until the years leading up to World War II, Grosse Hamburger Strasse was one of the main streets of Berlin's Jewish quarter. It was home to several Jewish schools, an old people's home and the city's oldest Jewish cemetery, established in 1672. The home was used during World War II as a detention centre for many thousands of Berlin Jews condemned to death in the camps at Auschwitz and Theresienstadt. The building was later destroyed, and in its place now stands a small monument representing a group of Jews being led to their deaths. A modest commemorative plaque is displayed nearby.

Nearby, at Grosse Hamburger Strasse No. 27, stands a Jewish school founded in 1778 by Moses Mendelssohn. Rebuilt in 1906, the building was reopened as a Jewish secondary school in 1993. The empty space once occupied by house No. 15–16, which was destroyed by World War II bombing, Is now an installation, *"The Missing House"* by Christian Boltanski, with plaques recording the names and professions of the former inhabitants of the house.

The Gedenkstätte Grosse Hamburger Strasse commemorating Berlin Jews murdered in the Holocaust

❼ Alter Jüdischer Friedhof

Old Jewish Cemetery

Grosse Hamburger Strasse. **Map** 9 B2. Ⓢ Hackescher Markt. 🚊 M1.

The Old Jewish Cemetery was established in 1672 and, until 1827 when it was finally declared full, it provided the resting place for over 12,000 Berliners. After this date Jews were buried in cemeteries in Schönhauser Allee and in Herbert-Baum-Strasse. The Alter Jüdischer Friedhof was destroyed by the Nazis in 1943, and in 1945 the site was turned into a park. Embedded in the original cemetery wall, a handful of Baroque *masebas* (or tombstones) continue to provide a poignant reminder of the past. A *maseba* stands on the grave of the philosopher Moses Mendelssohn *(see p104)*, erected in 1990 by members of the Jewish community.

❽ Sophienkirche

Grosse Hamburger Str. 31. **Map** 9 B1. **Tel** 308 79 20. Ⓢ Hackescher Markt. Ⓤ Weinmeisterstrasse. 🚊 M1, M4, M5, M6. **Open** May–Sep: 3–6pm Wed, 3–5pm Sat. 🕙 10am Sun.

A narrow passageway and a picturesque gate take you through to this small Baroque church. Founded in 1712 by Queen Sophie Luisa, this was the first parish church of the newly developed Spandauer Vorstadt area *(see p101)*. Johann Friedrich Grael designed the tower which was built between 1729 and 1735.

Interior of the Sophienkirche with its original 18th-century pulpit

Eighteenth-century buildings along Sophienstrasse

In 1892 the building was extended to include a presbytery, though the church still retains its original Baroque character. A modest, rectangular structure, Sophienkirche is typical of its period, with the tower adjoining the narrower side elevation. The interior still contains a number of its original 18th-century furnishings, including the pulpit and the font.

Several gravestones, some from the 18th century, have survived in the small cemetery surrounding the church.

❾ Sophienstrasse

Map 9 B1. Sammlung Hoffmann Sophienstrasse 21. **Tel** 284 99 120. Ⓢ Hackescher Markt. Ⓤ Weinmeisterstrasse. 🚊 M1, M4, M5, M6. **Open** 11am–4pm Sat, by appointment. 📷

The area around Sophienstrasse and Gipsstrasse was first settled at the end of the 17th century. In fact, Sophienstrasse was once the main street of Spandauer Vorstadt. The area underwent extensive restoration during the 1980s that preserved its small-town character. Today, the narrow lanes and three-storey buildings are reminiscent of Prague's Old Town. It was one of the first parts of East Berlin in which renovation was chosen in favour of large-scale demolition

and redevelopment. Now these modest but charming 18th-century Neo-Classical buildings are home to a number of different arts and crafts workshops, cosy bars, unusual boutiques, a puppet theatre and interesting art galleries.

One building with a particularly eventful history is Sophienstrasse No. 18. The house was erected in 1852, although its striking and picturesque terracotta double doorway dates from the time of its extensive restoration, undertaken in 1904 by Joseph Franckel and Theodor Kampfmeyer on behalf of the Crafts Society. Founded in 1844, the Crafts Society moved its headquarters to Sophienstrasse in 1905. On 14 November 1918 the very same house was used as the venue for the first meeting of the Spartacus League *(see p136)*, which was later to become the Communist Party of Germany. Today, No. 18 houses a modern dance and theatre company.

The main door of the house at Sophienstrasse No. 21 leads into a long row of interior courtyards running up as far as Gipsstrasse. In one of these courtyards is a private modern art gallery, the **Sammlung Hoffmann**, which can be reached by passing through a brightly-lit tunnel.

❿ Alte and Neue Schönhauser Strasse

Map 9 B1, 9 C1. Ⓢ Hackescher Markt. Ⓤ Weinmeisterstrasse. 🚋 M1.

Alte Schönhauser Strasse is one of the oldest streets in the Spandauer Vorstadt district, running from the centre of Berlin to Pankow and Schönhausen. In the 18th and 19th centuries this was a popular residential area among wealthy merchants. The proximity of the neighbouring slum area of the Scheunen-viertel *(see pp102–5)* to the west, however, lowered the tone of the neighbourhood quite considerably.

For a long time, bars, small factories, workshops and retail shops were the hallmark of the neighbourhood around Alte Schönhauser Strasse. Small private shops survived longer here than in most other parts of Berlin, and the largely original houses maintained much of their pre-1939 atmosphere.

Much has changed, however, since the fall of the Berlin Wall. Some of the houses have been restored, and many old businesses have been replaced by fashionable new shops, restaurants and bars, making it one of the most expensive retail areas in the city. Throughout the district, the old and the new now stand side by side. One

One of the Neo-Renaissance buildings on Neue Schönhauser Strasse

poignant example is at Neue Schönhauser Strasse No. 14. This interesting old house in the German Neo-Renaissance style was built in 1891 to a design by Alfred Messel. The first-floor rooms were home to the first public reading-room in Berlin, while on the ground floor was a *Volkskaffeehaus*, a soup-kitchen with separate rooms for men and women. Here the poor of the neighbourhood could get a free bowl of soup and a cup of ersatz (imitation) coffee.

Ironically, in the 1990s, the building became home to one of Berlin's most fashionable restaurants.

⓫ Volksbühne

People's Theatre

Rosa-Luxemburg-Platz. **Map** 10 D1. **Tel** 24 06 55. Ⓤ Rosa-Luxemburg-Platz. 🚌 100, 200. 🚋 M8.

Founded during the early years of the 20th century, this theatre owes its existence to the efforts of the 100,000 members of the Freie Volks-bühne (Free People's Theatre Society). The original theatre was built to a design by Oskar Kaufmann in 1913, a time when the Scheunenviertel district was undergoing rapid redevelopment. During the 1920s the theatre became famous thanks to the director Erwin Piscator (1893–1966), who later achieved great acclaim at the Metropol-Theater on Nollendorfplatz.

Destroyed during World War II, the theatre was eventually rebuilt during the early 1950s to a design by Hans Richter.

⓬ Torstrasse

Torstrasse. **Map** 1 B8–9, 2 D5–E5. Ⓤ Oranienburger Tor, Rosenthaler Platz, Rosa-Luxemburg-Platz. 🚌 142. 🚋 M1, M8.

Formerly a customs road and Berlin's northern border around 1800, Torstrasse is now a main thoroughfare connecting Prenzlauer Allee and Friedrich-strasse. From 1949 to 1990, the street was named Wilhelm-

Café in bustling Torstrasse

Pieck-Strasse after East Germany's first president, and some old buildings were replaced by prefabs. Although it is a busy, noisy and sometimes polluted street, Torstrasse has its charms and is transforming from a largely working-class bohemian area into a more appealing location, particularly for young urbanites.

The 19th-century residential buildings lining the street have been gentrified to make way for happening bars, trendy cafés and gourmet restaurants, art galleries, and fashion shops with numerous bargains to be found. "Soto", the area south of Torstrasse has the highest concentration of eclectic independent designers and brand outfitters in the city.

⓭ Kollwitzplatz

Ⓤ Senefelderplatz.

This green square is named after the German painter and sculptress Käthe Kollwitz (1867–1945), who once lived nearby. It was here that the socially engaged artist observed and painted the daily hardships of the working-class people living in overcrowded tenements. One of her sculptures stands on the square which is now the socializing hub of the district, with a Thursday organic farmers' market, cool bars, restaurants and shops that extend into the surrounding streets. Käthe Kollwitz's work can be seen at the Käthe-Kollwitz-Museum *(see p158)*.

⓮ Synagogue Rykestrasse

Rykestrasse 53. **Map** 2 F4. **Tel** 88 02 81 47. **Ⓤ** Senefelderplatz. **Open** for services only: Apr–Oct: 7pm Fri; Nov–Mar: 6pm Fri, 9:30am Sat.

This synagogue is one of the few reminders of old Jewish life in Berlin, and one of the few in Germany left almost intact during the Nazi terror regime. Built in 1904, the red-brick synagogue has a basilica-like nave with three aisles and certain Moorish features. Due to its location inside a huge tenement area, Nazi SA troops did not set it on fire during the *"Kristallnacht"* pogrom on 9 November 1938, when hundreds of other synagogues were razed to the ground. The synagogue welcomes visitors to its public services.

⓯ Wasserturm

Knaackstrasse/Belforter Strasse. **Map** 2 F4. **Ⓤ** Senefelderplatz.

The unofficial symbol of the district is a 30-m (98-ft) high water tower, standing high on the former mill hill in the heart of Prenzlauer Berg. It was here that some of the windmills, once typical in Prenzlauer Berg, produced flour for the city's population. The distinctive brick water tower was built in 1874 by Wilhelm Vollhering and served as a water reservoir for the country's first running water system. In the 1930s, the basement served as a make-shift jail, where Nazi SA troops held and tortured Communist opponents. This dark period is marked by a plaque.

The giant Wasserturm looming high in Knaackstrasse

Gravestones in the peaceful Jüdischer Friedhof

⓰ Jüdischer Friedhof
Jewish Cemetery

Schönhauser Allee 22–25. **Map** 2 E4. **Tel** 441 98 24. **Ⓤ** Senefelderplatz. **Open** 8am–4pm Mon–Thu, 7:30am–2:30pm Fri. **Closed** Sat, Sun & public hols.

This small Jewish cemetery is hidden behind thick walls on Schönhauser Allee, but the serene atmosphere, with tall trees and thick undergrowth, is a welcome oasis. The cemetery was laid out in 1827, though the oldest gravestone dates back to the 14th century. It was Berlin's second largest Jewish cemetery after the Jüdischer Friedhof Weissensee *(see p173)*. Among the many prominent Berliners resting here are the painter Max Liebermann (1847–1935); the composer and musical director of the Staatsoper Unter den Linden, ; and the author David Friedländer (1750–1834). The lapidarium displays historic gravestones from various Jewish cemeteries.

⓱ Kulturbrauerei

Schönhauser Allee 36–39. **Map** 2 E3. **Tel** 44 31 51 52. **Ⓤ** Eberswalder Strasse. 🚋 12, M1, M10.

This vast Neo-Gothic, industrial red-and-yellow-brick building was once Berlin's most famous brewery, Schultheiss, built by architect Franz Schwechten in 1889–92. Now housing the Kulturbrauerei, the huge complex with several courtyards has been revived as a cultural and entertainment centre with concert venues, restaurants and cafés, a cinema, as well as artists' ateliers. Inside the Kulturbrauerei, the **Museum Alltagsgeschichte der DDR** (Museum of Everyday Life in the GDR) features exhibitions on the former East Germany. It is currently closed, as some pieces are on loan to other museums, but will reopen in 2014.

⓲ Prater

Kastanienallee 7–9. **Map** 2 E3. **Tel** 448 56 88. **Ⓤ** Eberswalder Strasse. 🚋 12, M1.

Prater has been one of Berlin's best known entertainment institutions for more than a century. The building, along with its quiet courtyard, was constructed in the 1840s and later became the city's oldest and largest beer garden *(see p249)*. It now houses a restaurant, serving Berlin specialities, and stages a wide variety of pop, rock and folk concerts and theatre shows.

⓳ Zionskirche

Zionskirchplatz. **Map** 2 D4. **Tel** 88 70 98 70. **Ⓤ** Senefelderplatz, Rosenthaler Platz. 🚋 12, M1. **Open** irregular opening hours; call ahead.

Located in the square of the same name, Zionsplatz, this Protestant church was built between 1866 and 1873 – a tranquil oasis in the middle of this lively district. Both the square and the church have always been centres of political opposition. During the Third Reich, resistance groups against the Nazi regime congregated at the church, and when the communists were in power in East Germany the alternative "environment library" (an information and documentation centre) was established here. Church and other opposition groups active here played a decisive role in the transformation of East Germany in 1989–90.

⑳ Friedrichstadt-palast

Friedrichstadt Palace

Friedrichstrasse 107. **Map** 8 F2. **Tel** 23 26 23 26. 🚇 Oranienburger Tor. 🚈 Oranienburger Strasse or Friedrichstrasse. 🚌 147. 🚋 12, M1.

Multi-coloured glass tiles and a pink, plume-shaped neon sign make up the gaudy but eye-catching façade of the Friedrichstadtpalast. Built in the early 1980s, this gigantic theatre complex specializes in revues and variety shows. Nearly 2,000 seats are arranged around a huge podium, used by turns as a circus arena, a swimming pool and an ice-rink. In addition, a further huge stage is equipped with every technical facility. There is also a small cabaret theatre with seats for 240 spectators.

The original and much-loved Friedrichstadtpalast suffered bomb damage during World War II and was later condemned and replaced with the existing version. Built as a market hall, the earlier building was

later used as a circus ring. In 1918 it became the Grosse Schauspielhaus, or Grand Playhouse, opening on 28 November 1919 with a memorable production of Aeschylus' *The Oresteia* directed by the extraordinary Max Reinhardt *(see p112)*.

The building itself was legendary, its central dome supported by a forest of columns and topped with an Expressionist, stalactite-like decoration. An equally fantastical interior provided seating for 5,000 spectators.

㉑ Berliner Ensemble

Bertolt-Brecht-Platz 1. **Map** 8 F2. **Tel** 28 40 81 55. 🚈 & 🚇 Friedrichstrasse. 🚌 147. 🚋 12, M1.

Designed by Heinrich Seeling in the Neo-Baroque style and built from 1891 to 1892, this theatre has been witness to many changes in Berlin's cultural life. First known as the Neues Theater am Schiffbauerdamm, it soon became famous for staging important premieres. In 1893 it put on the first performance of *The Weavers,* by Gerhart Hauptmann. Later on, the theatre was acclaimed for its memorable productions by Max Reinhardt. These included Shakespeare's *A Midsummer Night's Dream* in 1905 which, for the first time, used a revolving stage and real trees as part of the set. In 1928 the theatre presented the world premiere of Bertolt Brecht's *The Threepenny Opera*. The building was destroyed during World

Bertolt Brecht's monument in front of the Berliner Ensemble

War II and subsequently restored with a much simpler exterior, but its Neo-Baroque interior, including Ernst Westphal's decorations, survived intact. After 1954 the theatre returned to prominence with the arrival of the Berliner Ensemble under the directorship of Bertolt Brecht and his wife, the actress Helene Weigel. The move from its former home, the Deutsches Theater, to the new venue was celebrated in November 1954, by staging the world premiere of *The Caucasian Chalk Circle*, written by Brecht in 1944/5. After Brecht's death his wife took over running the theatre, maintaining its innovative tradition.

㉒ Sammlung Boros

Reinhardtstrasse 20. **Map** 8 E2. **Tel** 28 40 81 55. 🚈 & 🚇 Oranienburger Tor. 🚌 147. 🚋 M1, M12. 🕐 Thu–Sun; book in advance. 🌐 **sammlung-boros.de**

This former air-raid bunker, built by architect Albert Speer, is an intriguing gallery location. The bunker has a chequered history; once used as a POW prison by the Red Army, it later became a warehouse, then in the 1990s it was a popular club.

In 2003, art collector Christian Boros bought the building and converted it into a gallery space. It houses the Boros Collection, which features modern art. No more than 12 guests can visit at one time and advance online registration is required.

The eye-catching façade of the Friedrichstadtpalast theatre complex

㉕ Dorotheenstädtischer Friedhof

This small cemetery, established in 1763, is the final resting place of many famous Berlin citizens. It was enlarged between 1814 and 1826, but in 1899, following the extension of Hannoversche Strasse, the southern section of the cemetery was sold and its graves moved. Many of the monuments are outstanding works of art, coming from the workshops of some of the most prominent Berlin architects, including Karl Friedrich Schinkel *(see p181)* and Johann Gottfried Schadow. A tranquil, tree-filled oasis, the cemetery is reached via a narrow path, leading from the street, between the wall of the French Cemetery and the Brecht- Weigel-Gedenkstätte house *(see p113)*.

★ **Johann Gottfried Schadow** (1764–1850)
Schadow created the famous *Quadriga*, which adorns the Brandenburg Gate.

Friedrich August Stüler (1800–1865)
Damaged during World War II, the grave of this famous architect was rebuilt in a colourful, post-modernist style.

Heinrich Mann (1871–1950)
This famous German novelist died in California but was buried in Berlin. The portrait is the work of Gustav Seitz.

Bertolt Brecht (1898–1956)
The grave of this famous playwright is marked with a rough stone. Beside him rests his wife, the actress Helene Weigel.

Hermann Wentzel (1820–1889)
This architect designed his own tombstone; the bust was carved by Fritz Schaper.

Main entrance

KEY

① **Luther's statue** is a copy of the monument designed by JG Schadow.

② **Chapel**

BIRKENALLEE

BRECHTWEG

Friedrich Hoffmann
(1818–1900)
The tomb of this engineer, best known as the inventor of the circular brick-firing kiln, takes the form of a colonnade faced with glazed bricks.

★ Karl Friedrich Schinkel
(1781–1841)
Schinkel was the most prominent German architect of his time, and the creator of many of Berlin's best-loved buildings.

Johann Gottlieb Fichte (1762–1814)
A well-known philosopher of the Enlightenment era, Fichte was also the first Rector of Berlin University.

YENALLEE

Georg Wilhelm Friedrich Hegel
(1770–1831)
Probably the greatest German philosopher of the Enlightenment era, Hegel worked for many years as a professor at Berlin University.

0 metres 20
0 yards 20

Elegant 19th-century façade of the Deutsches Theater

❷❸ Deutsches Theater

Schumannstrasse 13A. **Map** 8 E2.
Tel 28 44 12 25. Kammerspiele **U**
Oranienburger Tor. 🚌 147. 🚊 12, M1.

The theatre building was designed by Eduard Titz and built between 1849 and 1850 to house the Friedrich-Wilhelm Städtisches Theater. In 1883, following substantial reconstruction, it was renamed Deutsches Theater and opened with Friedrich Schiller's *Intrigue and Love*. The theatre became famous under its next director, Otto Brahm, and it was here that Max Reinhardt began his career as an actor, before eventually becoming director from 1905 until 1933. On Reinhardt's initiative the theatre's façade was altered and in 1906 the adjacent casino was converted into a compact theatre – the Kammerspiele. At the time, the first-floor auditorium was decorated with a frieze by Edvard Munch (now in the Neue Nationalgalerie).

Another famous figure associated with the theatre was Bertolt Brecht who, until 1933, wrote plays for it; after World War II he became the director of the Berliner Ensemble, whose first venue was the Deutsches Theater. Brecht's debut as director was his play, *Mother Courage and Her Children*.

Huge 19th-century building complex housing Charité hospital

❷❹ Charité

Chariteplatz 1. **Map** 8 E1, E2. **U**
Oranienburger Tor. 🚌 147. 🚊 12, M1.
Berliner Medizinhistoriches Museum der Charité **Tel** 450 53 61 56. **Open** 10am–5pm Tue, Thu, Fri, Sun; 10am–7pm Wed & Sat.

This huge building complex near Luisenstrasse contains the Charité hospital. Germany's oldest teaching hospital, it was first established in 1726 and has been attached to the Humboldt University *(see p62)* since its foundation in 1810. The oldest buildings of the current complex date back to the 1830s. Over the years, Charité has been associated with many

famous German doctors and scientists who worked here, including Rudolf Virchow and Robert Koch.

In 1899 Virchow founded the Museum der Charité, next to the Institute of Pathology. Its collection consists of some 23,000 specimens, which are available for public viewing. Although many artifacts were destroyed in World War II, the museum itself has survived and reopened in 1999.

❷❺ Dorotheenstädt-ischer Friedhof

See pp110–111.

❷❻ Brecht-Weigel-Gedenkstätte

Brecht-Weigel Memorial

Chausseestrasse 125. **Tel** 200 571 844.
Map 1 A5, 8 E1. **U** Naturkunde-museum or Oranienburger Tor. 🚌 147, 245. 🚊 M6, 12. **Open** 10–11:30am, 2–3:30pm Tue,10–11:30am Wed & Fri, 10–11:30am, 5–6:30pm Thu, 10am–3:30pm Sat, 11am–6pm Sun. 📷 compulsory. Every half hour (every hour on Sun). **Closed** Mon, public hols. 🅿

Bertolt Brecht, one of the greatest playwrights of the 20th century, was associated with Berlin from 1920, but emigrated in 1933. After the war, his left-wing views made him an attractive potential resident of the newly created German socialist state. Lured by the promise of his own theatre he returned to Berlin in 1948, with his wife, actress Helene Weigel. He directed the Berliner Ensemble until his death, concentrating mainly on the production of his plays.

He lived in a first-floor apartment at Chausseestrasse 125 from 1953 until his death in 1956. He is buried in Dorotheenstädtischer Friedhof *(see pp110–11)*. His wife lived in the second-floor apartment, and after Brecht's death moved to the ground floor. She also founded an archive of Brecht's works which is located on the second floor of the building.

Max Reinhardt (1873–1943)

This actor and director became famous as one of the 20th century's greatest theatre reformers. He worked in Berlin, first as an actor in the Deutsches Theater, and then from 1905 as its director. As well as setting up the Kammerspiele, he produced plays for the Neues Theater am Schiffbauerdamm (renamed the Berliner Ensemble) and the Schumann Circus (later to become the Friedrichstadtpalast), which was converted specially for him by Hans Poelzig. His experimental productions of classic and modern works brought him world-wide fame. Forced to emigrate because of his Jewish origins, he left Germany in 1933 and settled in the United States, where he died in 1943.

Remains of the Berlin Wall on
Bernauer Strasse

㉗ Gedenkstätte Berliner Mauer

Berlin Wall Memorial

Bernauer Strasse 111. **Map** 1 B4. Ⓢ
Nordbahnhof. Ⓤ Bernauer Strasse.
Ⓣ M8, M10. 🚌 245, 247. Wall
Documentation Center: **Tel** 467 98 36
66. **Open** Apr–Oct: 9:30am–7pm Tue–
Sun; Nov–Mar: 9:30am–6pm Tue–Sun.
📷 call ahead.

On the night between 12 and
13 August 1961 the East German
authorities decided to close the
border around the western
sectors of Berlin. Initially the
Berlin Wall *(die Mauer)* consisted
simply of rolls of barbed wire.
However, these were soon
replaced by a 4-m (13-ft) wall
safeguarded by a second wall
made from reinforced concrete.
This second wall was topped
with a thick pipe to prevent
people from reaching the top
of the Wall with their fingers.
Along the Wall ran what was
known as a "death zone", an area
controlled by guards with dogs.
Where the border passed close
to houses, the inhabitants were
relocated. Along the border
with West Berlin there were 293
watchtowers along with 57
bunkers and, later on, alarms.

On 9 November 1989, with
the help of Soviet leader Mikhail
Gorbachev, the Berlin Wall was
finally breached. Dismantling it
took much longer, however,
with more than a million tons
of rubble to be removed.

Only small fragments of the
Wall have survived. One of
these, along Bernauer Strasse
between Acker- and Bergstrasse,

is now an official place of
remembrance. The location of
the memorial is poignant, as
the Wall was cut in two here at
Bernauer Strasse. This resulted
in people jumping to the West-
side from upper-floor buildings
that stood right on the dividing
line, while border guards were
bricking up doors and windows
facing west. Today, the memorial
is a grim reminder of the hard-
ship the division inflicted on the
city. It includes a museum and
various installations along a mile
of the former border. The
Chapel of Reconciliation
replaces the original church,
which was demolished in 1985.

During the Wall's 28-year
existence, about 5,000 people
managed to escape into West
Berlin; a total of 192 people
were killed by the Eastern
border guards while attempting
to do so.

㉘ Museum für Naturkunde

Natural History Museum

Invalidenstrasse 43. **Map** 8 E1.
Tel 20 93 85 91. Ⓤ Naturkunde-
museum. 🚌 147, 245. **Open**
9:30am–6pm Tue–Fri, 10am–6pm
Sat, Sun, public hols. 📷

One of the biggest natural
history museums in the world,
the collection here contains
over 30 million exhibits.

Occupying a purpose-built
Neo-Renaissance building,
constructed between 1883 and
1889, the museum has been
operating for over a century,
and despite several periods of
renovation, has maintained its
old-fashioned atmosphere.

The highlight of the museum
is the world's largest original
dinosaur skeleton which is
housed in the glass-covered
courtyard. This colossal 23-m
(75-ft) long and 12-m (39-ft)
high brachiosaurus was
discovered in Tanzania in 1909
by a German fossil-hunting
expedition. Six other smaller
reconstructed dinosaur
skeletons and a replica of the
fossilized remains of an
archaeopteryx, thought to be
the prehistoric link between
reptiles and birds, complete this
fascinating display.

The adjacent rooms feature
extensive collections of
colourful shells and butterflies,
as well as taxidermy, including
birds and mammals. Particularly
popular are the dioramas –
scenes of mounted animals set
against the background of their
natural habitat. A favourite with
children is Bobby the Gorilla, who
was brought to Berlin Zoo in
1928 as a 2-year old and lived
there until 1935. The museum
also boasts an impressive
collection of minerals and
meteorites.

Brachiosaurus skeleton in the Museum für Naturkunde

❷ Hamburger Bahnhof

This art museum is situated in a specially adapted Neo-Classical building that was built in 1847 as a railway station. Following extensive refurbishment by Josef Paul Kleihues, it was opened to the public in 1996. At night, the façade is lit up by a neon installation by Dan Flavin. The museum has an ever-changing rotation of artworks including pieces by Joseph Beuys and a selection from the world-renowned Friedrich Christian Flick Collection of Art from the second half of the 20th century, as well as from the Marx and Marzona collections. The result is one of the best modern and contemporary art museums in Europe, which features film, video, music and design alongside painting and sculpture.

Restaurant
This stylish restaurant, run by chef Sarah Wiener, provides a welcome respite for visitors.

Museum façade
The museum's impressive Neo-Classical façade is flanked by two towers and has a grand entrance hall and inner courtyard.

Main entrance

First Time Painting (1961)
This work by American artist Robert Rauschenberg was created while he worked with John Cage at Black Mountain College.

★ Richtkräfte (1974–77)
Joseph Beuys' work – often a record of his thoughts – created an archive of the artist's vision.

Volk Ding Zero (2009)
This 3-m (9-ft) high bronze sculpture by Georg Baselitz was inspired by African, German and Polish folk art.

VISITORS' CHECKLIST

Practical Information
Invalidenstrasse 50/51.
Map 8 D1.
Tel 397 83 411.
W hamburgerbahnhof.de
Open 10am–6pm Tue–Fri,
11am–8pm Sat, 11am–6pm Sun.
Closed 24 & 31 Dec. ♿ 👫 🎒 📷 🚫

Transport
Ⓢ & Ⓤ Hauptbahnhof. 🚌 120,
123, 147, 240, 245, TXL, M41, M85.

★ **Mao** (1972)
This well-known portrait by Andy Warhol initially elevated the Chinese communist leader to the rank of pop icon.

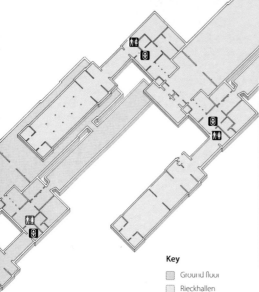

Key

- ▨ Ground floor
- ▨ Rieckhallen
- ▨ First floor
- ▨ Second floor

Main Hall
The main hall is used for unusual installations and even fashion shows. Here, models are showcasing the latest collections at the 2010 BOSS Black Fashion Show.

Gallery Guide

The gallery has more than 10,000 sq m (108,000 sq ft) of exhibition space. All the works on display at the Hamburger Bahnhof are temporary and exhibits described here may not necessarily be on display. The Rieckhallen shows selected works from the Friedrich Christian Flick Collection in rotation.

TIERGARTEN

Once a royal hunting estate, the Tiergarten became a park in the 18th century. In the 19th century a series of buildings, mostly department stores and banks, was erected at Potsdamer Platz. During World War II many of these buildings were destroyed. The division of Berlin changed the character of the area. The Tiergarten area ended up on the west side of the Wall, and later regained its glory

with the creation of the Kulturforum and the Hansaviertel. The area around Potsdamer Platz fell in East Berlin and became a wasteland. Since reunification, however, this area has witnessed exciting development. Together with the government offices near the Reichstag, this ensures that the Tiergarten area is at the centre of Berlin's political and financial district.

Sights at a Glance

Museums and Galleries

2 Musikinstrumenten-Museum
4 Kunstgewerbemuseum pp122–5
5 Kupferstichkabinett
6 Kunstbibliothek
8 Gemäldegalerie pp126–9
9 Neue Nationalgalerie
12 Bendlerblock (Gedenkstätte Deutscher Widerstand)
14 Bauhaus-Archiv

Districts, Squares and Parks

10 Potsdamer Platz pp132–5
15 Diplomatenviertel
16 Tiergarten
17 Grosser Stern

19 Hansaviertel
22 Regierungsviertel

Historic Buildings

1 Staatsbibliothek
3 Philharmonie und Kammermusiksaal
7 St-Matthäus-Kirche
11 Shell-Haus
13 Villa von der Heydt
20 Schloss Bellevue
21 Haus der Kulturen der Welt
23 Reichstag

Monuments

18 Siegessäule
24 Sowjetisches Ehrenmal

Restaurants

see pp235–6

1 Angkor Wat
2 Cafe am Neuen See
3 Cafe Mohring
4 Facil
5 Gaststatte Ambrosius
6 Kafers Dachgarten
7 Lanninger
8 Lindenbrau
9 Lutter & Wegner in Kaisersaal
10 OM
11 Rikes Gasthaus
12 Teehaus Tiergarten

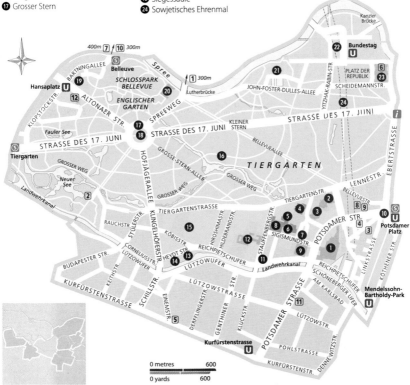

◄ **View of the Sony Centre, Potsdamer Platz**

For map symbols see back flap

Street-by-Street: Around the Kulturforum

The idea of creating a new cultural centre in West Berlin was first mooted in 1956. The first building to go up was the Berlin Philharmonic concert hall, built to an innovative design by Hans Scharoun in 1961. Most of the plans for the various other components of the Kulturforum were realized between 1961 and 1987, and came from such famous architects as Ludwig Mies van der Rohe. The area is now a major cultural centre which attracts millions of visitors every year.

❹ ★ Kunstgewerbemuseum
Among the collection at the Museum of Arts and Crafts you can see this intricately carved silver and ivory tankard, made in an Augsburg workshop in around 1640.

❺ Kupferstichkabinett
The large collection of prints and drawings owned by this gallery includes this portrait of Albrecht Dürer's mother.

❻ Kunstbibliothek
The Art Library boasts a rich collection of books, graphic art and drawings, many of which are displayed in its exhibition halls.

❽ ★ Gemäldegalerie
Among the most important works of the Old Masters exhibited in this gallery of fine art is this *Madonna in Church* by Jan van Eyck (circa 1425).

REICHPIETSCHUFER

LANDWEHRKANAL

❾ Neue Nationalgalerie
Sculptures by Henry Moore and Alexander Calder stand outside this streamlined building, designed by Ludwig Mies van der Rohe.

| 0 metres | 50 |
| 0 yards | 50 |

Key

— Suggested route

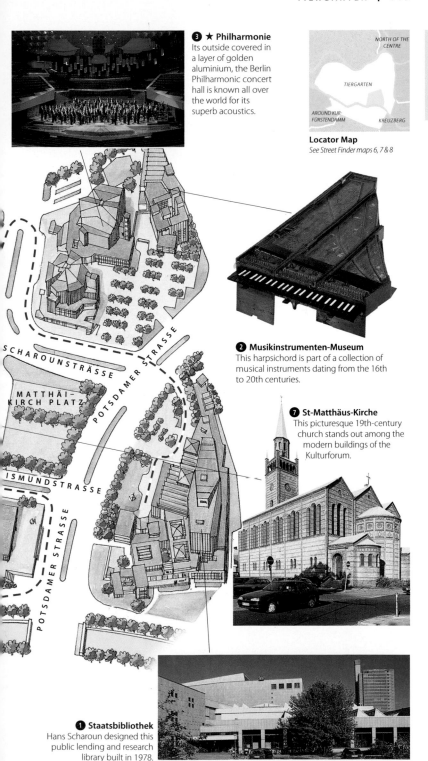

3 ★ Philharmonie
Its outside covered in a layer of golden aluminium, the Berlin Philharmonic concert hall is known all over the world for its superb acoustics.

Locator Map
See Street Finder maps 6, 7 & 8

2 Musikinstrumenten-Museum
This harpsichord is part of a collection of musical instruments dating from the 16th to 20th centuries.

7 St-Matthäus-Kirche
This picturesque 19th-century church stands out among the modern buildings of the Kulturforum.

1 Staatsbibliothek
Hans Scharoun designed this public lending and research library built in 1978.

The main reading room in the Staatsbibliothek

❶ Staatsbibliothek
State Library

Potsdamer Strasse 33. **Map** 8 D5.
Tel 2660. Ⓢ & Ⓤ Potsdamer Platz.
🚌 200, M29, M48, M85. **Open**
9am–9pm Mon–Fri, 9am–7pm Sat.

An unusual shaped building
with an east-facing gilded
dome, the Staatsbibliothek is
home to one of the largest
collections of books and manuscripts in Europe and is fondly
referred to by Berliners as the
Stabi. After World War II, East
and West Berlin each inherited
part of the pre-war state library
collection and the Staatsbibliothek was built to house the
part belonging to West Berlin.
The building itself was
designed by Hans Scharoun
and Edgar Wisniewski and
constructed between 1967
and 1978.

It is a building where the
disciplines of function and
efficiency took precedence to
that of form. The store rooms
hold about five million
volumes; the hall of the vast
reading room is open plan,
with an irregular arrangement
of partitions and floor levels;
general noise and the sound
of footsteps is muffled by fitted
carpets, making the interior a
very quiet and cosy place in
which to work.

The library itself houses more
than four million books, and an
excellent collection of
manuscripts. The Staatsbibliothek has been formally linked
to the Staatsbibliothek on
Unter den Linden *(see p63)*.

❷ Musikinstrumen-
ten-Museum
Museum of Musical Instruments

Tiergartenstrasse 1. **Map** 8 D5. **Tel** 25
48 11 78. Ⓢ & Ⓤ Potsdamer Platz.
🚌 200, M48, M85. **Open** 9am–5pm
Tue–Fri (to 10pm Thu), 10am–5pm Sat
& Sun. Wurlitzer Organ demonstration
noon Sat. 🎦 ♿ 🛍 🖼

Hidden behind the Philharmonie,
in a small building designed by
Edgar Wisniewski and Hans
Scharoun between 1979 and
1984, the fascinating Museum
of Musical Instruments houses
over 750 exhibits in a collection
dating from 1888. Intriguing
displays enable you to trace
each instrument's development

from the 16th century to the
present day. You can marvel at
the harpsichord of Jean
Marius, once owned by
Frederick the Great, and the
violins made by Amati
and Stradivarius.

Most spectacular of all is the
silent-film era cinema organ, a
working Wurlitzer dating from
1929. With a range of sounds
that extends even to locomotive impressions, the
Saturday demonstrations of its
powers attract enthusiastic
crowds. However, during the
the week the sounds of
exhibited instruments can be
heard on tapes. The museum
also has an excellent archive
and library open to the public.

❸ Philharmonie
und Kammer-
musiksaal
*Philharmonic and Chamber
Music Hall*

Herbert-von-Karajan-Str. 1. **Map** 8 D5.
Tel 25 48 89 99. Ⓢ & Ⓤ Potsdamer
Platz or Ⓤ Mendelssohn-Bartholdy-
Park. 🚌 200, M48, M85.

Home to one of the most
renowned orchestras in Europe,
this unusual building is among
the finest postwar architectural
achievements in Europe. The
Philharmonie, built between
1960 and 1963 to a design by
Hans Scharoun, pioneered a
new concept for concert hall
interiors. The orchestra's podium
occupies the central section of
the pentagonal-shaped hall,
around which are galleries for
the public, designed to blend
into the perspective of the five
corners. The exterior reflects
the interior and is

The tent-like gilded exterior of the Philharmonie and Kammermusiksaal

reminiscent of a circus tent. The gilded exterior was added between 1978 and 1981.

The Berlin orchestra was founded in 1882, and has been directed by such luminaries as Hans von Bülow, Wilhelm Furtwängler, the controversial Herbert von Karajan, who led the orchestra from 1954 until his death in 1989, and Claudio Abbado. The current director is Sir Simon Rattle. The orchestra attained renown not only for the quality of its concerts but also through its prolific symphony recordings.

Between the years 1984 to 1987 the Kammermusiksaal, which was designed by Edgar Wisniewski on the basis of sketches by Scharoun, was added to the Philharmonie. This building consolidates the aesthetics of the earlier structure by featuring a central multi-sided space covered by a fanciful tent-like roof.

❹ Kunstgewerbe-museum

Museum of Arts and Crafts

See pp122–5.

❺ Kupferstich-kabinett

Print Gallery

Matthäikirchplatz 8. **Map** 7 C5. **Tel** 266 42 42 42. Ⓢ & Ⓤ Potsdamer Platz or Ⓤ Mendelssohn-Bartoldy-Park. 🚌 200, M29, M41, M48, M85. Exhibitions: 10am–6pm Tue–Fri, 11am–6pm Sat & Sun. 🎨 ♿ 📷 👜 ✏ 🖼

The print collections of galleries in the former East and West Berlin were united in 1994 in this building located in the Kulturforum. These displays originate from a collection started by the Great Elector in 1652, which has been open to the public since 1831. Despite wartime losses it has an imposing breadth and can boast around 2,000 engraver's plates, over 520,000 prints and around 110,000 drawings and watercolours. Unfortunately, only a small fraction of these delicate treasures can be even

Edvard Munch's *Girl on a Beach*, a coloured lithograph

briefly exposed to daylight; therefore the museum does not have a permanent exhibition, only galleries with temporary displays of selected works. For those with a special interest, items in storage can be viewed in the studio gallery by prior arrangement.

The collection includes work from every renowned artist from the Middle Ages to contemporary times. Well represented is the work of Botticelli (including illustrations for Dante's *Divine Comedy*), Dürer, Rembrandt and the Dutch Masters, Watteau, Goya, Daumier and painters of the Brücke art movement.

❻ Kunstbibliothek

Art Library

Matthäikirchplatz 6. **Map** 7 C5. **Tel** 266 42 41 41. Ⓢ & Ⓤ Potsdamer Platz or Ⓤ Mendelssohn-Bartoldy-Park. 🚌 200, M29, M41, M48, M85. **Open** 10am–6pm Tue–Sun. 🎨

The Kunstbibliothek is not only a library with a vast range of books and periodicals about the arts, making it a tremendous resource for researchers, it is also a museum with a huge collection of posters, advertisements and an array of other forms of design. Worth seeing is a display on the history of fashion, as well as a vast collection of items of archi-tectural interest. The latter includes around 30,000 original plans and drawings by

architects such as Johann Balthasar Neumann, Erich Mendelssohn and Paul Wallot.

The exhibitions can be seen in the reading and studio rooms, although parts of the collection are also exhibited in the library's own galleries.

❼ St-Matthäus-Kirche

St Matthew's Church

Matthäikirchplatz. **Map** 7 C5. **Tel** 262 12 02. Ⓢ & Ⓤ Potsdamer Platz or Ⓤ Mendelssohn-Bartoldy-Park. 🚌 148, 200, M41, M48, M85. **Open** noon–6pm Tue–Sun, and for services.

St Matthew's Church once stood in the centre of a small square surrounded by buildings. After bomb damage in World War II, the structure was restored, making it the focal point of the Kulturforum. The church was originally built between 1844 and 1846 to a design by Friedrich August Stüler and Hermann Wentzel in a style based on Italian Romanesque temples.

Each of the three naves is covered by a separate two-tier roof, while the eastern end of the church is closed by a semi-circular apse. The exterior of the church is covered in a two-tone brick façade arranged in yellow and red lines. Ironically, this picturesque church with its slender tower now creates quite an exotic element among the many ultramodern and sometimes extravagant buildings of the Kulturforum complex.

The colourful exterior of the St-Matthäus-Kirche

Kunstgewerbemuseum

The Museum of Decorative Arts embraces many genres of craft and decorative art, from the early Middle Ages to the modern day. Goldwork is especially well represented. Among the most valuable exhibits is a collection of medieval goldwork from the church treasuries of Enger near Herford, and the Guelph treasury from Brunswick. The museum also takes great pride in its collection of late Gothic and Renaissance silver from the town of Lüneberg's civic treasury. There are also fine examples of Italian majolica, and 18th- and 19th- century German, French and Italian glass, porcelain and furniture. While the museum is closed for renovations, until 2014, the medieval collection will be on display at the Bode-Museum.

★ **Domed Reliquary** (1175–80)
From the Guelph treasury in Brunswick, the figures in this temple-shaped reliquary are made from walrus ivory.

Minneteppich (c.1430)
The theme of this famous tapestry is courtly love. Amorous couples, accompanied by mythical creatures, converse on topics such as infidelity, their words extending along the banners they hold.

Main entrance

★ **Goblet** (c.1480)
This glass goblet was made in Venice and is decorated with scenes from the lives of Adam and Eve.

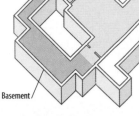

Lüneburg Lion *(1540)*
From the civic treasury in Lüneburg, this gold-plated silver jug in the form of a lion was crafted in the workshop of Joachim Worm.

Basement

Candelabra (1900)
This striking Art Nouveau
candelabra made from
silver, ivory and onyx
is the work of Belgian
artists Egide Rombaux
and Frans Hoosemans.

Wedding Dress (c.1780)
Made from brocade, with a lace
collar and cuffs, this Rococo
wedding dress is thought to have
belonged to Eleonor Schuster
from Breslau (now Wrocław).

Second
floor

First floor

Ground floor

★ **Harlequin Group** (c.1740)
These highly decorative, comic
porcelain characters from
Meißen are just one of the
treasures from the cabinets of
curiosities and Baroque collections
to be found on the second floor.

Key

▢ Middle Ages
▢ Renaissance
▢ Baroque
▢ Neo-Classical, Art Nouveau
▢ 20th century
▢ Temporary exhibitions

Gallery Guide

*The entrance to the museum is on the first floor, where
there is also an information gallery. In the basement is an
exhibition of contemporary design, on the ground floor
are exhibits from the Middle Ages and the Renaissance,
and on the second floor are handicrafts from the
Renaissance through to Art Nouveau.*

Exploring the Kunstgewerbemuseum

Opened in 1868, the Museum of Decorative Arts was the first of its kind in Germany. It was housed initially in the Martin-Gropius-Bau *(see p144)*, then from 1921 to 1939 occupied the Stadtschloss *(see p76)*. In 1940 it was moved to Schloss Charlottenburg *(see pp164–65)*. The current building, completed in 1985, is closed for renovations until 2014. The medieval collection is on display at the Bode-Museum, and another collection is on show in the Schloss Köpenick *(see p183)*.

Middle Ages

A large part of this collection is devoted to sacred art, much of it originating from church treasuries. A fine 8th-century reliquary in the shape of a burse (the container used in the Roman Catholic mass to hold the white linen cloth on which the bread and the wine are placed), comes from the treasury of a church in Enger in Westphalia. More reliquaries, many in the form of crosses, date from the 11th and 12th centuries. Two of the most interesting are the Heinrichskreuz, a gift to the cathedral in Basel from the Roman Emperor Heinrich II, and the Welfenkreuz, which comes from the Guelph treasury in Brunswick. Also from the latter comes a beautiful domed reliquary in the form of a small temple, and a portable altarpiece decorated with enamelwork, produced around 1150 by the craftsman Eilbertus of Cologne.

Exhibits from the Gothic period (12th to 16th centuries) include the stunning reliquary of St George of Elbing, made around 1480. Also fascinating are examples of secular art from this period, including caskets, vessels, a mirror, a knight's amulet and the renowned Minneteppich. This tapestry depicts a number of love scenes, and is designed to hang on the wall above a seat as a decorative means of keeping out draughts.

11th-century reliquary cross

Renaissance

The arts and crafts of the Renaissance period are well represented here. Especially valuable is a collection of Italian majolica, a type of pottery glazed in bright metallic oxides, imported into Tuscany from Majorca in the 15th century. Majolica workshops flourished during the 16th century, and many, including those of Faenza, Cafaggiolo and Urbino, are on show here.

Other interesting exhibits in this section are the 15th- and 16th-century Venetian glass, porcelain decorated with enamel work from Limoges in central France, and fine furniture and tapestry collections.

The highlight of the collection is a set of 32 magnificent, richly decorated goblets, bowls and jugs from the civic treasury at Lüneburg in northern Germany, acquired by the museum in 1874. Made of gold-plated silver, the set is the work of the skilled metalworkers of the town; some take the form of lions. Also notable are the works of the Nürnberg master craftsmen, above all the renowned Wenzel Jamnitzer and his nephew Christoph Jamnitzer.

As a result of the 16th-century fashion for *Kunst-kammern*, or curiosity cabinets, the collection also includes rare examples of naturalistic and exotic creations from other cultures, as well as some unusual technical equipment. Look out for a few pieces from the Pommersche Kunstschrank (curio cabinet), made for a 16th-century Pomeranian prince, Phillip II, as well as a display of 17th-century clocks and scientific instruments.

Baroque

Treasures from the Baroque period include an exquisite collection of German and Bohemian glass. A few of the pieces are made from so-called "ruby glass", a technique that was pioneered by Johann Kunckel in the second half of the 17th century.

A varied and rich collection of 18th-century ceramics includes some German faïence work, with amusingly decorated jugs and tankards. The porcelain display begins with a series of Böttger ceramics, the result of some of the very first European

Sixteenth-century tapestry entitled *The Triumph of Love*

Desk-board (c.1610–17) from the Pommersche Kunstschrank

experiments in porcelain production, undertaken by Johann Friedrich Böttger with the assistance of Ehrenfried Walther von Tschirnhaus.

Among some of the finest works from a variety of European factories, the porcelain from the Meißen factory is particularly well represented, with several pieces by one of the most famous Meißen modellers and designers, Johann Joachim Kändler.

Also on show is a fascinating selection of artifacts from the Königliche Porzellan- Manufaktur (Royal Porcelain Factory) in Berlin (see p137), which is well-known for its porcelain pieces depicting views of the city.

The collection of porcelain is complemented by a display of silver dishes produced in European workshops at the same period, and some decorative tableware.

Neo-Classical Revival And Art Nouveau

A comprehensive collection of late 18th- and early 19th-century Neo-Classical artifacts includes porcelain from some of the most famous European and Russian factories, French and German silver, as well as comprehensive exhibitions of glassware and furniture.

The Revival movement in central European art and crafts took place during the second half of the 19th century and is well represented here. A high standard of craftsmanship is seen in the sophisticated Viennese glass and jewellery. The collection also includes furniture made from papier-mâché. This interesting technique was first applied to furniture in England around 1850 and involves a wooden or wire frame which is covered in layers of paste and paper. Decorative techniques include painting and inlaying with mother-of-pearl.

The Secessionist and Art Nouveau movements of the 1890s and 1900s are represented by various artists including Henri van der Velde and Eugène Gaillard. Many pieces were acquired at the

Baroque clock by Johann Gottlieb Graupner (1739)

various World Fairs that occurred at this time. Of note are the frosted glass vases by French artist Emile Gallé, and pieces by the American Louis Comfort Tiffany, creator of the Favrile style of iridescent stained glass. Also displayed are pieces by the legendary René Lalique, including jewellery and glassware.

An interesting diversion is offered by two entertaining pieces of furniture, both dating from 1885, by the Italian designer Carlo Bugatti. Taking inspiration from Native American, Islamic and Far Eastern art, Bugatti made unique and spectacular use of rare woods and delicate inlays.

The 20th Century

The years between the two World Wars were a time of mixed trends in the decorative arts. On the one hand the traditions of the 19th-century Historical movement were continued, while on the other many artists were developing a completely new perspective on both form and decoration.

Art Nouveau vase, Emile Gallé (1900)

This part of the museum includes pieces that embody both approaches, but the strongest emphasis is placed on the innovative Art Deco style. Notable examples include a small porcelain tea service by Gertrud Kant, and a silver coffee set decorated with inlaid ebony, designed by Jean Puiforcat.

The museum's unique 20th-century collection has been continually updated since 1945, aiming to document developments in 20th- and 21st-century decorative arts. On display are a wide range of ceramics, furniture by well-known designers, and a variety of items in daily use.

❽ Gemäldegalerie

The Gemäldegalerie collection is exceptional in the consistently high quality of its paintings. Unlike those in many other collections, they were chosen by specialists who, from the beginning of the 19th century, systematically acquired pictures to ensure that all the major European schools of painting were represented. Originally part of the Altes Museum collection *(see p77)*, the paintings achieved independent status in 1904 when they were moved to what is now the Bodemuseum *(see p81)*. After the division of Berlin in 1945, part of the collection was kept in the Bode-Museum, while the majority ended up in the Dahlem Museums *(see p185)*. Following reunification, with the building of a new home as part of the Kulturforum development, this unique set of paintings was united again.

★ **Cupid Victorious** (1602)
Inspired by Virgil's *Omnia vincit Amor*, Caravaggio depicted a playful god, trampling over the symbols of Culture, Fame, Knowledge and Power.

Madonna with Child (c.1477)
A frequent subject of Sandro Botticelli, the Madonna and Child depicted here are surrounded by singing angels holding lilies, symbolizing purity.

Circular lobby leading to the galleries

Birth of Christ (c.1480)
This beautiful religious painting is one of the few surviving paintings on panels by Martin Schongauer.

Portrait of Hieronymus Holzschuher (1529)
Albrecht Dürer painted this affectionate portrait of his friend, who was the mayor of Nuremberg.

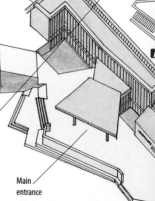

Main entrance

The Glass of Wine
(c.1658–61)
Jan Vermeer's carefully composed picture of a young woman drinking wine with a young man gently hints at the relationship developing between them.

VISITORS' CHECKLIST

Practical Information
Matthäikirchplatz 4–6.
Map 7 C5.
Tel 266 42 30 40.
Open 10am–6pm Tue–Sun (to 10pm Thu).
Closed 24 & 31 Dec. 🎨 🛝 👫 ♿ ♻ 📷

Transport
Ⓢ & Ⓤ Potsdamer Platz.
Ⓤ Mendelssohn-Bartholdy-Park.
🚌 200, M29, M41, M48, M85.

Love in the French Theatre
This picture has a companion piece called *Love in the Italian Theatre (see p25)*. Both are the work of French painter, Jean-Antoine Watteau.

Key
- 13th–16th-century German painting
- 14th–16th-century Dutch and French painting
- 17th-century Flemish and Dutch painting
- 18th-century French, English and German painting
- 17th–18th-century Italian painting, 17th-century German, French and Spanish painting
- 13th–16th-century Italian painting
- 16th–18th-century miniatures
- Digital gallery
- Non-exhibition space

★ Portrait of Hendrickje Stoffels (1656–7)
This portrait of Rembrandt's lover, Hendrickje Stoffels, is typical in that the painter focuses on the subject and ignores the background.

★ Dutch Proverbs (1559)
Pieter Bruegel managed to illustrate more than 100 proverbs in this painting.

Gallery Guide

The main gallery contains about 1,000 masterpieces grouped according to their country of origin and period. The educational gallery on the lower floor houses about 400 13th–18th-century European paintings and another digital gallery.

Visiting the Gemäldegalerie

The Gemäldegalerie's Modern building was designed by Heinz Hilmer and Christoph Sattler and its exhibition space offers a superb environment in which to view the paintings. The pictures are gently lit by the diffused daylight that streams in from above, while the walls are covered in light-absorbing fabric. The vast hall which occupies the centre of the building allows the visitor to take a break from sightseeing at any time. The hall, with a futuristic sculpture by Walter de Maria set in a water-filled pool, provides an ideal setting for a few moments of quiet contemplation and rest.

Frans Hals' portrait, *Malle Babbe* or *Crazy Babette* (c.1629–30)

Hans Holbein's *Portrait of Georg Gisze* (1532)

German Painting

German paintings are exhibited in several areas of the gallery. The first group comprises art from the 13th–16th centuries. A fine body of religious paintings and altar-pieces contains a historic 13th-century rectangular altarpiece from Westphalia. Other religious artifacts include the side panels of the 15th-century *Wurzach Altar*, ascribed to Hans Multscher, which vividly depict the torment of Christ and the life of the Virgin Mary. A real rarity is the *Nativity* by Martin Schongauer. Often thought of primarily as an engraver, he was one of the most significant painters of the late 15th century but few of his paintings have survived.

Another artist known for his engravings as well as paintings, Albrecht Dürer was a major figure in Renaissance art in northern Europe. His works displayed here include *Madonna with the Siskin*, painted in 1506 while he was visiting Italy, and two later portraits of Nürnberg patriarchs. There are also exhibits by Hans Süss von Kulmbach,

Hans Baldung Grien and Albrecht Altdorfer. Among the many works by Lucas Cranach the Elder is the delightful *Fountain of Youth*, from which old women emerge young and beautiful, while men regain their youth through amorous liaisons with the women. Another excellent painting in this collection is a portrait of the Danzig merchant Georg Gisze, painted by Hans Holbein the Younger at a time when both men were living in London. 17th- and 18th-century paintings, including the works of Adam Elsheimer and Johann Heinrich Tischbein, are on show elsewhere.

Dutch and Flemish Painting

The gallery with Dutch and Flemish paintings begins with the captivating canvases of Jan van Eyck. In addition to his precise portraits, you can see here the celebrated *Madonna in a Church*. The high quality of

paintings is maintained with the works of Petrus Christus and Rogier van der Weyden. Among the pictures by Hugo van der Goes, the most prized is *The Adoration of the Magi*, once the centre panel of a triptych.

The collection has four paintings by Hans Memling, and also the small *Madonna with Child* painted by one of his pupils, Michel Sittow. There is a large group of paintings by Gerard David, Jan Gossaert and Joos van Cleve. Try to keep an eye out for a modest picture by Hieronymus Bosch called *St John on Patmos*. One of the most outstanding paintings of the collection is Pieter Bruegel the Elder's *Dutch Proverbs*. However, in order to fully appreciate the mastery and humour in this work, make sure you use the accompanying board which explains all the one hundred or so proverbs illustrated here.

Within the large collection of excellent Flemish paintings you can marvel at the Baroque vitality and texture evident in the canvases of friends and

Salomon van Ruysdael's *Dutch Landscape with a Raid* (1656)

sometime collaborators Petrus Paulus Rubens, Jacob Jordaens, Jan Brueghel the Elder and Frans Snyders. The exceptional portraits of Anton van Dyck, who painted complex, psychologically revealing studies, are indicative of the artist at the height of his powers.

The gallery of 17th-century Dutch paintings probably holds the richest collection in the museum. Included among these are the portraits by Frans Hals, which perfectly illustrate his enormous artistic talents. Excellent examples of his varied work are the vigorous *Malle Babbe (c.1629–30)* – a portrait of the "crazy Babette" of Haarlem.

In fact, all the most famous Dutch painters are represented here but, of course, the works of Jan Vermeer and the master, Rembrandt, attract the greatest amount of interest. The works of Rembrandt include the paintings *Samson and Delilah, Susanna and the Two Elders,* and *Joseph and the Wife of Potiphar.* It is also worth taking time to view the *Man in the Golden Helmet,* a sad yet noble painting originally attributed to Rembrandt. Carbon dating has shown it to be the work of members of his studio. It is a magnificent tribute to his skill as a teacher.

Jean Baptiste Siméon Chardin's *The Draughtsman* (1737)

French, English and Spanish Painting

The collection of French art can be found in various parts of the gallery. Paintings of the 15th and 16th century are exhibited alongside Dutch paintings of that era. The oldest works date from the beginning of the 15th

Titian's *Venus with the Organ Player* (1550–52)

century, and the *Madonna with Child,* dating from c.1410, is one of the oldest preserved works of art painted on a canvas. One of the most valuable French works is by Jean Fouquet, entitled *Étienne Chevalier with Saint Stephen.* Comprising half of the *Diptych of Melun* this is one of Fouquet's few non-miniature paintings.

Nicolas Poussin, the mainspring of the French Classical tradition, and Claude Lorrain, famous for his idealized landscapes, represent 17th-century French painting. Eighteenth-century painting is strongly represented by the canvases of Jean-Antoine Watteau, Jean Baptiste Siméon Chardin and François Boucher.

Two areas in which this collection is less complete are Spanish and English painting. Nevertheless, there is a portrait by Diego Velázquez which is worth seeing, while the English pictures include good portraits by rivals Sir Joshua Reynolds and Thomas Gainsborough.

Sir Joshua Reynolds' *Portrait of Lady Sunderlin* (1786)

Italian Painting

The collection of Italian paintings is fairly comprehensive. There are exemplary works by 14th-century masters, including *Laying the Body to Rest in the Grave* by Giotto and parts of *Scenes from the Life of St Humilitas* by Pietro Lorenzetti. Paintings by Piero della Francesca, Fra Angelico, Masaccio, Andrea del Verrocchio, Sandro Botticelli, and Antonio del Pollaiuolo all represent the 15th century. In this collection you will also find later works by Raphael, including the *Madonna di Casa Colonna,* and the *Madonna di Terranuova,* painted after Raphael's arrival in Florence around 1505. There is also a collection of works by the Venetian Renaissance painter, Giovanni Bellini.

Indeed, the Venetian school in general is well represented: *Portrait of a Young Man* by Giorgione is a vibrant and colourful study; there is also Titian's *Venus and the Organ Player* and Tintoretto's *Virgin and the Child Adored by Saints Mark and Luke.* It is worth comparing Caravaggio's *Cupid Victorious,* whose provocative and distinctly human sexuality contrasts with the spiritual orthodoxy of *Heavenly and Earthly Love,* by Giovanni Baglione. Similar in style, the two paintings convey opposing ideologies. Cardinal Giustiani, whose brother owned Caravaggio's controversial canvas, commissioned the latter painting. Works by Giovanni Battista Tiepolo, Francesco Guardi and Antonio Canaletto represent the art of 18th-century Venice.

Karl Schmidt-Rottluff's *Farm in Daugart* (1910), Neue Nationalgalerie

❾ Neue Nationalgalerie
New National Gallery

Potsdamer Strasse 50. **Map** 7 C5.
Tel 266 424 242. 🔲 & Ⓢ Potsdamer
Platz or 🔲 Mendelssohn-Bartholdy-
Park. 🚌 200, M29, M41, M48, M85.
Open 10am–6pm Tue–Fri (to 10pm
Thu), 11am–6pm Sat & Sun. 🅿 ♿

The magnificent collection of modern art housed in the Neue Nationalgalerie has a troubled history. The core of the collection consisted of 262 paintings that belonged to banker JHW Wagener. In the late 1860s, when Wagener died, he bequeathed them to Crown Prince William, who housed them in the National galerie on Museum Island.

However, in 1937, a Nazi programme of cultural cleansing meant that over 400 of the works in the collection, which had grown to include paintings by Monet, Manet and Renoir, were confiscated.

After World War II the Berlin municipal authority decided to rebuild the collection and authorized the construction of a suitable building in West Berlin to house it. A commission was given to the elder statesman of modern architecture, the 75-year-old Mies van der Rohe. The result was the first museum in what would later become known as the Kulturforum. The national gallery is a striking, minimalist building with a flat steel roof over a glass hall, which appears to float in mid-air supported only by six slender interior struts. The permanent collection is housed in the basement of the museum, while the spacious ground-level glass hall plays host to temporary exhibitions.

The collection of the Neue Nationalgalerie comprises largely 20th-century art, but begins with artists of the late 19th century, such as Edvard Munch, Ferdinand Hodler and Oskar Kokoschka. German movements, such as Die Brücke, are well represented, with pieces by Ernst Ludwig Kirchner (notably his *Potsdamer Platz*) and Karl Schmidt-Rottluff.

As well as the Bauhaus movement, represented by Paul Klee and Wassily Kandinsky, the gallery shows works by exponents of a crass realism, such as Otto Dix and Georg Grosz. The most celebrated artists of other European countries are also included in the collection – Pablo Picasso, Ferdinand Léger, and the Surrealists Giorgio de Chirico, Salvador Dalí, René Magritte and Max Ernst. Post-World War II art is represented by the works of Barnett Newman and Frank Stella, among many others. The sculpture garden houses a variety of important works, both figurative and abstract.

Following reunification, a number of new works by artists from the former East Germany were added to the collection. Some of the art is sometimes on display at the Hamburger Bahnhof *(see pp114–15)* as both museums draw on the same collection.

❿ Potsdamer Platz

See pp132–5.

⓫ Shell-Haus

Reichpietschufer 60. **Map** 13 C1.
🔲 Mendelssohn-Bartholdy-Park.
🚌 200, M29, M48, M85.

This is undoubtedly a gem for lovers of the architecture developed during the period between World Wars I and II. This modernist office block was designed by Emil Fahrenkamp. Built from 1930 to 1932, it was one of the first buildings in Berlin to use a steel-frame construction.

The most eye-catching wing extends along Landwehrkanal with a zig-zag elevation; from a height of five storeys it climbs upwards in a series of steps, finishing up ten storeys high.

Damaged during World War II, Shell-Haus went through several stages of restoration and several incarnations, including as headquarters of the German navy and as a military hospital. Beautiful proportions and original design place the structure among the finest of Berlin's buildings of its era.

The impressive exterior of the Shell-Haus office building

The German State Naval Office, now part of the Bendlerblock complex

⓬ Bendlerblock (Gedenkstätte Deutscher Widerstand)

Stauffenbergstrasse 13–14. **Map** 7 B5, 7 C5. **Tel** 26 99 50 00. **U** Potsdamer Platz or Kürfurstenstrasse. M29, M48. **Open** 9am–6pm Mon–Fri (to 8pm Thu), 10am–6pm Sat & Sun. **Closed** 1 Jan, 24, 25 & 31 Dec.

The collection of buildings known as the Bendlerblock was originally built during the Third Reich as an extension to the German State Naval Offices. During World War II these buildings were the head-quarters of the Wehrmacht (German Army). It was here that a group of officers planned their famous and ultimately unsuccessful assassination attempt on Hitler on 20 July 1944. When the attempt led by Claus Schenk von Stauffenberg failed, he and his fellow conspirators were quickly rounded up and arrested. The death sentences on these men were passed at the Plötzensee prison (see p180). General Ludwig Beck was forced to commit suicide, while Stauffenberg, Friedrich Olbricht, Werner von Haeften and Ritter Mertz von Quirnheim were shot in the Bendlerblock courtyard.

A monument commem-orating this event, designed by Richard Scheibe in 1953, stands where the executions were carried out. On the upper floor of the building there is an exhibition documenting the history of the German anti-Nazi movements.

⓭ Villa von der Heydt

Von-der-Heydt-Strasse 18. **Map** 13 B1. **Tel** 266 41 28 88. **U** Nollendorfplatz. 100, 200, M29.

This fine villa, built in a late Neo-Classical style, is one of the few surviving reminders that the southern side of the Tiergarten was one of the most expensive and beautiful residential areas of Berlin.

Designed by Hermann Ende and GA Linke, the villa was built from 1860 to 1862. The neatly manicured gardens and railings around the villa are adorned with busts of Christian Daniel Rauch and Alexander von Humboldt. The statues, by Reinhold Begas, originally lined the Avenue of Triumph in the Tiergarten before being moved here. After restoration in 1980, the villa became the head-quarters of one of the most influential cultural bodies, the Stiftung Preussischer Kulturbesitz (Foundation of Prussian Cultural Heritage).

The captivating, streamlined buildings of the Bauhaus-Archiv

⓮ Bauhaus-Archiv

Klingelhöferstrasse 14. **Map** 13 A1. **Tel** 254 00 20. **U** Nollendorfplatz. 100, 106, 187, M29. **Open** 10am–5pm Wed–Mon.

The Bauhaus school of art, started by Walter Gropius in 1919, was one of the most influential art institutions of the 20th century. The belief of the Bauhaus group was that art and technology should combine in harmonious unity.

Originally based in Weimar, and from 1925 in Dessau, this school provided inspiration for numer-ous artists and architects. Staff and students included Mies van der Rohe, Paul Klee, Wassily Kandinsky, Theo van Doesburg and László Moholy-Nagy. The school moved to Berlin in 1932, but was closed down by the Nazis in 1933.

After the war, the Bauhaus-Archiv was relocated to Darmstadt. In 1964 Walter Gropius designed a building to house the collection, but it was never realized. The archive was moved to Berlin in 1971 and the design had to be adapted to the new site. Because the maestro was no longer alive, the project was taken over by Alexander Cvijanovic. The gleaming white building with its distinctive glass-panelled gables was built between 1976 and 1979 and houses the archive, library and exhibition halls for temporary displays.

Neo-Classical façade of the elegant Villa von der Heydt

⑩ Potsdamer Platz

To experience the vibrant energy of the new Berlin, there is no better place to visit than Potsdamer Platz. During the Roaring Twenties it was Europe's busiest plaza and a bustling entertainment centre, but during World War II it was bombed into a mountain of rubble. After the war, the square was left as a derelict wide open space, a no-man's-land beside the Berlin Wall. With reunification, the square was redeveloped by various international business concerns, such as DaimlerChrysler and Sony, who subsequently sold the properties. This building project is Berlin's largest to date. Berlin's old hub is once again a dynamic centre, a jewel of modern architecture created by architects such as Renzo Piano, Helmut Jahn and Arata Isozaki.

View of modern-day Potsdamer Platz

Beisheim Center
Lenné-, Bellevue- and Ebertstrasse.
W beisheim-center.de

Otto Beisheim, the founder and owner of the Metro retail chain, and one of Europe's wealthiest entrepreneurs, has created a glass and steel monument on Potsdamer Platz – the Beisheim Center. The two elegant high-rise towers on the northern edge of the square encompass several de luxe apartments. The largest was sold for around $5 million, to an American émigrée returning to her home city, and is probably Berlin's most expensive apartment. The center also incorporates a luxurious Ritz-Carlton and an elegant Marriott hotel.

The building was designed by the Berlin architectural team Hilmer, Sattler & Albrecht, although parts of the building were also created by architect David Chipperfield. The sandstone appearance of the small 19-floor skyscrapers, with

receding façades on the upper levels, is meant to be a modern reinterpretation of New York's Rockefeller Center.

Filmmuseum Berlin
Potsdamer Strasse 2 (at Sony Center).
Tel 30 09 030. **Open** 10am–6pm Tue–Sun, 10am–8pm Thu. 🏛 ♿ 🎞
W filmmuseum-berlin.de

In a city once famous for its world-class film industry, the film museum takes visitors backstage to Hollywood and the historic UFA (Universal Film AG) film studios.

Located in the Sony Center and run by the Freunde der Deutschen Kinemathek, a non-profit-making association for film-lovers, the museum chronicles the development of cinema from the first silent movie hits to the latest science-fiction productions. However, the main focus is on German films from the glorious UFA days in the 1920s, when Germany's leading film company produced one smash hit after another at the Babelsberg studios *(see p207)*. Films such as *The Cabinet of Dr Caligari*, directed by Friedrich Wilhelm Murnau (1888–1931), or *M* and *Metropolis* by Fritz Lang (1890–1976) are presented with costumes, set sketches, original scripts, models and photos. The Nazi era, when film making became a propaganda machine, is particularly interesting, and the museum documents the life and work of the actor Kurt Gerron, who died in Auschwitz, as well as other exhibits relating to the uses of propaganda in film.

One of the treasure troves of the museum is the collection of personal effects of the Berlin-born diva Marlene Dietrich (1901–1992). The exhibition presents her gowns, personal correspondence and complete luggage set. A unique item is a minute cigarette case, given to her as a gift by the director Josef von Sternberg (1894–1969), bearing the inscription: "To Marlene Dietrich, woman, mother and actress as there never was one before". Also on display are personal possessions from German film and television stars such as Heinz Rühmann (1902–1994) and Hans Albers (1891–1960).

The museum features a range of exhibitions with changing themes and special film programmes.

Façade of the Filmmuseum Berlin

Arkaden, one of Berlin's favourite shopping centres

Potsdamer Platz Arkaden

Alte Potsdamer Str. 7. **Tel** 25 59 270.
Open 10am–9pm Mon–Sat.
CinemaxX: Potsdamer Str. 5. **Tel**
Programme info: 25 92 21 11; reser-
vations: (0180) 524 63 62 99. 🖳

This entertainment and
shopping complex is hugely
popular with visitors. Spread
over three floors, the building
includes around 140 shops,
restaurants and boutiques. The
basement houses a food court
with many budget eateries
offering regional specialities
from all over Germany, as well
as several grocery shops. Berlin's

largest cinema, the **CinemaxX**,
is nearby. With 19 screens it
can accommodate up to
3,500 filmgoers.

Theater am Potsdamer Platz

Marlene-Dietrich-Platz 1. **Tel** (0180)
544 44. **Open** 8am–8pm daily. 🖳
Spielbank Berlin: Marlene-Dietrich-
Platz 1. **Tel** 25 59 90.
Open 11am–5am daily. 🖳

Situated in a square dedicated to
the famous actress Marlene
Dietrich, Berlin's largest musical
stage is housed in the modern
Theater am Potsdamer Platz,
designed by Renzo Piano as part

of the Daimler Quartier *(see
pp134–5)*. It stages German
versions of Broadway hit
musicals and shows such as
Beauty and the Beast.

The exclusive Adagio nightclub
is located in the basement of
this building and Berlin's most
popular casino, **Spielbank
Berlin**, can be found here too.

The theatre complex is also
the main forum for the **Berlin
Filmfestspiele**, known as
Berlinale. One of the film
industry's most important
festivals, it is held throughout
the city each February *(see p53)*.
Over the course of the 10-day-
long event, around 400 films are
broadcast, most of which are
world and European premieres.
Perhaps the most important part
of the festival are the Golden and
Silver Bears awards, which are
awarded to noteworthy major
international films. Tickets for
screenings can be hard to
come by, so plan ahead if
you wish to attend.

Bluemax Theater, the Blue
Man Group's Berlin location,
is found on the opposite side
of Marlene-Dietrich-Platz.
The famous mute performers
hold seven shows a week.

Historic Potsdamer Platz

Potsdamer Platz first evolved from a green park in 1831 and was named after one of the city's gates, the
Potsdamer Tor, located to the east of today's square. Thanks to a new railway station of the same name,
where the city's first ever train made its maiden journey in 1838, the square developed into a major
traffic hub at the intersection of Potsdamer Strasse and other thoroughfares. Later an underground train
line, along with a total of 31 tram and bus lines, added to the traffic chaos here. At the beginning of the
20th century it became the centre of Berlin's celebrated nightlife, with legendary, huge entertainment
venues such as Haus Vaterland and the Café Josty (a meeting place for famous artists including author
Theodor Fontane and painter Adolph
von Menzel), as well as several luxury
hotels. Germany's first radio trans-
mission was broadcast in 1923 at the
Vox Haus. The square was almost
destroyed by Allied bombardments
during the final Battle of Berlin in
April 1945. It became a vast open
space in the shadow of the Berlin
Wall where Western tourists, standing
on high observation platforms, could
peek over the wall. The empty square
featured in Wim Wenders' 1987 hit
film, *Wings of Desire*.

Development commenced in
1992, and Potsdamer Platz rose to
become Europe's largest
construction site where a total of $25
billion has been invested.

Bustling Potsdamer Platz in the 1930s

Sony Center

Potsdamer Strasse 2. **Open** 24 hrs.

The Sony Center, designed by the German-American architect Helmut Jahn, is one of Berlin's most exciting architectural complexes. Built between 1996 and 2000, the glitzy steel-and-glass construction covers a breathtaking 4,013 sq m (43,195 sq ft).

The piazza at the heart of the Center has become one of Berlin's most popular attractions. Set under a soaring tent-like roof, it is dominated by a pool with constantly changing fountains where the water sprays high into the air, then falls back to rise again in a different location. The light and airy piazza is surrounded by the offices of Sony's European headquarters, as well as apartment complexes, several restaurants, cafés and shops including the Sony style store. There is also the Cinestar (see pp264–5), a huge multiplex cinema with eight different screens, in addition to the Filmmuseum Berlin (see p132). The integrated IMAX cinema shows nature and science films on imposing 360° screens.

Inside the Sony Center is the small but magnificent **Kaisersaal**, a historic architectural gem that is set behind a glass façade. This dining hall, one of the city's finest, but private, function locations, was once part of the Grand Hotel Esplanade. The

Interior of the cupola of the Sony Center, designed by Helmut Jahn

epitome of luxury in pre-war Berlin, it was almost destroyed during World War II. When the site was sold to Sony by the City of Berlin in the early 1990s, the Berlin magistrate stipulated that the Kaisersaal, stairways, bathrooms and several other smaller rooms should be restored and integrated into the Sony Center. The historic ensemble originally stood some 46 m (150 ft) away and was carefully moved on air cushions to its present location in 1996. The fully restored Kaisersaal is dominated by a portrait of Kaiser Wilhelm II, the last German emperor, whose frequent visits to the original hotel gave this hall its name, although he never actually dined in this particular room.

Daimler Quartier

Around Alte Potsdamer Strasse. Panorama Punkt observation platform: Potsdamer Platz 1. **Tel** 25 93 70 80. **Open** 10am–6pm daily.

This vast complex was built between 1993 and 1998 and comprises 19 modern buildings, all designed in different styles according to an overall plan by architects Renzo Piano and Christoph Kohlbecker. The buildings form a long, narrow column of modern architectural jewels leading south from Potsdamer Platz all the way down to the Landwehr Canal.

Standing on either side of Alte Potsdamer Strasse, the red-brick high-rise block and its sister building opposite mark the entrance to this city quarter, and were designed by Berlin architect Werner Kollhoff. The western skyscraper is topped by a 96-m (315-ft) high observation platform called **Panorama Punkt** (Panorama Point). It offers a breathtaking view which can be reached via Europe's fastest elevator.

The green traffic-light tower in front of the Daimler Quartier is a replica of the first automatic traffic light in Berlin (and Europe), which was erected on the same spot in 1924. In pre-war days, Potsdamer Platz was an intricate crossing of several major streets and avenues, making it Europe's busiest traffic junction at the time.

The glass façade of the Kaisersaal, part of the Sony Center

At the southern end of this complex is yet another high-rise tower block, the **Debis-Haus** (formerly the Daimler-Chrysler software subsidiary). This 90-m (295-ft) high, 22 floor, yellow and green skyscraper is topped by a striking green cube and was designed by Renzo Piano and Hans Kollhoff *(see p47)*. A captivating sculpture by Jean Tinguely, entitled *Meta-Maxi*, adorns its soaring atrium. The sculpture is powered by 16 engines and symbolizes the constant movement of time.

Various works of art were commissioned for this complex and these can be seen throughout the public areas.

The red-brick office block of Daimler House

Leipziger Platz
Leipziger Platz, a small square just east of Potsdamer Platz, is being reconstructed and a huge shopping complex on the site of the former Wertheim department store is scheduled to open by autumn 2014. At the southern end of the square lies the Dali Museum. The original octagonal but rather bland square was created between 1732 and 1734 and later renamed Leipziger Platz in commemoration of the Battle of Leipzig in 1813 (the first decisive defeat of Napoleon). In the 19th century, the architects Karl-Friedrich Schinkel (1781–1841) and Peter Joseph Lenné (1789–1866) transformed the square into an architectural gem with landscaped gardens, surrounded by some of the most elegant city palaces and mansions in the whole of Berlin.

At the beginning of the 20th century the modern buildings, most notably the Kaufhaus Wertheim by Alfred Messel (1853–1909) built 1897–1905, made Leipziger Platz one of the

major, and more fashionable, shopping districts in pre-war Berlin.

Unfortunately, there are no historic remnants left. The current buildings have a modern look but are restricted to a maximum height of only 35 m (115 ft), the same height as the original buildings. They house various shops and restaurants, the Canadian Embassy and further international company headquarters.

Haus Huth
Alte Potsdamer Strasse 5.
Tel 25 94 14 20.
Open 11am–6pm daily.
Sammlung Daimler Chrysler Contemporary: **Open** as Weinhaus Huth. 🔲 6pm daily.

The only historic building on Potsdamer Platz to escape destruction in World War II was the grey limestone building of the Haus Huth. Originally a restaurant and wine shop, it was one of the first buildings in Berlin to be erected with a steel frame, intended to support the weight of the wine. It was designed by architects Conrad Heidenreich and Paul Michel in 1912. After the war, it stood alone on the vast eroded square. Today however, the offices of the famous car manufacturers DaimlerChrysler are located here, along with the

Rauschenberg's sculpture *Riding Bikes*, with Weinhaus Huth in the background

Diekmann im Haus Huth restaurant, a small café and Hardy's, an upmarket wine shop.

Haus Huth is also home to the **Sammlung DaimlerChrysler Contemporary**, a small exhibition featuring the latest additions to the corporation's collection of 20th-century art, which mostly consists of abstract and geometric paintings by German and international artists.

The best view of the building is from its south side where a jubilant, bright light installation by Robert Rauschenberg called *Riding Bikes* can be found.

The historic Haus Huth on Leipziger Platz

⑮ Diplomaten-viertel

Diplomatic Quarter

Map 6 F5, 7 A5, B5, C5. **U**
Nollendorfplatz or Potsdamer Platz.
🚌 100, 106, 187, 200.

Although a number of consulates existed in the Tiergarten area as early as 1918, the establishment of a diplomatic district along the southern edge of the Tiergarten, between Stauffenbergstrasse and Lichtensteinallee, did not take place until the period of Hitler's Third Reich between 1933 and 1945. During the years 1938 to 1943 large embassies representing the Axis Powers, Italy and Japan, were built here.

Despite the fact that these monumental buildings were designed by a number of different architects, the Fascist interpretation of Neo-Classicism and the influence of Albert Speer as head architect meant that the group was homo-genous, if bleak. Many of the buildings did not survive World War II bombing.

A diplomatic area has now emerged along Tiergarten-strasse. The Austrian embassy designed by Hans Hollein stands at the junction of Stauffenbergstrasse, next door to the embassies of India and the Republic of South Africa. At Tiergartenstrasse Nos. 21–3 the pre-World War II Italian embassy still stands, while next door is a copy of the first Japanese embassy. Between Klingel-höferstrasse and Rauchstrasse stands an imposing complex of five embassies. Completed in 1999, these represent Norway, Sweden, Denmark, Finland and Iceland. The complex has an art gallery and café which are open to the public.

⑯ Tiergarten

Map 6 E4, 7 A3, 8 D3. **S** Tiergarten or Bellevue. 🚌 100, 106, 187, 200.

This is the largest park in Berlin. Situated at the geographical centre of the city it occupies a surface area of more than 200 ha (495 acres). Once a forest used as the Elector's hunting reserve, it

One of many tranquil areas within the Tiergarten

was transformed into a landscaped park by Peter Joseph Lenné in the 1830s. A half-kilometre Triumphal Avenue was built in the eastern section of the park at the end of the 19th century, lined with statues of the country's rulers and statesmen.

World War II inflicted huge damage on the Tiergarten, including the destruction of the Triumphal Avenue, many of whose surviving monuments can now be seen in the Lapidarium *(see p148)*. Replant-ing, however, has now restored the Tiergarten which is a favourite meeting place for Berliners. Its avenues are now lined with statues of figures such as Johann Wolfgang von Goethe and Richard Wagner.

By the lake known as Neuer See and the Landwehrkanal are memorials to the murdered leaders of the Spartacus movement, Karl Liebknecht and Rosa Luxemburg *(see p30)*. Also worth finding is a collection of gas lamps, displayed near the Tiergarten S-Bahn station.

⑰ Grosser Stern

Great Star

Map 7 A4. **S** Bellevue.
U Hansaplatz. 🚌 100, 106, 187.

This vast roundabout at the centre of the Tiergarten has five large roads leading off it in the shape of a star. At its centre is the enormous Siegessäule (Triumphal Column). Surrounding it are various monuments brought over from the nearby Reichstag building *(see pp138–9)* during the

late 1930s. At the same period the Strasse des 17 Juni was widened to twice its size, the square surrounding the roundabout was enlarged and much of the existing statuary removed.

In the northern section of the square stands a vast bronze monument to the first German Chancellor, Otto von Bismarck (1815–98). Around it stand allegorical figures, the work of late-19th-century sculptor Reinhold Begas. Other statues represent various national heroes including Field Marshal Helmuth von Moltke (1800–91), chief of the Prussian general staff between the years 1858 and 1888, who won the Franco-German war.

Monument to Otto von Bismarck at the Grosser Stern

⑱ Siegessäule

Triumphal Column

Grosser Stern. **Map** 7 A4. **Tel** 391 29 61. **S** Bellevue. **U** Hansaplatz. 🚌 100, 106, 187. **Open** Apr–Oct: 9:30am–6:30pm daily; Nov–Mar: 10am–5pm daily. 🚻

The triumphal column is based on a design by Johann Heinrich Strack, and was built to commemorate victory in the Prusso-Danish war of 1864. After further Prussian victories in wars against Austria (1866) and France (1871), "Goldelse", a gilded figure by Friedrich Drake representing Victory, was added to the top. The monument stood in front of the Reichstag building until the Nazi government moved it to its present location in 1938. The base is decorated with bas-reliefs commemorating battles. Higher up the column a mosaic frieze by Anton von Werner depicts the 1871 founding of the German Empire. An observation terrace at the top offers magnificent vistas over Berlin.

Königliche Porzellan-Manufaktur

Established in 1763, the Königliche Porzellan-Manufaktur (Royal Porcelain Factory) was soon producing items of the highest artistic quality, competing with the products of the older Meissen factory in Saxony. The Berlin factory is particularly renowned for its Neo-Classical urns and plates decorated with views of the city. Large collections of porcelain with the markings KPM can be seen at the Ephraim-Palais *(see p93)*, in the Kunstgewerbemuseum *(see pp122–5)* and at the Belvedere within the grounds of Schloss Charlottenburg *(see pp164–5)*. It is also worth visiting the factory, located at Wegelystrasse 1, which is still producing porcelain, and includes a sales gallery and exhibition hall.

Neo-Classical vase with a view of the Gendarmenmarkt

Siegessäule (Triumphal Column)

⑲ Hansaviertel

Map 6 E3, E4, F3. Ⓢ Bellevue. Ⓤ Hansaplatz. ▣ 100, 106, 187. Akademie der Künste Hanseatenweg 10. **Tel** 20 05 72 00 0. **Open** 11am–8pm Tue–Sun. ▨

This area to the west of Schloss Bellevue is home to some of the most interesting modern architecture in Berlin, built for the 1957 Internationale Bauausstellung (International Architectural Exhibition). Taking on a World War II bomb site, prominent architects from around the world designed 45 projects, of which 36 were realized, to create a varied residential development set in an environment of lush greenery. The list of distinguished architects involved in the project included Walter Gropius (Händelallee Nos. 3–9), Alvar Aalto (Klopstockstrasse Nos. 30–32) and Oskar Niemeyer (Altonaer Strasse Nos. 4–14). The development also includes a school, a commercial services building and two churches.

In 1960, a new headquarters for the **Akademie der Künste** (Academy of Arts) was built at Hanseatenweg No. 10. Designed by Werner Düttmann, the academy has a concert hall, an exhibition area, archives and a library. In front of the main entrance is a magnificent piece, *Reclining Figure*, by eminent British sculptor Henry Moore.

⑳ Schloss Bellevue

Bellevue Palace

Spreeweg 1. **Map** 7 A3. Ⓢ Bellevue. ▣ 100, 187. **Closed** to the public.

This captivating palace with its dazzlingly white Neo-Classical façade is now the official residence of the German Federal President. Built in 1786 to a design by Michael Philipp Boumann for the Prussian Prince August Ferdinand, the palace served as a royal residence until 1861. In 1935 it was refurbished to house a Museum of German Ethnology. Refurbished again in 1938, it became a hotel for guests of the Nazi government.

Following bomb damage during World War II, the palace was carefully restored to its former glory, with the oval ballroom rebuilt to a design by Carl Gotthard Langhans. The palace is set within an attractive park laid out to the original late 18th-century design, though unfortunately the picturesque garden pavilions did not survive World War II.

Imposing façade of Schloss Bellevue, now the official Berlin residence of the German President

Haus der Kulturen der Welt or "pregnant oyster" as it is also known

㉑ Haus der Kulturen der Welt
House of World Culture

John-Foster-Dulles-Allee 10.
Map 7 C3. **Tel** 39 78 70. Ⓢ & Ⓤ
Hauptbahnhof & Bundestag.
🚌 100. **Open** 10am–7pm Mon–Sun.
Exhibitions 11am–7pm Wed–Mon. 🏛

This former congress hall's squat structure and parabolic roof has given rise to its affectionate nickname "the pregnant oyster". Built between 1956 and 1957 to a design by the American architect Hugh Stubbins, it was intended as the American entry in the international architecture competition "Interbau 1957" (from which the Hansaviertel apartment blocks originated). It soon became a symbol of freedom and modernity in West Berlin during the Cold War, particularly when compared to the GDR-era monumental buildings of Karl-Marx-Allee in East Berlin *(see pp174–5)*. However, its roof failed to withstand the test of time and the building partially collapsed in 1980.

After reconstruction it was re-opened in 1989, with a change of purpose. It is now used to bring world cultures to a wider German audience, and stages various events and performances to this effect. It is known for its jazz festivals in particular *(see pp50–53)*.

Standing nearby is the black tower of the Carillon, built in 1987 to commemorate the 750th anniversary of Berlin. Suspended in the tower is the largest carillon in Europe, comprising 67 bells. Daily at noon and 6pm, the bells give a brief computer-controlled concert.

㉒ Regierungsviertel
Government District

Map 8 D2, E2. Ⓢ Brandenburger Tor.
Ⓤ Bundestag. 🚌 100, 248.

This bold concept for a government district in keeping with a 21st-century capital was the winning design in a competition held in 1992. Construction of the complex began in 1997 and was completed in 2003. Axel Schultes and Charlotte Frank's grand design proposed a rectangular site cutting across the meander of the Spree river just north of the Reichstag.

While many of the buildings have been designed by other architects, their plans fitting within the overall concept, Schultes and Frank designed the Bundeskanzleramt, situated opposite the Reichstag, which is the official residence of the German Chancellor. The offices – Alsenblock and Luisenblock – are the work of Stephan Braunfels, as is the office Dorotheenblöcke, built by a consortium of five architects. The whole project is complemented by the neighbouring

Hauptbahnhof railway station, an impressive glass-and-steel construction with several levels above and underground. In 2009 the city's newest U-Bahn line, the U55, was completed, connecting Hauptbahnhof to the Bundestag and Brandenburger Tor. This will eventually be extended to Alexanderplatz to meet with the U5 line.

㉓ Reichstag

Platz der Republik. **Map** 8 D3, E3.
Ⓤ Bundestag. 🚌 100, 248. **Tel** 227 32 152. Dome: **Open** by appointment only via 🌐 **bundestag.de**. Assembly Hall: **Open** by appointment only.
🕐 10:30am, 1:30, 3:30 & 6:30pm daily when parliament is not sitting.
Closed 1 Jan, 24–26 & 31 Dec.

Built to house the German Parliament, the Reichstag was intended as a symbol of national unity and the aspirations of the new German Empire, declared in 1871. The Neo-Renaissance design by Paul Wallot captured the prevailing spirit of German optimism. Constructed between the years 1884 and 1894, it was funded by money paid by the French as wartime reparations.

On 23 December 1916, the inscription *"Dem Deutschen Volke"* ("To the German People") was added to the façade. The Reichstag became a potent symbol that would be exploited in the years to come.

In 1918 Philipp Scheidemann declared the formation of the Weimar Republic from the building. The next time the

The Bundeskanzleramt, the official residence of the Federal Chancellor

The Reichstag crowned by a dome designed by Sir Norman Foster

world heard about the Reichstag was on the night of 28 February 1933, when a fire destroyed the main hall. The Communists were blamed, accelerating a political witch-hunt driven by the Nazis, who subsequently came to power.

With the onset of World War II, the building was not rebuilt. Yet its significance resonated beyond Germany, as shown by the photograph of the Soviet flag flying from the Reichstag in May 1945, which became a symbol of the German defeat.

Between 1957 and 1972, the dome and most of the ornamentation was removed. As well as providing a meeting-place for the lower house of the German Bundestag (Parliament), the Reichstag also made a spectacular backdrop for huge festivals and rock concerts, much to the annoyance of the East German authorities.

On 2 December 1990, the Reichstag was the first meeting-place of a newly-elected Bundestag following German reunification. On 23 June 1995 the artist Christo and his wife Jeanne-Claude wrapped the Reichstag in glistening fabric – an artistic statement that lasted for two weeks.

The latest phase of rebuilding, between 1995 and 1999 to a design by Sir Norman Foster, transformed the Reichstag into a modern meeting hall beneath an elliptical dome. Visits to the cupola's viewing gallery are free and the views are breathtaking. The first parliamentary meeting in the new building took place on 19 April 1999.

㉔ Sowjetisches Ehrenmal
Monument to Soviet Soldiers

Strasse des 17 Juni. **Map** 8 D3. Ⓢ & Ⓤ Brandenburger Tor. 🚌 100, 248.

This huge monument near the Brandenburg Gate was unveiled on 7 November 1945, on the anniversary of the start of the October Revolution in Russia. Flanked by the first two tanks into the city, the monument commemorates over 300,000 Soviet soldiers who perished in the battle for Berlin at the end of World War II. The vast column was made from marble taken from the headquarters of the

Chancellor of the Third Reich, when it was being dismantled. The column was designed by Nicolai Sergievski, while the imposing figure on top, a soldier cast in bronze, is the work of Lew Kerbel. This monument is also a cemetery for around 2,500 Soviet casualties. Following the partition of Berlin, the site ended up in the British sector, but formed a kind of non-territorial enclave to which Soviet soldiers posted to East Berlin had access.

The sculpture of a Soviet soldier atop the Sowjetisches Ehrenmal

Berlin's Bridges

Despite wartime damage, Berlin's bridges are still well worth seeing. The Spree river and the city's canals have some exemplary architecture on their banks, while many of the bridges were designed and decorated by famous architects and sculptors. Probably the most renowned bridge is the Schlossbrücke designed by Karl Friedrich Schinkel *(see p76)*. Further south along the Kupfergrabenkanal, the Schleusenbrücke dates from c.1914, and is decorated with reliefs of the early history of the city's bridges and sluices. The next bridge, heading south, is the Jungfernbrücke dating from 1798, which is the last drawbridge in Berlin. The next bridge along is the Gertraudenbrücke *(see p87)*. Where Friedrichstrasse crosses the Spree river is the Weidendammer Brücke, originally built in 1695-7 and subsequently rebuilt in 1923, with an eagle motif decorating its balustrade. On the Spree near the Regierungsviertel is the magnificent Moltkebrücke (1886–91). The bridge is guarded by a huge griffin wielding a shield adorned with the Prussian eagle, while cherubs dressed in a military fashion hold up lamps. On the arches of the bridges are portraits of leaders designed by Karl Begas.

Ornamental feature of a bear on the Liebknechtbrücke

KREUZBERG

The area covered in this chapter is only a part of the district of the same name. The evolution of Kreuzberg began in the late 19th century when it was a working-class area. After World War II unrepaired buildings were abandoned by those who could afford to move, leaving a population of artists, foreigners, the unemployed and members of a variety of sub-cultures.

Kreuzberg is now an area of contrasts, with luxury apartments next to dilapidated buildings. Some parts of Kreuzberg are mainly Turkish, while others are inhabited by affluent young professionals. The district's attractions are its wealth of restaurants and Turkish bazaars, as well as an interesting selection of nightclubs, cinemas, theatres and galleries.

Sights at a Glance

Museums
2 Martin-Gropius-Bau
3 Topographie des Terrors
4 Checkpoint Charlie
5 Berlinische Galerie
6 Jüdisches Museum
8 Lapidarium
9 Deutsches Technikmuseum Berlin

Historic Buildings
1 Anhalter Bahnhof
11 Riehmers Hofgarten
13 Flughafen Tempelhof

Squares, Parks and Cemeteries
7 Mehringplatz
10 Friedhöfe vor dem Halleschen Tor
12 Viktoriapark

See also Street Finder maps
8, 9, 14, 15

Restaurants
see pp236–7
1 Altes Zollhaus
2 Bar Centrale
3 Cafe do Brasil
4 Cafe Stresemann
5 e.t.a. hoffmann
6 Golgotha
7 Gropius
8 Seerose
9 Tim Raue
10 Tomasa
11 Yorckschlosschen

◀ The Jüdisches Museum (Jewish Museum)

For map symbols see back flap

Street-by-Street: Mehringplatz and Friedrichstrasse

The areas north of Mehringplatz are the oldest sections of Kreuzberg. Mehringplatz, initially called Rondell, together with the Oktogon (Leipziger Platz) and the Quarré (Pariser Platz), were laid out in 1734 as part of the enlargement of Friedrichstadt. World War II totally changed the character of this area. It is now full of modern developments such as the Friedrichstadt Passagen – a huge complex of shops, apartments, offices, galleries and restaurants. Only a few buildings recall the earlier splendour of this district.

④ ★ Checkpoint Charlie
This small hut marks the place of the notorious border crossing between East and West Berlin.

❸ Topographie des Terrors
A shocking exhibition detailing Nazi crimes is housed within the former Gestapo and SS headquarters.

Key

— Suggested route

❷ Martin-Gropius-Bau
This interesting, multi-coloured Neo-Renaissance building is now the main temporary art exhibition space in the city.

Deutsches Technikmuseum

Haus am Checkpoint Charlie
Butterflies on a piece of the Berlin Wall mark the entrance to this museum.

Springer-Hochhaus
This shopping and restaurant complex is located inside the Axel-Springer-Hochhaus, a 1960s highrise built adjacent to the Berlin Wall as a highly-visible political statement.

Locator Map
See Street Finder maps 14 & 15

Märkisches
Museum →

RUDI · DUTSCHKE STRASSE

MARKGRAFENSTRASSE

❻ ★ Jüdisches Museum
Windows made to resemble cracks create a striking effect in the metallic facing of this building by architect Daniel Libeskind.

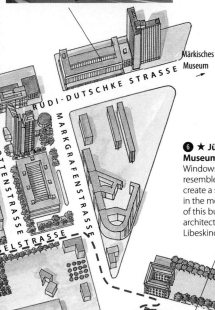

| 0 metres | 150 |
| 0 yards | 150 |

❼ Mehringplatz
The former Rondell was known for many years as Belle-Alliance-Platz. Completely destroyed during World War II, it was rebuilt by Hans Scharoun, who followed the original design.

❶ Anhalter Bahnhof

Askanischer Platz 6–7. **Map** 14 E1.
Ⓢ Anhalter Bahnhof. Ⓤ Potsdamer
Platz. Ⓤ Mendelssohn-Bartholdy-
Park. 🚌 M29, M41.

Only a tiny fragment now
remains of Anhalter Bahnhof,
which was named after the
Saxon Royal Family. It was once
Berlin's largest and Europe's
second largest railway station.

The hugely ambitious
structure was designed by
Franz Schwechten and
constructed in 1880. The station
was intended to be the largest
and most elegant in Europe in
order to impress official visitors
to the capital of the German
Empire. Some of the most
famous people to alight at
Anhalter Bahnhof were the
Italian king Umberto, who was
welcomed by Kaiser Wilhelm II
himself, and the Russian tsar
Nicholas. The station was taken
out of public use in 1943 after
its roof was destroyed by Allied
bombing. Only the front
portico remains, crowned by
still-damaged sculptures and
the hole that housed a large
electric clock, as well as
fragments of its once glorious
façade. On the vast grounds
behind it is the tent-like
entertainment venue,
Tempodrom (see p269).

❷ Martin-Gropius-Bau

Niederkirchnerstrasse 7 (corner of
Stresemannstrasse). **Map** 14 E1.
Tel 25 48 60. **Open** 10am–7pm
Wed–Mon. Ⓢ & Ⓤ Potsdamer Platz.
🚌 200, M29, M41. 🚶

The innovative Martin-Gropius-
Bau was originally built to fulfil
the requirements of an arts and
crafts museum. It was designed
by Martin Gropius with the
participation of Heino
Schmieden and constructed in
1881. The building is in a style
reminiscent of an Italian
Renaissance palace, with a
magnificent glazed interior
courtyard, an impressive atrium
and unusual, richly decorated
elevations. Located between

Exhibition documenting Nazi crimes at the Topographie des Terrors

the windows are the crests of
German cities, and within the
friezes are reliefs illustrating the
different arts and crafts. In the
plaques between the windows
of the top storey are beautiful
mosaics containing allegorical
figures representing the
cultures of different eras
and countries.

From 1922 Martin-Gropius-
Bau accommodated the
Museum of Ethnology, but
after World War II the building
was abandoned and left in
ruins. Although plans for an
inner-city motorway
threatened it until the 1970s,
a reconstruction programme
eventually commenced in
1981, led by architects
Winnetou Kampmann and
Ute Westroem. This was
followed in 1999 by a further
refurbishment, and since
then the building has housed
a changing series of exhibitions on art, photography
and architecture.

Allegorical mosaic on display in
the Martin-Gropius-Bau

❸ Topographie des Terrors

Stresemannstrasse 110 (entrance on
Niederkirchnerstrasse 8). **Map** 8 F5, 14
F1. **Tel** 25 45 09 50. Ⓢ & Ⓤ
Potsdamer Platz, Kochstrasse. Ⓢ
Anhalter Bahnhof. 🚌 M29, M41.
Open 10am–8pm daily. 🚶
🅦 topographie.de

During the Third Reich Prinz-
Albrecht-Strasse was probably
the most frightening address
in Berlin. In 1934 three of the
most terrifying Nazi political
departments had their headquarters in a block between
Stresemann-, Wilhelm-,
Anhalter-, and Prinz-Albrecht-
Strasse (now Niederkirchner
Strasse), making this area the
government district of
National Socialist Germany.

The Neo-Classical Prinz-
Albrecht palace at
Wilhelmstrasse No. 102 became
the headquarters of Reinhard
Heydrich and the Third Reich's
security service (SD). The arts
and crafts school at Prinz-
Albrecht-Strasse No. 8 was
occupied by the head of the
Gestapo, Heinrich Müller, while
the Hotel Prinz Albrecht at No. 9
became the headquarters of the
Schutzstaffel, or SS, with
Heinrich Himmler in command.
It was from the buildings in this
area of the city that decisions
about the Germanization of the
occupied territories were made,
as well as plans on the genocide
of European Jews. After World
War II, the buildings were pulled

down. In 1987, however, in some surviving cellars that were once torture cells, an exhibition was mounted that documented Nazi crimes. An exhibition building was added in 2010.

A preserved section of the Berlin wall runs along-side the grounds of the Topographie des Terrors at Niederkirchner Strasse.

❹ Checkpoint Charlie

Friedrichstrasse 43–45. **Map** 9 A5. **Tel** 253 72 50. **U** Kochstrasse. M29. Haus am Checkpoint Charlie: **Open** 9am–10pm daily.

A Alpha, B Bravo, C Charlie. Not many people remember that the name of this notorious border crossing between the American and Soviet sectors stemmed from the word that signifies the letter C in the international phonetic alphabet.

Between 1961 and 1990, Checkpoint Charlie was the only crossing point for foreigners between East and West Berlin. During that time, it represented a symbol of both freedom and separation for the many East Germans trying to escape from the DDR's Communist regime.

Little remains of the former crossing point, which was witness to a number of dramatic events during the Cold War, including a tense two-day standoff between Russian and American tanks in 1961.

In 1990, the checkpoint was formally closed with an official ceremony attended by the foreign ministers of the four occupying powers: the US, Great Britain, France and the Soviet Union.

Today, there are no longer any gates, barriers or barbed wire to be seen; instead there is a replica checkpoint booth, complete with sand bags and the famous, huge sign on the old Western side that reads "You are leaving the American Sector". There is also an exhibition space called the BlackBox, housing the Zentrum Kalter Krieg (Cold War Centre), which documents and explores the period after World War II up until 1989.

The replica booth at the former Checkpoint Charlie

Also on Friedrichstrasse are two large photographs of an American and a Russian soldier, that form part of a well-known series by the Berlin photographer Frank Thiel. His portraits commemorate the departure of the Allies.

One of the original watchtowers is worth visiting at the museum nearby – **Haus am Checkpoint Charlie**. The museum's rich collection details Cold War border conflicts, and the construction of the Berlin Wall. Of special interest are the exhibits connected with the escape attempts of East Germans to the West. The ingenuity and bravery of these escapees is astonishing, using devices such as secret compartments built into cars, and specially constructed suitcases.

A separate exhibition illustrates the peaceful campaigns carried out in the name of democracy in many totalitarian countries.

❺ Berlinische Galerie

Alte Jakobstrasse 124–28. **Map** 9 C5. **Tel** 78 90 26 00. **U** Kochstrasse. 248, M29. **Open** 10am–6pm Wed–Mon.

The city's museum for modern art, design and architecture is one of the finest regional museums in the country. Themed exhibitions, which are regularly changed, draw upon its huge collection of German, East European and Russian paintings, photographs, graphics and architectural artifacts.

One of the highlights is the 5,000-strong painting collection, which covers all the major art movements from the late 19th century until today. It includes works by Max Liebermann, Otto Dix, Georg Baselitz, Alexander Rodtschenko, Iwan Puni and Via Lewandowsky.

The museum's collection of sketches, prints and posters encompasses the Berlin Dadaists George Grosz, Hannah Höch and Werner Heldt, as well as works by Ernst Ludwig Kirchner and Hanns Schimansky.

Amongst the architectural items held by the Galerie are drawings and models for buildings that were never built, offering fascinating glimpses into how the city might have looked. A fine example is the shell-like Expressionist Sternkirche (Star Church), designed by Otto Bartning in 1922.

Kühn Malvessi's *Letter Field* in front of the Berlinische Galerie

❻ Jüdisches Museum Berlin

The Jewish Museum designed by Daniel Libeskind, a Polish-Jewish architect based in the United States, is an exciting and imaginative example of late 20th-century architecture. The plan, shape, style, and interior and exterior arrangement of the building are part of a complicated philosophical programme to illustrate the history and culture of Germany's Jewish community, and the repercussions of the Holocaust. The exhibition has gathered together many artifacts, such as books and photographs, to bring the memories and stories of Jewish life alive. The long, narrow galleries with slanting floors and sharp zig-zagging turns are designed to evoke the feeling of loss and dislocation. These are interspersed by "voids" that represent the vacuum left behind by the destruction of Jewish life.

★ **Moses Mendelssohn's Glasses**
These glasses are on show in the section entitled *"Moses Mendelssohn and the Enlightenment"*, which details the philosopher's fight for religious tolerance in a time when Jews possessed no civil rights.

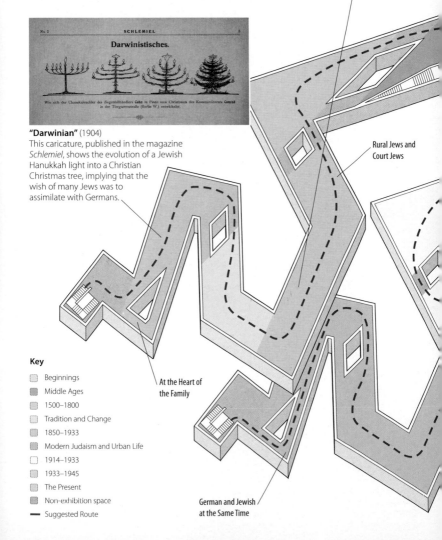

"Darwinian" (1904)
This caricature, published in the magazine *Schlemiel*, shows the evolution of a Jewish Hanukkah light into a Christian Christmas tree, implying that the wish of many Jews was to assimilate with Germans.

Rural Jews and Court Jews

Key
- Beginnings
- Middle Ages
- 1500–1800
- Tradition and Change
- 1850–1933
- Modern Judaism and Urban Life
- 1914–1933
- 1933–1945
- The Present
- Non-exhibition space
- Suggested Route

At the Heart of the Family

German and Jewish at the Same Time

Museum Guide

Entrance to the museum is via an underground path from the former Berlin Museum next door. Stairs lead up to the start of the exhibition which is divided into 14 sections, taking visitors through German Jewish history and culture from early history, through the Middle Ages and up to the present day.

Entrance to exhibition via underground tunnel

World War I and Weimar Republic

Persecution Resistance– Extermination

Exit

East and West

★ **Daniel Libeskind's Design**
The extraordinary zinc-clad, jagged structure of the museum is likened to a deconstructed Star of David, and attracted over 350,000 visitors to the museum in the two years before the exhibitions were installed.

Electric Iron AEG
An iron made by one of Germany's largest electrical companies, founded by Emil Rathenau, forms part of the collection celebrating the dominant position of Jews in trade and industry in Berlin throughout the late 19th and early 20th centuries.

★ **Garden of Exile**
Comprising 49 tilted pillars to represent the foundation of the state of Israel in 1948 plus one for Berlin, the garden also symbolizes the forced exile of Germany's Jews.

A representation of Peace, by Albert Wolff, in Mehringplatz

❼ Mehringplatz

Map 15 A2. Ⓤ Hallesches Tor.
🚌 248, M41.

Mehringplatz was planned in the 1730s, when the boundaries of the city were extended. Its original name was Rondell, meaning circus, an appropriate name as Wilhelmstrasse, Friedrichstrasse and Lindenstrasse all converged here.

Rondell was the work of Philipp Gerlach then, in the 1840s, Peter Joseph Lenné designed the decoration of the square. At the centre is the Column of Peace, commemorating the Wars of Liberation in 1815. The column is crowned by the figure of Victory by Christian Daniel Rauch. Two sculptures were added in the 1870s: *Peace* by Albert Wolff; and *Clio* (the Muse of History) by Ferdinand Hartzer. In the 19th and early 20th centuries the area was populated with politicians, diplomats and aristocrats, and in 1947 the square was named after the writer Franz Mehring. The current buildings date from the 1970s.

❽ Lapidarium

Hallesches Ufer 78. **Map** 14 E2.
Ⓤ Mendelssohn-Bartholdy-Park.

This interesting building, decorated with an enchanting Oriental-style chimney, was once Berlin's pumping station. It was built from 1873 to 1876 and designed by Hermann Blankenstein. The original steam pumps have survived to this day. The Lapidarium once contained numerous sculptures, including virtually all the sculptures that once decorated the Avenue of Victory in the Tiergarten, known as "Puppenallee". These majestic statues of celebrated warriors and rulers stood side by side in their robes and weapons, only slightly diminished by the loss of many heads, arms and other body parts. In 2009 the Lapidarium was sold, and all the statues were transferred to the Zittadelle Spandau.

❾ Deutsches Technikmuseum Berlin

Trebbiner Strasse 9. **Map** 14 E2.
Tel 90 25 40. Ⓤ Gleisdreieck.
🚌 M29, M41. **Open** 9am–5:30pm Tue–Fri, 10am–6pm Sat–Sun. ♿ 🅿

The Technical Museum was first established in 1982 with the intention of grouping more than 100 smaller, specialized collections under one roof. The current collection is arranged on the site of the former trade hall, the size of which allows many of the museum's exhibits, such as locomotives, aircraft, boats, water towers and storerooms, to be displayed full-size and in their original condition.

Of particular interest in the collection are the dozens of locomotives and railway carriages from different eras as well as the vintage cars. There are also exhibitions dedicated to flying, the history of paper manufacture, printing, weaving, electro-technology and computer technology. There are also two windmills, a brewery and an old forge. The section called Spectrum is especially popular with children as it allows them to conduct "hands-on" experiments.

❿ Friedhöfe vor dem Halleschen Tor

Mehringdamm, Blücher-, Baruther & Zossener Strasse. **Map** 15 A3. **Tel** 691 6138. Ⓤ Hallesches Tor. 🚌 140, 248, M41. **Open** Dec & Jan: 8am–4pm daily; Feb & Nov: 8am–5pm daily; Mar & Oct: 8am–6pm; Apr & Sep: 8am–7pm; May–Aug: 8am–8pm.

Beyond the city walls, next to the Hallesches Tor, are four cemeteries established in 1735. Among the beautiful gravestones are great Berlin artists including the composer Felix Mendelssohn-Bartholdy, architects Georg Wenzeslaus von Knobelsdorff, David Gilly and Carl Ferdinand Langhans, and the writer, artist and composer ETA Hoffmann.

⓫ Riehmers Hofgarten

Yorckstr. 83–86, Grossbeerenstr. 56–57 & Hagelberger Strasse 9–12.
Map 14 F4. Ⓤ Mehringdamm.
🚌 140, 248, M19.

Riehmers Hofgarten is the name given to the 20 or so exquisite houses arranged around a

Headstone in the picturesque Friedhöfe vor dem Halleschen Tor

Renaissance-style façade in Riehmers Hofgarten

picturesque garden in the area bordered by the streets Yorck-, Hagelberger and Grossbeeren-strasse. These houses were built between 1881 and 1899 to the detailed designs of Wilhelm Riehmer and Otto Mrosk, respected architects who not only designed intricate, Renaissance-style and Neo-Baroque façades but also gave equal splendour to the elevations overlooking the courtyard garden. The streets of Riehmers Hofgarten have been carefully restored and Yorckstrasse also has quite a few cafés. Next to Riehmers Hofgarten is the church of St Bonifaz, which was designed by Max Hasak. Adjacent to the church is a similar complex of houses built in an impressive Neo-Gothic style.

To experience the authentic atmosphere of old Kreuzberg, you need to go no further than Bergmannstrasse. Here, entire districts of 19th-century houses have been restored to their original state. The atmosphere is further enhanced by antique streetlamps, a pedestrianized street, and bars and galleries. This is also true for

Marheinekeplatz, where there is a lively covered market.

⓫ Viktoriapark

Map 14 E4, E5, F5. Ⓤ Platz der Luftbrücke. 🚌 104, 140, M19.

This rambling park, with several artificial waterfalls, short trails and a small hill, was designed by Hermann Machtig and built between 1884 and 1894. The Neo-Gothic Memorial to the Wars of Liberation at the summit of the hill is the work of

Karl Friedrich Schinkel, created between 1817 and 1821. The monument commemorates the Prussian victory against Napoleon's army in the Wars of Liberation. The cast-iron tower is well ornamented. In the niches of the lower section are 12 allegorical figures by Christian Daniel Rauch, Friedrich Tieck and Ludwig Wichmann. Each figure symbolizes a battle and is linked to a historic figure – either a military leader or a member of the royal family.

⓭ Flughafen Tempelhof

Platz der Luftbrücke. **Map** 14 F5.
Ⓤ Platz der Luftbrücke. 🚌 104, 248.

Situated beyond Kreuzberg, Tempelhof airport was once Germany's largest. Built in 1923, it was enlarged during the Third Reich. The building is typical of Third Reich architecture, even though the eagles that decorate the buildings predate the Nazis. The additions to the original structure were designed by Ernst Sagebiel in 1939.

In 1951, a monument was added in front of the airport. Designed by Eduard Ludwig, it commemorates the airlifts of the Berlin Blockade. The three spikes on the top symbolize the air corridors used by Allied planes. Following heated political debate, the airport was permanently closed in late 2008.

The Berlin Blockade (1948–9)

On 24 June 1948, as a result of rising tensions between East Germany and West Berlin, Soviet authorities blockaded all the roads leading to West Berlin. In order to ensure food and fuel for the residents, US General Lucius Clay ordered that provisions be flown into the city. British and American planes made a total of 212,612 flights, transporting almost 2.3 million tons of goods, among which were parts of a power station. In April 1949, at the height of the airlift, planes were landing every 63 seconds. The blockade ended in May, 1949. Although the airlifts were successful, there were casualties: 70 airmen and 8 ground crew lost their lives.

Allied plane bringing supplies during the Berlin Airlift

AROUND KURFÜRSTENDAMM

The eastern area of the Charlottenburg region, around the boulevard known as Kurfürstendamm, was developed in the 19th century. Luxurious buildings were constructed along Kurfürstendamm (the Ku'damm), while the areas of Breitscheidplatz and Wittenbergplatz became replete with hotels and department stores. After World War II, with the old centre (Mitte) situated in East Berlin, Charlottenburg became the centre of West Berlin. Traces of wartime destruction were removed very quickly and this area was transformed into the heart of West Berlin, and dozens of new company headquarters and trade centres were built. The situation changed after the reunification of Berlin, and although many tourists concentrate on Mitte, the heart of the city continues to beat around Kurfürstendamm.

Sights at a Glance

Museums
6 Newton-Sammlung
10 Käthe-Kollwitz-Museum

Streets and Squares
4 Kurfürstendamm
9 Fasanenstrasse
11 Savignyplatz
14 Tauentzienstrasse

Parks
1 Zoologischer Garten

Historic Buildings
2 Europa-Center
3 *Kaiser-Wilhelm-Gedächtnis-Kirche pp156–7*
5 Ludwig-Erhard-Haus
7 Theater des Westens
8 Jüdisches Gemeindehaus
12 Universität der Künste
13 Technische Universität
15 KaDeWe

☐ Restaurants
see pp237–8

1 Baba Angora
2 Belmondo
3 Bleiburg's
4 Brasserie Le Faubourg
5 Brenner
6 Cafe-Restaurant Wintergarten im Literhaus
7 Calcutta
8 Dickie Wirtin
9 Die Quadriga
10 El Borriquito
11 Esswein am Fasanenplatz
12 Florian
13 Grune Lampe
14 La Mano Verde
15 Marjellchen
16 Namaskar
17 Restaurant 44
18 Sachico Sushi
19 Satyam
20 Tastees
21 Wilson's

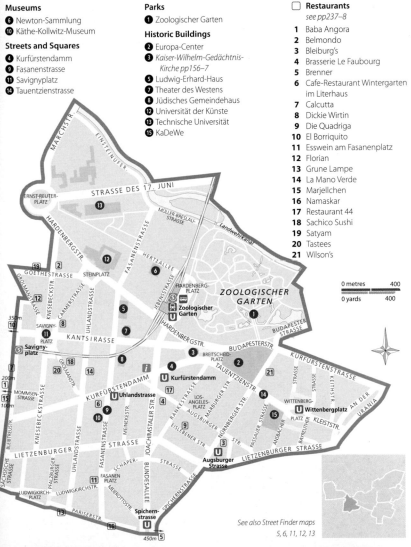

0 metres 400
0 yards 400

See also Street Finder maps
5, 6, 11, 12, 13

◀ View of the magnificent Kaiser-Wilhelm-Gedächtnis-Kirche

For map symbols *see back flap*

Street-by-Street: Breitscheidplatz and Ku'damm

The area surrounding the eastern end of the Ku'damm, especially Tauentzienstrasse and Breitscheidplatz, is the centre of the former West Berlin. Thirty years ago this ultramodern district, full of department stores and office blocks, attracted visitors from all over the world. Today, although the area still retains its unique atmosphere, it is becoming overshadowed by Potsdamer Platz and the arcades of Friedrichstrasse. However, nowhere else in Berlin is there a place so full of life as Breitscheidplatz, a department store with such style as KaDeWe, or streets as refined as Fasanenstrasse.

Kant-Dreieck
This building, containing only right angles, was designed by Josef Paul Kleihues. The "sail" on the roof makes it instantly recognizable.

8 Jüdisches Gemeindehaus
Some of the remaining fragments of the old synagogue have been incorporated into the façade of this building.

Literaturhaus contains a charming café and a good bookshop.

10 Käthe-Kollwitz-Museum
The museum is housed in one of the charming villas on Fasanenstrasse.

9 Fasanenstrasse
This tranquil street features some of the most expensive shops in Berlin.

Key

Suggested route

0 metres   400
0 yards   400

4 Ku'damm
A stroll along the Ku'damm is a stroll into the heart of Berlin, and an essential part of any visit to the city.

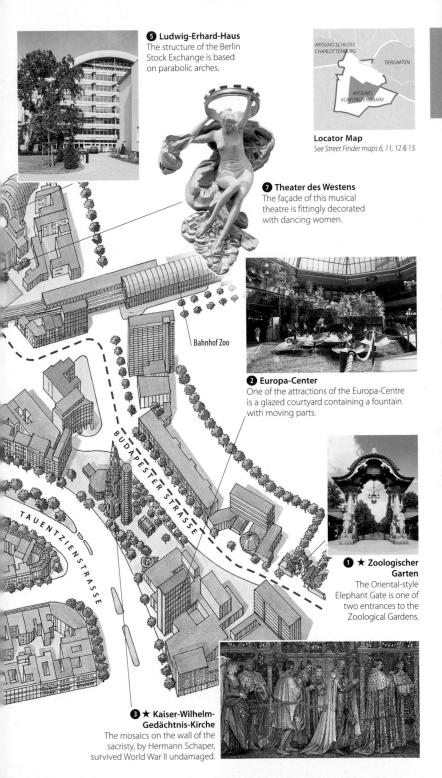

5 Ludwig-Erhard-Haus
The structure of the Berlin Stock Exchange is based on parabolic arches.

Locator Map
See Street Finder maps 6, 11, 12 & 13.

7 Theater des Westens
The façade of this musical theatre is fittingly decorated with dancing women.

Bahnhof Zoo

2 Europa-Center
One of the attractions of the Europa-Centre is a glazed courtyard containing a fountain with moving parts.

1 ★ Zoologischer Garten
The Oriental-style Elephant Gate is one of two entrances to the Zoological Gardens.

3 ★ Kaiser-Wilhelm-Gedächtnis-Kirche
The mosaics on the wall of the sacristy, by Hermann Schaper, survived World War II undamaged.

Hippopotamus House is spanned by fine-meshed glass domes

❶ Zoo Berlin

Zoological Garden

Hardenbergplatz 8 or Budapester Strasse 34. **Map** 6 E5, 12 E1. **Tel** 25 40 10. Ⓢ & Ⓤ Zoologischer Garten. 🚌 100, 109, 110, 200, 204, 245, 249, M45, M46, M49, X9, X10, X34. **Open** 21 Mar–3 Oct: 9am–7pm daily; 4 Oct–20 Mar: 9am–5pm daily. ♿
🌐 zoo-berlin.de

Zoo Berlin is one of Berlin's greatest attractions and many animal "stars" are to be found here. It is part of the Tiergarten and dates from 1844, which makes this zoo the oldest in Germany. You can enter from Harden-bergplatz through the Lion's Gate, and from Budapester Strasse through the decorative Oriental-style Elephant Gate.

The zoo offers a number of attractions, including the monkey house, which contains a family of gorillas, and a darkened pavilion for nocturnal animals. The hippopotamus pool has a glazed wall that enables visitors to observe these enormous animals under-water. The aquarium, one of the largest in Europe, contains sharks, piranhas and unusual animals from coral reefs. There is also a huge terrarium with an over-grown jungle that is home to a group of crocodiles.

❷ Europa-Center

Breitscheidplatz. **Map** 12 E1.
Ⓢ & Ⓤ Zoologischer Garten.
🚌 100, 109, 200, X9.

The Europa-Center stands on the site of the legendary Romanisches Café, a famous meeting place for Dada artists in the 1920s. The current building was established in 1965, and since that time it has been one of the largest complexes of its type in the whole of Germany. Designed by Helmut Hentrich and Hubert Petschnigg, the Europa-Center is a group of low-rise buildings housing a trade centre, numerous restaurants and pubs. The uninspiring edifice of the deluxe Hotel Palace Berlin has been incorporated into the centre, as well as a 22-storey office block.

Around the Center are dotted some amusing fountains, including the "Flow of Time Clock", designed by Bernard Gitton. Seconds, minutes and hours are measured in vials and spheres of green liquid. The Europa-Center also houses the political cabaret *Die Stachelschweine*.

❸ Kaiser-Wilhelm-Gedächtnis-Kirche

See pp156–7.

❹ Kurfürstendamm

Map 11 A2, B2, C3, 12 D1.
Ⓤ Kurfürstendamm or Uhlandstrasse or Zoologischer Garten.
🚌 109, 110, M19, M29.

This is undoubtedly one of the most elegant streets in Berlin. The wide avenue was established in the 1880s on the site of a former track that led to the Grunewald forest. It was quickly populated with imposing buildings and grand hotels. In the 20 years between World Wars I and II, the Ku'damm (as it is popularly called) was renowned for its great cafés, visited by famous writers, directors and painters.

After World War II, the damaged houses were replaced with modern buildings, but this did not change the essential character of this fine street. During the Cold War years it became a symbol of free-market consumerism and the main shopping street in West Berlin. Today, elegant shops and cafés with pretty summer gardens continue to attract a chic crowd.

❺ Ludwig-Erhard-Haus

Fasanenstrasse 85. **Map** 6 D5. Ⓢ & Ⓤ Zoologischer Garten. 🚌 245, M45, M49, X9, X34.

The distinctive curve of this innovative building houses the headquarters of the Berlin stock exchange as well as a trade and industry centre. Completed in 1998, Ludwig-Erhard-Haus is the creation of British architect Nicholas Grimshaw and it has been compared to the skin of an armadillo, a giant skeleton and the ribbing of a shell.

The main structure of the building is composed of 15 elliptical arches, which extend above the roof and down through the glass walls on each side of the building.

A fountain representing Earth, outside the Europa-Center

❻ Newton-Sammlung

Jebensstrasse 2. **Map** 6 D5.
Tel 31 86 48 25. Ⓢ & Ⓤ
Zoologischer Garten.
Open 10am–6pm Tue, Wed &
Fri–Sun, 10am–10pm Thu.

After his death in 2004, the
society and art photographer
Helmut Newton (1931–2004)
bequeathed his life's work to the
city of Berlin. Newton, who was
born and received his first
training as a photographer in
Berlin, became one of the
20th-century's most well-known
photographers with his images of
nudes and portraits of the rich
and famous.

The museum is constantly
extending its collections so as to
serve as the city's museum of
photography. It exhibits selections of Newton's work, including
his early fashion and nude photography as well as self-portraits
and landscapes. There is also a
collection of Newton's cameras.

The façade of the Theater des
Westens on Kantstrasse

❼ Theater des Westens

Kantstrasse 9–12. **Map** 12 D1.
Tel (0180) 544 44. Ⓢ & Ⓤ
Zoologischer Garten. M49, X9, X10,
X34, 100, 109, 110, 200.

The Theater des Westens, one of
the most picturesque of all
Berlin's theatres, was built in
1896 to a design by Bernhard
Sehring. The composition of its
façade links Neo-Classical
elements with Palladian and Art
Nouveau details. The interior of
the theatre has been designed
in a splendid Neo-Baroque style,
while the back and the section

that houses the stage have
been rebuilt within a Neo-
Gothic structure, incorporating
the decorative elements of
a chess set.

From its very beginning the
theatre catered for lighter forms
of musical entertainment.
Operettas and vaudeville were
staged here, followed by
musicals such as Les Misérables.
Some of the world's greatest
stars have appeared on the
stage here, including Josephine
Baker, who performed her
famous banana dance in 1926.
Near the theatre is the
renowned Delphi cinema and
popular jazz club Quasimodo.

❽ Jüdisches Gemeindehaus
Jewish Community House

Fasanenstrasse 79/80. **Map** 12 D1.
Tel 880 280. Ⓢ & Ⓤ Zoologischer
Garten. Ⓤ Uhlandstrasse or Kurfürst-
endamm. 245, M49, X10, X34.

The Jewish community has its
headquarters in this building,
constructed on the site of a
synagogue that was burned
down during Kristallnacht on 9
November 1938 (see p31). The
original synagogue was
designed by Ehenfried Hessel in
a Romanesque-Byzantine style
and built in 1912. The ruins of
the synagogue were removed
only in the mid-1950s. The new

The entrance of the Jüdisches
Gemeindehaus

building, designed by Dieter
Knoblauch and Heinz Heise,
was constructed in 1959. The
only reminders of the
splendour of the former
synagogue are the portal at the
entrance to the building and
some decorative fragments
on the façade.

Inside there are offices, a
school, a kosher restaurant
called Arche Noah and a prayer
room covered by three glazed
domes. At the rear there is a
courtyard with a place of
remembrance. There is also an
emotive statue at the front of
the building, depicting a
broken scroll of the Torah (the
holy book of Jewish Law).

German Cinema

The 1920s were a boom time for the
arts, and German cinema gained
prominence throughout the world
with the rise of Expressionism. The
opening of the UFA film studios in
1919 in Babelsberg (see p207) was a
milestone in the development of
German cinema. The studios became
the heart of the film industry and
rivalled Hollywood as a centre for
innovation. Many famous films were
produced here, including the
Expressionist masterpiece The Cabinet
of Dr Caligari (1920) by Robert Wiene,
Ernst Lubitsch's Madame Dubarry (1919) with Pola Negri, and Nosferatu
(1922) by Friedrich Murnau. Other films released by the studios were
Fritz Lang's Doctor Mahuse (1922) and his futuristic film Metropolis (1927).
In April 1930, the studios premiered Josef von Sternberg's The Blue Angel,
featuring the young Marlene Dietrich in the lead role. After Hitler came
to power many directors and actors left Germany.

Marlene Dietrich in the well-known
film The Blue Angel

❸ Kaiser-Wilhelm-Gedächtnis-Kirche

This church-monument is one of Berlin's most famous landmarks, surrounded by a lively crowd of street traders, buskers and beggars. The vast Neo-Romanesque church was designed by Franz Schwechten. It was consecrated in 1895 but was destroyed by bombs in 1943. After World War II the ruins were removed, leaving only the massive front tower at the base of which the Gedenkhalle (Memorial Hall) is situated. This hall documents the history of the church and contains some of the original ceiling mosaics, marble reliefs and liturgical objects from the church. In 1961, Egon Eiermann designed an octagonal church in blue glass and a new freestanding bell tower.

Kaiser's Mosaic
Kaiser Heinrich I is depicted here in this elaborate mosaic, sitting on his throne.

Main Altar
The vast figure of Christ on the Crossis the work of Karl Hemmeter.

Mosaic Decoration
Original mosaics remain on the arches and the walls near the staircase. These feature the Dukes of Prussia among the other decorative elements.

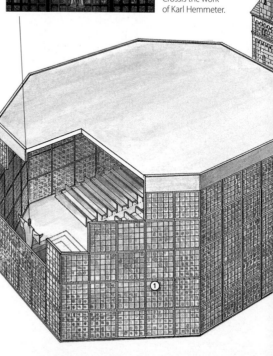

Key

① **Walls of** reinforced concrete and blue-coloured glass form a dense grid.

② **Rose window**

③ **The damaged tower** roof of the former church is one of the best-known symbols of Berlin.

④ **The figure of Christ** is a vast sculpture by Hermann Schaper and once decorated the church altar. It survived World War II damage.

⑤ **Kalser's Mosaic**

Bell Tower
The new hexagonal bell tower stands on the site of the former main nave of the destroyed church.

Tower Clock
The tower is decorated with a clock based on a Classical design.

★ Mosaic of the Hohenzollerns
The mosaic of the Hohenzollerns is in the vestibule. The family is led by Queen Luise and the centre is dominated by Kaiser Wilhelm I.

Orthodox Cross
This cross was a gift from the Russian Orthodox bishops from Volokolamsk and Yuryev, given in memory of the victims of Nazism.

Main entrance

★ Coventry Crucifix
This modest cross was fashioned from nails found in the ashes of Coventry Cathedral, England. The Cathedral was destroyed during German bombing raids in 1940.

Fasanenstrasse – one of the most elegant streets in Berlin

⑨ Fasanenstrasse

Map 11 C2, 12 D1, 12 D3. Ⓤ Uhlandstrasse. 🚌 109, 110, M49, X10, X34.

The discreet charm of Fasanenstrasse, particularly between Lietzenburger Strasse and Kurfürstendamm, has attracted the most exclusive designer shops in the world. Well maintained buildings, *fin-de-siècle* villas set in tranquil gardens, and elegant shop windows of jewellers, art galleries and fashion shops will all entice you to take an afternoon stroll along this street.

It is worth seeing the villas at No. 23–5, which are called the Wintergarten-Ensemble. The first one, No. 23, dates from 1889. Tucked away in a garden, the villa is home to the Literaturhaus, which organizes interesting exhibitions and readings. It has an excellent café that extends into a conservatory. At No. 24 is the Käthe-Kollwitz museum, and No. 25, built in 1892 by Hans Grisebach, accommodates an auction house and art gallery.

⑩ Käthe-Kollwitz-Museum

Fasanenstrasse 24. **Map** 11 C2. **Tel** 882 52 10. Ⓤ Uhlandstrasse or Kurfürstendamm. 🚌 109, 110, 204, 249, X10. **Open** 11am–6pm daily. 📷 🖼 **kaethe-kollwitz.de**

This small private museum provides a unique opportunity to become acquainted with the work of Käthe Kollwitz (1867–1945). Born in Königsberg, the artist settled in Berlin where she married a doctor who worked in Prenzlauer Berg, a working-class district (*see p101*). Her drawings and sculptures portrayed the social problems of the poor, as well as human tragedy and suffering. She frequently took up the theme of motherhood and war after losing a son and grandson in World Wars I and II.

The museum exhibits her work, including sculptures, posters and drawings, as well as letters and photographs.

Mother and Child, from the Käthe-Kollwitz-Museum

⑪ Savignyplatz

Map 11 C1. Ⓢ Savignyplatz. 🚌 M49, X34.

Savignyplatz is enclosed on the south side by the arcade of a railway viaduct, which appears in the film *Cabaret* by Bob Fosse. During the day the square does not look interesting – there are no remarkable buildings, only carefully tended greenery and flower beds. However, the area around the square truly comes alive at night. The dozens of cafés and restaurants fill up, while in summer the entire edge of the square and neighbouring streets turn into one big garden filled with tables and umbrellas. People come from outlying districts to visit popular restaurants and cafés such as Esswein am Fasanenplatz, or Dicke Wirtin (*see p237*). The arcades in the viaduct contain many cafés and bars, and one section has been taken up by the Bücherbogen bookshop (*see p254*).

⑫ Universität der Künste

University of the Arts

Hardenbergstrasse 32–33 and Fasanenstrasse 1b. **Map** 6 D5. Ⓢ Zoologischer Garten or Ⓤ Ernst-Reuter-Platz. 🚌 245, M45, X9. 🖼 **udk-berlin.de**

The Universität der Künste was originally called Preussische Akademie der Künste, which was established in 1696. It continued a long tradition of teaching artists in Berlin and has been headed by well-known figures including Johann Gottfried Schadow and Anton von Werner. As a result of a number of reforms between 1875 and 1882, the Academy was divided into two separate colleges. A complex of buildings was erected for them on Hardenbergstrasse and Fasanenstrasse. The Neo-Baroque buildings were built between 1897 and 1902 to a design by Heinrich Keyser and Karl von Grossheim.

After World War II, only two large buildings, both with decorative façades, survived. On the Hardenbergstrasse side was the Hochschule für Bildende Künste (College for Fine Art), while on the Fasanenstrasse side was the Hochschule für Musik und Darstellende Kunst (College for Music and Performing Arts). Unfortunately, the concert hall did not survive. A new one was built in 1955, designed by Paul Baumgarten.

Bas-relief sculpture on the façade of the Hochschule der Künste

A small *fin-de-siècle* building that looks like a castle, at Hardenbergstrasse No. 36, is a college for religious music which belongs to this group of college buildings.

⓭ Technische Universität
Technical University

Strasse des 17 Juni 135. **Map** 5 C4. Ⓤ Ernst-Reuter-Platz. 🚌 245, M45, X9.

The vast area that lies to the east of Ernst-Reuter-Platz along the Strasse des 17 Juni is occupied by the buildings of the Technische Universität. Officially called Technische Universität Berlin (TUB), it was established in 1879 after the unification of the School of Crafts and the renowned Bauakademie. From its inception the Technische Universität had five different departments, which were all housed, from 1884, in a Neo-Renaissance building designed by Richard Lucae, Friedrich Hitzig and Julius Raschdorff. After World War II, the ruined front wing was rebuilt as a flat block without any divisions, while the rear wings and three internal courtyards retained their original appearance.

It is worth continuing along Strasse des 17 Juni towards the colonnade of the Charlotten-burger Tor (or gate), dating from 1908. The colonnade is ornamented with the figures of Friedrich and Sophie Charlotte holding a model of Schloss Charlottenburg *(see pp164–5)* in their hands. Beyond the gate and to the right, on the island, is an unusual green building with a gigantic pink pipe. This is the centre that monitors water currents and caters to the needs of seagoing vessels.

⓮ Tauentzienstrasse

Map 12 E1. Ⓤ Wittenbergplatz. 🚌 M19, M29, M46.

This is one of the most important streets for trade and commerce in this part of Berlin. Some shops here are not as expensive or as elegant as on Kurfürstendamm – but they attract more visitors for this reason. One of the highlights of the street is the unusual façade of the department store Peek & Clopenburg. Designed by Gottfried Böhm, the walls of the building are covered with transparent, gently slanting and undulating "aprons".

Other highlights include the central bed of colourful flowers, as well as an interesting sculpture entitled *Berlin*. Created by Brigitte and Martin Matschinsky-Denninghoff, the sculpture was erected near Marburger Strasse in 1987 on the occasion of the 750th anniversary of Berlin.

⓯ KaDeWe

Tauentzienstrasse 21–24. **Map** 12 E2. **Tel** 21 21 0. Ⓤ Wittenbergplatz. 🚌 M19, M29, M46. **Open** 10am–8pm Mon–Thu, 10am–9pm Fri, 9:30am–8pm Sat. 🆆 kadewe.de

Kaufhaus des Westens, or KaDeWe, as it is popularly known, is the largest department store in Europe. It was built in 1907 to a design by Emil Schaudt, but it has been extended several times from the original building. From the very beginning KaDeWe was Berlin's most exclusive department store, with a comprehensive collection of goods for sale and with a slogan that ran "In our shop a customer is a king, and the King is a customer".

After World War II, KaDeWe effectively became the symbol of the economic success of West Berlin. You can buy everything here, however the main attraction must be the gourmet's paradise, with the largest collection of foodstuffs in the whole of Europe. Here there are exotic fruits and vegetables, live fish and seafood, 100 varieties of tea, more than 2,400 wines and a host of other gastronomic delights. KaDeWe also has a restaurant, the Wintergarten.

The sculpture *Berlin*, symbolizing the former divided Berlin

AROUND SCHLOSS CHARLOTTENBURG

The area surrounding Schloss Charlottenburg is one of the most enchanting regions of the city, full of greenery and attractive buildings dating from the end of the 19th century. Originally a small settlement called Lützow, it was only when Elector Friedrich III (later King Friedrich I) built his wife's summer retreat here at the end of the 17th century *(see p23)* that this town attained significance. Initially called Schloss Lietzenburg, the palace was renamed Schloss Charlottenburg after the death of Queen Sophie Charlotte. By the 18th century Charlottenburg had become a town, and was for many years an independent administration, inhabited by wealthy people living in elegant villas. It became officially part of Berlin in 1920, and despite World War II and the ensuing division of the city, the central section of this area has kept its historic character.

Sights at a Glance

Museums
❸ Neuer Flügel
❻ Gipsformerei Berlin
❾ Museum Scharf-Gerstenberg
❿ Museum Berggruen
⓫ Bröhan-Museum

Historic Buildings
❶ Schloss Charlottenburg pp164–5
❹ Neuer Pavillon (Schinkel-Pavillon)
❼ Mausoleum
❽ Belvedere
⓬ Schlossstrasse Villas
⓭ Luisenkirche

Parks and Gardens
❺ Schlosspark

Monuments
❷ Reiterdenkmal des Grossen Kurfürsten

☐ Restaurants
see pp238–9

1 Ana e Bruno
2 Brauhaus Lemke
3 Chenab
4 Don Giovanni
5 Engelbecken
6 Eosander
7 Genazvale
8 La Batea
9 Le Piaf
10 Natural'mente
11 Restaurant Kien-Du
12 Taverna Ambrosios

| 0 metres | 600 |
| 0 yards | 600 |

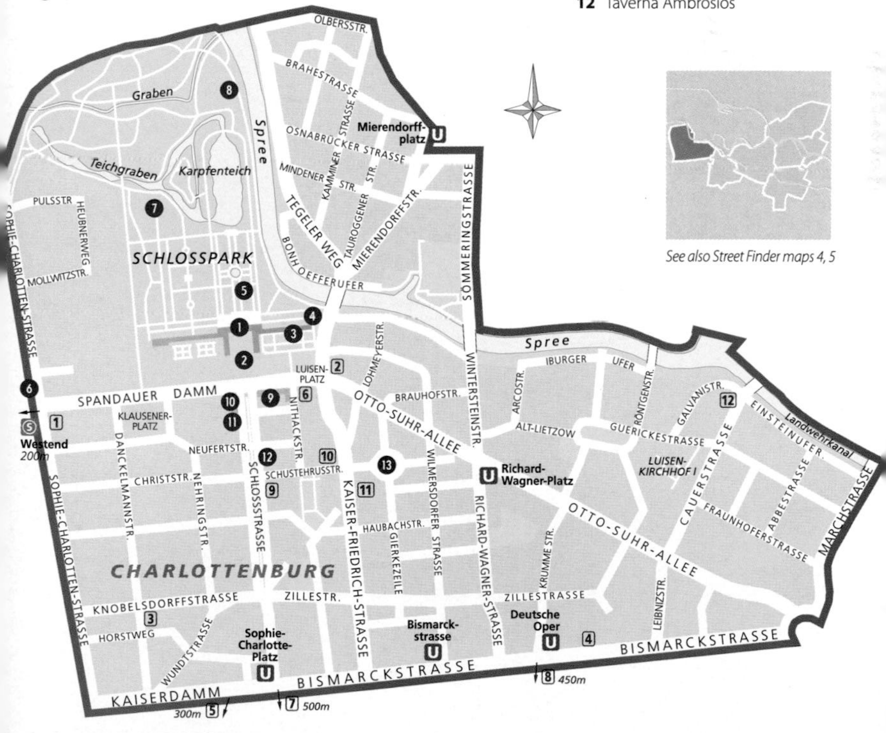

See also Street Finder maps 4, 5

◄ Porzellankabinett, the porcelain gallery inside Schloss Charlottenburg

For map symbols see back flap

Street-by Street: Around the Schloss

The park surrounding the former royal summer residence in Charlottenburg is one of the most picturesque places in Berlin. Visitors are drawn here by the meticulous post-war rebuilding of this luxury Baroque complex and outlying structures, whose marvellous interiors were once home to Prussian nobles. The wings of the palace and its pavilions house interesting exhibitions. After a stroll in the beautiful park, you can take refreshment in the Kleine Orangerie.

① ★ Schloss Charlottenburg
The central section of the palace is called Nering-Eosanderbau, in honour of the architects who designed the building.

② Reiterdenkmal des Grossen Kurfürsten
The momument to the Great Elector was funded by his son King Friedrich I and designed by Andreas Schlüter.

0 metres	150
0 yards	150

Kleine Orangerie

③ Neuer Flügel
The palace's new wing was once home to the royal art collection. Today the building houses changing art and history exhibits.

Key

— Suggested route

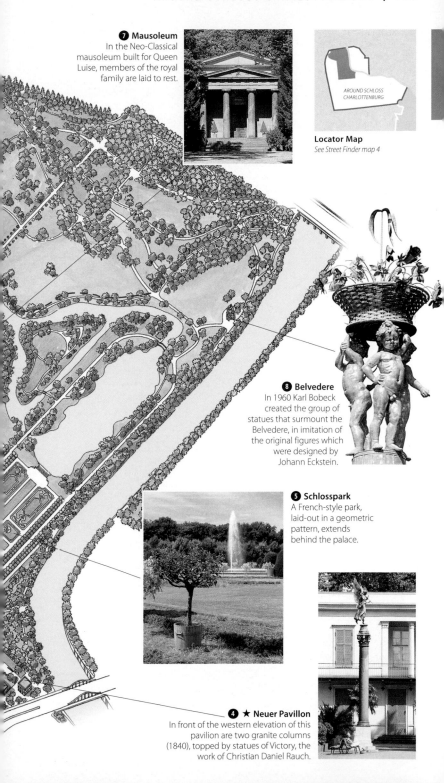

7 Mausoleum
In the Neo-Classical mausoleum built for Queen Luise, members of the royal family are laid to rest.

Locator Map
See Street Finder map 4

8 Belvedere
In 1960 Karl Bobeck created the group of statues that surmount the Belvedere, in imitation of the original figures which were designed by Johann Eckstein.

5 Schlosspark
A French-style park, laid-out in a geometric pattern, extends behind the palace.

4 ★ Neuer Pavillon
In front of the western elevation of this pavilion are two granite columns (1840), topped by statues of Victory, the work of Christian Daniel Rauch.

❶ Schloss Charlottenburg

The palace in Charlottenburg was intended as a summer home for Sophie Charlotte, Elector Friedrich III's wife. Construction began in 1695 to a design by Johann Arnold Nering. Between 1701 and 1713 Johann Friedrich Eosander enlarged the palace, crowning it with a cupola and adding the orangery wing. Subsequent extensions were undertaken by Frederick the Great (Friedrich II), who added the Neuer Flügel, designed by Georg Wenzeslaus von Knobelsdorff, between 1740 and 1746. Restored to its former elegance following World War II, its collection of richly decorated interiors is unequalled in Berlin.

Gallery Guide

The ground floor of Altes Schloss houses the opulent Baroque chambers of Frederick I, a Portrait Gallery and a Porcelain Cabinet. The upper floors incude the apartment of Friedrich Wilhelm IV and a silver and tableware collection.

First floor

Ground floor

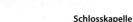

★ Porzellankabinett
This exquisite mirrored gallery has walls lined from top to bottom with a fine display of Japanese and Chinese porcelain.

Schlosskapelle
Only parts of the pulpit in the court chapel are original to the palace. All the other furniture and fittings, including the royal box, are reconstructions.

Main entrance

Façade
The central section of the palace is the oldest part of the building, and is the work of Johann Arnold Nering.

Cupola
The palace's tall, Baroque cupola completes the perspective from Schlossstrasse.

Fortuna
A sculpture by Richard Scheibe crowns the palace, replacing the original statue destroyed during World War II.

Key

- [ ] Official reception rooms
- [ ] Apartments of Sophie-Charlotte
- [ ] Neuer Flügel or Knobelsdorff-Flügel exhibition space
- [ ] Friedrich Wilhelm II's summer apartments
- [ ] Mecklenburg apartments
- [ ] Apartments of Friedrich Wilhelm IV
- [ ] Friedrich Wilhelm II's winter apartments
- [ ] Frederick the Great's apartments

VISITORS' CHECKLIST

Practical Information
Luisenplatz.
Map 4 E2. Altes Schloss (Nering-Eosanderbau):
Tel (0331) 96 94 200.
W spsg.de
Open 10am–6pm Tue–Sun (to 5pm Nov–Mar). compulsory on ground floor only.
Neuer Flügel (Knobelsdorff-Flügel):
Tel (0331) 96 94 200.
Open 10am–6pm Wed–Mon (to 5pm Nov–Mar).

Transport
U Richard-Wagner-Platz & Sophie-Charlotte-Platz. S Westend. 109, 145, 210, X21.

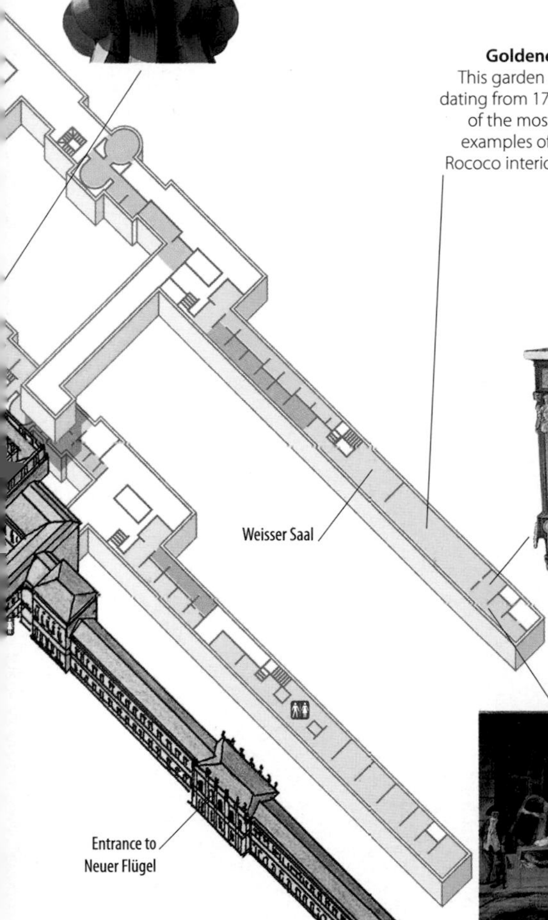

Goldene Galerie
This garden ballroom dating from 1746 is one of the most creative examples of Prussian Rococo interior design.

Weisser Saal

Entrance to Neuer Flügel

Neuer Flügel
The new wing holds the elegant apartments and exquisite furniture of Frederick Wilhelm III.

★ **Gersaint's Shop Sign** (1720)
An avid collector of French painting, Frederick the Great bought this and other fine canvases by Antoine Watteau for his collection.

The Monument to the Great Elector standing in front of Schloss Charlottenburg

❷ Reiterdenkmal des Grossen Kurfürsten

Monument to the Great Elector

Luisenplatz. **Map** 4 E2.
U Richard-Wagner-Platz & Sophie-Charlotte-Platz. **S** Westend.
🚌 109, 309, M45.

The statue of the Great Elector (Friedrich Wilhelm) is the finest in Berlin and was paid for by his son, Elector Friedrich III (later King Friedrich I). Designed by Andreas Schlüter to be cast in one piece, the statue was started in 1696 but not finished until 1703. It was initially erected near the former Berlin palace, by Lange Brücke (now called Rathausbrücke). The statue was moved to safety during World War II but ironically, on the return journey, the barge transporting the monument sank in the port of Tegel.

In 1949 the statue was retrieved intact from the water and erected in the courtyard of Schloss Charlottenburg. However, it lacked the original base which was left behind in East Berlin, so a copy was commissioned. The original base finally ended up in the Bode-Museum topped with a replica of the statue. The statue portrays the Great Elector as a warrior in ancient armour (albeit wearing a 17th-century wig) mounted on horse-back, triumphant over the figures of prisoners of war around the base. The base itself is decorated with patriotic reliefs of allegorical scenes. One scene depicts the kingdom surrounded by figures representing History, Peace and the Spree river; another shows the kingdom protected by embodiments of Faith, Bravery (in the form of Mucius Scaevola) and Strength (represented by the figure of Hercules).

❸ Neuer Flügel

Luisenplatz (Schloss Charlottenburg–Neuer Flügel). **Map** 4 E2. **Tel** (0331) 969 4200. **U** Richard-Wagner-Platz & Sophie-Charlotte-Platz. **S** Westend. 🚌 109, 309, M45. **Open** Apr–Oct: 10am–6pm Wed–Mon; Nov–Mar: 10am–5pm Wed–Mon.

Built between 1740 and 1747, the new wing of Schloss Charlottenburg used to house the popular Galerie der Romantik. The main part of this collection of Romantic paintings has now been returned to the Alte Nationalgalerie *(see p80)*. The rest have been moved to the Neuer Pavillon. In its place, the new wing houses Frederick the Great's private quarters. Items on display include paintings he acquired and curiosities such as his collection of snuff boxes. The wing also hosts temporary art and history exhibitions.

❹ Neuer Pavillon (Schinkel-Pavillon)

Luisenplatz (Schlosspark Charlottenburg). **Map** 4 F2. **Tel** (0331) 969 4200. **U** Richard-Wagner-Platz & Sophie-Charlotte-Platz. **S** Westend. 🚌 109, 309, M45. **Open** Apr–Oct: 10am–6pm Tue–Sun; Nov–Mar: 10am–5pm Tue–Sun. 🅿

This charming Neo-Classical pavilion, with its clean lines and first-floor balcony, was built for Friedrich Wilhelm III and his second wife, Princess Auguste von Liegnitz. During a visit to Naples, the king stayed in the Villa Reale del Chiamonte and was so impressed that he commissioned Karl Friedrich Schinkel to build him something similar. The pavilion was finished for the king's birthday on 3 August 1825. Schinkel designed a two-storey structure with a central staircase and ranged the rooms around it in perfect symmetry. Pillared galleries, on the first floor, added variety to the eastern and western elevations. A cast-iron balcony runs around the entire

The Neuer Pavillon which was modelled on a Neapolitan villa

French-style garden in the Schloss Charlottenburg park

structure. Like many other Schloss Charlottenburg buildings, the pavilion burned down totally in World War II and was rebuilt in 1960. It reopened after renovations in 2011.

The display inside the pavilion reveals the original splendour and atmosphere of the aristocratic interiors, enhanced with pictures and sculptures of the period. The prize picture is a renowned panorama of Berlin dated 1834, painted by Eduard Gärtner from the roof of the Friedrichs-werdersche Kirche *(see p65).* You can also admire paintings by Karl Friedrich Schinkel, who was not only a great architect but also a fine painter of fabulous architectural fantasies.

❺ Schlosspark
Palace Park

Luisenplatz (Schloss Charlottenburg). **Map** 4 D1. Ⓤ Richard-Wagner-Platz & Sophie-Charlotte-Platz. Ⓢ Westend. 109, 309, M45.

This extensive royal park surrounding Schloss Charlotten-burg *(see pp164–5),* criss-crossed with tidy gravel paths, is a favourite place for Berliners to stroll at the weekend. The park is largely the result of reconstruction work carried out after World War II, when 18th-century prints were used to help reconstruct the varied layout of the original grounds. Immediately behind Schloss Charlottenburg is a French-style Baroque garden, made to a

strict geometrical design with a vibrant patchwork of flower beds, carefully trimmed shrubs and ornate fountains adorned with replicas of antique sculptures. Further away from the palace, beyond the curved carp lake, is a less formal English-style landscaped park, the original layout of which was created between 1819 and 1828 under the direction of the renowned royal gardener, Peter Joseph Lenné. The lakes and waterways of the park are the habitat of various water fowl including herons. A bike path stretches along the Spree river from the palace park to the Grosses Tiergarten and beyond.

❻ Gipsformerei Berlin
Replica Workshop

Sophie-Charlotten-Strasse 17–18. **Map** 4 D3. **Tel** 326 769 11. Ⓤ Sophie-Charlotte-Platz. Ⓢ Westend. 309, M45. **Open** 9am–4pm Mon–Fri, 9am–6pm Wed.

Founded by Friedrich Wilhelm III in 1819, the Gipsformerei produces original-size replicas from items in Berlin museums and other collections. The first head of the workshop that also repairs damaged sculptures was renowned sculptor Christian Daniel Rauch.

Visitors are welcome to this modest brick building west of Schloss Charlottenburg and can purchase items on the spot or choose from catalogues to have them made to order and

shipped home. Sculptures are generally copied in white plaster or painted true to the original. Most moulds originate from the Middle Ages, the Renaissance and the 19th century.

❼ Mausoleum

Luisenplatz (Schlosspark Charlotten-burg). **Map** 4 D2. **Tel** 32 09 14 46. Ⓤ Richard-Wagner-Platz & Sophie-Charlotte-Platz. Ⓢ Westend. 109, 309, M45. **Open** Apr–Oct: 10am–6pm Tue–Sun. **Closed** Nov–Mar.

Queen Luise, the beloved wife of Friedrich Wilhelm III, was laid to rest in this dignified, modest building, set among the trees in Schlosspark. The mausoleum was designed by Karl Friedrich Schinkel, in the style of a Doric portico-fronted temple.

In the original design, the queen's sarcophagus was housed in the crypt while the tombstone (actually a cenotaph sculpted by Christian Daniel Rauch) stood in the centre of the mausoleum. After the death of Friedrich Wilhelm in 1840, the mausoleum was refurbished, an apse added and the queen's tomb moved to one side, leaving room for her husband's tomb, also designed by Rauch. The second wife of the king, Princess Auguste von Liegnitz, was also buried in the crypt of the mausoleum, but without a tombstone.

Between the years 1890 and 1894, the tombs of Kaiser Wilhelm I and his wife, Auguste von Sachsen-Weimar, were added to the crypt. Both monuments are the work of Erdmann Encke.

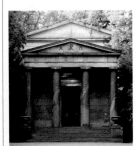

The Schinkel-designed Mausoleum, final resting place of German royalty

The Belvedere's Baroque flourishes and clean Neo-Classical lines

❽ Belvedere

Spandauer Damm 20–24 (Schlosspark Charlottenburg). **Map** 4 E1. **Tel** 32 09 14 45. ⓤ Richard-Wagner-Platz & Sophie-Charlotte-Platz. ⓢ Westend. 🚌 109, 309, M45. **Open** Apr–Oct: 10am–6pm Tue–Sun; Nov–Mar: noon–4pm Sat, Sun & hols.

The Belvedere is a summer house in the Schlosspark which served as a tea pavilion for Friedrich Wilhelm II and, in times of war, as a watchtower. It dates from 1788 and was designed by Carl Gotthard Langhans. The architect mixed Baroque and Neo-Classical elements, giving the building an oval central structure with four straight-sided annexes. The building is crowned by a low dome topped with a sculpture of three cherubs dragging a basket of flowers.

Ruined during World War II, the summer house was reconstructed between 1956 and 1960 and adapted to serve as exhibition space. The exhibition is a large collection of porcelain from the Berlin Königliche Porzellan-Manufaktur (Royal Porcelain Workshop), which has pieces from the Rococo period up to late Biedermeier, including some outstanding individual items.

❾ Museum Scharf-Gerstenberg

Schlossstrasse 70. **Map** 4 E3. **Tel** 266 42 42 42. ⓤ Richard-Wagner-Platz & Sophie-Charlotte-Platz. ⓢ Westend. 🚌 309, M45. **Open** 10am–6pm Tue–Sun. 🎨

The two pavilions on either side of Schlossstrasse were intended as officers barracks for the King's Guard du Corps. Built between the years 1851 and

Odilon Redon's work in pastel, Museum Scharf-Gerstenberg

1859 by Friedrich August Stüler, they were inspired by a design by King Friedrich Wilhelm IV. The eastern pavilion joins the stable block and once housed the Ägyptisches Museum (Egyptian Museum), which has now moved to its original location, the Neues Museum, on Museum Island.

Since the departure of the Egyptian Museum, the Marstall (stable block) has housed the Museum Scharf-Gerstenberg. Titled "Surreal World", the museum presents paintings, sculptures and works on paper by Surrealist artists such as Goya, Piranesi and Redon, but also modern works by Dalí, Magritte, Max Ernst, Paul Klee and Dubuffet. More than 250 objects are presented over three floors, explaining the history of surreal art, with pieces from almost all the leading Surrealists. A film programme features classic Surrealist films by Luis Buñuel and Salvador Dalí.

❿ Museum Berggruen

Schlossstrasse 1. **Map** 4 E3. **Tel** 266 42 42 42. ⓤ Richard-Wagner-Platz & Sophie-Charlotte-Platz. ⓢ Westend. 🚌 109, 309, M45. **Open** 10am–6pm Tue–Sun. 🏛 ♿ 📷

Heinz Berggruen assembled this tasteful collection of art dating from the late 19th and first half of the 20th century. Born and educated in Berlin, he emigrated to the US in 1936, spent most of his life in Paris, but finally entrusted his collection to the city of his birth. The museum opened in what was once the west pavilion of the barracks using space freed up by moving the Antikensammlung to Museum Island (see p77). The exhibition halls were modified according to the designs of Hilmer and Sattler, who also designed the layout of the Gemäldegalerie. The Museum Berggruen is particularly well known for its large collection of quality paintings, drawings and gouaches by Pablo Picasso.

Pablo Picasso's *Woman in a Hat* (1939), Museum Berggruen

The collection begins with a drawing from his student days in 1897 and ends with works he painted in 1972, one year before his death. In addition to these, the museum displays more than 60 works by Swiss artist Paul Klee and more than 20 works by Henri Matisse. The museum also houses paintings by other major artists, such as Van Gogh, Braque and Cézanne. The collection is supplemented by some excellent sculptures, particularly those of Henri Laurens and Alberto Giacometti.

⓫ Bröhan-Museum

Schlossstrasse 1a. **Map** 4 E3. **Tel** 32 69 06 00. Ⓤ Richard-Wagner-Platz & Sophie-Charlotte-Platz. Ⓢ Westend. 🚌 109, 309, M45. **Open** 10am–6pm Tue–Sun. **Closed** 24 & 31 Dec. 🅿 🕸 **broehan-museum.de**

Located in a late Neo-Classical building which, like the Museum Berggruen, was formerly used as army barracks, is this small but interesting museum. The collection of decorative arts was amassed by Karl H Bröhan, who from 1966 collected works of art from the Art Nouveau (Jugendstil or Secessionist) and Art Deco styles. The paintings of the artists particularly connected with the Berlin Secessionist movement, such as Karl Hagermeister and Hans

Art Deco vase, Brohan-Museum

The Great Elector (1620–88)

The Elector Friedrich Wilhelm was one of the most famous rulers of the Hohenzollern dynasty. He inherited the position of Elector of Brandenburg in 1640. Brandenburg-Prussia, founded in 1618, was subject to the Polish crown. One of his first duties was to rebuild the region after the devastation of the 30 Years' War *(see p23)* and in 1660 he wrested the territory from Poland. During the course of his reign, Berlin became a powerful city. Rich families from all over Europe, fleeing persecution in their own land, chose to settle in Berlin – wealthy Dutch merchants, Huguenots from France and Jews from Vienna following the Edict of Potsdam (1685).

Baluschek, are especially well represented. Alongside the paintings there are fine examples of other media and crafts: furniture, ceramics, glass-ware, silverwork and textiles. Each of the main halls features an individual artist, but often using an array of artistic media. There is also a display of furniture by Hector Guimard, Eugène Gaillard, Henri van de Velde and Joseph Hoffmann, glasswork by Emile Gallé, and porcelain from the best European manufacturers.

⓬ Schlossstrasse Villas

Schlossstrasse 65–6/. **Map** 4 E3. Ⓤ Sophie-Charlotte-Platz. 🚌 309.

Most of the historic villas and buildings that once graced Schlossstrasse no longer exist. However, careful restoration of a few villas enables the visitor to get a feel for what the atmosphere must have been like at the end of the 19th century. It is worth taking a stroll down Schlossstrasse to look at three of the reno-vated villas – No. 65, No. 66 and especially No. 67. The latter villa was built in 1873, in a Neo-Classical style to a design by G Töbelmann. After World War II, the building was refurbished to return it to its former splendour. The front garden,

however, a characteristic of the area, was only returned to its original state in 1986, when several villas had their gardens restored. If you continue the walk down the nearby Schustehrusstrasse, there is an interesting school building at No. 39–43 linked to the Villa Oppenheim since the end of the 19th century.

⓭ Luisenkirche
Luise Church

Giekerplatz 4. **Map** 4 F3. **Tel** 341 90 61. Ⓤ Richard-Wagner-Platz & Sophie-Charlotte-Platz. 🚌 109, M45. **Open** 9am–1pm Mon, Tue, Thu & Fri, 2–6pm Wed & during Sunday service (10am).

This small church has undergone a series of re-designs and refurb-ishments in its lifetime. The original plans by Philipp Gerlach were first adapted by Martin Böhme, before the church was built (1713–16). Its Baroque styling was removed in the next course of rebuilding, undertaken by Karl Friedrich Schinkel from 1823 to 1826, when the church was renamed in memory of Queen Luise, who died in 1810. The last refurbishment took place after the church suffered major damage during World War II.

The shape of the church is based on a traditional Greek cross, with a tower at the front. The interior fixtures and fittings are not the originals, and the elegant stained-glass windows were only made in 1956.

FURTHER AFIELD

Berlin is an extensive city with a totally unique character, shaped by its history. Up until 1920 the actual city of Berlin consisted only of the present districts Mitte, Tiergarten, Wedding, Prenzlauer Berg, Friedrichshain and Kreuzberg. It was surrounded by satellite towns and villages, which for many years had been evolving independently. Each of these had its own administrative centre, parish church and individual architecture. Some of these town's residents still speak of "going to Berlin" when ultimately they are simply hopping on a bus a few stops.

In 1920, as part of great administrative reforms, seven towns were incorporated into Berlin, along with 59 communes and 27 country estates. This reform effected the creation of an entirely new city occupying around 900 sq km (348 sq miles), with a population that had expanded to 3.8 million.

In this way the range of the metropolis extended and Berlin now had leafy suburbs and boroughs of medieval origins, such as Spandau. Villages, private estates and palaces, such as Schloss Britz and Schloss Schoenhausen were absorbed into Berlin. (Even Schloss Charlottenburg was outside the city limits until 1920.) Industralization called for workers and means of transporting and housing them. Residential and commerical construction boomed following the city enlargement.

Over the following decades the faces of many of these boroughs changed. Modern housing developments have arisen together with industrial centres, although some places have kept their small-town or rural character. Thanks to this diversity, a stay in Berlin can equal visiting several cities simultaneously. A short journey by S-Bahn enables you to travel from the cosmopolitan city centre of the 21st century to the vast forests of the Grunewald, Peacock Island or the beach at Wannsee. You can explore everything from Dahlem's tranquil streets lined with villas, to Spandau's Renaissance citadel, cobbled lanes and vast Gothic church of St Nicholas – all just half an hour away from the centre and well worth a visit.

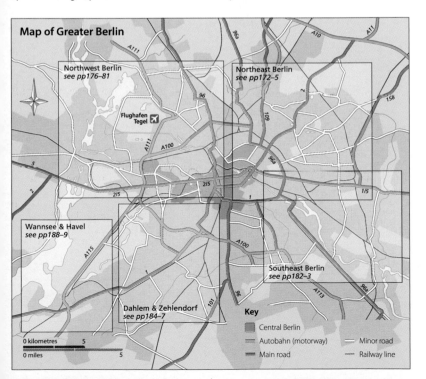

Map of Greater Berlin

Northwest Berlin
see pp176–81

Northeast Berlin
see pp172–5

Flughafen Tegel

Wannsee & Havel
see pp188–9

Southeast Berlin
see pp182–3

Dahlem & Zehlendorf
see pp184–7

Key

Central Berlin

Autobahn (motorway)

Main road

Minor road

Railway line

0 kilometres 5

0 miles 5

◄ Statue of Kaiser Wilhelm inside Grunewaldturm *(see p189)*

For additional map symbols *see back flap*

Northeast Berlin

To the north, the Baroque palace of Schönhausen is a real attraction in the middle of Pankow's Schlosspark gardens. From here it is worth visiting the Weissensee district, which has one of the largest Jewish cemeteries in Europe. Walking the partly neglected grounds is a haunting experience. Hohenschön-hausen in the very east of the district is home to the Stasi Gedenkstätte, a museum and memorial on the grounds of East Germany's main secret service prison.

A section of the garden elevation of Schloss Niederschönhausen

❶ Schloss Schönhausen

Tschaikowskistrasse 1. **Tel** (0331) 96 94 200. Ⓢ & Ⓤ Pankow. 🚌 150, 250. 🚊 M1. **Open** Apr–Oct: 10am–6pm Thu–Sun; Nov–Mar: 10am–5pm Sat, Sun & hols. 🎫

This palace, located in an extensive and picturesque park, belonged to the von Dohna family during the 17th century. Ownership of the estate passed to the Elector Friedrich III in 1691, for whom Johann Arnold Nering designed the palace. In 1704 it was extended to a design by Johann Friedrich Eosander von Göthe, who added side wings. The palace was home to Queen Christine, estranged wife of Frederick the Great, between 1740 and 1797. In 1763 further extensive refurbishment was undertaken by architect Johann Boumann. The property remained in the hands of the Prussian royal family for the next hundred years. Among those who resided here were Princess Auguste von Liegnitz, following the death of her husband, King Friedrich Wilhelm III.

After World War II the rebuilt palace was occupied by the president of the German Demo-cratic Republic, Wilhelm Pieck. In 1990 Round Table discussions were held here and the treaty to reunify Germany was signed here on 3 October that year.

Make time for a stroll through the vast park, which has kept the character bestowed by Peter Joseph Lenné in the 1820s.

❷ Gethsemane-kirche

Stargader Strasse 77. **Tel** 44 57 745. Ⓤ & Ⓢ Schönhauser Allee. 🕚 11am Sun.

This Neo-Gothic red-brick church is the most famous church in the area as it played a crucial role in East Germany's peaceful revolution. The neighbourhood is dominated by the Protestant Gethsemanekirche, which dates back to 1890. The church was

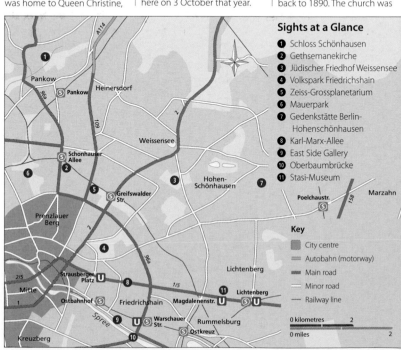

Sights at a Glance

❶ Schloss Schönhausen
❷ Gethsemanekirche
❸ Jüdischer Friedhof Weissensee
❹ Volkspark Friedrichshain
❺ Zeiss-Grossplanetarium
❻ Mauerpark
❼ Gedenkstätte Berlin-Hohenschönhausen
❽ Karl-Marx-Allee
❾ East Side Gallery
❿ Oberbaumbrücke
⓫ Stasi-Museum

Key

▪ City centre
▬ Autobahn (motorway)
▬ Main road
— Minor road
— Railway line

0 kilometres   2
0 miles   2

one of several built on the order of Emperor Wilhelm II, who wanted to increase religious worship among the mostly Social Democratic working-classes living in Prenzlauer Berg and other areas. The building was designed by August Orth (1828–1911), one of the period's most important architects of churches and railway stations.

The Protestant community here is proud to have pioneered civil rights movements, and hosted political Anti-Nazi rallies from 1933–45. The congregation also questioned the Socialist regime after World War II, while the church itself served as an assembly hall for peaceful opponents in October 1989. On 2 October that year, the praying crowd was brutally attacked by the East German secret service police, marking the start of the Communist regime's demise.Today, the square is surrounded by beautiful restored buildings, housing many sidewalk restaurants, cafés and quaint little shops. Only a few steps away is Kollwitzplatz (see p107), a welcoming, leafy square with an atmosphere reminiscent of Paris. Nearby Kollwitzstrasse is home to an organic farmers' market on Saturdays.

Entrance to the red-brick Gethsemanekirche

❸ Jüdischer Friedhof Weissensee

Herbert-Baum-Strasse 45. **Tel** 925 33 30. Ⓢ Greifswalder Strasse, then 🚋 12, M4, M13. 🚌 156, 200. **Open** Apr–Sep: 7:30am–5pm Mon–Thu, 7:30am–2:30pm Fri, 8am–5pm Sun; Oct–Mar: 7:30am–4pm Mon–Thu, 7:30am–2:30pm Fri, 8am–4pm Sun. **Closed** Sat & public hols.

This extensive Jewish cemetery, established in 1880 according to a design by Hugo Licht, is the final resting place for more than 115,000 Berliners, many of whom were victims of Nazi persecution. It is chilling to note that many surnames listed on gravestones simply no longer exist in Germany, due to whole familes being eradicated or driven out of the country.

By the main entrance is a place of remembrance for the victims of the Holocaust, with plaques bearing the names of the concentration camps. Buried here are renowned figures from Berlin's Jewish cultural and commercial past. Among others here rest the publisher Samuel Fischer and the restaurateur Berthold Kempinski.

Some tombstones are out-standing works of art, such as that of the Panowsky family, designed by Ludwig Hoffmann, or the Cubist tombstone of Albert Mendel, designed by Walter Gropius. Some family graves are adorned with temple-like structures. The Nazis left this burial ground largely unharmed.

In 1999 the cemetery was desecrated in an act of anti-Semitic vandalism. Over 100 headstones were kicked over and some were smeared with swastikas.

Still in use today, most of the new graves belong to Jewish immigrants from the former Soviet Union, who outnumber the German-born Jews in Berlin.

Neo-Baroque Märchenbrunnen in Volkspark Friedrichshain

❹ Volkspark Friedrichshain

Am Friedrichshain/Friedenstrasse. **Map** 10 F1. 🚌 142, 200. 🚋 M5, M6, M8, M10.

This extensive park complex of Friedrichshain, with its picturesque nooks and crannies, was one of Berlin's first public parks. It was laid out in the 1840s on the basis of a design by landscape architect Peter Joseph Lenné, with the idea of creating an alternative Tiergarten for the inhabitants of the eastern districts of the city. The greatest attraction of the park is the Fountain of Fairy Tales – Märchenbrunnen by Ludwig Hoffmann, built from 1902 until 1913. It is a spectacular feature, in a Neo-Baroque style with fountain pools made from Tivoli stone, decorated with small statues of turtles and other animals. The fountain is surrounded by well-known characters from the fairy tales by the Brothers Grimm. The park's frequent redesigns included, during World War II, the construction of two large bunkers. After the war the site was covered with a mound of earth.

Between the years 1969 and 1973 a sports and games area was established in the park, although there is still plenty of room for leisurely strolls. For the adventurous, there is a challenging outdoor climbing wall.

Silvery dome of the Zeiss-Grossplanetarium

❺ Zeiss-Gross-planetarium

Prenzlauer Allee 80 (Ernst-Thälmann-Park). Tel 42 18 450 (reservations). Ⓢ Prenzlauer Allee, then 🚌 156. 🚊 M2. **Open** call for details. 📷

The silvery dome visible from afar is the huge planetarium, built in the grounds of a park dedicated to the memory of the inter-war communist leader Ernst Thälmann, who died at Buchenwald concentration camp. The foyer of the planetarium houses an exhibition of optical equipment and various accessories produced by the renowned factory of Carl-Zeiss-Jena.

❻ Mauerpark

Mauerpark, Gleimstrasse. Ⓤ Bernauer Strasse, Eberswalder Strasse. 🚊 M10. Flea market: **Open** 10am-6pm Sun, Bernauer Strasse.

Mauerpark is a largely tree-less expense of lawn, one of the very few extended green spaces in Prenzlauer Berg and a magnet for young locals and tourists alike. Although a little claustrophobic on warm days, it is a great spot for people-watching. On Sundays, aspiring pop stars can attempt karaoke at the amphitheatre and perform to a packed audience. Children love the park and an artificial rock can be climbed under professional supervision. The giant eclectic flea market held on weekends next to the park attracts huge crowds of

mostly 20-somethings looking for a special bargain from Berlin, be it junk or vintage. Vegan burgers and cold beers complete the experience, which can be a welcome treat after seeing the haunting Wall Memorial nearby (see p113). The Mauerweg, a shared walking and bicycle path, follows the path of the old Wall right across Mauerpark.

❼ Gedenkstätte Berlin-Hohen-schönhausen

Genslerstrasse 13a. **Tel** 9860 82 30. Ⓤ & Ⓢ Lichtenberg, then 🚌 256 to Liebenwalderstrasse/Genslerstrasse. 🚊 16 to Genslerstrasse, M5 to Freienwalder, M6. **Open** 9am–6pm daily. 📷 (in German) 11am, 1pm, 3pm Mon–Fri, every hour from 10am–4pm Sat, Sun & hols. In English: 2:30pm Wed, Sat & Sun.

This museum was established in 1995 in the former custody building of the Stasi – the dreaded security service of the GDR. The custody building was part of a huge complex built in 1938. In May 1945 the occupying Russian authorities created a special transit camp here, in which they interned war criminals subsequently transported to Siberia. Shortly thereafter they started to bring anyone under political suspicion to the camp. During this time more than 20,000 people passed through here.

From 1946 this group of buildings was refashioned into the custody area for the KGB (Soviet Secret Service), and in 1951 it was given over for the use of the Stasi.

During a visit you can see prisoners' cells and interrogation rooms. Housed in the cellars was the "submarine" – a series of cells for the most "dangerous" suspects.

❽ Karl-Marx-Allee

Map 10 F3. Ⓤ Strausberger Platz, Frankfurter Tor or Weberwiese. 🚊 M10.

The section of Karl-Marx-Allee between Strausberger Platz and Frankfurter Tor is effectively a huge open-air museum of Socialist Realist architecture. The route leading east to Poland and Moscow, was named Stalinallee in 1949 and chosen as the site for the construction showpiece of the new German Democratic Republic. The avenue was widened to 90 m (300 ft) and in the course of the next ten years, huge residential

Façade of Gedenkstätte Berlin-Hohenschönhausen

tower blocks and a row of shops were built on it. The designers, led by architect Hermann Henselmann, succeeded in combining three sets of architectural guidelines. They used the style known in the Soviet Union as "pastry chef" according to the precept "nationalistic in form but socialist in content", and linked the whole work to Berlin's own traditions. Hence there are motifs taken from famous Berlin architects Schinkel and Gontard, as well as from the renowned Meissen porcelain.

The buildings on this street, renamed Karl-Marx-Allee in 1961, are now considered historic monuments. The buildings have been cleaned up and the crumbling details are gradually being restored.

The Eastern end of Karl-Marx-Allee continues as Frankfurter Allee. Its shabby side streets have yet to be gentrified unlike the Prenzlauer Berg or Kreuzberg districts. Street art is everywhere and many buildings are former squats, but the atmosphere here is vibrant and relaxed. There is a young feel to the area as most residents are in their mid-twenties, drawn to the alternative cafés and happening sub-culture bars.

Fragment of Socialist Realist decoration from Karl-Marx-Allee

❾ East Side Gallery

Mühlenstrasse. Ⓢ & Ⓤ Warschauer Strasse. Ⓢ Ostbahnhof. 🚌 140, 240. 🚊 M10.

Since 1990, this 1,300-m (1 mile) section of the Berlin Wall along Mühlenstrasse between Hauptbahnhof and Oberbaumbrücke has been known as the East Side Gallery. A huge collection of graffiti on display here, the work of 118

Exterior of the Stasi-Museum – headquarters of the secret service

different artists from 21 countries, organized by the Scottish artist Chris MacLean, was restored in 2009 to mark the 20th anniversary of the fall of the Wall.

❿ Oberbaumbrücke

Ⓢ & Ⓤ Warschauer Strasse Ⓤ Schlesisches Tor. 🚌 347. 🚊 M10.

This pretty bridge crossing the Spree river was built from 1894 to 1896 to a design by Otto Stahn. It is made from reinforced concrete, but the arches are covered with red brick. The central arch is marked by a pair of crenellated Neo-Gothic towers. The most decorative element of the bridge, a Neo-Gothic arcade, supports a line of the U-Bahn.

The bridge was not open to traffic for 12 or so years prior to reunification, as it linked districts from opposing sides of the Berlin Wall. Only pedestrians with the relevant documents were able to use this bridge. After reunification and renovation, it was returned to full working order.

The picturesque Neo-Gothic archway of Oberbaumbrücke

⓫ Forschungs- und Gedenkstätte Normannenstrasse (Stasi-Museum)

Ruschestrasse 103 (Haus 1). **Tel** 553 68 54. Ⓤ Magdalenenstrasse. **Open** 11am–6pm Mon–Fri, 2–6pm Sat & Sun. 🚗 🌐 **stasimusem.de**

Under the German Democratic Republic, this huge complex of buildings at Ruschestrasse housed the Ministry of the Interior and the infamous Stasi (GDR secret service) headquarters. The Stasi's "achievements" in infiltrating its own community were without equal in the Eastern bloc.

Since 1990 one of the buildings has housed a museum that describes the organizational structure, history and ideology of the Stasi. It includes photographs and documents depicting the Stasi's activities. The break up of the Stasi is covered, as well as an overview of subsequen events, leading up to the reunion of Germany.

A model of the headquarters is on display, as well as equipment used for bugging and spying on citizens. You can also walk around the office of the infamous Stasi chief Erich Mielke, the commander of Ministry for State Security. A "big-brother"-like figure, Mielke's legacy of suffering still lives on in the memory of millions of German citizens. The interior is just as it was when the Stasis used the complex.

Northwest Berlin

A visit to this part of the city provides a chance to see the grandeur of the Olympiastadion, which was inspired by the monumental architecture of ancient Rome. Nearby stands the monolithic Le Corbusier Haus, once regarded as the model for future housing. The historic town of Spandau has some pretty medieval streets and a well-preserved Renaissance citadel. Another attraction is the Messegelände, home of renowned trade fairs, and crowned by the Funkturm radio tower.

Le Corbusier Haus, by the renowned French architect

❶ Le Corbusier Haus

Flatowallee 16. Ⓢ Olympiastadion. 🚌 149, 218. 📷 1st Sat of month in summer, register online.
🄌 **corbusierhaus-berlin.de**

This apartment building by Le Corbusier, on a hill near the site of the Olympiastadion, was this architect's entry to the 1957 Interbau Exhibition (see p137). Following World War II, there was a housing shortage all over Europe. Le Corbusier's innovative design for what he called a *Unité d'Habitation* was his attempt to create fully self-sufficient housing estates in answer to this problem. He built three of these complexes, the most famous being in Marseilles. For his Berlin design, Le Corbusier wanted to build over 500 two-storey apartments with integral services, such as a post office, shops, a sports hall and nursery school. The structure fell short of Le Corbusier's aspirations as financial pressure meant the estate lacked some service elements; in addition, structural alterations changed the building's proportions from the original plans. Nevertheless, the monolithic building was a milestone for West-Berlin's post-war architecture. For some, it has always remained the "Wohnmaschine" (dwelling machine) and they criticise the jail-like hallways, called "streets" by the architect. Others praise the Bauhaus-inspired clear lines, airy, light-filled apartments and the architectural departure from ornamental features.

Functionality triumphs in this "vertical city" and the view over the Grunewald and to the TV tower in the east is spectacular. Most of the 1,000 residents own condos in the building.

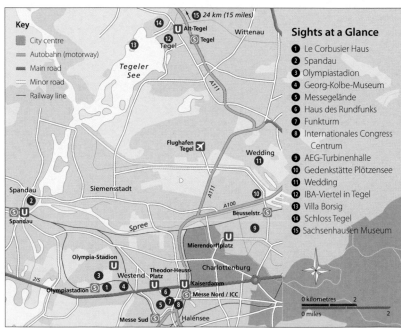

Key

▨ City centre
▬▬ Autobahn (motorway)
▬▬ Main road
∷∷∷ Minor road
— Railway line

Sights at a Glance

❶ Le Corbusier Haus
❷ Spandau
❸ Olympiastadion
❹ Georg-Kolbe-Museum
❺ Messegelände
❻ Haus des Rundfunks
❼ Funkturm
❽ Internationales Congress Centrum
❾ AEG-Turbinenhalle
❿ Gedenkstätte Plötzensee
⓫ Wedding
⓬ IBA-Viertel in Tegel
⓭ Villa Borsig
⓮ Schloss Tegel
⓯ Sachsenhausen Museum

0 kilometres   2
0 miles   2

❷ Spandau

Zitadelle Spandau Am Juliusturm 64.
Tel 354 94 40. 🚇 Zitadelle.
🚌 X33. **Open** 10am–5pm daily. 🅿
🌐 **zitadelle-spandau.de**

Spandau is one of the oldest towns within the area of greater Berlin, and it has managed to retain a distinct character for itself. Evidence of the earliest settlement dates back to the 8th century, although the town of Spandau was only granted a charter in 1232. The area was spared the worst of the World War II bombing, so there are still some interesting sights to visit. The heart of the town is a network of medieval streets with a picturesque market

The Hohenzollern coat of arms above the main gate of the citadel

Interior of the Gothic St-Nikolai-Kirche in Spandau

square and a number of original timber-framed houses; in the north of Spandau sections of town wall still stand, dating from the 15th century. In the centre of town is the magnificent Gothic St-Nikolai-Kirche dating from the 15th century. The church holds many valuable ecclesiastical furnishings, such as a splendid Renaissance stone altar from the end of the 16th century, a Baroque pulpit from around 1700 which came from a royal palace in Potsdam, a Gothic baptismal font and many epitaphs. A castle was first built on the site of the Zitadelle Spandau (citadel) in the 12th

Crowned black Prussian eagle

century, but today only the 36-m (120-ft) Juliusturm (tower) remains. In 1560 the building of a fort was begun here, to a design by Francesco Chiaramella da Gandino. It took 30 years to bring to completion, however, and most of the work was supervised by architect Rochus Guerrini, Graf zu Lynar. Though the citadel had a jail, Rudolf Hess, Spandau's most infamous resident, was incarcerated a short distance away in a military prison after the 1946 Nuremberg trials. In 1987 the former deputy leader of the Nazi party died, and the prison was torn down.

Zitadelle Spandau

This magnificent and perfectly proportioned 16th-century citadel stands at the confluence of the Spree and Havel rivers. Both the main citadel and its various 19th-century additions are still in excellent condition. The "Iron Chancellor", Otto von Bismarck *(see p26)*, moved the gold treasure of the Reichskriegsschatz (Imperial War Fund) here in 1874, where it remained until 1919. The citadel now holds museums of local history, and an observation terrace on the crenellated Juliusturm (tower).

Key

① Bastion Kronprinz
② Bastion Brandenburg
③ Palace
④ Main gate
⑤ Bastion König
⑥ Bastion Königin
⑦ Juliusturm
⑧ Ravelin Schweinekopf

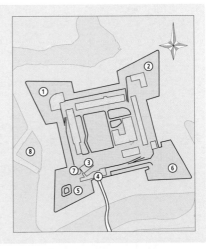

❸ Olympiastadion

Olympischer Platz. **Tel** 25 00 23 22. Ⓢ & Ⓤ Olympiastadion. 🚌 218, M49. **Open** 20 Mar–31 May: 9am–7pm daily; 1 Jun–15 Sep: 9am–8pm daily; 16 Sep–31 Oct: 9am–7pm daily; 1 Nov–19 Mar: 9am–4pm daily.

The Olympiastadion, or Reichs-sportfeld, as it was originally known, was built for the 1936 Olympic Games in Berlin. It was designed by Werner March in the Nazi architectural style and was inspired by the architecture of ancient Rome. The Olympiastadion was immortalized in the final scenes of István Szabó's classic film *Mephisto*. To the west lie the Maifeld and the Waldbühne. The former is an enormous assembly ground surrounded by grandstands and fronted by the Glocken-turm, a 77-m (250-ft) tower, while the latter is an open-air amphitheatre. To the north are swimming pools and sports grounds.

Following a €236-million refurbishment, including a seemingly free-floating roof, the stadium was reopened in 2004 as a high-tech arena. The Deutsches Sportmuseum next to the stadium hosts concerts and shows.

Two sculptures of athletes decorating the Olympiastadion

Fountain in the garden of the sculptor Georg Kolbe's villa

❹ Georg-Kolbe-Museum

Sensburger Allee 25. **Tel** 304 21 44. Ⓢ Heerstrasse. 🚌 218, X34, X49. **Open** 10am–6pm Tue–Sun. 🔲 georg-kolbe-museum.de

One of the most renowned German sculptors, Georg Kolbe (1877–1947) bequeathed the house in which he lived and worked almost his entire life to the city of Berlin. The villa was built by the Swiss architect, Ernst Reutsch, between 1928 and 1929 in a Functionalist style. Extended a few years later by the architect Paul Lindner, it was given an old-fashioned styling with rooms that open onto a large hall. Kolbe also left the city 180 of his sculptures and his art collection, which includes works by the Expressionist painter Ernst Ludwig Kirchner and the sculptor Wilhelm Lehmbruck. Visiting here is not only a rare chance to get to know Kolbe's works but also an opportunity to see his house and workshop, which display the tools and various devices for lifting a heavy or large sculpture.

Workshops with sculptors are held here regularly and controversial exhibitions on challenging and topical subjects, for example contemporary body image, draw large audiences.

❺ Messegelände

Hammarskjöldplatz. Ⓢ Messe Nord/ICC. Ⓤ Kaiserdamm. 🚌 104, 139, 349, X49.

The pavilions of the vast exhibition and trade halls which lie south of Hammarskjöldplatz cover more than 160,000 sq m (1,700,000 sq ft). Many of the international events organized here, including the food and agricultural fair Grüne Woche, are among the largest events of their kind in Europe. Even so, the exhibition areas are constantly enlarged and updated.

The original exhibition halls on this site were built before World War I, but nothing of these buildings remains. The oldest part is the Funkturm and the group of pavilions which surround it. The huge building at the front – Ehrenhalle – was built in 1936 to a design by Richard Ermisch, and is one of the few surviving buildings in Berlin designed in a Fascist architectural style.

The straight motorway that lies at the rear of the halls, in the direction of Nikolassee, is the famous Avus, the first German autobahn, built in 1921. It was adapted for motor racing and became Germany's first car-racing track. It was here that the world speed record was broken before World War II. Now it forms part of the autobahn system.

Monumental façade of the Ehrenhalle, part of the Messegelände

Clean, geometric shapes in the Art Deco lobby, Haus des Rundfunks

❻ Haus des Rundfunks

Masurenallee 8–14. Ⓢ Messe Nord/ICC. Ⓤ Theodor-Heuss-Platz. 🚌 104, 218, X34, X49.

This building's depressing, flat, brick-covered façade hides an interior of startling beauty. The huge edifice was constructed as a radio station between 1929 and 1931 to a design by Hans Poelzig. The building has a triangular shape, with three studio wings radiating from the central five-storey hall. The impressive Art Deco interiors, which are spectacularly lit from above, are enhanced by geometrically-patterned rows of balconies and large, pendulous, octagonal lamps. They represent one of the finest architectural achievements of this era in Berlin.

From the studio concert hall, concerts are often broadcast on radio RBB (Rundfunk Berlin-Brandenburg).

❼ Funkturm

Hammarskjöldplatz. **Tel** 30 38 29 96. Ⓢ Messe Nord/ICC. Ⓤ Kaiserdamm. 🚌 104, 218, 349, X34. Observation Terrace: **Open** 10am– 8pm Mon, 10am–11pm Tue–Sun (may vary due to weather).

The radio tower, resembling Paris' Eiffel tower, has become one of Berlin's most recognizable landmarks. Built in 1924

to a design by Heinrich Straumer, it rises 150 m (500 ft) into the air. It now operates as both an air-traffic control tower and a radio mast. Visitors can enjoy views on the observation terrace at 125 m (400 ft), or dine at the Funkturm's lofty restaurant at 55 m (180 ft).

❽ Internationales Congress Centrum

Messedamm 19. Ⓢ Messe Nord/ICC. Ⓤ Kaiserdamm. 🚌 104, 218, 349, X34, X49. 🆆 icc-berlin.de

This silver futuristic structure stands on a peninsula of land, surrounded on two sides by a continuous stream of fast moving cars. The Internationales Congress Centrum (ICC) marked yet another stage in the rivalry between East and West Berlin – it was built in reply to the East's Palast der Republik.

Constructed between 1973 and 1979, to a design by Ralf Schüler and Ursulina Schüler-Witte, the building is a mass of angular aluminium shapes that disguise its well-thought-out construction. The conference area is separate from the concert halls, for good sound-proofing. One of the most modern buildings of its type in the world, it has a state-of-the-art electronic security system and an advanced means of

Nighttime view of the Funkturm, Berlin's radio tower

co-ordinating and directing the several thousand people who come here to attend various meetings and conferences. More than 80 rooms and halls enable the venue to host a variety of events, from rock concerts for up to 5,000 spectators to a small artistic workshop or seminar.

The building also has a roof garden, where you can rest during intervals. In front of the main entrance stands *Alexander the Great in front of Ekhatana*, by French sculptor Jean Ipoustéguy (born 1920).

The impressive and modern AEG-Turbinenhalle

❾ AEG-Turbinenhalle

Huttenstrasse 12–19. Ⓤ Turmstrasse, then 🚌 M27.

This building is one of the most important textbook examples of modern architecture dating from the beginning of the 20th century. It was commissioned by the electronics company AEG in 1909 and designed by Peter Behrens in conjunction with Karl Bernhardt. While former Berlin's industrial buildings were mostly red-brick and fortress-like, the Turbinenhalle was among the earliest structures not to incorporate any element, decorative or otherwise, that reflected previous architectural styles. A huge hangar of a building, it has enormous windows and stretches 123 m (400 ft) down Berlichingenstrasse. The principal design imperative for this structure was to maintain a streamlined profile, while making no effort to disguise the materials used in its construction.

⑩ Gedenkstätte Plötzensee

Plotzensee Memorial

Hüttigpfad. **Tel** 344 32 26.
Ⓢ Beuselstrasse, then 🚌 123.
Open Mar–Oct: 9am–5pm; Nov–Feb: 9am–4pm. 🆆 **gedenkstaette-ploetzensee.de**

A narrow street leads from Saatwinkler Damm to the site where nearly 2,500 people convicted of crimes against the Third Reich were hanged. The Gedenkstätte Plötzensee is a simple memorial in a brick hut, which still has the iron hooks from which the victims were suspended. The main figures in the unsuccessful assassination attempt against Hitler, on 20 July 1944, were executed in Bendlerblock *(see p131)*, although the remainder of the conspirators were killed here. Count Helmut James von Moltke, one of the leaders of the German resistance movement, was also executed here. The count organized the Kreisauer Kreis – a political movement which gathered together and united German opposition to Hitler and the Third Reich.

⑪ Wedding

Wedding. Ⓤ & Ⓢ Wedding, Gesundbrunnen. Ⓤ Seestrasse, Osloer Strasse. 🚌 133, 222, 224, then a 15-minute walk.

Wedding, part of the Mitte district, is an interesting, up-and-coming area. Artists are taking over abandoned industrial buildings, a theatre and gallery scene is developing, and the area is becoming more attractive to renters and buyers. Volkspark Rehberge, a beautiful, park, is a hidden gem.

⑫ IBA-Viertel in Tegel

Karolinenstrasse & Am Tegeler Hafen.
Ⓤ Alt Tegel.

The development around the southern edge of the port of Tegel is an essential stop for

The Villa Borsig façade viewed from the garden

lovers of modern, and particularly post-modern, architecture. This complex developed out of the IBA (Internationale Baustellung) building exhibition in 1987. Over 30 architects were involved in the project, although the main designers were Charles Moore, John Ruble and Buzz Yudell. Within this complex stands the Humboldt-Bibliothek, which draws on Neo-Classical themes. In 1997 a monument was established to the eminent scientists Wilhelm and Alexander von Humboldt in front of this library.

Running the length of Am Tegeler Hafen street is a large housing estate where each unit has been designed by a different architect. For instance, at No. 8, the house by Stanley Tigerman recalls a style popular in Hanseatic architecture, while the red house at No. 10, designed by Paolo Portoghesi, looks as though it has been cracked lengthwise in two.

To the north, the IBA-Viertel estate borders another modern building, the Hotel Sorat, carefully built around the remaining section of an old windmill that was once part of the Humboldt estate.

⑬ Villa Borsig

Reiherwerder. Ⓤ Alt Tegel. 🚌 133, 222, 224, then a 15-minute walk.

This villa sits on a peninsula which cuts into the Tegeler See and is reminiscent of Schloss Sanssouci in Potsdam. It was built much later, however, between 1911 and 1913. It was designed by Alfred Salinger and Eugen Schmohl for the Borsig family, one of the wealthiest industrialist families in Berlin. This villa is particularly picturesque when observed from the lake, so it is worth looking out for it while cruising in a boat.

⑭ Schloss Tegel

Adelheidallee 19–21. **Tel** 886 71 50.
Ⓤ Alt Tegel. 🚌 133, 222.
Open (tours only) May–Sep: 10am, 11am, 3pm, 4pm Mon.

Schloss Tegel is one of the most interesting palace complexes in Berlin. In the 16th century there was already a manor house on this site, which in the second half of the 17th century was rebuilt into a hunting lodge for the Elector Friedrich Wilhelm. In 1766 the ownership of the

The elegant Neo-Classical façade of Schloss Tegel

property passed to the Humboldt family, and between the years 1820 and 1824, Karl Friedrich Schinkel thoroughly rebuilt the palace, giving it its current style.

There are tiled bas-reliefs decorating the elevations on the top floor of the towers. These were designed by Christian Daniel Rauch and depict the ancient wind gods. Some of Schinkel's marvellous interiors have survived, along with several items from what was once a large collection of antique sculptures. The palace is still privately owned by descendants of the Humboldt family, but guided tours are offered when the palace is open. It is also worth visiting the park. On its western limits lies the Humboldt family tomb designed by Schinkel and decorated with a copy of a splendid sculpture by Bertel Thorwaldsen; the original piece stands inside the palace.

🅑 Sachsenhausen Museum

Strasse der Nationen 22, Oranienburg. **Tel** 03301/2000. Ⓢ Oranienburg, then 🚌 804, 821. **Open** mid-Mar–mid-Oct: 8:30am–6pm daily; mid-Oct–mid-Mar: 8:30am–4:30pm daily; museum closed Mon. 📷 Ⓦ stiftung-bg.de

Built by the Nazis in 1936, the concentration camp at Sachsenhausen was liberated in 1945 by the Russians. Up to 200,000 people were incarcerated in this camp during its nine-year existence.

However, when the Soviet Army entered Sachsenhausen, there were only 3,000 inmates in the camp, mostly women and sick people.

The iron gate at the entrance bears a sign that reads *"Arbeit macht frei"* ("Work will set you free"), and indeed, many early prisoners were released upon demonstrating that they had learned how to be "good German citizens". By 1939, however, fewer prisoners were being released. It is estimated that over 30,000 people died in the camp, killed by hunger, disease or mass extermination.

Sachsenhausen is now a memorial and museum. Each area of the camp hosts an exhibit – for example, the one in the former infirmary focuses on medicine and racism under the Nazi regime. Other exhibits illustrate the daily life of the prisoners, or the way Sachsenhausen worked as a Soviet Special Camp between 1945 and 1950, when it housed Nazi functionaries and political undesirables.

Former entrance to the Sachsenhausen Prison Camp

Karl Friedrich Schinkel (1781–1841)

Schinkel was one of the most renowned German architects; even today his work forms an essential element of the architectural landscape of Berlin. He graduated from the Berlin Bauakademie, and for many years held a high-profile position in the Prussian Building Ministry. He was equally skilled in producing both Neo-Classical and Neo-Gothic designs. In Berlin and Potsdam he designed a few dozen buildings – palaces, civic buildings and churches, many of which still stand today. He also excelled at painting and even designed scenery for the opera house on Unter den Linden, among others. You can admire his paintings in the Galerie der Romantik in Schloss Charlottenburg. Schinkel's creativity had a truly enormous influence on the next generation of architects working in Prussia.

Southeast Berlin

An expedition to Berlin's furthest corners provides an occasion to visit the building in which Germany surrendered from World War II, now home to the Deutsche-Russisches Museum. However, you can just as easily stroll through the zoological garden in the park at the Baroque Schloss Friedrichsfelde or enjoy a leisurely break in Köpenick, which has retained the atmosphere of a small town.

Gigantic wreath commemorating the Red Army in Treptower Park

❶ Treptower Park

Archenhold-Sternwarte, Alt-Treptow 1.
Ⓢ Treptower Park. 🚌 166, 265.
Archenhold Sternwarte: **Tel** 536 06 37
19. **Open** 2–4:30pm Wed–Sun. 🗷
8pm Thu, 3pm Sat & Sun.

The vast park in Treptow was laid out in the 1860s on the initiative and design of Johann Gustav Meyer. In 1919 it was where revolutionaries Karl Liebknecht, Wilhelm Pieck and Rosa Luxemburg assembled a 150,000-strong group of striking workers.

The park, however, is best known for the colossal monument to the Red Army. Built between 1946 and 1949, it stands on the grave of 5,000 Soviet soldiers killed in the battle for Berlin in 1945. The gateway is marked by a vast granite sculpture of a grieving Russian Motherland surrounded by

statues of Red Army soldiers. This leads to the mausoleum, topped by an 11-m (35-ft) high figure of a soldier rescuing a child and resting his mighty sword on a smashed swastika. The whole scheme was the work of architect Jakow Biełopolski and sculptor Jewgien Wuczeticz.

In the farthest section of the park it is worth going to see the astronomical observatory, **Archenhold Sternwarte**, built for a decorative arts exhibition held here in 1896. Given a permanent site here in 1909, the observatory was used by Albert Einstein for a lecture on the Theory of Relativity in 1915. It is also home to the longest refracting telescope in the world (21-m or 70-ft) and a small planetarium.

Beyond Treptower Park lies another park, Plänterwald, while the Spree river provides an ideal place for a stroll or boat ride.

❷ Tierpark & Schloss Friedrichsfelde

Am Tierpark 125. Ⓤ Tierpark. 🚌 194, 296, 396. 🚋 27, 37, M17. Schloss: **Tel** 51 53 14 07. **Open** Tue, Thu, Sat, Sun & hols. Tierpark: **Tel** 51 53 10. **Open** 1 Jan–16 Mar: 9am–5pm; 17 Mar–24 May: 9am–6pm; 25 May–9 Sep: 9am–7pm; 10 Sep–21 Oct: 9am– 6pm; 22 Oct–31 Dec: 9am–5pm. 🗷

This charming Baroque palace was built for the Dutchman Benjamin von Raule around 1695, to a design by Johann Arnold Nering. Under successive owners, it underwent major renovations. It was redesigned in 1719 by Martin Heinrich Böhme, and

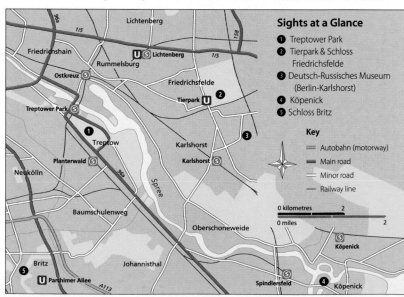

Sights at a Glance

❶ Treptower Park
❷ Tierpark & Schloss Friedrichsfelde
❸ Deutsch-Russisches Museum (Berlin-Karlshorst)
❹ Köpenick
❺ Schloss Britz

Key

═══ Autobahn (motorway)
▬▬▬ Main road
─── Minor road
─── Railway line

| 0 kilometres | 2 |
| 0 miles | 2 |

again in 1786, by Peter Biron. It was this renovation which gave the residence its current appearance.

The well-balanced structure, typical of the style during the transition from Baroque to Neo-Classical, was extensively restored in the 1970s. It now houses a museum of interiors, and is chiefly furnished with 18th and 19th-century pieces. The palace's park was re-designed into the zoological garden of East Berlin in 1957.

The façade of Schloss Friedrichsfelde

❸ Deutsch-Russisches Museum (Berlin-Karlshorst)

Zwieseler Strasse 4/Rheinsteinstrasse **Tel** 50 15 08 10. Ⓢ Karlshorst. 🚋 27, 37, M17. 🚌 296. **Open** 10am–6pm Tue–Sun.

This building was erected in the 1930s as the casino of the Wehrmacht (armed services of the Third Reich). It was here on the night of 8 May 1945 that Hitler's successor Grossadmiral Karl Dönitz, Field Marshal Wilhelm Keitel, Admiral Hans Georg von Friedeburg and General Hans-Jürgen Stumpff signed the unconditional surrender of Germany's armed forces. You can visit the renowned hall in which the surrender was signed, the office of Marshal Zhukov, and see an exhibition documenting the history of World War II.

❹ Köpenick

Kunstgewerbemuseum: Schlossinsel 1. **Tel** 266 42 42 42. Ⓢ Spindlersfeld, then 🚌 167, or Ⓢ Köpenick, then 🚌 164. 🚋 60, 61, 62, 67, 68. **Open** 10am–6pm Thu–Sun.

Köpenick is much older than Berlin. Already in the 9th century AD this island contained a fortified settlement called Kopanica. It was inhabited by Slavs from the Łaba river region, which in the 12th century was ruled by Duke Jaksa, who was waging a war against the Ascanian Albrecht the Bear over Brandenburg (see p21). From the late 12th century Köpenick belonged to the Margrave of Brandenburg, also an Ascanian. In about 1240 a castle was built, around which a town began to evolve, though over the years it lost out in importance to Berlin. Craftsmen settled here, and after 1685 a large colony of Huguenots also settled here. In the 19th century Köpenick recreated itself as an industrial town. Despite wartime devastation it has retained its historic character. There are no longer any 13th-century churches, nevertheless it is worth strolling around the old town. By the old market square and nearby streets, such as Alt Köpenick and Grünstrasse, modest houses have survived which recall the 18th century, next to buildings from the end of the 19th century.

At Alt Köpenick No. 21 is a vast brick town hall built in the style of the Brandenburg Neo-Renaissance between the years 1901 and 1904 by Hans Schütte and Hugo Kinzer. It was here on 16 October 1906 that a famous swindle took place. Wilhelm Voigt dressed himself in a Prussian officer's uniform and proceeded to arrest the mayor and then fraudulently empty everything from the city treasury. This incident inspired a comedy, *The Captain from Köpenick* by Carl Zuckmayer, which is still popular.

Köpenick's greatest attraction is a magnificent palace on the island in the southern part of town. It was built between 1677 and 1681 for the heir to the throne Friedrich (later King Friedrich I), to a design by the Dutch architect Rutger van Langfeld. The three-storey Baroque building that resulted was extended to a design by Johann Arnold Nering, but until 1693 only part of the extension was completed: the chapel, entrance gate and a small gallery wing.

In 2004 the **Kunstgewerbemuseum** *(see pp122–25)* opened a series of Renaissance and Baroque rooms in the Köpenick palace. This collection also includes some examples of magnificent furniture.

❺ Schloss Britz

Alt-Britz 73. **Tel** 60 97 92 30. Ⓤ Parchimer Allee. 🚌 181, M44, M46. **Open** 11am–6pm Tue–Sun. 🌐 schlossbritz.de

Originally a small manor house built in 1706 for Sigismund von Erlach, Schloss Britz was extended to its current size between 1880 and 1883 to a design by Carl Busse. It is a one-storey palace with a modest Neo-Classical aspect adorned with Baroque statues at the front and a tower on the garden side. As well as housing a museum, the building is often used as a venue for concerts and exhibitions. The palace displays furnishings from the *Gründerzeit* – the years after the founding of the German Empire in 1871. The 19th-century interiors are excellent but it is also worth strolling through the park, where there is a bust of one of the former owners, Rüdiger von Ilgen, which once stood in the Tiergarten.

Next to the palace is a housing estate called Hufeisensiedlung (Horseshoe Colony), built in the late 1920s to a design by Bruno Taut and Bruno Schneidereit. The architects' aim was to create spacious and affordable housing for Berliners.

Zehlendorf and Dahlem

With nearly half of Zehlendorf covered by forests, lakes and rivers, the region has a rustic, quiet atmosphere. One of the more interesting suburbs here is Dahlem, a settlement first mentioned in 1275. Retaining its Gothic parish church and its manor house, Dahlem was transformed into an affluent, tranquil city suburb with grand villas and museums, designed by Bruno Paul, at the beginning of the 20th century. The district was confirmed as a major cultural and educational centre after World War II with the establishment of the Freie Universität and the completion of the museum complex.

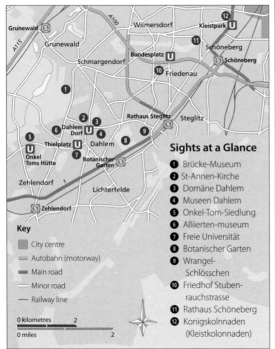

Key

- City centre
- Autobahn (motorway)
- Main road
- Minor road
- Railway line

0 kilometres 2
0 miles 2

Sights at a Glance

1. Brücke-Museum
2. St-Annen-Kirche
3. Domäne Dahlem
4. Museen Dahlem
5. Onkel-Tom-Siedlung
6. Alliierten-museum
7. Freie Universität
8. Botanischer Garten
9. Wrangel-Schlösschen
10. Friedhof Stuben-rauchstrasse
11. Rathaus Schöneberg
12. Konigskolnnaden (Kleistkolonnaden)

❶ Brücke-Museum

Bussardsteig 9. **Tel** 831 20 29.
🚌 115. **Open** 11am–5pm Wed–Mon.

One of the more interesting museums dedicated to 20th-century art is hidden away on a leafy, tranquil street lined with picturesque villas. The elegant Functionalist building was built by Werner Düttmann in 1966 to 1967. The museum houses a collection of German Expressionist painting linked to the artistic group known as Die Brücke, which originated in Dresden in 1905 and was based in Berlin from 1910. The members of this group included Karl Schmidt-Rottluff, Emil Nolde, Max Pechstein, Ernst Ludwig Kirchner and Erich Heckel. The collection is based on almost 80 works by Schmidt-Rottluff bequeathed to the town in 1964. The collection quickly grew, thanks to donations and acquisitions. In addition to displaying other works of art contemporary to Die Brücke (which was disbanded in 1913), there are also some paintings from the later creative periods of these artists, as well as works of other closely associated artists. Nearby, at Käuzchensteig No. 8, lie the foundation's head-quarters, established in the former studio of the sculptor Bernhard Heliger. The garden, which borders the Brücke-Museum, has a display of his metal sculptures.

❷ St-Annen-Kirche

Königin-Luise-Strasse 55. **Tel** 841 70 50. 🚇 Dahlem Dorf. 🚌 110, X11, X83. **Open** 11am–1pm Sat & Sun.

At the centre of a small leafy cemetery stands the Gothic 14th-century St-Annen-Kirche. The church was built initially with a plain roof. The chancel was completed in the 15th century, the vaulting in the 17th century and the tower was added in the 18th century.

Inside the church, 14th-century wall paintings depict scenes from the life of St Anna, alongside items of ecclesiastical furnishings. These include a 15th-century painting called *The Crucifixion* and 11 late Gothic figures of saints.

The cemetery, which dates back to the 13th century, is also worth exploring. It has a 1996 monument dedicated to the victims of Nazi tyranny. During the war, the congregation's pastor was Martin Niemöeller, a founder of the Confessing Church, a protestant movement that resisted the Nazification of churtches. Activist Martin Niemöeller was sent to a concentration camp in 1938 and survived imprisonment.

Gothic St-Annen-Kirche dating back to the 14th century

The combined museum and working farm of Domäne Dahlem

❸ Domäne Dahlem
Dahlem City farm

Königin-Luise-Str. 49. **Tel** 66 63 000.
🇺 Dahlem Dorf. 🚌 110, X11, X83.
Open 10am–6pm Wed–Mon.
🦽 (museum only). 🆆 **domaene-dahlem.de**

Domäne Dahlem, a manor house and farming estate, is a rare oasis of country life in the Berlin suburbs. The Baroque house was built for Cuno Johann von Wilmersdorff around 1680 and still retains its original character. Part of the Stadtmuseum Berlin (Museum of the City of Berlin), the manor house boasts period interiors, while the 19th-century farm buildings hold a collection of agricultural tools. Also on show is a large and varied collection of beehives.

Domäne Dahlem is a farm and a museum with a garden, workshops and farm animals. Festivals and markets held here demonstrate rural crafts and skills – you can learn how to shoe a horse or milk a cow, or, if you prefer, you can just relax with a glass of cold beer. There is an organic food market on Saturday mornings.

❹ Museen Dahlem

Museum für Asiatische Kunst, Ethnologisches Museum (formerly Museum für Völkerkunde), Museum Europäischer Kulturen Lansstrasse 8 and Arnimallee 25. **Tel** 266 424 242. 🇺 Dahlem Dorf. 🚌 110, X11, X83. **Open** 10am–6pm Tue–Fri, 11am–6pm Sat & Sun. **Closed** Mon, Dec 24 & 31. 🦽

Dahlem's first museums were built between 1914 and 1923. After World War II, with many of Berlin's collections fragmented, a large miscellany of art and artifacts was put on display here. In the 1960s the museums were extended considerably: the Museen was created to rival East Berlin's Museum Island. Reunification in 1990 meant the collections could be reunited and reorganized. Paintings were moved to the Kulturforum *(see pp126–9)*, and sculptures to the Bode-Museum *(see p81)*. Three museums are now housed at Dahlem: Museum für Asiatische Kunst (Museum of Asian Art); Ethnologisches Museum (Museum of Ethnology); and Museum für Europäischer Kulturen (Museum of European Culture).

The Museum für Asiatische Kunst shows the world's most important East Asian and Indian art collections from 4000 BC onwards and pays special homage to the art along the Silk route and early Indian sculptures. Among the many exquisite pieces is a collection of Japanese paintings and East Asian lacquered art. The Ethnologisches Museum displays about 500,000 objects from pre-industrial societies around the world with a focus on non-European cultures. A highlight

Japanese woodcut from the Museum für Asiatische Kunst

East Prussian carpet from the Museum Europäischer Kulturen

is the gold Inca jewellery. There are plans to move the Asian and non-European ethnological collections from Museen Dahlem to the Humboldt Forum *(see p76)*, a project roughly estimated to take place in 2016.

The Museum Europäischer Kulturen is an ethnographic museum that specializes in European folk art and culture, and documents the daily life of its inhabitants. It hosts long-running but temporary exhibitions, often in conjunction with museums from other European countries. Among the exhibits on display are earthenware items, costumes, jewellery, toys and tools.

Country Churches

The establishment of Greater Berlin in 1920 swallowed up nearly 60 villages, some of which were older than the city itself. Now they have evolved into large residential estates, and many of the parish churches (more than 50) have survived. The most treasured, dating from the 13th century, can be seen in the south of Berlin, for instance in Britz by Backbergstrasse, Buckow (Alt-Buckow) or in Mariendorf (Alt Mariendorf). The oldest church, dating from the 13th century, has survived in Marienfelde (Alt Marienfelde).

St Anna's in Dahlem

Wittenau

Marienfelde

Henry-Ford-Bau, the rector's office and library at the Freie Universität

➎ Onkel-Tom-Siedlung

Riemeister Strasse/Argentinische Allee. 🚇 Onkel-Toms-Hütte.

This housing estate, known as "Uncle Tom's Estate", represents one of the most interesting urban architectural achievements of the Weimar Republic. It was built from 1926 to 1932, to a design by Bruno Taut, Hugo Häring and Otto Rudolf Salvisberg. Their primary intention was to solve the city's housing shortage by building large developments that were both pleasant to live in and fairly inexpensive. This project in Zehlendorf was the realisation of the English concept of garden cities. The result is an enormous housing estate comprising single- and multiple-family houses. It is set in lush greenery on the borders of Grunewald and accommodates nearly 15,000 people.

➏ Alliierten-museum

Clayallee 135. **Tel** 818 19 90. 🚇 Zehlendorf, then 🚌 115. 🚇 Oskar-Helene-Heim. **Open** 10am–6pm Thu–Tue. 📷 by appointment.

In the heart of the former US military sector of Berlin is the Allied Museum, which combines exhibition space with open-air grounds.

A fascinating exhibition of everyday objects, military memorabilia, photographs and films explains life during the Cold War and the story of Berlin and its inhabitants between 1945 and 1994.

➐ Freie Universität

Henry-Ford-Bau Garystrasse 35–39. **Tel** 83 85 11 11. 🚇 Thielplatz. 🚌 110. 🌐 **fu-berlin.de**

The Free University was established on 4 December 1948 on the initiative of a group of academics and activists, led by Ernst Reuter. This was a reaction to the restrictions introduced at the Humboldt-Universität in the Soviet sector and further evidence of the competition between the two halves of the city. The university was initially located in rented buildings. It was only thanks to the American Ford Foundation that the Henry-Ford-Bau, housing the rector's office, the auditorium and the library, was built. Designed by Franz Heinrich Sobotka and Gustav Müller, and built from 1951 to 1954, the building is distinguished by its fine proportions.

Another architectural highlight can be found at the

Humanities and Social Science building, designed by Norman Foster and finished in 2005. It has a glass-domed centrepiece, housing the Philological Library, which is nicknamed the "Berlin Brain" due to its cranial shape.

➑ Botanischer Garten
Botanical Garden

Unter den Eichen 5–10 & Königin-Luise-Strasse 6–8. **Tel** 83 85 01 00. 🚇 Dahlem-Dorf. 🚉 Botanischer Garten. 🚌 M48, X83. **Open** daily; Nov–Jan: 9am–4pm; Feb: 9am–5pm; Mar & Oct: 9am–6pm; Apr & Aug: 9am–8pm; May–Jul: 9am–9pm; Sep: 9am–7pm. Museum: **Open** 10am–6pm daily. 🌐 **botanischer-garten-berlin.de**

This park is one of the most beautiful places in Berlin. It was created towards the end of the 19th century and has a romantic character with gentle hills and picturesque lakes. Of particular interest is the 19th-century palm house, designed by Alfred Koerner. The greenhouses were built from 1984 to 1987 to a design by Engelbert Kremser. The most popular plants are the exotic species such as the orchids and cacti. By the entrance on the Königin-Luise-Platz side is the Botanisches Museum, home to an excellent collection of plant specimens.

The pleasantly cultivated spaces of the Botanischer Garten

❾ Wrangel-Schlösschen

Schlossstrasse 48. **Tel** 902 99 39 24. 🅄 Rathaus Steglitz. 🚍 M2, M48, M85.

This compact Neo-Classical palace derives its name from Field Marshal Wrangel, the building's mid-19th-century owner. However, the house was built much earlier, in 1804, following a design by Heinrich Gentz. The simplicity and clarity of its details make it a prime example of early Neo-Classical architecture. It currently houses the cultural centre for the district of Steglitz.

Wrangel-Schlösschen, a fine example of Neo-Classical architecture

❿ Friedhof Stubenrauchstrasse

Stuberauchstrasse cemetery

Stubenrauchstrasse 43–45/Südwestkorso. 🄪 & 🅄 Bundesplatz. 🚍 248.

This small cemetery in the shadow of a motorway achieved renown in 1993 as the burial place of Marlene Dietrich, who died on 6 May. Born Maria Magdalena von Losch in 1901, she grew up at Leberstrasse No. 65 in Schöneberg. For a few years she struggled to make a career as an actress, playing small parts. In 1929 she was discovered in Berlin by Hollywood director Josef von Sternberg who was filming *The Blue Angel*, based on Heinrich Mann's novel *Professor Unrat*. The ensuing role of Lola took Marlene to the height of fame. She sang only

once more in Berlin, giving a concert at the Titania-Palast in 1960. Although she died in Paris, she was laid to rest in the city of her birth.

Rathaus Schöneberg – the site of President Kennedy's speech

⓫ Rathaus Schöneberg

Schoneberg town hall

John-F-Kennedy-Platz 1. 🅄 Rathaus Schöneberg. 🚍 104, M46.

The gigantic building with a tower is the Schöneberg town hall, built between 1911 and 1914. From 1948 to 1990 it was used as the main town hall of West Berlin. Here, on 26 June 1963, the US President John F Kennedy gave his famous speech. More than 300,000 Berliners assembled to hear the

young president say *"Ich bin ein Berliner"* – "I am a Berliner", intended as an expression of solidarity from the democratic world to a city defending its right to freedom.

While Kennedy's meaning was undoubtedly clear, pedants were quick to point out that, strictly speaking, he said "I am a small doughnut".

⓬ Königskolonnaden (Kleistkolonnaden)

Potsdamer Strasse **Map** 13 B4. 🅄 Kleistpark. 🚍 106, 204, M46.

A short walk north of U-Bahn Kleistpark, the unremarkable architecture of Potsdamer Strasse suddenly transforms dramatically. Leading to the park, the elegant sandstone Königskolonnaden captivates the passer-by with its Baroque ornamental sculptures. The royal colonnade, designed by Carl von Gontard and built between 1777 and 1780, once graced the route from Königsstrasse to Alexanderplatz. In 1910, to protect it from traffic, it was moved to this new site.

The huge Kammergericht at the far boundary of the park was built between 1909 and 1913 to a design by Carl Vohl, Rudolf Mönnich and Paul Thömer. The site of the notorious Nazi Volksgericht or "People's Court", it was also used to try members of the failed July 1944 Bomb Plot against Hitler *(see p131)*.

Elegant façade of Königskolonnaden

Wannsee & Havel

Some of Berlin's most affluent neighbourhoods are scattered along the Wannsee lakeside and Havel shores, but above all it is the natural beauty of the area that attracts Berliners and visitors alike and makes it the city's most popular recreation spot. It is worth cycling or walking *(see pp210–213)* here to enjoy the views of sailing boats on Havel and Wannsee, and to see stunning summer houses and royal parks. The museum in the Haus der Wannsee-Konferenz is poignant; the building was originally where the Nazis made their most shocking decisions.

Sights at a Glance

1. Strandbad Wannsee
2. Haus der Wannsee-Konferenz
3. Villenkolonie Alsen
4. Grabstätte von Heinrich von Kleist
5. Museumsdorf Düppel
6. Grunewaldturm

Key

- ▦▦▦ Autobahn (motorway)
- ▬ Main road
- — Minor road
- — Railway line

0 kilometres 2

0 miles 2

❶ Strandbad Wannsee

Wannseebadweg 2s. Ⓢ Nikolassee. 🚌 218.

The vast picturesque lake of Wannsee, situated on the edge of Grunewald, is a principal destination for Berliners who are looking for some kind of recreation. Here you can take part in water sports, enjoy a lake cruise, bathe, or simply enjoy relaxing on the shore. The most developed part is the south-eastern corner of the lake. Here, near S-Bahn Wannsee, there are yachting marinas and harbours,

while further north is one of the largest inland beaches in Europe – Strandbad Wannsee. It has been in use since the beginning of the 20th century, and was developed between 1929 and 1930 by the construction of a complex of changing rooms, shops and cafés on top of man-made terraces.

On sunny summer days, sun-worshippers completely cover the sandy shore, while the lake is filled with yachts and windsurfers. It is also quite pleasant to take a walk around Schwanenwerder island. It has many elegant villas, one of which, Inselstrasse No. 24/26, was built for Axel Springer, the German newspaper publisher.

❷ Haus der Wannsee-Konferenz

Am Grossen Wannsee 56/58. **Tel** 805 00 10. Ⓢ Wannsee, then 🚌 114. **Open** 10am–6pm daily.

This is one of the most beautiful of the luxury Alsen holiday villas, and yet the most abhorrent. Designed by Paul Baumgarten between 1914 and 1915, it is in the style of a small Neo-Baroque palace with an elegant portico. In 1940 the villa was sold to the Nazi SS. On 20 January 1942, a meeting took place between Richard Heydrich and 14 other officers from the secret service and the SS, among them Adolf Eichmann. It was then that the decision was taken about "the final solution on the question of Jews". Their plans for the outright extermination of 11 million Jews embraced the whole of Europe, including Great Britain and neutral countries.

Since 1992 this has been a museum and place of remembrance. An exhibition depicts the history of the

Boarding point for lake cruises on the Wannsee

The exterior of Haus der Wannsee-Konferenz

Holocaust with some shocking documents and photographs from the ghettos and extermination camps. For security reasons, the gate to the villa is always locked, and to enter the park you have to announce yourself through the intercom.

❸ Villenkolonie Alsen

Am Grossen Wannsee. Ⓢ Wannsee, then 🚌 114. Max-Liebermann Villa: **Closed** Tue. 🅿️ 📷 Ⓦ **max-liebermann.de**

This clutch of villas forms a delightful holiday resort – the oldest of its kind in Berlin. The villas are thought to be the most beautiful, not just because of their picturesque lakeside location, but also because of the quality of their architecture.

Strolling along Am Grossen Wannsee, it is worth looking at the villa at No. 39/41, known as Haus Springer. It was designed by the architect Alfred Messel in 1901 and is covered with shingles which reflect contemporary American designs.

Another must-see villa stands at No. 42, designed by Paul Baumgarten in 1909 for the painter Max Liebermann (1845–1935). Liebermann spent many summers here painting in the garden on the shores of Wannsee. The villa is now a museum and houses around 40 of Liebermann's paintings.

❹ Grabstätte von Heinrich von Kleist

Grave of Heinrich Von Kleist

Bismarckstrasse (near No. 3).
Ⓢ Wannsee. 🚌 114, 316, 318.

A narrow street running from Königstrasse at the viaduct of the S-Bahn Wannsee leads to the spot where the playwright Heinrich von Kleist committed suicide. On 21 November 1811 he shot his companion Henriette Vogel and then turned the pistol on himself. They are both buried here. A stone marks their grave, on which flowers are left by well-wishers.

Reconstructed medieval settlement at the Museumsdorf Düppel

❺ Museumsdorf Düppel

Clauerstrasse 11. **Tel** 802 66 71.
Ⓢ Mexikoplatz or Ⓤ Krumme Lanke, then 🚌 118, 622. **Open** late Mar–early Oct: 3–7pm Thu, 10am–5pm Sun. 🅿️ Ⓦ **dueppel.de**

A visit here is like a trip back in time. A reconstruction of a medieval village has been made on the site of a 13th-century settlement, discovered in the 1940s. It is a living village surrounded by still cultivated gardens and fields, where traditional breeds of pigs and sheep are raised in the sheds and pigsties.

On Sundays the village puts on displays of traditional crafts. Here you can see how primitive saucepans and tools were fashioned; how wool was spun, dyed and woven; and how baskets were made.

❻ Grunewaldturm

Havelchaussee 61. 🚌 218.

The Neo-Gothic tower built on a hill at the edge of the Havel river is one of the most prominent features of the area. This type of tower became popular in Germany during the 19th century as a way of commemorating important events or people. The Grunewaldturm was built in 1899 on the centenary of the birth of Wilhelm I. After 1871 he was the first Emperor of the Second Reich and the tower was initially named "Kaiser-Wilhelm-Turm". The 56-m (185-ft) tower was designed by Franz Schwechten and is made of red brick with plaster details. The tower is made all the more striking by the green background provided by the surrounding leafy trees.

Currently used as an observation tower, the view from the top of this structure is well worth climbing the 204 steps for. There is a popular restaurant in the base of the tower.

The impressive red-brick Neo-Gothic Grunewaldturm

GREATER BERLIN

POTSDAM

Potsdam is an independent city bordering Berlin. It is also the capital of Brandenburg, with almost 140,000 inhabitants. The first historical reference to Potsdam dates from AD 993. The town blossomed in the 1600s, during the era of the Great Elector *(see p22)*, and then again during the 18th century. Potsdam suffered very badly during World War II, particularly on the nights of 14 and 15 April 1945, when the Allies bombed the town's centre. Today, despite its wartime losses, Potsdam is one of the most interesting cities in Germany. Tourists flock to see the royal Park Sanssouci and palaces such as the Marmorpalais and Schloss Cecilienhof. It is also worth strolling around Neuer Garten and the historic area around the Rathaus. The Russian colony of Alexandrowka, the Holländisches Viertel, the film studios of Babelsberg and Babelsberg park *(see pp212–13)* also rate among the attractions of Potsdam.

Sights at a Glance

Historic Buildings
1. Neues Palais pp196–7
3. Communs
4. Schloss Charlottenhof
5. Römische Bäder
6. Chinesisches Haus
7. Orangerie
9. Neue Kammern
10. Schloss Sanssouci pp202–203
11. Bildergalerie
12. Historische Mühle
15. Schloss Cecilienhof
16. Marmorpalais
21. Altes Rathaus
24. Wasserwerk Sanssouci

Historic Areas
13. Alexandrowka
17. Holländisches Viertel

Churches
8. Friedenskirche
18. Peter und Paul Kirche
19. Französische Kirche
20. Nikolaikirche

Parks and Theme Parks
2. Park Sanssouci
14. Neuer Garten
25. Telegrafenberg
26. Filmpark Babelsberg

Museums
22. Potsdam-Museum
23. Marstall (Filmmuseum)

Restaurants
see p243
1. Alexandrowka
2. Krongut Bornstedt
3. Maison Charlotte
4. Massimo 18
5. Speckers Landhaus

0 metres 750
0 yards 750

◀ Terraced vineyard leading to the Sanssouci Palace, Park Sanssouci

For map symbols *see back flap*

Street-by-Street: Park Sanssouci

The enormous Park Sanssouci, covering an area of 287 hectares, is among the most beautiful palace complexes in Europe. The first building to be constructed was Schloss Sanssouci, the summer palace of Frederick the Great. It was built between 1744 and 1747 on the site of an orchard. Over the years, Park Sanssouci was expanded and enriched by the addition of other palaces and pavilions. Allow yourself at least a whole day to enjoy the park fully.

❸ Communs
This house for the palace staff has an unusually elegant character, and is situated next to a pretty courtyard.

❶ ★ Neues Palais
This monumental building of the New Palace, constructed between 1763 and 1769, is crowned by a massive dome.

0 metres   200
0 yards   200

❺ Römische Bäder
The Roman baths include a mock-Renaissance villa and a suite of Roman-style rooms.

❹ Schloss Charlottenhof
This Neo-Classical palace gained its name from Charlotte von Gentzkow, the former owner of the land on which the palace was built.

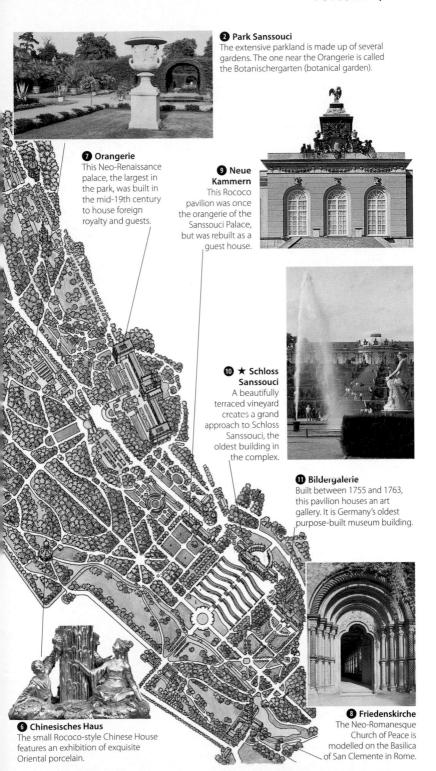

2 Park Sanssouci
The extensive parkland is made up of several gardens. The one near the Orangerie is called the Botanischergarten (botanical garden).

7 Orangerie
This Neo-Renaissance palace, the largest in the park, was built in the mid-19th century to house foreign royalty and guests.

9 Neue Kammern
This Rococo pavilion was once the orangerie of the Sanssouci Palace, but was rebuilt as a guest house.

10 ★ Schloss Sanssouci
A beautifully terraced vineyard creates a grand approach to Schloss Sanssouci, the oldest building in the complex.

11 Bildergalerie
Built between 1755 and 1763, this pavilion houses an art gallery. It is Germany's oldest purpose-built museum building.

6 Chinesisches Haus
The small Rococo-style Chinese House features an exhibition of exquisite Oriental porcelain.

8 Friedenskirche
The Neo-Romanesque Church of Peace is modelled on the Basilica of San Clemente in Rome.

❶ Neues Palais

This imposing Baroque palace, on the main avenue in Park Sanssouci, was built at the request of Frederick the Great. The initial plans were prepared in 1750 by Georg Wenzeslaus von Knobelsdorff. However, construction only began in 1763, after the Seven Years' War *(see p23)*, to a design by Johann Gottfried Büring, Jean Laurent Le Geay and Carl von Gontard. The result was a vast two-storey building, decorated with hundreds of sculptures and more than 200 richly adorned rooms, which together make up one of Germany's most beautiful palaces.

Façade
The entrance to the Neues Palais is through the gate on the western façade. The imposing gate is flanked by stone sentry boxes.

Study
This Rococo-style study was part of Frederick the Great's personal apartment.

KEY

① **The Schlosstheater** was completed in 1768, and designed by JC Hoppenhaupt.

② **Bas-reliefs** on the triangular tympanum depict figures from Greek mythology, including Minerva, the Muses and Pegasus.

Upper Gallery
The Rococo interior, with a beautiful inlaid floor, is decorated with Italian paintings.

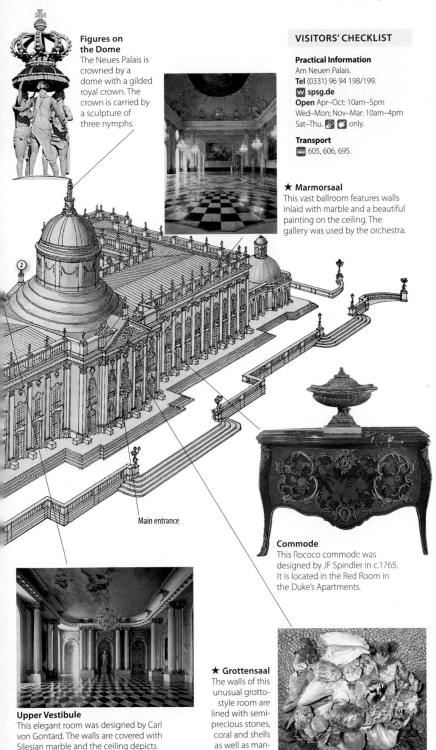

Figures on the Dome
The Neues Palais is crowned by a dome with a gilded royal crown. The crown is carried by a sculpture of three nymphs.

VISITORS' CHECKLIST

Practical Information
Am Neuen Palais.
Tel (0331) 96 94 198/199.
w **spsg.de**
Open Apr–Oct: 10am–5pm
Wed–Mon; Nov–Mar: 10am–4pm
Sat–Thu. 🦽 📷 only.

Transport
🚌 605, 606, 695.

★ **Marmorsaal**
This vast ballroom features walls inlaid with marble and a beautiful painting on the ceiling. The gallery was used by the orchestra.

Main entrance

Commode
This Rococo commode was designed by JF Spindler in c.1765. It is located in the Red Room in the Duke's Apartments.

Upper Vestibule
This elegant room was designed by Carl von Gontard. The walls are covered with Silesian marble and the ceiling depicts Venus and the Graces.

★ **Grottensaal**
The walls of this unusual grotto-style room are lined with semi-precious stones, coral and shells as well as man-made stalactites.

❷ Park Sanssouci

Schopenhauerstrasse/Zur
Historischen Mühle. 🚌 612, 614, 695.

This vast park, covering some
287 ha (700 acres), was
established in 1725 on the site of
an orchard. However, it was only
transformed into an enormous
landscaped park when
construction work began on
Schloss Sanssouci (see pp202–
203). Today, the park is made up
of smaller gardens dating from
different eras, each of which has
been maintained in the original
style. At the foot of Schloss
Sanssouci is the oldest section of
the park, containing the Dutch
garden, a number of fountains
and the French-style Lustgarten
(pleasure garden), with a
symmetrical layout and lovely
rose beds. Surrounding
Friedenskirche is the Marly-
garten, created in the mid-19th
century by Ludwig Persius.

The eastern part of the park is
called the Rehgarten, a
beautifully landscaped park in
the English style, designed by
Peter Joseph Lenné, and
established on the site of former
hunting grounds. This park
extends right up to the Neues
Palais. To the south, surrounding
the small palace, extends the

Charlottenhof Park, also
designed by Lenné. In the
northern section of the park,
next to the Orangerie, is the
Nordischer Garten and the
Paradiesgarten.

The range of different garden
styles makes a simple stroll
through this park particularly
pleasant. There are also a large
number of sculptures, columns,
obelisks and grottoes for the
visitor to explore. The
perspectives that suddenly open
up across the park and the
picturesque groupings of trees
are also beautiful.

❸ Communs

Am Neuen Palais. 🚌 605, 695.

This area of the park consists of
a pair of two-storey pavilions
linked by a semi-circular
colonnade. They are unusually
elegant buildings considering
they were used for servants'
quarters and the palace
kitchens. However, they also
served to screen from view the
cultivated fields that extended
past the park from the palace.

The Communs were built
between 1766 and 1769 by Carl
von Gontard, to a design by
Jean Laurent Le Geay. The

Elegant façade of the Communs, the
servants' quarters

buildings are enclosed by an
elegant courtyard reflected in
the style of the buildings. The
kitchen was in the south
pavilion, linked to the palace by
an underground passageway,
and the north pavilion
accommodated the servants of
the king's guests. Today, the
rectors' offices of the University
of Potsdam are located here in
the Communs.

❹ Schloss Charlottenhof

Charlottenhof Palace

Geschwister-Scholl-Strasse 34a (Park
Charlottenhof). **Tel** (0331) 969 42 28.
🚌 605, 606. 🚊 91, 94. **Open** 1 May–
31 Oct: 10am–5pm Tue–Sun.

This small Neo-Classical palace
is located in the southern
extension of Park Sanssouci,
Park Charlottenhof. It was
designed by Karl Friedrich
Schinkel in 1829 for the heir to
the throne, later King Friedrich
Wilhelm IV. This small one-storey
building was built in the style of
a Roman villa. The rear of the
palace has a portico that opens
out onto the garden terrace.

Some of the wall paintings
which were made in the
so-called Pompeiian style,
designed by Schinkel, are still
in place. The most interesting
part of the interior is the blue-
and-white-striped Humboldt
Room, also called the Tent
Room due to its resemblance
to a tent. The palace is
surrounded by a picturesque
landscaped park designed by
Peter Joseph Lenné.

One of the many sculptures on display in Park Sanssouci

❺ Römische Bäder
Roman Baths

Lenné-Strasse (Park Charlottenhof).
Tel (0331) 969 42 00. 605, 606.
91, 94, 98. **Open** May–Oct:
10am–6pm Tue–Sun.

This picturesque group of pavilions, situated by the edge of a lake, forms the Roman Baths, which actually served as accommodation for the king's guests. It was designed by Karl Friedrich Schinkel, with the involvement of Ludwig Persius, between 1829 and 1840. At the front is the gardener's house, which is adjacent to an asymmetrical low tower in the style of an Italian Renaissance villa. In the background, to the left, extends the former bathing pavilion, which is currently used for temporary exhibitions. All of the pavilions are arranged around an internal garden planted with a multi-coloured carpet of shrubs. A closer look will reveal that many of these colourful plants are actually vegetables.

❻ Chinesisches Haus
Chinese House

Ökonomieweg (Rehgarten). **Tel** (0331) 969 42 00. 606, 695. 91, 94.
Open May–Oct: 10am–6pm Tue–Sun.

The lustrous, gilded pavilion that can be seen glistening from a distance is the Chinese House. Chinese art was popular during the Rococo period – people wore Chinese silk, rooms were wallpapered with Chinese designs, furniture was lacquered, drinks were served in Chinese porcelain, and Chinese pavilions were built in gardens.

The Chinesisches Haus was built in Park Sanssouci between 1754 and 1756 to a design by Johann Gottfried Büring. It is circular in shape with a centrally located main hall surrounded by three studies. Between each of these are pretty *trompe l'oeil* porticos. Ornaments, together with gilded figures of Chinese gentlemen and ladies, surround

The Chinesisches Haus, now housing a collection of porcelain

the pavilion. Originally the Chinesisches Haus served as a tea room and a summer dining room. Today, it houses a collection of porcelain.

❼ Orangerie

Maulbeerallee (Nordischer Garten).
Tel (0331) 969 42 00. 695.
Open Apr: 10am–6pm Sat, Sun & hols;
May–Oct: 10am–6pm Tue–Sun.
Observation terrace: **Open** Apr:
10am–6pm Sat, Sun & hols; May–Oct:
10am–6pm Tue–Sun.

Towering above the park is the Orangerie, designed in the Italian Renaissance style and crowned by a colonnade. The Orangerie was built to house guests, not plants. It was constructed between 1851 and 1860 by Friedrich August Stüler on the initiative and direction of Friedrich Wilhelm IV. The final

Long flight of stairs leading to the Renaissance-style Orangerie

design was partly based on the plans of Ludwig Persius. It served as a guest residence for the king's sister and her husband Tsar Nicholas I. The rooms were grouped around the Raphael Hall, which was based on the Regia Hall in the Vatican and decorated with copies of the works of Italian artist Raphael. It is also worth climbing up to the observation terrace, from where the view extends over Potsdam.

❽ Friedenskirche

Am Grünen Gitter. **Tel** (0331) 97 40 09.
695. 91, 94. **Open** late Apr:
11am–5pm Mon–Sat, noon–5pm Sun;
May–1 Oct: 10am–6pm Mon–Sat,
noon–6pm Sun; 2–16 Oct: 11am–5pm
Mon–Sat, noon–5pm Sun; 17 Oct–late
Apr: 11am–4pm Sat, 11:30am–5pm Sun.

Close to Schloss Sanssouci is Friedenskirche, or the Church of Peace. The foundation stone was laid by King Friedrich Wilhelm IV in 1845 and the church was completed in 1848. Designed by Ludwig Persius, Friedrich August Stüler and Ludwig Hesse, the church is based on San Clemente in Rome.

Inside, the vaulted ceiling of the apse is covered by a 12th-century mosaic depicting the figure of Christ as a judge. This Byzantine mosaic was originally located in the church of San Capriano on the island of Murano in Venice. Next to the church is a mausoleum containing the tombs of Friedrich Wilhelm I, Friedrich Wilhelm IV and Kaiser Friedrich III.

❾ Neue Kammern

New Chambers

Zur Historischen Mühle (Lustgarten). **Tel** (0331) 969 42 00. 695. **Open** Apr–Oct: 10am–6pm Wed–Mon; Nov–Mar: 10am–5pm Wed–Mon.

The Neue Kammern contains residential apartments. It is the mirror image of the Bildergalerie and was originally built as an orangery in 1747 to a design by Georg Wenzeslaus von Knobelsdorff. In 1777 Frederick the Great (Friedrich II) ordered the building to be remodelled as guest accommodation. The architect, Georg Christian Unger, left the elegant Baroque exterior of the orangery largely untouched and instead concentrated on converting the interior. As well as the sumptuous guest suites, the new design included four elegant halls. The best of these is the Ovidsaal, with its rich reliefs and marble floors. The interior decor has been maintained in Frederick's Rococo style. The building also houses a collection of Meissen figurines.

❿ Schloss Sanssouci

See pp202–203.

Detail of Caravaggio's *Doubting Thomas*, in the Bildergalerie

⓫ Bildergalerie

Zur Historischen Mühle. **Tel** (0331) 969 42 00. 695. **Open** May–Oct: 10am–6pm Tue–Sun.

The picture gallery housed in the building adjacent to Schloss Sanssouci is the first purpose-built gallery in Germany. It was constructed between 1755 and 1764 to a design by JG Büring. The garden elevation reveals an allegorical tableau representing Art, Education and Crafts, while busts of renowned artists have been placed in the windows.

The gallery contains an exhibition of Baroque paintings once owned by Frederick the Great, although part of the collection can be found in the Gemäldegalerie *(see pp126–9)*. Highlights include Caravaggio's *Doubting Thomas* and Guido Reni's *Cleopatra's Death*, as well as a number of canvases by Rubens and van Dyck.

⓬ Historische Mühle

Historic Windmill

Mauelbeerallee 5. **Tel** (0331) 550 68 51. 695. **Open** Apr–Oct: 10am–6pm daily; Nov, Jan–Mar: 10am–4pm Sat & Sun.

A mill has been located here since the early 18th century, although this is actually a reconstruction, dating from 1993. According to local legend, the original windmill was so noisy that Frederick the Great ordered it to be dismantled. However, a court upheld the miller's cause and the mill stayed. In 1790 a new windmill was built in its place, which lasted until 1945. The mill currently houses a museum of mechanical windmills.

⓭ Alexandrowka

Russische Kolonie Allee/ Puschkinallee. 92, 96. 604, 609, 692, 697.

A trip to Alexandrowka takes the visitor into the world of Pushkin's stories. Wooden

A Russian-style wooden house in the settlement of Alexandrowka

houses made from logs, decorated with carved motifs and set in their own gardens, create a very pretty residential estate. Although they appear to be picturebook, traditional Russian houses, they were constructed in 1826 under the direction of a German military architect called Captain Sneth-lage. What is interesting is that the estate was created for the singers of a Russian choir. The choir was set up in 1812 to entertain the troops and was recruited from over 500 Russian prisoners of war, who had fought with Napoleon. In 1815, when the Prussians and the Russians joined forces, the choir was retained by Friedrich Wilhelm III.

Peter Joseph Lenné was responsible for the overall appearance of the estate, and it was named Alexandrowka after the Tsarina, the Prussian Princess Charlotte. It is based on the shape of the cross of St Andrew inscribed within an oval. In all, 12 houses were built here, as well as an outhouse which now contains a small museum. Some of the dwellings are still owned by the descendants of the choir. To the north of this estate stands the Russian Orthodox church of Alexander Nevski (1829).

Orange growing in the Neuer Garten's Marmorpalais

⑭ Neuer Garten
New Garden

Am Neuen Garten. 🚌 692.

Running along the edge of Heiliger See, on what was once the site of palace vineyards, is a park laid out between 1787 and 1791. It was landscaped originally by Johann August Eyserbeck on the instructions of Friedrich Wilhelm II, while

Schloss Cecilienhof, summer residence of the Hohenzollern family

the current layout was created by Peter Joseph Lenné in 1816. It is a Romantic park ornamented with numerous pavilions and sculptures. The charming Marmorpalais stands beside the lake, while the northern section contains the early 20th-century Schloss Cecilienhof. Elsewhere you can see the red and green gardeners' houses, the pyramid-shaped ice house and a Neo-Gothic library pavilion completed in 1794.

⑮ Schloss Cecilienhof

Am Neuen Garten. **Tel** (0331) 969 42 00. 🚌 692. **Open** Apr–Oct: 10am–6pm Tue–Sun; Nov–Mar: 10am–5pm Tue–Sun.

The Cecilienhof residence played a brief but important part in history because the 1945

Potsdam Conference took place here. Built between 1914 and 1917, the palace is the most recent of the Hohenzollern dynasty buildings and was designed by Paul Schultze-Naumburg in the style of an English country manor. It is a sprawling, asymmetrical building with wooden beams making a pretty herringbone pattern on its walls. The gatehouse passageways leading to the courtyards are decorated with Baroque reliefs.

The palace was the Hohen-zollern family residence after they lost the crown; the family remained in Potsdam until February 1945. It now functions as a first-class hotel and restaurant, where history lovers can relax amid carefully tended shrubbery. Most of the historic furnishings used during the famous Potsdam conference are on display.

The Potsdam Conference of 1945

On 17 July 1945 the heads of government for Great Britain (Winston Churchill, later represented by Clement Attlee), the United States (Harry Truman) and the Soviet Union (Joseph Stalin) met in Schloss Cecilienhof to confirm the decisions made earlier that year at Yalta. The aim of both conferences was to resolve the problems arising at the end of World War II. They decided to abolish the Nazi Party, to limit the size of the German militia and monitor it indefinitely, and also to punish war criminals and establish reparations. They also revised the German borders and arranged the resettlement of Germans from Poland. The conference played a major part in establishing the political balance of power in Europe, which continued for the next 45 years.

Attlee, Truman and Stalin at Cecilienhof

❿ Schloss Sanssouci

The name Sanssouci is French for "without a care" and gives a good indication of the flamboyant character of this enchanting Rococo palace, built in 1745. The original sketches, made by Friedrich II (Frederick the Great) himself, were finalized by Georg Wenzeslaus von Knobelsdorff. The glorious interiors were designed by Knobelsdorff and Johann August Nahl. The king clearly loved this palace, as his final wishes were that he should be buried here, near the tomb of his Italian greyhounds. He was actually interred in the Garnisonkirche, Potsdam, but his final wishes were carried out in 1991.

Bacchanalian Figures
The carved male and female bacchanalian figures on the pilasters are the work of Friedrich Christian Glume.

Voltaire Room
This room is decorated with naturalistic carvings of birds, flowers and fruit.

Domed Roof
The oxidized green dome covers the Marmorsaal. It is decorated with Baroque sculptures.

KEY

① **The wings** were added to the building between 1841 and 1842.

② **The colonnade** frames the view of the artificial ruins on the hill.

Marmorsaal
The imposing marble hall is decorated with pairs of columns made from Carrara marble. Frederick the Great wanted this room to be loosely based on the Pantheon in Rome.

Arbour
The palace design is completed by picturesque arbours and pergolas decorated with sun motifs.

VISITORS' CHECKLIST

Practical Information
Park Sanssouci.
Tel (0331) 96 94 198/199.
🅦 spsg.de
Open 1 Apr–31 Oct: 9am–5pm Tue–Sun; Nov, Jan–31 Mar: 9am–4pm Tue–Sun.
Damenflügel: May–Oct: 10am–6pm Sat–Sun. 🅿 🗺 compulsory.

Transport
🚌 612, 614, 650, 695. 🚊 91, 94, X98.

Weimar Urn (1785)
This Neo-Classical urn from the Berlin company KPM *(see p137)* is a copy of the original urn, which was presented to the Duchess of Weimar.

★ **Fêtes Galantes** (c. 1715)
The real jewels in the palace are the enchanting paintings by Antoine Watteau. He was one of Frederick the Great's favourite artists.

Bibliothek
The library of Frederick the Great contains about 2,100 books. The walls are lined with cedar panelling to create a contemplative atmosphere.

★ **Konzertzimmer**
The walls of the salon are decorated with paintings by Antoine Pesne, based on Greek mythology.

⑯ Marmorpalais
Marble Palace

Am Ufer des Heiligen Sees (Neuer Garten). **Tel** (0331) 969 42 00. 🚌 692, 695. **Open** Apr: 10am–6pm Sat, Sun & hols; May–Oct: 10am– 6pm Tue–Sun; Nov–Mar: 10am–4pm Sat, Sun & hols.

The Marmorpalais is situated on the edge of the lake in Neuer Garten *(see p201)*, a park northeast of the centre of Potsdam. This small palace is a beautiful example of early Neo-Classical architecture and owes its name to its façade, which is lined with Silesian marble.

The square main body of the palace was the initiative of King Friedrich Wilhelm II. The original building was completed in 1791 to a design by Carl von Gontard, under the direction of Carl Gotthard Langhans. The single-storey building had small rooms around a central staircase, but this turned out to be too small, and in 1797 it was extended. An extra floor and two projecting wings were added. This gave the Marmorpalais the character of a Palladian villa.

The main part of the palace contains Neo-Classical furnishings from the late 1700s, including furniture from the workshops of Roentgen and porcelain from Wedgwood, the English firm. The interiors of the wings date from slightly later, from the 1840s. The concert hall in the right-hand wing is particularly beautiful. King Friedrich Wilhelm II died in this palace in 1797.

Neo-Classical Marmorpalais, with its inlaid marble façade

The historic Dutch district known as the Holländisches Viertel

⑰ Holländisches Viertel
Dutch Quarter

Friedrich-Ebert-/Kurfürsten-/Hebbel-/Gutenbergstr. 🚌 604, 609, 692. 🚊 91, 92, 94, 96.

Just as amazing as the Russian district of Alexandrowka *(see pp200–201)* is this Dutch district. The area is popular with tourists, with numerous shops, galleries, cafés and beer cellars, especially along the central Mittelstrasse.

Dutch workers, invited by Friedrich Wilhelm I, arrived in Potsdam at the beginning of the 18th century. Between 1733 and 1742 a settlement was built for them, comprising 134 gabled houses arranged in four groups, according to plans by Johann Boumann the Elder. They were built from small red bricks and finished with stone and plaster details. These houses are typically three-storey, with picturesque roofs and gables.

⑱ Peter und Paul Kirche

Bassinplatz. **Tel** (0331) 230 79 90. 🚌 604, 609, 612. 🚊 91, 92, 94, 96. **Open** Mon–Sat; opening hours vary so call ahead. 🚏 10am Sun.

This 19th-century church was the first large Catholic church built in Potsdam, at the initiative of Friedrich Wilhelm IV. The first designs came from Friedrich August Stüler, but the final version is the work of Wilhelm Salzenberg. The church was built in 1870, in the shape of a Neo-Romanesque cross. Its slender tower is a copy of the campanile of San Zeno Maggiore in Verona, Italy. Inside are three beautiful paintings by Antoine Pesne.

The colonnaded portico of the Französische Kirche

⑲ Französische Kirche
French Church

Bassinplatz. **Tel** (0331) 29 12 19. 🚌 604, 609, 612. 🚊 93, 94, 99. **Open** late Mar–Oct: 1:30–5pm daily.

This church, reminiscent of the Pantheon in Rome, was built especially for the Hugenots in 1752. Following their expulsion from France, they were given the option of settling in Prussia in 1685 *(see p23)*. Those who settled in Potsdam benefited from the hospitality of other churches, then eventually the Französische Kirche was built for them. It was designed by Johann Boumann the Elder in the shape of an ellipse. The front elevation is supported by a grand columned portico. The side niches, which are the entrances of the church, are decorated with the allegorical figures of Faith and Knowledge.

The interior dates from the 1830s and is based on designs by Karl Friedrich Schinkel.

⑳ Nikolaikirche

Am Alten Markt. **Tel** (0331) 270 86 02. 🚌 604, 605, 609, 610, 695. 🚊 91, 92, 93, 94, 96, 99, X98. **Open** Oct–Apr: 9am–5pm daily; Mar–Sep: 9am–7pm daily.

This imposing church, built in a late Neo-Classical style, is the most beautiful church in Potsdam. It was designed in 1830 by Karl Friedrich Schinkel and the building work was overseen by Ludwig Persius. The main body of the church is based on a square cross, with a semicircular presbytery.

It was decided only in the 1840s to crown the church with a vast dome, supported on a colonnaded tambour (wall supporting a dome). Schinkel had envisaged this from the beginning of the project, but it was not included in the orders of the king. Initially it was thought that the dome would be supported by a wooden structure, though ultimately it was built using iron between 1843 and 1848, according to a design by Persius and Friedrich August Stüler. The interior decoration and the furnishings of the church date back to the 1850s, and in the main area of the church they were based on the earlier designs by Schinkel.

In front of the church stands an obelisk built between 1753 and 1755 to a design by Prussian architect Georg Wenzeslaus von Knobelsdorff. Initially it was decorated by medallions depicting the portraits of Prussian rulers, but during the post-World War II restorations, they were replaced with portraits of renowned Prussian architects.

㉑ Altes Rathaus
Old Town Hall

Am Alten Markt. 🚌 604, 609, 692, 694. 🚊 90, 92, 93, 96, 98.

This elegant, colonnaded building, located on the eastern side of Alter Markt, is the old town hall. Designed by Johann Boumann the Elder, it was built in 1753 on the site of an earlier building that served a similar purpose. The uppermost storey, which features an ornamental attic roof, is decorated with the crest of Potsdam and allegorical sculptures. At the summit of the small tower are two

Atlas at Altes Rathaus

gilded figures of Atlas, each carrying a globe of the earth. The Altes Rathaus is currently used as a cultural centre. The interior of the neighbouring mid-18th-century building was also refurbished, and a glassed-in passageway was built, linking the two buildings.

The Potsdam Royal Palace was located at one time on the west side of Alter Markt. It was a massive two-storey building with three wings. There was also an elegant courtyard and a superb gateway crowned by a tower. The palace was built in 1662 on the site of a former castle, on the initiative of the Great Elector. Over the following years the palace was greatly enlarged and modernized for members of the royal family, including Frederick the Great (Friedrich II). After a bombing raid in 1945 the palace remained in ruins for many years, but the East German Government decided finally to pull down the remains in 1960. It is now the home of the Potsdam-Museum.

Potsdam Town Gates

The city of Potsdam was enclosed by a wall in 1722. This wall did not serve a defensive purpose – it was supposed to contain criminals and stop soldiers deserting. When the borders of the town were extended in 1733, new districts were also enclosed by the wall. There was a total of five city gates, of which three have survived. Jägertor has survived in its original condition and dates from 1733. Featuring solid, wide pillars, the gate is crowned with a group of sculptures depicting hunting dogs attacking a deer. Nauener Tor was redesigned in 1755 by Johann Gottfried Büring and, interestingly, it is one of the earliest examples of Neo-Gothic design occurring outside Great Britain. The most imposing of the gates is the Brandenburger Tor. It was rebuilt in 1770 in a Neo-Classical style to commemorate victory in the Seven Years' War (see p23). The designers, Gontard and Unger, gave it the appearance of an ancient triumphal arch. At the very top is a number of different groups of sculptures. These include figures from Greek mythology, such as Hercules and Mars.

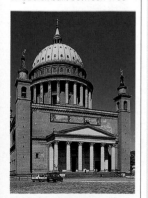
Nikolaikirche's imposing exterior, with its green, weathered dome

Nauener Tor   Jägertor   Brandenburger Tor

㉒ Potsdam-Museum

In the Altes Rathaus, Am Alten Markt. **Tel** (0331) 289 68 00. 📧 609, 692. 🚋 92, 96, 98. **Open** 10am–6pm Tue–Sun. ♿

The Potsdam-Museum was founded in 1909 by the citizens of the city, and has been bequeathed a sizeable collection of art and artifacts. Its changing collection is a reflection of local history and tells the story of Potsdam's development, from the earliest historical reference to the present day. A nearby branch of the museum, Memorial Linde 54/55, is a former prison and interrogation centre used by both the Nazi and East German regimes.

The impressive façade of the Potsdam-Museum

㉓ Marstall (Filmmuseum)

Breite Str 1A. **Tel** (0331) 27 18 10. 📧 605, 695. 🚋 91, 92, 96, 98. **Open** 10am–6pm Tue–Sun. ♿

This Baroque pavilion, once used as a royal stables, hence the name Marstall, is the only remaining building of a former royal residence. It was first established in 1714 by refashioning the orangery built by Johann Nering in 1685. In 1746 it was extended and refashioned once more, according to a design by the architect GW von Knobelsdorff. It suffered extensive damage in World War II and in 1977, after major restoration, it was converted to a film museum.

Stately building of the Marstall (Filmmuseum)

As well as temporary exhibitions, this museum documents the history and work of the Babelsberg studios, Germany's earliest film studios. Exhibits include old projectors, cameras and other equipment as well as props used in some of the most famous German films.

㉔ Wasserwerk Sanssouci

Breite Strasse 28. **Tel** (0331) 969 42 25. 📧 605, 606. 🚋 91, 94, X98. **Open** May–Oct: 10am–6pm Sat, Sun & hols. ♿

Although Potsdam once boasted a Russian and a Dutch community, the remarkable mosque (also called Dampfmaschinenhaus) was not built to serve the needs of an Islamic community, but to hide the special steam pump that serviced the fountains in Park Sanssouci. This Moorish-style building, with its minaret and Oriental dome, was designed by Ludwig Persius in 1842. The dome does not serve any useful

Moorish Wasserwerk Sanssouci, complete with minaret

purpose, although within the minaret there is a huge chimney. While visiting you can see the preserved steam-powered machinery made by the Borsig company.

㉕ Telegrafenberg

Albert-Einstein-Strasse. Ⓢ Potsdam Hauptbahnhof. Einsteinturm: **Tel** (0331) 74 99 469. **Open** May–Oct, by appointment only. ♿ compulsory.

The buildings on the Telegrafenberg are considered to be some of the best 20th-century structures in the world and attract many admirers of modern architecture. The hill received its current name in 1832, when an optical telegraph station linking Berlin and Koblenz was built here. In the late 19th century, various educational institutes were located here, including the Institute of Astrophysics, for which the complex of buildings in yellow brick was built.

The meandering avenues lead to a picturesque clearing where the small Einsteinturm (Einstein's Tower) breaks through the surrounding trees. Specially designed to observe the solar system, the tower was intended to provide information that would support Einstein's Theory of Relativity. It was built in 1920 by Erich Mendelsohn and is regarded as one of the finest architectural examples of German Expressionism. Its fantastical appearance was intended to show what could be achieved with reinforced concrete. However, the costs of the complicated form limited the use of concrete, and above the first storey the building is made from brick-work covered in plaster.

㉖ Filmpark Babelsberg

This amazing theme park was laid out on the site of the film studios where Germany's first films were produced in 1912. From 1917 the studio belonged to Universum-Film-AG (UFA), which produced some of the most renowned films of the silent era, such as *Metropolis (see p155)*. Nazi propaganda films were also made here. The studio is still operational today, although part of the complex is open to visitors. Expect to see the sets from old films, special effects at work and stuntmen in action.

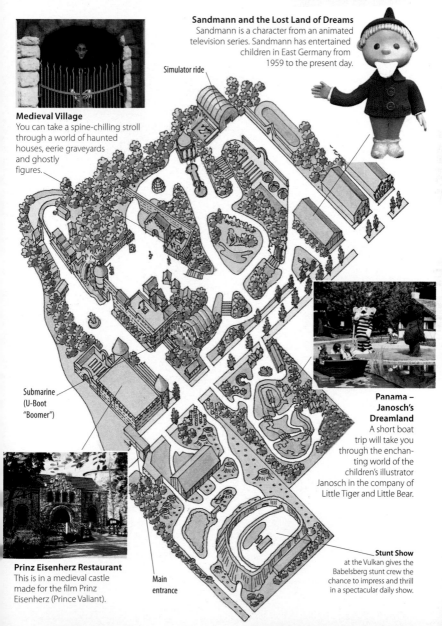

Medieval Village
You can take a spine-chilling stroll through a world of haunted houses, eerie graveyards and ghostly figures.

Simulator ride

Sandmann and the Lost Land of Dreams
Sandmann is a character from an animated television series. Sandmann has entertained children in East Germany from 1959 to the present day.

Submarine (U-Boot "Boomer")

Panama – Janosch's Dreamland
A short boat trip will take you through the enchanting world of the children's illustrator Janosch in the company of Little Tiger and Little Bear.

Prinz Eisenherz Restaurant
This is in a medieval castle made for the film Prinz Eisenherz (Prince Valiant).

Main entrance

Stunt Show
at the Vulkan gives the Babelsberg stunt crew the chance to impress and thrill in a spectacular daily show.

THREE GUIDED WALKS

Berlin is full of enchanting parks, gardens, lakes and interesting monuments, and one of the best ways to enjoy them is by going on a guided walk. The three walks suggested in this chapter provide for relaxation far from the hustle and bustle of the city centre. The first takes you onto the picturesque Pfaueninsel (Peacock Island), which at the end of the 18th century was refashioned into a romantic English-style park with garden pavilions and an enchanting little palace. After visiting the island you can pay a short visit to Nikolskoe – a Russian-style *dacha* (country house) built for the future Tsar Nicholas I and his wife, the daughter of King Friedrich Wilhelm III. The second walk begins in Berlin and takes you first through the grounds of the Klein Glienicke

Park, which was laid out in the 1820s for Prince Karl of Prussia. This route continues across the former border between East and West Germany, in an area which is now part of Potsdam. There you can visit the Romantic-era park of Babelsberg, and the Neo-Gothic palace designed for Prince Wilhelm by Karl Friedrich Schinkel. The third walk, around the forest called Grunewald, takes you initially through a deluxe villa resort of the late 19th century, and then along forest paths to the Grunewaldsee. On the shores of this lake stands an enchanting hunting lodge. From there you can continue walking to the Brücke-Museum. Because each of these three walks leads you across unpaved paths, remember to wear comfortable shoes.

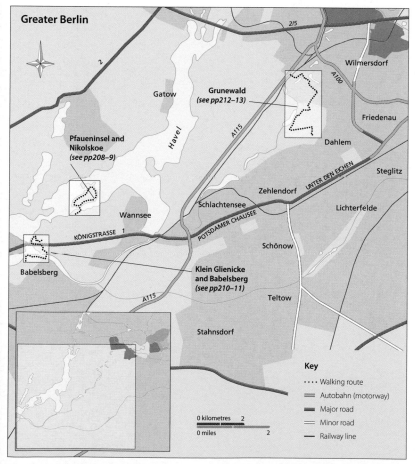

Greater Berlin

Wilmersdorf

Gatow

Grunewald
(see pp212–13)

Friedenau

Pfaueninsel and Nikolskoe
(see pp208–9)

Havel

Dahlem

Steglitz

UNTER DEN EICHEN

Zehlendorf

Lichterfelde

Schlachtensee

Wannsee

POTSDAMER CHAUSEE

KÖNIGSTRASSE

Schönow

Babelsberg

Klein Glienicke and Babelsberg
(see pp210–11)

Teltow

Stahnsdorf

Key

•••• Walking route

▭ Autobahn (motorway)

▬ Major road

═ Minor road

— Railway line

0 kilometres 2

0 miles 2

◀ The picturesque Neo-Gothic Babelsberg palace

For map symbols *see back flap*

Pfaueninsel and Nikolskoe

This walk takes you around Pfaueninsel (Peacock Island). This picturesque park, now a nature reserve, was laid out in 1795 according to a design by Johann August Eyserbeck. Its final form, which you see today, is the work of the renowned landscape architect Peter Joseph Lenné. This pleasant, relaxing walk allows you to explore several interesting sights, and to encounter the peacocks for which the island is named. Afterwards you can have refreshments at the lakeside, or head straight to Nikolskoe, the location of one of Berlin's finest restaurants.

James's Well, deliberately built to resemble a picturesque ruin

One of the colourful peacocks on Pfaueninsel (Peacock Island)

Around Pfaueninsel

At the jetty ① you board a small passenger ferry which takes you to the island in a few minutes. After disembarking, follow the path which leads to the left. It continues along the edge of the island, gently uphill to the Castellan's House ② and further on to the Swiss House, dating from 1830, in which the gardener lived. Continue along the path to the extensive clearing with a picturesque flower garden, beyond which is the small romantic palace of Schloss Pfaueninsel ③. Dating from 1794, it was designed by Johann Gottlieb

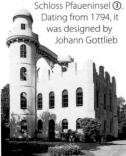

The Neo-Gothic Schloss Pfaueninsel designed by Johann Brendel

Brendel for Friedrich Wilhelm II and his mistress Wilhelmine Encke (the future Countess Lichtenau). The palace was built of wood, with a façade (hidden away) fashioned in the form of a ruined medieval castle. The façade was visible from Neuer Garten in Potsdam. The cast-iron bridge which links the towers was built in 1807. During the summer months you can go inside the palace to see its furnishings from the 18th and 19th centuries.

After leaving the palace follow the path that leads along the edge, passing by the kitchen pavilion ④ on the left, which is set amid greenery. At the next junction turn gently right into the depths of the island. You will pass by the James's Well ⑤ which was built to resemble an ancient ruin, and cross a meadow heading towards a small wood which contains the Kavalierhaus ⑥. This building was used to provide the royal household with accommodation. At the front of the

house, Karl Friedrich Schinkel installed an authentic façade from a late Gothic house brought over from Danzig (now Gdansk) in Poland. From here you proceed further in the same direction, and

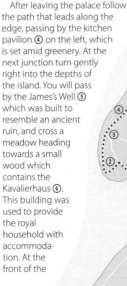

PFAUENINSELCHAUSSE

Wannsee
4km / 2.5 miles

NIKOLSKOER WEG

| 0 metres | 200 |
| 0 yards | 200 |

Key

• • • Suggested route

– – Ferry route

emerge again in a large clearing. To the left you can marvel at the Parschenkessel bay ⑦ in the distance, surrounded by dead trees on which cormorants nest. Take the path on the left to the Neo-Gothic Dairy ⑧ and the Dutch House ⑨. This was a cow shed and dates from 1802, while

Guests on the terrace of the Blockhaus Nikolskoe in summer

further along the edge of the lake, while on the right side among the trees you pass the stone commemorating Johannes Kunckel, an alchemist who lived on Pfaueninsel in the 17th century. In his quest to uncover how to make gold he, in fact, discovered a method of producing ruby coloured glass. Carry on further through the forest, passing the Gothic Bridge ⑪, and then take the path to the right up towards the hill of the Aviary ⑫, home to multi-coloured parrots and pheasants. From here you continue towards the tall column of a Fountain ⑬ designed by Martin Friedrich Rabe in 1824. Next, walk onward to the jetty, passing the market gardens with their hothouses on the way.

From the Jetty to Nikolskoe
Once you've taken the little ferry back to the mainland, head off to the right, going south. When you come to the fork take the left hand path leading gently uphill. This leads to the

Tips for Walkers

Beginning of the walk: the jetty for the ferry to Pfaueninsel.
Length: 4.4 km (2.7 miles).
Duration: 2.5–3 hours.
Getting there: Bus 218 or 316 from S-Bahn Wannsee; or ferry from Wannsee or Potsdam.
Stops: Pfaueninsel has no restaurants. "Wirtshaus zur Pfaueninsel" is by the jetty; "Blockhaus Nikolskoe" is in Nikolskoe. Schloss Pfaueninsel: **Open** Apr–Oct: 10am–5:30pm Tue–Sun. **Tel** 805 86 830.
Ⓦ spsg.de

church of Saints Peter and Paul ⑭, which rises above a large terrace from where there are pretty views of Pfaueninsel. The church was built between the years 1834 and 1837, according to a design by Friedrich August Stüler. The small, orderly, body of the church is fronted by a tower crowned by an onion-shaped dome, which reflects Russian Orthodox sacral architecture. This links to the adjacent Blockhaus "Nikolskoe" ⑮, a Russian-style wooden *dacha* (country house), built in 1819 by the architect Snethlage, who created the Alexandrowka estate in Potsdam. The *dacha* was a present from King Friedrich Wilhelm III to his daughter and son-in-law, the future Tsar Nicholas I. Following a fire in 1985 the *dacha* was reconstructed, and it currently houses a restaurant. Nearby you will find a bus-stop where you can catch buses back to the S-Bahn Wannsee.

Havel

the Dairy is an artificial ruin of a medieval abbey dating from 1795. From here take the path along the edge of the lake heading south; you can marvel at the wonderful views. To the right by the edge of the forest you can see Luisentempel ⑩ in the form of a Greek temple. Its sandstone portico at the front was moved to the island from the mausoleum in Schlosspark Charlottenburg *(see p167)* in 1829. The path leads

The little ferry on the Havel river which takes passengers to Pfaueninsel

For map symbols *see back flap*

Glienicke and Babelsberg

This guided walk takes you through an area covered by two interesting palace-park complexes – Glienicke and Babelsberg. They were built originally for members of the royal family during the mid-19th century. The buildings of Glienicke were designed by Schinkel, Persius and von Arnim in a Neo-Classical style. Peter Joseph Lenné created the charming park in which they are located. Babelsberg has a more romantic park that was completed by Hermann von Pückler-Muskau. It is maintained in a completely different style, with regal Neo-Gothic pavilions.

Mosaic from the Klosterhof in the gardens of Klein Glienicke

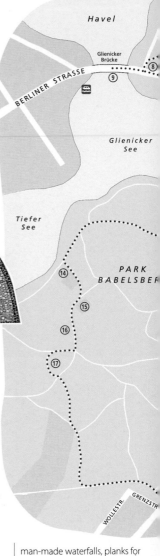

Around Glienicke

The walk begins by the main gate leading into the park. The southern section of the park has the feel of an Italianate Arcadian garden. Soon on the left you will see the Stibadium ①, a roofed pavilion designed by Ludwig Persius. Nearby you can marvel at the imposing Fountain of Lions ②, decorated with gilded figures of these royal beasts. The fountain stands on the axis of the palace ③ which was built in 1825, according to a design by

The reconstructed Gothic Gerichtslaube (arcaded courthouse)

Karl Friedrich Schinkel for Prince Carl of Prussia. During the summer, you can visit the palace between 10am and 6pm. Beyond the symmetrical, Neo-Classical building extends an irregular cluster of buildings, grouped around a courtyard with a veranda, which include a pergola and staff cottages. You pass by the palace and approach the Coach House ④, designed by Schinkel but refurbished several times. This now houses the Coach House restaurant.

Beyond the Coach House you can see the orangery and greenhouses built by Persius. A path leads in the direction of the lake, but on the way it is worth diverting to the right to the Klosterhof ⑤, a mock monastery with pavilions, also by Persius. In the walls of these buildings are numerous Byzantine and Romanesque architectural elements from Italy. Further to the north extends a second "wild" section of the park created to resemble an alpine and Carpathian landscape, with

man-made waterfalls, planks for crossing the water, and hunting lodges. You can return in the direction of the lake and go up to the Casino ⑦, which once contained guest apartments. From here a path extending along the lake takes you to the Grosse Neugierde ⑧, a circular pavilion with a roof supported by Doric columns, based on the Athenian monument to Lysikrates from the 4th century BC. From here there are beautiful views across the Havel river and Glienicker Brücke ⑨, known

From Glienicke to Babelsberg

On leaving the park you cross to the other side of Potsdamer Chaussee and proceed along Mövenstrasse, passing the massive building of the Jagdschloss Glienicke ⑪ on the right. Located on the site of an earlier hunting lodge, its Neo-Mannerist appearance is the result of a massive rebuilding process undertaken in 1889 by Albert Geyer, on behalf of Prince Friedrich Leopold. It now houses an international meeting centre as well as an academy of folk art. Passing the Jagdschloss you turn right into Waldmüllerstrasse, then right again into Lankestrasse, which leads you to the bridge linking Glienicke with Babelsberg.

Around Schloss Babelsberg

From the bridge you head right towards the engine house ⑫, designed by Persius to look like a medieval castle with a tall tower covering the chimney. From here you head towards Schloss Babelsberg ⑬, designed by Karl Friedrich Schinkel for the future Kaiser Wilhelm I of Germany. The palace was built between 1833 and 1835 in a Neo-Gothic style and shows the influence of English architecture on Schinkel. This beautiful, irregular building with many towers and bay windows is one of

Babelsberg's Neo-Gothic Flatowturm dating from 1853 to 1856

Schinkel's greatest works. Visitors can go inside.

From here, take the path leading along the edge of the Havel to the so-called Kleines Schloss ⑭. Another Neo-Gothic palace, although much smaller in scale, this was where ladies of the court once resided. It now houses a café.

From here you proceed further to the edge of the lake, taking the left branch to the Neo-Gothic stable ⑮, and further to the Gerichtslaube (Gothic arcaded courthouse) ⑯ which was moved here from Berlin. The final sight on this walk is the Flatowturm ⑰, a Neo-Gothic tower dating from 1853 to 1856, from which there are marvellous views of the surrounding area. From here follow the path to the park exit at Grenzstrasse. Turning left, you reach the bus stop for the No. 694 which goes to S-Bahn Babelsberg station.

paradoxically as the bridge of unity under the East German regime. The border with West Berlin ran across this bridge, where the exchange of spies was conducted during the Cold War. You return via a path along the wall of the main gate, passing the Kleine Neugierde ⑩, a pavilion serving as a tea room. This was built in the form of an ancient temple, and its walls contain original Roman and Byzantine fragments.

0 metres	300
0 yards	300

Key

• • • Suggested route

For map symbols *see back flap*

The Neo-Gothic Schloss Babelsberg, designed by KF Schinkel

Tips for Walkers

Beginning of the walk: bus stop at Glienicker Brücke.
Length: 4.2 km (2.6 miles).
Duration: 3 hours.
Getting there: bus 316 from S-Bahn station Wannsee or ferry from Wannsee or Potsdam.
Stops: Café at Park Babelsberg; Coach House at Glienicke. Schloss Babelsberg: **Open** Apr–Oct: 10am–6pm Sat, Sun & hols. **Tel** (0331) 969 42 50 for latest information. Ⓦ spsg.de

Grunewald

This walk leads initially through one of Berlin's most elegant residential areas, established in 1889. Once the haunt of politicians, wealthy industrialists, renowned artists and academics, some villas now serve as the headquarters of academic institutes. This walk continues through the forest to a small hunting lodge with an interesting art collection, and ends at the edge of the Grunewald in a residential estate of elegant villas, home of the Brücke-Museum.

The elegant villa at Winklerstrasse No. 11

From Bahnhof Grunewald to Hagenstrasse

From the S-Bahn Grunewald station follow the signs to "Grunewald (Ort)". Be sure to take a close look at the station itself ① – this picturesque wooden framed building was built in 1899. The station has a dark past, though, as Berlin's Jews were transported from here to the concentration camps. From the square in front of the station go along Winklerstrasse, which turns left. Along the way you will pass stunningly beautiful villas. The Neo-Classical house at No. 15, dating from 1899, was home to architect Ewald Becher ②. Not much further on the same side of the road, at No. 11, is a villa dating from 1906 ③. It was designed by Hermann Muthesius, who transplanted onto German soil the style of English rustic building. On the right at No. 12 is Villa Maren, dating from 1897, an example of a Neo-Renaissance building in the style of an Italian

palazzo with *sgraffito* decorations ④. The villa at No. 8–10, dating from 1902, boasts costly stone elevations, which fan out richly with decorations in the German Renaissance style ⑤. By this villa turn right into Hasensprung, which leads across the bridge decorated with running hares, dividing Dianasee from Königssee. You reach Königsallee and turn left before immediately turning right into Lassenstrasse, and then right again into Bismarckstrasse, which leads to a small square where you can marvel at the picturesque Neo-Gothic Grunewald-Kirche ⑥. From here go left into Furtwänglerstrasse, where it is worth looking at the villa at No. 15, a beautiful example of a southern German country house ⑦. Next turn right into Hubertusbader Strasse, where at No. 25 an interesting villa has survived with Neo-Classical motifs ⑧, which is the work of

Rose window, Grunewald-Kirche

Arnold Hartmann dating from 1896. He is also responsible for the villa at No. 23 Seebergsteig, featuring fantastic elevations decorated with Secessionist motifs ⑨. From here continue along Hubertusbader Strasse to Hagenstrasse.

From Hagenstrasse to the Brücke-Museum

You cut through Hagenstrasse and continue further, straight into Wildpfad, where you turn left in Waldmeisterstrasse, which leads along the fence of the grounds of private clubs. Turn right into Eichhörn-

Key

• • • Suggested route

chensteig, which gradually becomes surrounded by forest and changes from being a road into a forest path. Once past the grounds of the private clubs, follow a road which goes gently to the right, and down to the edge of the picturesque Grunewaldsee. Turn left and continue along its edge to Jagdschloss Grunewald ⑩. This is one of the oldest civic buildings to survive in Berlin. It was built for the Elector Joachim II in 1542, and around 1700 it was rebuilt in a Baroque style. Through the gate you enter a courtyard enclosed on three sides with household buildings. In the small palace is Berlin's only surviving Renaissance hall. It houses a collection of paintings, with canvases by Rubens and van Dyck among others. In the east wing is the small Waldmuseum, with illustrations that depict forest life. Following a fire, which destroyed the roof and other parts of the building, the Jagdschloss underwent extensive renovation work and reopened in 2009.

From the palace you proceed further along the edge to Forsthaus Paulsborn ⑪ (see p242). This picturesque building was constructed in 1905, according to a design by Friedrich Wilhelm Göhre. The entire building is maintained in the style of a hunting lodge with decorations that reflect hunting themes. During the

The household buildings in the hunting lodge in Grunewald

summer the garden is filled with tables, where you can enjoy a tasty meal and have a rest, following the walk. From Paulsborn you return to Jagdschloss Grunewald; at the crossroads you should take the central avenue sign-posted "Wilmersdorf". This leads through the forest and emerges on Pücklerstrasse. Passing modern deluxe villas you continue straight on, and then turn right into Fohlenweg, then turn right again into Bussardsteig, at the end of which is the Brücke-Museum (see p184) ⑫. It is also worth looking at the exhibition of sculptures by Bernhard Heliger arranged in the garden surrounding the villa at Käuzchensteig No. 8. From here you continue to Clayallee where buses on the No. 115 route operate.

Restaurant in the Forsthaus Paulsborn near Jagdschloss Grunewald

Tips for Walkers

Beginning of the walk: Grunewald S-Bahn station.
Distance: 3 km (1.8 miles).
Duration: 2.5–3 hours.
Getting there: S-Bahn line 3 or 7; U-Bahn Oskar-Helene-Heim; Bus 115.
Museum: Jagdschloss Grunewald. **Tel** 813 35 97.
Open Apr–Oct: 10am–6pm Thu–Sun; Nov–Mar: guided tours only, 11am, 1pm, 3pm Sat–Sun & hols.
Stops: The Grunewald area has numerous cafés and restaurants, including Forsthaus Paulsborn near Jagdschloss Grunewald.

0 metres 400
0 yards 400

TRAVELLERS' NEEDS

WHERE TO STAY

Berlin has a good selection of hotels to suit any budget. Many of the expensive hotels belong to well-known international chains, but you can also find reasonably priced rooms in and around the centre. There are good-quality mid-range hotels in eastern Berlin, where many new hotels have been built recently. There is no lack of luxurious hotels in eastern Berlin, either, particularly around Unter den Linden. Many of the more affordable hotels in the western part of Berlin require urgent repairs. The area around Grunewald is an oasis of peace that will guarantee a good rest. From the numerous hotels in Berlin, this section highlights some of the best; these have been categorized according to themes, location and price. Details about each of the hotels can be found on pages 222–5. Information about alternative ways of spending a night can be found on pages 220–21.

The elegant lobby of the Hotel Adlon Kempinski *(see p225)*

Where to Look

There are a few areas in Berlin with large concentrations of hotels. In each area there is usually at least one luxury hotel as well as several more affordable places. In Charlottenburg, around Kurfürstendamm and Tauentzienstrasse, are well-known hotels, such as the Kempinski Hotel Bristol Berlin, Savoy, Palace Berlin and the Steigenberger. Bear in mind that this part of Berlin was severely damaged during World War II and the majority of these hotels occupy modern buildings; hotels in old buildings, like the Brandenburger Hof, are a rarity. Inexpensive hotels and pensions can be found in the side streets off the main road, but ask to see the rooms before you decide. Good hotels are also situated in the east part of Tiergarten, around Lützowufer.

The most luxurious hotels can be found in Eastern Berlin, where many first-class hotels occupy lavishly restored historic landmark buildings. The Adlon (now called Hotel Adlon Kempinski), Regent and Hotel de Rome, situated in the western part of Mitte around Unter den Linden, are the most luxurious. In the eastern part of this area, around Alexanderplatz, the hotels are more reasonably priced but still offer good-quality rooms.

Grunewald is an oasis of peace far from the bustle of Berlin. There is the luxurious Schloss-hotel Berlin, as well as cosy pensions and little hotels, some set in 19th-century villas and palaces.

If you don't mind staying outside the centre of Berlin, you should head for Neukölln. Here, close to Treptower Park, is the enormous Estrel – the largest hotel in Germany.

Hotel Prices

Hotel prices in Berlin do not alter much with the season. However, major events and trade fairs do push up prices. Many more luxurious hotels offer weekend discounts and often, if you just turn up without a reservation, you can find yourself a good deal. If you intend to stay for an extended period of time, try to negotiate a better rate. Many hotels offer discounts if you book ahead via their website.

Hidden Extras

In Germany, taxes are included in hotel room rates, but you are expected to tip for any additional services, such as bringing luggage to the room or booking a theatre ticket. Hotels from the Dorint chain are an exception: they provide a range of services (such as free bicycle hire) at no additional cost.

There is also no hard and fast rule about breakfast: it is best to ask if it is included in the price when making a

Swimming pool at the Hotel de Rome *(see p224)*

◀ Galeries Lafayette, Friedrichstrasse

One of the artist-decorated rooms in the Arte Luise Kunsthotel *(see p224)*

reservation. Most Berlin hotels have their own parking spaces, but rates are sometimes exorbitant. Ask about telephone charges before using the phone in your room and check the exchange rates before using this service. Items from the minibar and paid-television channels can also turn out to be surprisingly costly. Wi-Fi is available at most hotels, however you may be charged for using the Internet.

Facilities

There is no standardized system of categorizing hotels by stars in Germany, although the price of a room usually reflects the quality. Small hotels usually include breakfast – typically rolls, jam, chocolate spread, cereal, cold meats, cheese and coffee. They will probably not have a restaurant and their services are limited. Larger hotels tend to provide a full American buffet on top of the traditional German fare.

If you are staying for a longer period, consider an Aparthotel – an apartment, complete with a fully-equipped kitchen – or a private apartment (see www.craigslist.org/berlin). This is a good idea of you are travelling with a small group.

Saunas and Spas

Many of the more expensive hotels are equipped with spa and sauna facilities. These are usually unisex (though some spas have women's days) and it is very unusual for either sex to

wear a swimsuit. Guests should be prepared to only wear towels and for other sauna users to be in the nude. In fact, wearing swimsuits in sauna areas is often considered rude and unhygienic, particularly in Finnish or steam saunas, as well as in whirlpools. Spa etiquette usually also calls for silence in the room. In dry Finnish saunas, an "Aufguss", the repeated infusion of fresh herbs and heat is usually announced.

When entering a steam sauna, clean the seat before you sit down. There is usually a water hose at the entrance for this purpose. After 8–15 minutes in the sauna, shower or rinse off with ice-cold water (the cold-water bath is only suitable for the physically fit). Rest and then continue the cycle once or twice. Do not drink alcohol when visiting a sauna, and make

Conference room in the Hotel Villa Kastania *(see p224)*

sure you take in fluids and vitamins (usually offered in the form of water and lemon slices).

Hotel spas, such as those at the Grand Hyatt, Hotel de Rome and Hotel Intercontinental are exceptional. In winter, try the Badeschiff Arena, a sauna and swimming pool complex built on pontoons on the Spree river *(see p272)*.

How to Book

You can book a room in Berlin by telephone, email or online. If you prefer, you can use the city's tourist service **Berlin Tourismus Marketing** *(see p221)*, www.visitberlin.de. This company can make your booking in hotels throughout Berlin. When making a reservation be prepared to give your credit card details

If you are already in Berlin and would like to find a comfortable room, your best option is to go to one of the large tourist information bureaux. Some of the best of these are situated in the **Neues Kranzler-Eck**, at the **Brandenburg Gate**, and at **Hauptbahnhof** *(see 221)*.

Private Rooms

Bed & Breakfast-style accommodation is not particularly popular in Berlin, although this kind of service can be found in some of the residential districts far from the city centre. You can obtain information about them from tourist information bureaux and the other organizations whose numbers are listed in the Directory *(see p221)*.

Travelling with Children

Travelling with children in Berlin should not present a problem. A cot can be requested in most hotels, and there is usually no extra charge for having a small child in the room, although an extra bed for an older child may sometimes incur a cost. In better hotels, a reliable babysitter can be obtained at a few hours' notice. In hotel restaurants, high chairs for children are standard.

The luxurious lounge at the Kempinski Hotel Bristol Berlin

Disabled Travellers

Nearly all top-quality and luxury hotels are able to accommodate disabled travellers – at least one entrance will have wheelchair access and some rooms will have specially adapted bath-rooms. Unfortunately, the situation in mid-range and lower standard hotels is not as promising; special equipment is a rarity. In very old buildings, there may not be an elevator. The **Hotel Mondial** *(see p223)*,

The elegant lobby area of the Marriott Hotel

located near Kurfürstendamm, is recommended for disabled travellers. It has many facilities for wheelchair users in all its public rooms and has as many as 22 bedrooms equipped for people with special needs.

Deposits

In many Berlin hotels, a deposit may be requested either when reserving the room or upon checking in at the hotel. A credit card is the most common way to secure a room over the telephone. Otherwise, be prepared to use cash to pay about 20 to 40 per cent of the price for one night's stay. The amount you pay as a deposit should always be credited to the final bill. In some smaller hotels or pensions, don't be surprised if you are asked to pay for your first night's accomm-odation in full on arrival.

Youth Hostels

It is easy to find inexpensive accommodation in Berlin at a youth hostel. The **DJH (Landesverband Berlin-Brandenburg)**, an organization that belongs to the International Youth Hostels Association, gives discounts to all its members. Membership is usually inexpensive and you will have to join to stay at a hostel. The DJH has hostels in different locations throughout Berlin. There are also many independent youth hostels and hotels for students in Berlin that do not belong to any organization. You can find them at www.hostelworld.com.

The type of accommodation offered usually consists of dormitory-style rooms with bunk beds. There is often a communal bathroom on each floor and a kitchen is usually available for cooking your own meals. Most youth hostels have a dining room where breakfast and a hot evening meal are served. Some youth hostels are closed during the day, allowing no access to the rooms; confirm this in advance.

Camping

Camping is a popular pastime throughout Germany, and the **Deutscher Camping Club** has a lot of information about campsites in and around Berlin. This organisation also provides information about indepen-dently run campsites in Berlin.

Campsites are open usually from the beginning of April until the end of October. There are two exceptions: the Berlin-Kladow in Spandau and the Am Krossinsee in Köpenick, which are open year-round. The majority of people staying at campsites are young, particularly during the Oktoberfest *(see p52)* and in June, when the Christopher Street Day Parade takes place *(see p51)*. During these times some campsites can be very busy and noisy.

Illuminated façade of the Westin Grand

Organized Youth Groups

Berlin has a large base of accommodation for organized youth groups. Most of these are hostel-style accommodation, situated on the outskirts of the city. They were established not only for the purpose of school trips but also for children from West Berlin; until the unification of Germany in 1990, it was difficult for youth groups to organize trips to the countryside so they had to opt for trips to the Grunewald instead. Information about availability and bookings is offered by **Berlin Tourismus Marketing** and by larger tourist information centres, such as at Neues Kranzler Eck.

The spacious lobby of the Hotel Palace

Recommended Hotels

The hotels on pages 222–25 of this guide are a selection of the best budget, business, charming and luxury hotels in Berlin. They are first listed according to theme, and then alphabetically by area. Most of the hotels are spread across the main tourist areas, although a number that are further afield are included if they offer particularly good value for money, facilities, service or charm. There are also B&Bs, guesthouses and apartments included. What they all have in common is that, regardless of category and price, they have something special to offer.

Where a hotel has an exceptional feature, such as great-value rates, or spectacular views it has been highlighted as a DK Choice.

DIRECTORY

Information and Booking

Berlin Tourismus Marketing
Am Karlsbad 11, Berlin.
Map 14 D1.
Tel 25 00 25.
🖳 visitberlin.de

Brandenburg Gate
Pariser Platz,
southern building.
Map 8 E3.
Open 9:30am–6pm daily.

Hauptbahnhof
Europaplatz 1, level 0,
northern entrance.
Map 8 D1.
Open 8am–10pm daily.

Potsdam Tourismus Service
Am Neuen Markt 1.
Tel (0331) 27 55 88 99.
🖳 potsdamtourismus.de

Tourist Information
Neues Kranzler-Eck,
Kurfürstendamm 22.
Map 12 D1.
Open 10am–8pm Mon–Sat, 9:30am–6pm Sun.

Private Rooms

Bed & Breakfast in Berlin
Tel 44 05 05 82.
🖳 bed-and-breakfast-berlin.de

Coming Home
Tel 21 79 800.
🖳 coming-home.org

Erste Mitwohnzentrale
Sybelstrasse 53,
10629 Berlin-Charlottenburg.
Map 11 A2.
Tel 324 30 31.
🖳 mitwohn.com

Fine and mine
Neue Schönhauser Str. 20,
10178 Berlin.
Map 9 C2.
Tel 23 55 120.

Wohnwitz
Holsteinische Strasse 55,
10717 Berlin-Wilmersdorf.
Map 11 C4, C5.
Tel 861 82 22.
🖳 wohnwitz.com

Disabled Travellers

Berliner Behindertenverband
Jägerstrasse 63d,
10117 Berlin-Mitte.
Tel 204 38 47.

Der Landesbeauftragte für Menschen mit Behinderung
Oranienstrasse 106, 10997 Berlin. **Tel** 90 28 29 17.

Youth Hostels

DJH (Landesverband Berlin-Brandenburg)
Service centre:
Kluckstrasse 3, 10785 Berlin.
Tel 264 95 20.
Open 8am–6pm Mon–Fri.
Hostelworld
🖳 Hostelworld.com

Jugendherberge Berlin am Wannsee
Badeweg 1, 14129 Berlin.
Tel 803 20 34

Jugendherberge Berlin International
Kluckstrasse 3, 10785 Berlin. **Map** 13 C1.
Tel 747 68 79 10.

Jugendherberge Ernst Reuter
Hermsdorfer Damm 48,
13467 Berlin.
Tel 404 16 10.

Camping

DCC-Campingplatz Berlin-Gatow
Kladower Damm 213–17,
14089 Berlin.
Tel 365 43 40.
Open Apr–Sep: am–1pm, 3–10pm daily; Oct–Mar: 8am–1pm, 3–9pm daily.

DCC-Campingplatz Berlin-Kladow
Krampnitzer Weg 111,
14089 Berlin.
Tel 364 22 97.
Open Apr–Sep: 6am–1pm, 3–10pm daily; Oct–Mar: 8am–1pm, 3–9pm daily.

Deutscher Camping Club
Kladower Damm 207–213,
14089 Berlin.
Tel 218 60 71.
🖳 dccberlin.de

Where to Stay

Budget

Around Unter den Linden

City Hostel Berlin €
Glinkastrasse 5, 10117
Tel *238 866 85* **Map** 8 F5
🆆 cityhostel-berlin.com
Modern rooms with en suite bathrooms. Free breakfast and Wi-Fi. Great terrace bar.

Intermezzo für Frauen €
Gertrud-Kolmar-Strasse 5, 10117
Tel *224 890 96* **Map** 8 E4
🆆 hotelintermezzo.de
A hotel that caters to women. Bright and spacious rooms, and a good breakfast spread.

East of the Centre

Alameda €
Michaelkirchstrasse 15, 10179
Tel *308 683 30* **Map** 10 E5
🆆 hotel-alameda-berlin.de
Seventeen well-equipped and comfortable attic rooms, some with balconies. Great location.

City Stay €
Rosenstrasse 16, 10178
Tel *236 240 31* **Map** 9 C2
🆆 citystay.de
Loft-style rooms, a lobby bar, a cobbled courtyard and free Wi-Fi. Elaborate breakfast spread.

North of the Centre

A&O Berlin Hauptbahnhof €
Lehrter Strasse 11, 10557
Tel *322 920 42 00* **Map** 7 C1
🆆 aohostels.com
Dorms, singles and doubles (with private showers available). Comfortable lounge area. Pet friendly.

DK Choice

Circus €–€€
Rosenthaler Strasse 1, 10119
Tel *200 039 39* **Map** 9 B1
🆆 circus-berlin.de
This fun hotel often wins accolades for its high standards of service and unbeatable value for money. The location on Rosenthaler Platz is another big plus for those drawn to the city's nightlife. Circus also offers guests numerous extras, from bike rentals to rickshaw tours and baby-sitting. Enjoy the elaborate breakfast spread, or a coffee at the Circus Cafe.

Generator €
Storkower Strasse 160, 10407
Tel *417 24 00*
🆆 generatorhostels.com
Large hostel with private rooms and female dorms. Just 10 minutes from Alexanderplatz.

Hotel Albrechtshof €
Albrechtstrasse 8, 10117
Tel *30 30 88 60* **Map** 8 F2
🆆 hotel-albrechtshof.de
Reasonably priced rooms that are simple and tastefully done. Pleasing garden and rooftop views.

Transit Loft €
Immanuelkirchstrasse 14a, 10405
Tel *484 937 73* **Map** 2 F4
🆆 transit-loft.de
Medium-sized, family-friendly hotel in a converted factory. Clean, well-maintained rooms.

Tiergarten

Familie Herfort €
Flensburger Strasse 27, 10557
Tel *399 043 33* **Map** 6 F2
🆆 fewobe-berlin.de
Nine spacious and well-equipped apartments. Convenient location and impeccable service.

Hotel am Schloss Bellevue €
Paulstrasse 3, 10557
Tel *391 12 27* **Map** 7 B2
🆆 hotelamschlossbellevue.de
Small, cosy hotel with innovative rooms decorated by a young local grafitti artist.

Meininger City Hotel €
Ella-Trebe-Strasse 9, 10557
Tel *666 361 00* **Map** 8 D1
🆆 meiningerhotels.com
Modern and functional rooms with free Wi-Fi. There is a games room. Excellent transport links.

Price Guide
Prices are based on one night's stay in high season for a standard double room, inclusive of service charges and taxes.

€	up to €80
€€	€80–€180
€€€	over €180

Kreuzberg

Three Little Pigs Hostel Berlin €
Stresemannstrasse 66, 10963
Tel *263 958 80* **Map** 14 F1
🆆 three-little-pigs.de
Set in an old convent building in a vibrant, multicultural area. Free parking.

Around Kurfürstendamm

Air in Berlin hotel €
Ansbacher Strasse 6, 10787
Tel *212 99 20* **Map** 12 F1
🆆 hotelairinberlin.de
Three-star hotel with clean rooms in an excellent location.

ArtHotel Connection €–€€
Fuggerstrasse 33, 10777
Tel *210 21 88 00* **Map** 12 F2
🆆 arthotel-connection.de
Gay-friendly hotel in an Art Nouveau building. Great service.

Berolina an der Gedächtniskirche €
Rankestrasse 35, 10789
Tel *236 396 82* **Map** 12 E1
🆆 berolinahotels.de
No-frills hotel with cosy rooms. Close to West End restaurants.

City Pension €
Stuttgarter Platz 9, 10627
Tel *327 74 10* **Map** 11 A1
🆆 city-pension.de
Small, friendly hotel with spacious, well-appointed rooms. Some have en suite showers.

Bold interior design in Circus

Hotel Bogota €–€€
Schlüterstrasse 45, 10707
Tel *881 50 01* **Map** 11 B2
ⓦ bogota.de
Clean and comfortable rooms with
oodles of character and charm.
Warm and personable staff.

Hotel Pension Kürfurst €–€€
Bleibtreustrasse 34/35, 10707
Tel *885 68 20* **Map** 11 B2
ⓦ kurfuerst.com
Beautiful Art Nouveau mansion
with generously sized rooms that
are tastefully furnished.

Pension Funk €€
Fasanenstrasse 69, 10719
Tel *882 71 93* **Map** 12 D2
ⓦ hotel-pensionfunk.de
Early 20th-century town house
with period features. Decent-
sized rooms.

Further Afield

East Side Hotel €
Mühlenstrasse 6, 10243
Tel *251 71 59*
ⓦ eastsidehotel.de
Single, double and twin rooms
in a historic building. Excellent
on-site restaurant.

Michelberger Hotel €–€€
Warschauer Strasse 39/40, 10243
Tel *297 785 90*
ⓦ michelbergerhotel.com
Quirky but comfortable rooms,
and a friendly vibe. Enjoy live
music in the bar.

Pension Rotdorn €
Heerstrasse 36, 14055
Tel *300 992 92* **Map** 3 A5
ⓦ pension-rotdorn.de
Family-run pension set in a
grand old mansion. Decent-sized
rooms. Free parking and Wi-Fi.

Business

Around Unter den Linden

Arcotel John F €€
Werderscher Markt 11, 10117
Tel *405 04 60* **Map** 9 B4
ⓦ arcotelhotels.com
Modern hotel with large rooms
and an unbeatable location.
Great restaurant. Excellent service.

Meliá Hotel €€
Friedrichstrasse 103, 10117
Tel *206 079 00* **Map** 8 F3
ⓦ meliaberlin.com
Spanish chain hotel perfectly
located for major sights. Plush,
comfortable rooms and a fully
equipped gym.

The plush and inviting lobby of Derag
Livinghotel Henriette

East of the Centre

Derag Livinghotel Henriette €€
Neue Rossstrasse 13, 10179
Tel *246 009 00* **Map** 9 C4
ⓦ deraghotels.de
Reputable chain hotel with
comfortable, cosy rooms. Classy
decor and great service.

North of the Centre

Adina Apartment Hotels €€
Platz vor dem Neuen Tor 6, 10115
Tel *200 03 20* **Map** 8 E1
ⓦ adina.eu
Well-furnished studios and
apartments equipped with all
modern amenities.

Kastanienhof €€
Kastanienallee 65, 10119
Tel *44 30 50* **Map** 2 D4
ⓦ kastanienhof.biz
Friendly hotel with modern,
tastefully decorated rooms.

Maritim proArte Hotel €€
Friedrichstrasse 151, 10117
Tel *203 344 10* **Map** 8 F3
ⓦ maritim.de
Large, contemporary hotel with
clean and generous sized rooms.

Mercure Hotel Berlin City €€
Invalidenstrasse 38, 10115
Tel *30 82 60* **Map** 1 A5
ⓦ accorhotels.com
Luxurious three-star rooms in a
modern, centrally located hotel.

Tiergarten

Ameron Hotel Abion €€
Alt Moabit 99, 10559
Tel *39 92 00* **Map** 6 F2
ⓦ abion-hotel.de
Slick hotel, great for corporate
travellers. Spa service available.

Hotel Tiergarten €€
Alt-Moabit 89, 10559
Tel *39 98 96* **Map** 6 F1
ⓦ hotel-tiergarten.de
Bright, spacious rooms set in a
19th-century apartment block.
Great breakfast buffet.

Maritim Hotel Berlin €€
Stauffenbergstrasse 26, 10785
Tel *206 50* **Map** 7 C5
ⓦ maritim.de
Glitzy hotel with comfortable
rooms in a tranquil setting.
Excellent service.

Novotel am Tiergarten €€
Strassse des 17 Juni 106, 10623
Tel *60 03 50* **Map** 6 E4
ⓦ accorhotels.com
Comfortable large hotel with
every possible four-star amenity.

Around Kurfürstendamm

Ellington Hotel €€
Nürnberger Strasse 50–5, 10789
Tel *68 31 50* **Map** 12 E2
ⓦ ellington-hotel.com
Historic 19th-century building
with superior double rooms.
Great service standards.

H10 Kudamm €€
Joachimstaler Strasse 31, 10719
Tel *322 92 23 00* **Map** 12 D2
ⓦ hotelh10berlinkudamm.com
Modern hotel in a converted
19th-century school building.
Beauty and fitness centre on site.

Mondial €€
Kurfürstendamm 47, 10707
Tel *88 41 10* **Map** 11 B2
ⓦ hotel-mondial.com
Bright, spacious and pleasantly
decorated rooms at this hotel.
Disabled-friendly.

Further Afield

Andel's €€
Landsberger Allee 106, 10369
Tel *453 05 30* **Map** 10 F2
ⓦ vi-hotels.com
Award-winning, British-designed
hotel with great views over
Berlin. Chic and spacious rooms.

Charming Hotels
North of the Centre

Jurine €€
Schwedter Strasse 15, 10119
Tel *443 29 90* **Map** 2 D4
ⓦ hotel-jurine.de
Family-run hotel in a quiet
location. Enjoy the healthy
breakfast spread. Free Wi-Fi.

Myer's Hotel €€
Metzer Strasse 26, 10405
Tel *44 01 40* **Map** 2 E5
ⓦ myershotels.de
Classy hotel with a touch of
elegance. Unwind in the tea
room or on the outdoor terrace.

For more information on types of hotels *see pp218–21*

Tiergarten

DK Choice

Altberlin €€
Potsdamer Strasse 67, 10785
Tel *26 06 70* **Map** 13 C1
w altberlin-hotel.de
All 50 rooms at this cosy hotel
converted from a town house,
are furnished in authentic
period style. The excellent on-
site restaurant offers traditional
cuisine. Great modern amenities
in an enviable location.

Hansablick €€
Flotowstrasse 6, 10555
Tel *390 48 00* **Map** 6 E3
w hansablick.de
It's worth paying a little extra for
the deluxe doubles. Free Internet
in the lounge, plus a fitness room.

Kreuzberg

Hotel Johann €€
Johanniterstrasse 8, 10961
Tel *225 07 40* **Map** 15 B3
w hotel-johann-berlin.de
Bright, sunny rooms with barrel-
vaulted ceilings. Breakfast is
served in the garden in summer.

Riehmers Hofgarten €€
Yorckstrasse 83, 10965
Tel *780 988 00* **Map** 14 F4
w riehmers-hofgarten.de
A grand mansion with elegant
decor set in 19th-century courtyards. All modern amenities.

Around Kurfürstendamm

Art Nouveau €€
Leibnizstrasse 59, 10629
Tel *327 74 40* **Map** 11 A1
w hotelartnouveau.de
Spacious, tastefully furnished
rooms and suites with stucco
ceilings and wooden floors.

Axel €€
Lietzenburger Strasse 13/15, 10789
Tel *210 028 93* **Map** 12 F2
w axelhotels.com
Oriented towards the gay
community but open to everyone.
Great views from the skybar.

DK Choice

Louisa's Place €€€
Ku'damm 160, 10709
Tel *63 10 30* **Map** 11 A2
w louisas-place.net
This modernized and well-
furnished 1900s apartment
building preserves all its original
architectural features. The

suites are lavish and vary in
size. Relax in the hotel spa and
heated indoor pool or enjoy the
massage services on offer.

Mark Hotel Meineke €€€
Meinekestrasse 10, 10719
Tel *880 028 32* **Map** 12 D2
w berlinmarkhotels.de
Charming 19th-century town
house, minutes from Ku'damm.
Relax in the garden terrace.

Further Afield

Ostel Hostel €
Wriezener Karree 5, 10243
Tel *257 686 60*
w ostel.eu
Set in a 1980s apartment block,
this fun hotel recreates East Berlin
decor of the 70s and 80s.

Hotel Pension Enzian €€
Hortensienstrasse 28, 12203
Tel *832 50 75*
w hotel-pension-enzian.de
A charming hotel with spacious
rooms near the Botanical Garden.
Excellent on-site restaurant.

Schloss Hotel im Grunewald €€€
Brahmsstrasse 10, 14193
Tel *89 58 40*
w schlosshotelberlin.com
Luxurious mansion with opulent
rooms and impeccable service.

Honigmond Garden Hotel €€€
Invalidenstrasse 122, 10115
Tel *284 455 77*
w honigmond-berlin.de
Individually decorated rooms
and a secluded courtyard garden.
Convenient location.

Entrance to the luxurious Brandenburger
Hof hotel

Design/ Boutique
Around Unter den Linden

Cosmo €€
Spittelmarkt 13, 10117
Tel *585 822 22* **Map** 9 B5
w designhotels.com
A haven of tranquility amid the
bustle of the Mitte. Sleek rooms.

Hotel Gendarm Nouveau €€
Charlottenstrasse 61, 10117
Tel *206 06 60* **Map** 9 A4
w hotel-gendarm-berlin.de
Small hotel with tastefully
furnished rooms and great
service.

East of the Centre

Arte-Luise Kunsthotel €€
Luisenstrasse 19, 10117
Tel *28 44 80* **Map** 8 E2
w luise-berlin.com
Appealing rooms, individually
decorated by local artists. Excellent
on-site restaurant.

Lux 11 €€
Rosa-Luxemburg-Strasse 9–13, 10178
Tel *936 28 00* **Map** 10 C2
w lux-eleven.com
A minimalist hotel with clean,
bright and spacious rooms and
apartments. Fantastic service.

North of the Centre

DK Choice

Ackselhaus €€
Belforter Strasse 21, 10405
Tel *443 376 33* **Map** 2 E4
w ackselhaus.de
A beautifully restored 19th-
century property with lots of
charm and a lovely breakfast
garden. The rooms and suites
are individually designed and
decorated with flair. There is
also a special honeymoon suite
that can be requested. Relax in
the lovely Thai garden.

Casa Camper €€€
Weinmeisterstrasse 1, 10178
Tel *200 034 10* **Map** 9 C1
w casacamper.com
Sleek design and spacious rooms
at this hotel. Excellent on-site
restaurant and free Wi-Fi.

Tiergarten

Mandala €€€
Potsdamer Strasse 3, 10785
Tel *590 05 12 34* **Map** 8 D5
w themandala.de
Luxurious living in studio rooms,
suites or penthouses with views.

Nhow's striking and quirky interior design

Around Kurfürstendamm

Artemisia Frauen Hotel €€
Brandenburgische Strasse 18, 10707
Tel *860 93 20* **Map** 11 A3
W frauenhotel-berlin.de
A women-only hotel with a pleasant roof terrace. Great breakfast spread.

Askanischer Hof €€
Kurfürstendamm 53, 10707
Tel *881 80 33* **Map** 11 B2
W askanischer-hof.de
Art Deco features and glitzy interiors. Rooms vary in size but all are decorated with antiques.

Bleibtreu €€
Bleibtreustrasse 31, 10707
Tel *88 47 40* **Map** 11 B2
W bleibtreu.com
Well-equipped rooms with pine wood furnishings. Deli-restaurant, fitness centre and on-site spa.

Q Hotel €€
Knesebeckstrasse 67, 10623
Tel *810 06 60* **Map** 11 C1
W designhotels.com
Surprisingly affordable designer hotel aimed mainly at corporate travellers. Futuristic decor.

Brandenburger Hof €€€
Eislebener Strasse 14, 10789
Tel *21 40 50* **Map** 12 D2
W brandenburger-hof.com
A charming luxury hotel with lavish rooms and elegant decor. Soothing Japanese winter garden.

Further Afield

DK Choice

Nhow Berlin €€
Stralauer Allee 3, 10245
Tel *290 29 90*
W nhow-hotels.com
An amazing cantilevered structure jutting out over the Spree, this offbeat hotel will delight all lovers of design and music, which are the dominant themes. Nhow offers guitar and keyboard loans to rooms. There's also a rooftop sound studio.

Propeller Island City Lodge €€
Albrecht-Achilles-Strasse 58, 10709
Tel *891 90 16*
W propeller-island.com
Themed rooms, whimsically designed and furnished in a rather offbeat manner. Good service.

Villa Kastania €€€
Kastanienallee 20, 14052
Tel *300 00 20* **Map** 3 A5
W villakastania.com
Rooms are decorated with great attention to detail. Spa services available. Impeccable service.

Luxury Hotels
Around Unter den Linden

DK Choice

Adlon Kempinski €€€
Unter den Linden 77, 10117
Tel *226 115 55* **Map** 8 F3
W kempinski.com
The Adlon has won numerous plaudits, both for its impeccable standards of service and for being the final word in luxury. It offers exquisitely decorated bedrooms, and facilities such as Michelin-starred gourmet dining and an enormous spa in which to be pampered.

Hotel de Rome €€€
Behrenstrasse 37, 10117 **Map** 8 F4
Tel *460 60 90*
W roccofortecollection.com
Classy furnishings and alfresco dining on a rooftop terrace.

Regent €€€
Charlottenstrasse 49, 10117
Tel *203 38* **Map** 9 A4
W regenthotels.com
A celebrity magnet, this hotel boasts a Michelin two-star restaurant and other luxurious amenities. Workout in the state-of-the-art health club.

North of the Centre

Soho House €€€
Torstrasse 1, 10119
Tel *405 04 40* **Map** 10 E1
W sohohouseberlin.de
Rooms of various sizes in a prestigious private members club.

Tiergarten

Grand Hotel Esplanade €€
Lützowufer 15, 10785
Tel *25 47 80* **Map** 13 A1
W esplanade.de
Excellent amenities at this plush hotel. Convenient location.

Grand Hyatt €€€
Marlene-Dietrich-Platz 2, 10785
Tel *255 317 72* **Map** 8 D5
W berlin.grand.hyatt.de
Large business hotel with comfortable rooms and a charming sun-bathing terrace.

Around Kurfürstendamm

Savoy €€
Fasanenstrasse 9–10, 10623
Tel *31 10 30* **Map** 12 D1
W hotel-savoy.com
Historic hotel famous for its refined decor. Well-stocked bar.

Concorde €€€
Augsburger Strasse 41, 10789
Tel *800 99 90* **Map** 12 D1
W berlin.concorde-hotels.com
Sleek high rise in a great location. Unwind at the wellness centre, which has a sauna and solariums.

Swissôtel €€€
Augsburger Strasse 44, 10789
Tel *22 01 00* **Map** 12 D1
W sotel.com
Geared mainly towards business travellers. Large, well-lit rooms and warm service.

Waldorf Astoria €€€
Hardenbergstrasse 28, 10623
Tel *814 00 00* **Map** 12 D1
W placeshilton.com
Located in the Zoofenster Tower. Rooms have panoramic views and marble bathrooms.

Further Afield

Aspria Ku'damm €€€
Karlsruher Strasse 20, 10711
Tel *890 68 88 10* **Map** 5 A5
W aspria-berlin.de
Superb concept hotel that offers varied fitness facilities. Well-appointed rooms. Great service.

For more information on types of hotels *see pp218–21*

WHERE TO EAT AND DRINK

Given that Berlin is so cosmopolitan, you will find a wider range of restaurants here than in any other city in Germany. This includes Indian, Greek, Chinese, Thai and Turkish as well as Alsatian and Cambodian. Recently, new places have been opened by famous chefs, which maintain high European standards of international-style cuisine. There are also plenty of restaurants specializing in local dishes: the food can be a little heavy, but it is usually very tasty and served in large portions. Wherever you are in Berlin, you won't have to travel far to find somewhere to eat – every area has its own cluster of restaurants, cafés and bars, covering a range of styles and prices. Some of the best places are listed on pages 232–43. These have been chosen for their delicious food and/or good value. The listings on pages 244–9 should help those who would like a bite to eat but want the more relaxed setting of a café or bar.

The elegant interior of Margaux *(see p232)*

Where to Go

Although good restaurants and cafés can be found all over Berlin, some of the best gourmet restaurants tend to be located in exclusive hotels, including **Facil** in the Mandala *(see p236)* or **Fischer's Fritz** in the Regent *(see p232)*. Alternatively, some good restaurants, such as the excellent **Margaux Berlin** *(see p232)*, can also be found on quiet streets.

The largest concentrations of restaurants are in a number of well-known districts. In the former West Berlin, for example, the most famous restaurants are clustered around Savignyplatz. Good places to eat in the centre can be found in and around Oranienburger Strasse. One of the top spots in Berlin that is popular with young people is Prenzlauer Berg, near Kollwitzplatz. In the eastern part of Berlin, restaurants in Kreuzberg (particularly along Oranienstrasse) are among the busiest in the city. The places in these areas are all consistently good and offer a wide choice in style and price.

What to Eat

In the morning, nearly all eateries, including those in most hotels, will offer a sub-stantial breakfast. This usually consists of eggs, ham or cold cuts and different kinds of cheese. On Sundays some places also serve a German buffet-style brunch (breakfast combined with lunch) until 2pm. At lunchtime, it's easy to find an elaborate salad or a bowl of steaming soup almost anywhere. In addition many restaurants may also offer their standard menus with slightly reduced prices.

The options for an evening meal are practically unlimited. In a restaurant serving local food options may be a tasty pork knuckle or potato soup *(see pp228–9)*. Lovers of Italian cuisine can easily find a good pizzeria or a restaurant serving regional Italian dishes. Fans of Oriental food can choose between many Asian national cuisines, a great variety of which are situated along Prenzlauer Berg and around Savignyplatz. Berlin also has very good Mexican restaurants, particularly around Oranienburger Strasse and in Kreuzberg, and the food served at Greek restaurants is usually quite good and very inexpensive. Vegetarians can easily find something suitable at most restaurants; vegetarian restaurants are marked in the listings *(see pp232–43)*.

Prices and Tipping

Menus, showing meals and their prices, are usually on display outside restaurants and cafés. Prices can vary a great deal. It is possible to eat a three-course meal, without alcohol, for €20, but in the centre of Berlin the price rises to €25–€30. In a top-

Outside Oxymoron *w(see p235)*, in the Hackesche Höfe

Outside Dressler, Unter den Linden
(see p232)

notch establishment the cost of a meal can be over €150. The price of alcohol varies as well, but the cheapest drink is beer. Although prices include service and tax, many Germans will round up the bill. In more expensive restaurants a 10 per cent tip is customary. Some restaurants add "service not included" to their menus and bills. Although it is not legal to demand a tip, it is polite to leave some extra for the waiting staff.

Eating Hours

In general, cafés open at 10am and restaurants at noon; the latter sometimes also close between 3 and 6pm. However, there are a lot of places that stay open late, sometimes until 2 or 3am. Some of the most expensive and best restaurants are only open in the evening and may be closed on one day during the week as well.

Booking

In the most upmarket restaurants, reservations are usually required – in popular places it is advisable to book well in advance. For the majority of good restaurants it is necessary to book only for Friday or Saturday evenings.

Disabled Diners

In order to avoid any problems in advance, you should discuss wheelchair access when booking. Bear in mind, however,

that even if a dining room may be accessible on the ground floor, the toilets may be up or down stairs or through a narrow corridor.

Children

Casual restaurants usually welcome children, though this may not be the case in more upmarket establishments. Those that do cater for children may provide high chairs as well as light dishes, particularly during lunchtime. Some places will offer a separate children's menu with small portions. Children are also allowed in pubs and bars.

Reading the Menu

Menus are often written out in German and English, and some restaurants will provide menus in French as well. If you find yourself in a restaurant or bar, where the menu is hand-written, ask a waiter for help. Many restaurants offer a menu of the day with seasonal dishes or the chef's specials, which are always worth considering.

Smoking

Smoking is banned in all public places, including restaurants, bars, pubs and clubs, but a handful of restaurants have a separate smoking area or room. In some parts of Berlin, such as Kreuzberg and Friedrichshain, the ban appears to have been ignored.

The stylish Bocca di Bacco (see p232)

Recommended Restaurants

The restaurants on pages 232–43 of this guide cover a range of cuisine styles and prices, and are the best of their kind. They are listed by area, mostly in the main tourist districts, although there are a number that merit a special trip further afield. Within these areas, they are listed alphabetically in each of the three price categories.

Berlin's restaurant scene offers a huge variety of cuisine types (see What to Eat, p226).

Where a restaurant is in some way exceptional – perhaps for its cooking, its good-value menus, or family-friendly facilities – it has been highlighted as a DK Choice.

The elegant interior of Facil (see p236)

The Flavours of Berlin

To treat your senses in Berlin, you need do nothing more than stroll through the street markets, historic market halls and speciality food shops. Spicy, hot sausages such as *Currywurst* or *Thüringer* will lure you into the traditional German butcheries. The scent of freshly baked rolls and breads wafts from the corner bakeries. Fresh herbs, typical German garden vegetables such as red or green cabbage, and wild mushrooms are spectacularly displayed. Freshwater fish from the region's many lakes and rivers glisten on their beds of ice; particularly popular are pike-perch, eel, trout and even sweet river crabs.

Harzer Roller and Emmenthaler cheeses

Wild mushrooms, one of the region's most famous products

Berlin's Hearty Heritage

Historically, Berlin has never been a gourmet capital, and neither has the surrounding, rural Brandenburg region. The Hohenzollern court focused more on its army than on culture and cuisine. But the Great Electors were formidable hunters, and game such as wild boar, rabbit, and duck, as well as goose and birds of prey were (and remain) an integral part of Berlin's cuisine. Later, in the 19th century, both the evolving Prussian well-to-do and the working class preferred hearty and simple food over fine dining – not only because Berlin was then a comparatively poor city, but also because of the long and hard winters and generally inclement weather.

Bread and Potatoes

There is an enormous variety of breads and rolls to be found on today's menus. Many are unique to Berlin, such as the wholewheat and rye, dark, crusty *Schusterjungen*

Mehrkornbrötchen (mixed grain roll)

Berliner Landbrot (mild rye bread)

Laugenbrötchen (salty sourdough rolls)

Graubrot (sourdough rye bread)

Semmel (milk-dough roll)

Selection of typical German loaves and bread rolls

Local Dishes and Specialities

Berliners have many ways of preparing pork, making it the most popular main dish. As *Kasseler*, created by Berlin butcher Cassel in the late 19th century, the meat is salted and then dried before being served with sauerkraut, mashed potatoes and very spicy mustard. Berlin's traditional pork knuckle, also accompanied by sauerkraut and potatoes, isn't complete without a portion of split pea purée (called *Erbspuree* in Berlin). Pork sausages include *Currywurst* – a post-World War II invention by Berlin Imbiss (food stall) owner Hedwig Mueller – which are served with a spicy sauce of curry, tomatoes and chili along with a roll or French fries. You can find this filling snack at Imbisse throughout the city.

Zanderfilet, or Havel-Zander, is pan-fried pike-perch with a vegetable sauce and onions, served with mashed potatoes.

Display of traditional German sausages in a Berlin butcher's shop

("shoemaker's boy") or *schrippen*, the cheap roll eaten daily at every meal.

Potatoes were introduced by Frederick the Great. They appear at most German meals, alongside fish or meat or cooked in a broth for dishes such as *Kartoffelsuppe*.

The Brandenburg Influence

Berlin's restaurants only rediscovered the region's true heritage after the fall of the Wall, absorbing culinary traditions from the Mark Brandenburg, the suddenly re-accessible rural countryside surrounding Berlin with its thick forests, rivers and lakes. Today, the fresh produce provided by the region's farms are an integral part of Berlin's cuisine. Old recipes have returned to modern kitchens. Freshwater fish like pike-perch, or game such as wild

boar or duck, are flavoured with fresh herbs such as dill and parsley, and the famous Brandenburger Landente (Brandenburg country duck), stuffed with apples, onions and herbs, slowly roasted and coated with a honey-oil to make it perfectly crusty, is once again a favourite on Berlin menus.

Fresh vegetables from the Mark Brandenberg region

Berlin's Fine Dining Revolution

With the city's reunification came a new international influence, which gave birth to many Michelin-starred and other gourmet restaurants. Restaurants often prepare Berlin signature dishes with a more healthy or an exotic twist, giving traditional dishes a modern flavour. One of the Mark Brandenberg's most important products, fresh wild mushrooms, such as *Pfifferlinge* or *Steinpilze*, figure prominently, and classic ingredients like sauerkraut, cabbage and beet may be paired with Mediterranean fish or Asian spices.

Best Local Food

Restaurants: Altes Zollhaus (*p236*); Nante-Eck (*p232*); Lorenz Adlon Esszimmer (*p232*); Zur Letzten Instanz (*p233*); Dressler (*p232*).

Shops and markets: Marheineke-Markthalle; Turkish Market, Maybachufer; KaDeWe gourmet food floor (*p258*); Rogacki Gourmet Centre (*p258*); Butter Lindner delicatessen chain.

Imbisse (food stalls): Konnopke (below train tracks, Eberswalder Strasse subway, Prenzlauer Berg); Ku'damm 195 Imbiss, Kurfürstendamm; Currywurstbude, Wittenbergplatz, Charlottenburg.

Kasseler Nacken is salted and dried pork served with sauerkraut or green cabbage and mashed potatoes.

Berliner Leber is veal or pork liver on a bed of mashed potatoes, with fried onions and pan-fried apple slices.

Brandenburger Landente is stuffed duck served with red cabbage and potato dumplings or mashed potatoes.

What to Drink in Berlin

In Berlin, as throughout the rest of Germany, beer is the most widely drunk alcoholic beverage. There are no productive vineyards around Berlin, but wines from the Rhine and Mosel regions are always popular. As an *aperitif*, or with pork dishes, Berliners often enjoy a shot of rye vodka *(Korn)*, sometimes flavoured with herbs. With dessert, a glass of herbal liqueur often fits the bill.

A typical bar in Berlin

Pilsner beers from Berlin breweries

Lager (Pilsner)

Berliners drink beer on every occasion, and Germany's many beers are some of the best and purest in the world. Some of the best-known Berlin breweries are Schultheiss, Berliner Kindl, Berliner Pils and Engelhardt, but beers brewed in other parts of Germany are just as popular. Although beer is available in all sorts of venues and *"Ein Bier, bitte"* can be heard in pubs, cafés and restaurants, it is worth experiencing the atmosphere of an old-fashioned beerhouse, or *Kneipe*. The most highly esteemed beer is draught beer, drawn from the cask *(vom Fass)* and poured slowly into tall glasses. Pouring in a thin trickle is essential to achieve a thick head of foam, and a good barman will take a few minutes to fill your glass. Berliners drink mostly lager *(Pils)*, but other beers are also popular.

A *Brezel* makes a good snack with beer

Other Beers

In addition to the usual light, Pilsner-type beers, Berlin's breweries, many of them small and independent, also make a number of more adventurous brews. Dark, sweetish beer, known as *Schwarzbier* or black beer, is becoming more and more popular and has rather more than the standard four per cent alcohol. *Weizenbier* is made from wheat rather than barley, and is usually served in half-litre (one pint) glasses wth a slice of lemon. Another unusual drink is *Bock*, an especially strong beer made with barley. *Maibock* is a special version, available only in May.

Strong, dark Bock beer

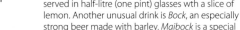

Berliner Weisse with raspberry and woodruff cordials

Berliner Weisse, a light malted-wheat beer

Berliner Weisse mit Schuss

A Berlin speciality, called *Berliner Weisse mit Schuss*, is a light, newly-fermented wheat beer that continues fermenting in the bottle. On its own, it is not very palatable as it is rather watery and sour, but when mixed with raspberry cordial it becomes fruity and delicious. Mixing with sweet woodruff syrup gives it a vivid green colour and a slightly medicinal flavour. *Berliner Weisse mit Schuss* is served in large wine glasses with a straw, and makes a very refreshing drink, particularly popular during the hot summer months.

Wine

No wine is produced around Berlin as the climate here is too cold for vines, but a variety of wines from Germany's southern and western regions are available in Berlin. The most famous are the white wines, particularly those made from Riesling grapes. Most expensive are those from the Rheingau region. The northern climate dictates that most German wines are white, but lovers of red wine can try the Rhine Assmanshausen Spätburgunder, made from Pinot Noir grapes. Although there is no regional system of classification like the French *Appellation d'Origine Contrôlée,* a national quality control system divides German wines into three categories: *Tafelwein* or table wine is the most basic; next comes

Qualitätswein, and the highest is *Qualitätswein mit Prädikat,* which includes wines made from specially selected grapes. *Trocken* means dry, *halbtrocken* means medium dry and *süss* means sweet. You can also find some very good sparkling wines known as *Sekts.*

A prize-winning bottle of German red wine

Riesling from Schloss Vollrads

Other Alcoholic Beverages

Vodka is often drunk with more substantial meals, particularly those based on pork. Especially recommended is one of the rye vodkas, such as *Weizendoppelkorn,* that are popular in Berlin. Many establishments also serve brandies, known generically as *Weinbrand.* In addition, various digestive liqueurs and vodkas flavoured with plant extracts are quite popular, particularly *Kümmerling, Jägermeister* and, a Berlin favourite, *Kaulzzdorferkräuter Likör.* In many restaurants you will come across a speciality honey liqueur from east Prussia known as *Bärenfang.* More of an acquired taste is *Goldwasser* from Danzig, a traditional herbal liqueur containing flakes of gold leaf. It is made according to a secret 16th-century German recipe.

Weizendoppelkorn rye vodka

Herbal digestive liqueur

Bitter-sweet Jägermeister liqueur

Non-Alcoholic Cold Drinks

Although Berlin tap water is safe to drink, it is not usually served with restaurant meals. If you want water you should order a bottle of mineral water *(Mineralwasser)* adding *"ohne Kohlen-Säure"* if you prefer still water. A wide variety of canned sparkling soft drinks, ubiquitous across Europe and the US, are popular in Berlin. Fruit juices are also widely drunk and a wide selection is available in every restaurant and café. Another popular soft drink is *Apfelschorle,* apple juice mixed in equal proportions with sparkling mineral water.

Apfelschorle

Peppermint and camomile, two widely available herbal teas

Coffee and Tea

Coffee is very popular in Berlin and is served in a variety of ways. The most usual is filter coffee, served by the cup or the pot, generally with condensed milk and sugar. If you prefer something stronger and more aromatic you should go for an espresso. It is also easy to enjoy a good cup of tea in Berlin, herbal or otherwise. Germans drink a lot of herbal teas, two of the most common being peppermint *(Pfefferminztee)* and camomile *(Kamillentee).* If you want a cup of non-herbal tea, you can make a point of ordering *Schwarzen Tee.* If you want milk with your tea, then ask for *Tee mit Milch.*

Where to Eat and Drink

Around Unter Den Linden

Nante-Eck €
Traditional German **Map** 8 F3
Unter den Linden 35, 10117
Tel *22 48 72 57*
Berlin-style cheap eats are on offer in this homely pub on Unter den Linden. Fill up on Berlin calf's liver with port sauce or meatballs with mustard, washed down with local beer.

Zwölf Apostel €
Italian **Map** 9 A3
Georgenstrasse 2, 10117
Tel *201 02 22*
Rambling restaurant beneath the railway arches near Friedrichstrasse station. Serves 12 pizza flavours, named for the 12 apostles and cooked to perfection in a stone oven.

Augustiner am Gendarmenmarkt €€
Regional German **Map** 9 A4
Charlottenstrasse 55, 10117
Tel *204 540 20*
This Bavarian pub with wooden panelling and oak barrels overlooks Berlin's most beautiful square. It serves hearty German fare such as baked knuckle of pork with Bavarian sauerkraut and beef goulash in a beer sauce.

Chipps €€
German **Map** 9 B4
Jägerstrasse 35, 10117
Tel *364 445 88*
The serious breakfasts at this eatery include waffles and pancakes but above all eggs. Try Dancing Queen – poached egg with spinach and fresh chives in a Hollandaise sauce, on wholemeal bread. Weekend brunch.

Cookies Cream €€
Vegetarian **Map** 8 F4
Behrenstrasse 55, 10117
Tel *280 88 06*
The chef at this unpretentious yet hip veggie hangout uses only the freshest locally grown ingredients to create inventive dishes that change seasonally. Free entry to on-site nightclub on Tuesdays and Thursdays.

Einstein Café €€
German **Map** 8 F3
Unter den Linden 42, 10117
Tel *204 36 32*
Rub shoulders with German politicians and other movers and shakers while admiring the changing photo and art exhibitions in the atrium. Try the house speciality, apfelstrudel, for breakfast or elevenses.

Samâdhi €€
South Asian Vegetarian **Map** 8 E4
Wilhelmstrasse 77, 10117
Tel *224 888 50* **Closed** *Mon*
A short walk from the Brandenburger Tor, this vegetarian restaurant is very convenient for sightseers. Gluten-free dishes on request.

Bocca di Bacco €€€
Italian **Map** 8 F4
Friedrichstrasse 167, 10117
Tel *206 728 28*
Master chef Loriano Mura directs the kitchen of this classy Italian restaurant with an elegant ambience that attracts the glitterati. Superb wine list.

Borchardt €€€
French-German **Map** 9 A4
Französische Strasse 47, 10117
Tel *81 88 62 30*
German politicians and celebrities flock to this Gendarmenmarkt restaurant with retro decor from the early 1900s. Schnitzel is the mainstay of an ever-changing menu. Reservations advised.

Dressler €€€
French-International **Map** 8 F4
Unter den Linden 39, 10117
Tel *204 44 22*
The signature dish of the Art Deco Dressler is the Parisian Secret – a melt-in-the-mouth rump steak cooked in a mystery sauce.

DK Choice

Fischers Fritz €€€
Modern French **Map** 9 A4
Charlottenstrasse 49, 10117
Tel *203 363 63*
Fischers Fritz was awarded two Michelin stars in 2012 for the fifth year running, due to the creative flair of chef Christian Lohse. The meat dishes are tempting, but it is the fish and seafood dishes that get most of the accolades. Try the Breton lobster roasted with salt, chilli and coriander, or the fillet of Mediterranean red mullet with mashed potatoes, Nyons olives and tomatoes. The two-course lunch menu is more reasonable.

Lorenz Adlon Esszimmer €€€
German fine dining **Map** 8 E4
Unter den Linden 77, 10117
Tel *226 119 60*
Dine at Berlin's gourmet temple *par excellence*, with views of the Brandenburger Tor and the creations of Michelin-starred chef Hendrik Otto for company.

Margaux Berlin €€€
Modern French **Map** 8 E3
Unter den Linden 78, 10117
Tel *226 526 11* **Closed** *Sun*
Unforgettable food from Michelin-starred chef Michael Hoffmann,

Sophisticated interiors of the Michelin-starred Fischers Fritz restaurant

including glazed pollock served with artichoke and truffle and flavoured with fresh herbs and tiger nuts from his own garden.

Quarré €€€
French-German Map 8 E4
Unter den Linden 77
Tel *226 115 55*
This brasserie has great views of Pariser Platz and the Brandenburg Tor. The Berliner Klassiker menu offers an alternative gourmet take on regional Brandenburg cuisine.

Vau €€€
Modern French Map 9 A4
Jägerstrasse 54–55, 10117
Tel *202 97 30*
Celebrity TV chef Kolja Kleeberg won this classy restaurant a Michelin star with his inspired take on French cooking. The striking interior is best described as modern meets Art Nouveau.

Museum Island

Café im Bodemuseum €
German Map 9 A2
Geschwister-Scholl-Straße 6, 10117
Tel *202 143 30*
Break for lunch or coffee in the surroundings of the Bode-museum's Neo-Classical building while gazing down on Andreas Schlüter's magnificent equestrian statue of the Great Elector. No museum ticket required.

Ming Dynastie €€
Chinese Map 10 E4
Brückenstrasse 6, 10179
Tel *308 756 80*
Excellent Chinese restaurant serving an extensive menu, including regional dishes, plus dim sum to Peking Duck.

East of the Centre

Domklause €
Traditional German Map 9 E2
Karl-Liebknecht-Strasse 1, 10178
Tel *847 12 37 37*
The chef in the DDR Museum restaurant once cooked for East German politicians. Down-to-earth meat dishes such as Mock Hare and Hunter's Schnitzel.

Típica €
Mexican Map 9 C2
Rosenstrasse 19, 10178
Tel *250 994 40*
Authentic Mexican dishes in a traditional *taqueria* (roadside

Enjoy stunning city views from Fernsehtum Sphere in the TV tower

café) specializing in meat or vegetable tortillas served with black beans, salad and a plethora of sauces.

Fernsehturm Sphere Restaurant €€
German-International Map 9 C2
Panoramastrasse 1A, 10178
Tel *242 33 33*
This revolving restaurant in the TV tower serves typical Berlin-Brandenburg specialities including *kabeljau* (cod with beetroot and potato puree).

Zum Nussbaum €€
Traditional German Map 9 C3
Am Nussbaum 3, 10178
Tel *242 30 95*
Reconstructed country inn set in a Nikolaiviertel side street serving traditional Berlin cuisine including roll mop, *bouletten* (spicy meatballs), fish and vegetable pancakes, as well as local beers.

> ### DK Choice
>
> **Zur Letzten Instanz** €€
> **Traditional German** Map 10 D3
> *Waisenstrasse 14–16, 10179*
> **Tel** *242 55 28* **Closed** Sun
> Berlin's oldest pub, Zur Letzten Instanz dates from 1621. Beethoven and Napoleon are thought to have eaten here and Charlie Chaplin, Mikhail Gorbachev and Angela Merkel certainly did. The classic German fare, including *eisbein* (pork knuckle) and *rinderroulade* (beef olive), is served in a cosy wood-panelled room with a majolica tiled stove. There is a shady courtyard garden.

Reinhard's €€€
International Map 9 C3
Poststrasse 28, 10178
Tel *242 33 33*

Stylish Nikolaiviertel restaurant decorated with photographs of German artists and film stars of yesteryear. The house speciality is Secret of the Kaiser's Court – steak served in a sauce created for Max Liebermann.

North of the Centre

Anna Blume €
International Map 2 F3
Kollwitzstrasse 83, 10435
Tel *440 487 49*
This classy café-restaurant has a lovely terrace and lustre-lit interior. Some customers rave about the breakfast, others about brunch, while most crave the lime cheesecake dessert.

Beth Café €
Jewish Map 9 A1
Tucholskystrasse 40, 10117
Tel *281 31 35* **Closed** Fri eve & Sat
A kosher café in the New Synagogue area with a limited menu. Sample the speciality *kolbo platte* (salad with tahina, falafel and humus).

Cafe Fleury €
French Map 1 C5
Weinbergsweg 20, 10119
Tel *440 341 44*
Lovely French-owned café with distinctive flowery wallpaper and an outdoor terrace. Wonderful smell of freshly brewed coffee, croissants, brioches and other breakfast delicacies greets guests.

Dada Falafel €
Middle Eastern Map 8 F1
Linienstrasse 132, 10115
Tel *275 969 27*
Offers fast food worth lingering over, including arguably the best falafels this side of Damascus, as well as grat shawarmas and fresh salads.

For more information on types of restaurants see p227

Khushi €
Indian **Map** 2 E4
Kollwitzstrasse 37, 10405
Tel *484 937 90*
Delicious Indian food to eat in or take out, prepared with fresh ingredients. Moderately spicy dishes.

Sophieneck €
Regional German **Map** 9 B1
Große Hamburger Strasse 37, 10115
Tel *283 40 65*
Warm pub-restaurant near Sophienkirche. Regional cooking with fresh ingredients and an international twist. Tempting vegetarian options and a menu for kids as well.

Transit €
Southeast Asian **Map** 9 B1
Rosenthaler Strasse 68, 10119
Tel *247 816 45*
Food here is served in tapas-sized portions – three bowls should suffice. All dishes are MSG free, and have playful names including Duck in Pyjamas (crispy duck and plum sauce rolled in a pancake).

DK Choice

Yam Yam €
Korean **Map** 9 C1
Alte Schönhauser Strasse 6, 10119
Tel *246 324 85*
Popular with local fashionistas, this canteen-style restaurant run by Sumi Ha uses organic Korean vegetables and hot spices and flavouring typical of the region's cooking. Try *cha chang myun* (noodles with pork and black beans, served with pickled cabbage) or rise to the challenge of a *bibimbap* (beef, vegetables and fried egg mixed with a fiery red pepper paste.)

Zum Schusterjungen €
Traditional German **Map** 2 E2
Danziger Strasse 9, 10435
Tel *442 76 54*
Typical Berlin corner pub with quirky rustic touches. The home-cooked food includes large portions of liver and onions, knuckle of pork, and bacon wraps. Serves draught beer.

Al Contadino sotto Le Stelle €€
Italian **Map** 9 B1
August Strasse 36, 10119
Tel *281 90 23*
Stylish, upmarket *trattoria* with friendly service and the flavours of southern Italy. Home-made pasta and good fish and meat dishes. Try the grilled swordfish marinated in white wine vinegar, honey and oregano.

Brecht-Keller €€
Austrian **Map** 8 F1
Chausseestrasse 125, 10115
Tel *282 38 43*
Convivial cellar restaurant in the Brecht Museum where the simple Austrian cooking is inspired by recipes invented by Brecht's wife, Helene Weigel.

Cenacolo €€
Italian **Map** 2 E3
Sredzkistrasse 23, 10435
Tel *440 447 43*
The aroma of fresh herbs and pizzas cooked in a traditional stone oven greets diners at this popular Prenzlauer Berg restaurant. Book ahead.

Friedrichs106 €€
Austrian **Map** 8 F2
Friedrichstrasse 106, 10117
Tel *405 205 94*
Modern coffee house with terrace overlooking the Spree. Offers breakfasts, savoury and fruit strudels, steaks and classic Austrian dishes including *tafelspitz* (boiled beef).

Gambrinus €€
Traditional German **Map** 8 F1
Linienstrasse 133, 10115
Tel *282 60 43*
Traditional *kneipe* (pub) with old-fashioned tiles, dark wood furnishings, framed photos and posters of Old Berlin. Massive portions of German pub grub.

Gugelhof €€
Alsatian **Map** 2 E4
Knaackstrasse 37, 10435
Tel *442 92 29*
Former US president Bill Clinton visited this lively restaurant near Kollwitzplatz with Alsatian specialities such as tarte flambée and lamb cassoulet.

Habel Weinkultur and Brasserie €€
Modern German **Map** 8 E2
Luisenstrasse 19, 10117
Tel *28 44 80*
Upmarket brasserie inspired by Prussian culinary traditions, but with a Mediterranean twist. Impressive wine list.

Hackescher Hof €€
Modern German-International **Map** 9 B2
Rosenthaler Strasse 40–41, 10178
Tel *280 980 10*
Café-restaurant-patisserie with an interior reminiscent of a Viennese coffee house. Popular with office workers for its attractively priced two-course lunch menu. Stays open until 2am.

Mao Thai €€
Thai **Map** 2 F3
Wörther Strasse 30, 10405
Tel *441 92 61*
Popular with locals and visitors alike for its excellent, mildly spiced Thai food and alfresco seating in summer.

Monsieur Vuong €€
Vietnamese **Map** 9 C1
Alte Schönhauser Str. 46, 10119
Tel *99 29 69 24*
Oriental bistro with a two-course menu and specials up on the blackboard. Generous portions, efficient service and a tempting selection of scented teas.

Nola's am Weinberg €€
Swiss **Map** 1 C4
Veteranen Strasse 9, 10119
Tel *440 407 66*
Swiss cantonal cuisine featuring fondue, noodle and risotto dishes. Lovely summer terrace. Sunday brunch from 10am.

Casual outdoor seating on the tree-shaded pavement at, Gugelhof

Oxymoron   €€
Italian-French   **Map** 9 B2
Rosenthaler Strasse 40-41, 10178
Tel *283 918 86*
This fashionable Hackescher
Markt dining space and night
club attracts a young crowd. Art
Deco interior with glittering
lustres and wood-framed mirrors.

DK Choice

Pasternak   €€
Russian-Jewish   **Map** 2 F4
Knaackstrasse 22/24, 10405
Tel *441 33 99*
A long-time favourite with
Berlin's sizeable Russian
community, Pasternak prides
itself on its authentic cuisine.
Focus on the rich assortment of
zakuski (starters), but do not
overlook the *blini* (buckwheat
pancakes filled with spinach
and cheese, salmon and
horseradish, or caviar). The
warm dining space is adorned
with traditional wallpaper,
lamps and candles.

Restauration 1900   €€
Traditional   **Map** 2 E3
Husemannstrasse 1, 10435
Tel *442 24 94*
The granny's kitchen menu at
this Art Nouveau restaurant
features old Prussian favourites
such as *königsberger klops*
(meatballs in creamy caper
sauce). Weekend brunch buffet
from 10am; booking essential.

**Sarah Wiener Cafe and
Restaurant**   €€
Austrian-
Mediterranean   **Map** 8 D1
Invalidenstrasse 50–51, 10557
Tel *707 136 50*   **Closed** *Mon*
Refined dining in the Hamburger
Bahnhof museum. Tino Speer's
cuisine uses fresh organic
ingredients and serves some
of Berlin's best schnitzels.

Savanna   €€
African   **Map** 2 E3
Sredzkistrasse 26, 10435
Tel *443 186 21*
The wide-ranging menu here
features exotic antelope and
zebra steaks as well as vegetable
platters – fried yams, okra, lentils,
bananas and spinach served with
rice, couscous or *injera* (Eritrean
flat bread).

Yosoy   €€
Spanish   **Map** 9 B2
Rosenthaler Strasse 37, 10178
Tel *283 912 13*
Commendably affordable,
authentic tapas bar with Spanish

Range of Russian and Jewish goodies on offer at Pasternak

regional wines. Appetizing fish
and meat main courses.

DK Choice

Dos Palillos   €€€
International-
Asian   **Map** 9 B1
*Casa Camper Hotel,
Weinmeisterstrasse 1, 10178*
Tel *200 034 13*
Sit facing the open kitchen
of this cutting-edge restaurant
and watch Catalan master chef
Albert Raurich have his creative
way with Asian-style tapas.
The oysters cooked in sake are
delicious. The 12-course menu
costs €45 and is good value.
The steely interior was designed
by the Parisian Bouroullec
brothers. Book ahead.

Reinstoff   €€€
Fine dining   **Map** 1 A5
*Schlegelstrasse 26c/Edison Höfe,
10115*
Tel *308 812 14*
Daniel Achilles' sensational
Michelin-starred inventions
delight in unusual pairings – river
trout and rowanberry, Norway
lobster and rhubarb, carrot and
lemon ice cream.

Tiergarten

Angkor Wat   €
Cambodian   **Map** 7 B2
Paulstrasse 22, 10557
Tel *393 39 22*
This well-established restaurant
on the edge of the Tiergarten
draws diners with its exotic decor
and aromatic curries.

Cafe am Neuen See   €
German-Mediterranean   **Map** 6 F5
Lichtensteinallee 2, 10787
Tel *254 493 00*

In the heart of Tiergarten Park,
this café has lakeside terrace
views and a menu comprising
Bavarian snacks and draught
beers, as well as Italian mains
including fresh pizzas. Cosy
seating in winter, plus boat
rental and a sandpit
for kids.

Café Möhring   €
Traditional German   **Map** 8 D5
*Weinhaus Huth, Alte Potsdamer
Strasse 5, 10785*
Tel *259 270 07*
Relocated to the Huth-Haus, the
only surviving building from
the old Potsdamer Platz, Möhring
is one of the few remaining
traditional Berlin cafés. Pasta,
salads and tempting *torten*
(cream cakes).

Gaststätte Ambrosius   €
Traditional German   **Map** 13 A1
Einemstrasse 14, 10785
Tel *264 05 26*
Nourishing home cooking,
with specialities such as Berlin-
style liver, served with onions
and apple sauce, and tasty
potato soup.

Lindenbräu   €
Traditional German   **Map** 8 D5
Bellevuestrasse 3-5, 10785
Tel *257 512 80*
Popular watering hole on
Potsdamer Platz. Bavarian
specialities and home
brewed fruit-flavoured wheat
beer are served on a large
roof terrace.

OM   €
Nepalese-Indian   **Map** 7 A2
Kirchstrasse 16,
Tel *39749554*
Family-friendly restaurant close
to the Spree. Try the hot and
spicy lamb kebabs or opt for
milder dishes such as the crispy
duck in coconut sauce.

For more information on types of restaurants *see p227*

Teehaus Tiergarten €
International Map 5 A5
Altonaer Strasse 2/2a, 10557
Tel *394 804 00*
Lovely setting in the English
garden next to Schloss Bellevue.
Snacks, cakes and main courses
served in the teahouse or on the
terrace. Summer concerts Jul–Sep.

Lanninger €€
Modern German Map 6 F1
Alt-Moabit 99, 10559
Tel *399 207 98*
Smart modern restaurant and
cocktail lounge with terrace
views across a lovely, tree-fringed
stretch of the Spree.

Lutter & Wegner im Kaisersaal €€
German-Austrian Map 8 D5
Bellevuestrasse 1, 10785
Tel *263 903 72*
This illustrious restaurant,
founded over two centuries ago,
is located in the former Kaisersaal
dining room – a relic of Imperial
Germany. Sample refined
cooking and fine wines here.

Rikes Gasthaus €€
Traditional German Map 13 C1
*Hotel Alt-Berlin, Potsdamer Strasse
67, 10785*
Tel *26 06 70*
Old-world restaurant with menus
based on original recipes from
Frau Rike's grandmother's
cookbook including Coachman's
Goulash, beef cooked in beer.

Facil €€€
Modern Fusion Map 8 D5
Potsdamer Strasse 3, 10785
Tel *590 05 12 34*
Michelin-starred gourmet food in
the Mandala Hotel *(see p224)*
restaurant. A glass-roofed
pavilion is the backdrop for
master chef Michael Kempf's
inspired culinary cuisine, which
draws on the freshest market
produce and subtly exotic spices.

DK Choice

Käfers Dachgarten €€€
Modern German Map 8 D3
Platz der Republik, 11011
Tel *226 29 90*
Overlooked by many visitors
to Berlin, this lovely roof garden
restaurant in the Reichstag
building has a terrace with
spectacular views across the
city. Sample sophisticated
German dishes made with
the freshest regional produce
and accompanied by choice
wines. Book at least 3 hours in
advance and remember to
bring your passport.

Käfers Dachgarten restaurant, on the rooftop of the Reichstag building

Kreuzberg

Cafe do Brasil €
Brazilian Map 14 F4
Mehringdamm 72, 10961
Tel *780 068 87*
The party atmosphere at this
popular Kreuzberg restaurant
draws a lively international
crowd. Specialities include
Brazilian beach BBQ cooking,
delicious seafood stews
(*moquecas*) and caipirinha
cocktails. Sunday brunch.

Cafe Stresemann €
Traditional German Map 14 E1
Stresemannstrasse 90, 10963
Tel *261 17 60*
This modern pub restaurant is
handy for sights around
Potsdamer Platz. The menu
comprises classics such as
schnitzel, pork knuckle, and Berlin-
style liver served with stewed
apple, potatoes and sauerkraut.

Golgatha €
International Map 14 E5
Dudenstrasse 40-64, 10965
Tel *785 24 53*
Lively 1920s beer garden on
the edge of picturesque Viktoria
Park. Offers grills as well as ample
vegetarian options. Adventure
playground for children.

Gropius €
International Map 14 E1
Niederkirchnerstrasse 7, 10963
Tel *254 864 06*
Restaurant in the Martin Gropius
Bau with a summer terrace and a
seasonal menu that reflects the
temporary art exhibitions.

Seerose €
Vegetarian Map 14 F4
Mehringdamm 47, 10961
Tel *698 159 27*
The buffet features spinach
lasagne, pasta and rice dishes

with pick-and-mix side salads.
Delicious bio-wines, helpful
staff and indoor and outdoor
seating available.

DK Choice

Tomasa €
International Map 14 E4
Kreuzbergstrasse 62, 10965
Tel *810 098 85*
Great for families, this friendly
restaurant in a red-brick villa has
a well-stocked playroom and
a great kids' menu. For the
grown-ups, Tomasa caters for
every possible taste and is
especially strong on breakfast
and brunch choices. It is spread
out over two floors and has a
courtyard garden.

DK Choice

Yorckschlösschen €
International Map 14 F3
Yorckstrasse 15, 10965
Tel *215 80 70*
A Kreuzberg haunt with a
Bohemian interior featuring
velvet sofas, old wooden
furnishings and a beer garden.
The extensive menu offers 14
breakfast choices and includes
lighter meals and hearty
German favourites such as
leberkäse (meat loaf) served with
fried egg and salad. This spot
has been popular for more than
20 years with jazz musicians,
who regularly perform here.

Altes Zollhaus €€
Modern German Map 15 B3
Carl-Herz-Ufer 30, 10961
Tel *692 33 00*
Dine out in a charming half-
timbered house with a delightful
garden. Classic rustic cooking
features the famous Beelitzer
asparagus in season.

Bar Centrale €€
Italian **Map** 14 F4
Yorckstrasse 82, 10965
Tel *786 29 89*
This bar-restaurant in the heart of Kreuzberg has a loyal following. Refined Italian cuisine, including a tempting range of starters

E.T.A. Hoffmann €€€
Modern Austrian **Map** 14 F4
Yorckstrasse 83, 10965
Tel *780 988 09*
Tyrolean chef Thomas Kurt has his creative way with traditional Austrian and German recipes. Try the cushion of Brandenburg venison with Gatow radish and potato noodles.

Tim Raue €€€
Modern Asian fusion **Map** 9 A5
Rudi-Dutschke Strasse 26, 10969
Tel *259 379 30*
The Michelin-starred Tim Raue offers authentic Japanese, Thai and Chinese cooking. Minimalist interior with gallery lighting and American walnut furniture.

Around Kurfürstendamm

Baba Angora €
Turkish **Map** 11 B1
Schlüterstrasse 29, 10629
Tel *323 70 96*
Classic Anatolian cuisine such as spicy *Adana sis kebab* with yoghurt and herbs. Vegetarian and fish options as well. The unusual decor comprises ancient Hittite art. Large outdoor terrace.

Bleiberg's €
Jewish **Map** 12 E2
Nürnberger Strasse 45A, 10789
Tel *219 136 24*   **Closed** *Fri eve & Sat*
Kosher café with a relaxed vibe and a menu that includes vegetarian and vegan dishes as well as Russian *blinis*.

Dicke Wirtin €
Traditional German **Map** 11 C1
Carmerstrasse 9, 10623
Tel *312 49 52*
This authentic Berlin *kneipe* is a short walk from Savigny Platz. Try the Eintopf, a steaming hot pot, and the Berliner Kindl, one of the nine draught beers available.

Sachico Sushi €
Japanese **Map** 11 C1
Grolmanstrasse 47, Jeanne-Mammen-Bogen 584, 10623
Tel *313 22 82*
Handy refuelling stop after Ku'damm shopping, with a tempting business lunch of *kaitan* (conveyor belt) sushi; pay extra for sashimi and grills.

Satyam €
Indian Vegetarian **Map** 5 C5
Goethestrasse 5, 10623
Tel *318 061 11*
Vegetarian restaurant with specialities such as aubergine in lightly spiced tomato sauce with ginger and garlic. Some vegetables come directly from India.

Tastees €
Jamaican **Map** 11 C1
Grolmannstrasse 27, 10623
Tel *889 220 28*
Spicy Caribbean fare with specialities including patties, jerk chicken and curried shrimps with fried banana.

Brenner €€
German-International **Map** 12 E3
Regensburger Strasse 7, 10777
Tel *236 244 70*
Choice of Austrian, Italian and German dishes reflecting Tyrolean culinary influences. Congenial atmosphere in a wood-panelled interior.

Cafe-Restaurant Wintergarten im Literaturhaus €€
German-International **Map** 12 D2

Sleek and minimalist decor at Tim Raue, serving oriental cuisine

Fasanenstrasse 23, 10719
Tel *882 54 14*
Break from shopping on Ku'damm and visit this bolthole favoured by artists and intellectuals. Breakfast and international dishes are served in an Art Nouveau interior. Shady garden.

Calcutta €€
Indian **Map** 11 B1
Bleibtreustrasse 17, 10623
Tel *883 62 93*
Oldest Indian restaurant in Berlin reputed for its sophisticated dishes from all parts of the subcontinent. *Tandoori* dishes cooked in traditional wood-fired oven.

El Borriquito €€
Spanish **Map** 11 B1
Wielandstrasse 6, 10625
Tel *312 99 29*
A crowded Iberian-themed dining room where guests are entertained by Spanish guitarists and Flamenco dancers. Serves tapas, seafood and lamb specialities.

DK Choice

Esswein am Fasanenplatz €€
Modern German **Map** 11 C2
Fasanenstrasse 40, 10719
Tel *889 292 88*
Esswein is making waves within Berlin's culinary scene, thanks to its modern German cooking. The menu is seasonal but might feature *pfälzer wurstsalat* (Rhineland sausage with cheese and bread), with *ochsen fetzen* (ox slices baked in a râgout of grapes, mushrooms and chestnuts) to follow. Choose from a selection of more than 40 Mosel wines to accompany your meal for the makings of a memorable evening.

Warm interiors of E.T.A. Hoffmann, specializing in Austrian cuisine

For more information on types of restaurants see p227

The bright and grand interior
at Die Quadriga

Florian €€
Swabian Map 5 C5
Grolmanstrasse 52, 10623
Tel *313 91 84*
Small, pristine restaurant with an
understated charm that attracts
celebrities. Excellent Swabian
cuisine with a modern twist;
uses organic produce.

Grüne Lampe €€
Russian Map 11 C3
Uhlandstrasse 51, 10719
Tel *887 193 93*
Popular with Russian expats,
who love the authentic home
cooking. Large selection
of *zakuski* and *blini*. Some
vegetarian options.

La Mano Verde €€
Vegan Map 11 C1
*Kempinski Plaza,
Uhlandstrasse 181, 10623*
Tel *827 031 20*
A treat for serious non meat-
eaters, this strictly vegan
restaurant uses only plant-based
ingredients, and has several
gluten-free dishes, too. Inspired
daily specials.

Marjellchen €€
Regional German Map 11 B1
Mommsenstrasse 9
Tel *883 26 76*
Regional German cooking
traditions survive here thanks
to the original recipes of the
owner's grandmother.

Namaskar €€
Indian Map 12 D3
Pariser Strasse. 56/57, 10719
Tel *886 806 48*
Rated as one of the city's best
Indian restaurants. The menu
celebrates the rich diversity
of cooking on the subcontinent.
Great choice of dishes.

Belmondo €€€
French Map 11 C3
Knesebeckstrasse 93, 10623
Tel *362 872 61*
Red leather banquettes and
photos of the famous actor Jean-
Paul Belmondo bring a touch of
French elegance to this Charlot-
tenburg bistro. Excellent fish and
seafood dishes, and a sensational
bouillabaisse (fish soup).

Brasserie Le Faubourg €€€
French Map 12 D1
Augsburger Strasse 41, 10789
Tel *800 999 77 00*
Flagship restaurant of the
Concorde Hotel offering refined
French cooking at its best.
Friendly and efficient staff add to
a pleasurable dining experience.
Outdoor terrace seating.

Die Quadriga €€€
European Map 12 D2
Eislebener Strasse 14, 10789
Tel *214 056 51* **Closed** Sun
French and European creations
are served in the restaurant of
the Hotel Brandenburger Hof.

Restaurant 44 €€€
International Map 12 D1
Augsburger Strasse 44, 10789
Tel *22 01 00*
Upmarket gourmet dining in the
terrace restaurant of the Swissôtel.
Fine views of the Ku'damm.

Wilson's €€€
American Map 12 E1
*Hotel Crowne Plaza, Nürnberger
Strasse 65, 10787*
Tel *210 070 00*
The focus here is on succulent
prime ribs and steaks, using beef
imported from the US. Save room
for the home-made ice cream.
Romantic terrace.

Around Schloss
Charlottenburg

Chenab €
Indian Map 4 D4
Knobelsdorffstrasse 35, 14059
Tel *364 347 99*
Go for the tasty, mildly spiced
vegetarian dishes at this neighbourhood eatery. The banana
curry takes some beating. Great
value for money.

Natural'mente €
Vegetarian and Vegan Map 4 F3
Schustehrusstrasse 26, 10585
Tel *341 41 66* **Closed** Sat, Sun,
dinner daily
This bio-restaurant uses only
whole foods and organic
produce. The menu features

vegetable platters, soups, and
desserts. Drinks include organic
beers and wines.

Taverna Ambrosios €
Greek Map 5 B3
*Galvanistrasse 12A,
10587*
Tel *341 55 54*
Laid-back Greek taverna with
ochre walls, blue check tablecloths and wonderful food.
The weekday lunch menu
offered here is especially
good value.

Bräuhaus Lemke €€
Traditional German Map 4 F3
Luisenplatz 1, 10585
Tel *308 789 79*
Micro-brewery adjacent to
Schloss Charlottenburg with
views of the park from the pub
terrace. Hearty German fare
and a good choice of stout, ale
and pilsner beers.

Don Giovanni €€
Italian Map 4 A4
Bismarckstrasse 28, 10625
Tel *341 76 53*
Serves huge thin-crusted
pizzas as well as Tuscan meat
and fish specialities. An excellent
selection of German red wines
is available.

Engelbecken €€
Regional German Map 4 E5
Witzlebenstrasse 31, 14057
Tel *615 28 10*
Sample delectable Bavarian
white veal and pork sausages
with sweet mustard, or the
saddle of organic pork with
fried mushroom, carrots and
pureed nettle leaves. Bavarian
lager or dark beers can be
enjoyed outside on the
pavement terrace.

Eosander €€
International Map 4 E3
Spandauer Damm 3, 14059
Tel *437 296 01*
Restfully sedate café-restaurant
just across the road from Schloss
Charlottenburg. The Art Nouveau
decor gives it a touch of
sophistication and a nostalgic air.
Open for breakfast.

Genazvale €€
Georgian Map 4 E5
Windscheidstrasse 14, 10627
Tel *450 860 26*
Friendly restaurant featuring
dishes and flavours from the
Black Sea. Must-tastes include
chatschapuri (cheese bread),
saziwi (chicken in walnut sauce)
and the delicious Georgian
regional wines.

DK Choice

Le Piaf €€
French **Map** 4 E3
Schlossstrasse 60, 14059
Tel *342 20 40* **Closed** *Sun, Mon, lunch daily*
A classy bistro with a menu based on Alsatian and French recipes, including classics such as *confit de canard*, as well as frog legs and snails for the more adventurous. The wines are imported from the owner's favourite wineries. The cosy interiors, attentive French staff and a terrace make dining at Le Piaf a memorable experience.

Restaurant Kien-Du €€
Thai **Map** 4 F4
Kaiser-Friedrich-Strasse 89, 10585
Tel *341 14 47*
The oldest Thai restaurant in Berlin is known for its red and green curries and its garlanded Buddha shrine. Native draught beer is available.

Ana e Bruno €€€
Italian **Map** 4 D3
Sophie-Charlottenstrasse 101, 14059
Tel *325 71 10*
Bruno Pellegrini's inspired gourmet cooking at a reasonable price. Excellent wine list.

Further Afield

Amrit €
South Asian **Map** 16 E2
Oranienstrasse 202-3, 10999
Tel *612 55 50*
Popular Kreuzberg restaurant offering generous portions inspired by Indian, Thai and Malaysian flavours.

Baraka €
North African **Map** 16 F2
Lausitzer Platz 6, 10997
Tel *612 63 30*
Serves an appetizing range of Moroccan and Egyptian specialities including tajine, couscous and vegetarian dishes. Cavernous ambience and seating on banquettes and cushions.

Britzer Mühle €
Traditional German
Buckower Damm 130, Neukölln, 12349
Tel *604 18 19*
Bucolic views of a mill from the large beer garden and the cosy dining room. Huge portions of attractively priced German pub grub. Live music on Mondays.

Crêperie Bretonne €
French **Map** 16 E3
Reichenberger Strasse 30, 10999
Tel *600 311 92* **Closed** *Mon*
Savoury galettes filled with ham, Roquefort, and pear. Follow with sweet pancakes, and Breton cider from the Val de Rance served in porcelain cups.

Darjiling €
Indian
Alt-Tegel 25, 13507
Tel *430 045 65*
Exotic aromas of cardamom and coriander greet visitors. Chicken, mutton and fish standards come with a smile, and at low prices.

Golden Buddha €
Thai **Map** 1 C1
Gleimstrasse 26, Prenzlauer Berg, 10437
Tel *448 55 56*
Neighbourhood restaurant with a real buzz. Locals flock here for the soft Thai flavours, vegetarian specials, and friendly service.

Hasir Ocakbasi €
Turkish **Map** 16 E2
Adalbertstrasse 12, 10999
Tel *615 070 80*
Berlin's love affair with the döner kebab began here in 1971. Large selection of char-grilled meat and fish dishes, delicious mezzes and home-made desserts.

Henne €
Traditional German **Map** 16 D1
Leuschnerdamm 25, 10999
Tel *614 77 30*
Ample chicken dishes on the menu at this wonderfully atmospheric Kreuzberg pub, now more than a century old.

Il Casolare €
Italian **Map** 16 D3
Grimmstrasse 30, 10967
Tel *695 066 10*
Some of the best pizzas in Berlin, with wafer-thin crusts and delicious toppings. Bohemian ambience, tables overlooking the Landwehr Canal and famously brusque waiters. Book ahead.

Kurhaus Korsakow €
Traditional German
Grünberger Straße 81, 10245
Tel *547 377 86*
Home-cooking and draught beers in a cosy atmosphere. Place your orders for Berliner *leber* (liver) or *bouletten* with cabbage roulade.

Loretta am Wannsee €
Regional German
Kronprinzessinnenweg 260, 14109
Tel *801 053 33*
Traditional beer garden, grill and restaurant overlooking the Wannsee with lovely lake views. The house speciality is Hax'n: knuckle of pork cooked in dark beer.

Candlelit dining in a rustic and cosy setting at Kurhaus Korsakow

For more information on types of restaurants *see p227*

Well-stocked bar at the popular Max und Moritz pub

Lotus Lounge €
Vegetarian **Map** 3 C3
Soorstrasse 85, 14050
Tel *232 550 65* **Closed** *Sun & dinner daily*
Restaurant in the Tibetan-Buddhist Centre offering mains such as spinach and potato gratin flavoured with garlic and tomato.

Max und Moritz €
Traditional German **Map** 16 D1
Oranienstrasse 162, 10969
Tel *695 159 11*
Rustic-style pub grub with generous helpings of Berlin-style food. Try the meatballs with caper sauce or beef goulash with noodle dumplings.

Merhaba €
Turkish
Greifswalder Strasse 4, 10405
Tel *488 279 40*
Traditional Turkish restaurant with typical Anatolian mezzes and grilled specialities. Very boisterous at weekends, with live music and belly dancing.

Miss Saigon €
Vietnamese **Map** 16 F2
Skalitzer Strasse 38, 10999
Tel *695 333 77*
Small no-frills restaurant that surprises with the quality of its South Vietnamese seafood and vegetable dishes, seasoned and spiced with refinement.

Nirwana €
Indian **Map** E4
Schlossstrasse 49, 12165
Tel *793 16 59*
Excellent regional cooking and huge portions. The menu ranges from mild *korma* or *biryani* dishes to spicier *masalas* and *vindaloos*.

Noodles e Figli €
Italian **Map** 16 F2
Skalitzer Strasse 94b, 10997
Tel *616 712 14*
Overlooks Berlin's grand old overhead railway. The chef here has a whimsical take on traditional pasta and risotto dishes. Home-baked bread.

Obermaier €
Regional German **Map** 16 D2
Erkelenzdamm 17, 10999
Tel *616 568 62*
Authentic Bavarian and Alpine cooking in a typical Bavarian beer garden. Specialities include *schweinelende* (pork loin) served with cranberry sauce and fried dumplings.

Old Shanghai €
Chinese **Map** 8 F1
Chausseestrasse 32, Prenzlauer Berg, 10115
Tel *288 794 66*
The chef is from Shanghai and his wife can advise on the traditional Chinese menu. Try the oven-baked ocean perch, cooked Shanghai-style in sweet and sour sauce.

Shaan €
Indian
Richardplatz 20, Neukölln, 12055
Tel *680 893 82*
Friendly restaurant with a typical range of regional dishes. Try chicken marinated in more than 20 spices and cooked in an earthenware *tandoori* oven.

Sufissimo €
Middle Eastern-Persian **Map** 16 D4
Fichtestrasse 1, 10967
Tel *616 208 33*
Try the yoghurt soup with herbs, followed by turkey breast with almonds and raisins in an apricot and cardamom sauce. The decor features blue banquettes and Oriental silverware.

Tandir €
Turkish **Map** 16 E5
Hermannstrasse 157, 12051
Tel *625 67 05*
Neighbourhood *imbissbude* (takeaway) and small restaurant with outdoor seating. Serves grilled meat, falafel, soup and casseroles.

Taverna To Koutouki €
Greek **Map** 16 E3
Kottbusser Damm 9, 10967
Tel *692 52 17*
There's a welcoming glass of ouzo on arriving at this popular Greek restaurant with a candlelit interior and typical dishes including *bifteki* (cheese-filled meatballs) and a mixed grill platter.

Thüringer Stuben €
Regional German **Map** 2 F1
Stargarder Strasse 28, Prenzlauer Berg, 10437
Tel *446 33 39*
Stag heads adorn the wood-panelled walls in this mock-traditional Thuringian inn. Home-made potato dumplings, sausages and regional specialities.

Vux €
Vegan
Wipperstrasse 14, Neukölln, 12055
Closed *Mon & Tue*
Cosy Neukölln café with a nice selection of home-made bagels. Also serves soups, quiches and delicious biscuits and waffles.

Weltrestaurant Markthalle €
Traditional German **Map** 16 F2
Pücklerstrasse 34, 10997
Tel *617 55 02*
Wood-panelled dining room near Görlitzer U-bahn station serving generous helpings of Berlin pub grub and draught beers.

Wirtshaus zur Pfaueninsel €
German-International
Pfaueninselchaussee 100, 14109
Tel *805 22 25*
Beer garden-restaurant with great views of the Havel. Ideally situated for a riverside stroll or for the ferry hop to Peacock Island. Asparagus, mushroom and pumpkin dishes in season.

Yellow Sunshine €
Vegetarian **Map** 16 F3
Wiener Strasse 19, 10999
Tel *695 987 20*
Vegan *currywurst* is on the menu at this roomy Kreuzberg bistro, along with organic fries, soya burgers and a large choice of topping and sauces.

Key to prices *see p232*

Yogi-Haus €
Indian **Map** 13 A5
Belziger Strasse 42, 10823
Tel *782 92 23*
Popular Schöneberg restaurant specializing in North Indian cuisine, mainly chicken and mutton dishes. Large dining space with an open kitchen.

Zum Bayernmichel €
Traditional German
Bornholmer Strasse 87, Prenzlauer Berg, 10439
Tel *444 30 44*
Traditional Bavarian-style inn with a beer garden serving Paulaner on draught. The Bauerngrillpfanne is a combo of Nuremberg sausages, pork medallions, chicken breast and bacon-wrapped runner beans – simply mouthwatering.

Austria €€
Austrian **Map** 15 A5
Bergmannstraße 30, 10961
Tel *694 44 40*
Famous with Berliners long before Pulitzer prize-winning author Jeffrey Eugenides gave it a plug in *Middlesex*. Wiener schnitzel is the house speciality, served in mammoth portions.

DK Choice

Blockhaus Nikolskoe €€
German
Tel *805 29 14*
This restaurant is idyllically located, with the Grunewald forest as its backdrop and the broad expanse of Havel and Peacock Island ahead. The restaurant occupies a wooden *dacha* (country house) built for the heir to the Russian throne in 1819. The food, especially the fresh fish and local game, suit the spectacular views and waterside setting.

Brauhaus in Rixdorf €€
Traditional German
Glasower Straße 27, Neukölln, 12051
Tel *626 88 80*
Beer garden and restaurant in a converted 19th-century villa. Serves locally brewed beer and traditional dishes such as *eisbein* (knuckle of pork) served with sauerkraut and boiled potatoes.

Cape Town €€
South African
Schönfliesser Strasse 15, Prenzlauer Berg, 10439
Tel *400 576 58*
A meat-eater's paradise a short walk from Schönhauser Allee

S-bahn. Generous portions of springbok and wildebeast. South African wines also available.

Castel Montecroce €€
Italian **Map** 15 A5
Friesenstrasse 14, 10965
Tel *628 454 71*
Unassuming but endearing *trattoria* offering candlelit dining. Excellent home-made pasta and a selection of meat and fish dishes, but leave room for the tiramisu. Discreet but attentive staff.

Fischerhütte €€
Regional German
Fischerhüttenstraße 136, 14163
Tel *367 526 34*
Picturesque views of the Schlachtensee from this lakeside beer garden and restaurant. There is a bio-grill and a kids' play area.

Fisherman's €€
Fish
Eisenhammerweg 20, 13507
Tel *437 464 70*
Fish and scallops come in inspired variations, accompanied by Rieslings. The view of the lake is priceless.

Freischwimmer €€
German
Vor dem Schlesischen Tor 2a, 10997
Tel *610 743 09*
Lively waterside café-bar set on floating stages overlooking the Spree and the Landwehrkanal. A young crowd gathers for Sunday brunch, and on summer evenings for the electronic and techno music on the opposite bank.

Funkturm Restaurant €€
German-Continental **Map** 3 B5
Hammarskjöldplatz 1, 14055
Tel *303 829 00*

Large glasses of frothy beer on offer in the popular Austria restaurant

Set in a 52-m (171-ft) high radio tower dating from the 1920s, with original Art Deco interiors. Panoramic views over West Berlin from the champagne bar.

Haus Sanssouci €€
German
Am Grossen Wannsee 60, 14109
Tel *805 30 34*
Smart, elegant restaurant with mouthwatering fish, seafood and game specialities. Located in the world's first pre-fabricated wooden villa. Large summer garden with fabulous views over Wannsee.

Hax'nhau €€
Regional German
Alt-Tegel 2, 13507
Tel *433 90 34*
Decked out as a traditional Bavarian inn, with dark-wood furnishings and beamed ceilings. Hearty helpings of regional meat and fish specialities. There is a buffet as well.

Hugo €€
International **Map** 12 D4
Bundesallee 161, 10715
Tel *311 713 38*
A Neighbourhood restaurant that is popular locally for its reasonably priced prime cuts of Argentine and Black Angus beef.

DK Choice

Jolesch €€
Austrian **Map** 16 F2
Muskauer Strasse 1, 10997
Tel *612 35 81*
Tobias Janzen shows a deft touch in his subtle reinterpretation of traditional Austrian cooking in this gourmet temple. The menu is seasonal but Austrian specialities are recommended. Try Emperor Franz-Josef's favourite *tafelspitz* (boiled beef) served here with creamed spinach, apple-horseradish, chive sauce and fried potatoes. Wash it down with excellent Grüner Veltliner. The pine-green walls and plum-coloured banquettes create a calming ambience.

Juleps New York Bar & Restaurant €€
American **Map** 11 A1
Giesebrechtstrasse 3, 10629
Tel *881 88 23*
Shades of an American speakeasy in this brick-walled diner and cocktail bar. The burgers are made with imported American beef.

For more information on types of restaurants *see p227*

Diners at the elegant Restaurant Volt, popular for its regional cuisine

Le Mano Verde   €€
Vegan   **Map** 5 C5
Kempinski Plaza, Uhlandstrasse 181,
10623
Tel *827 031 20*
A wide choice of creative vegan
options, with an emphasis on
raw food, all of organic origin.
In a very central yet slightly
hidden location.

Little Otik   €€
American   **Map** 16 D4
Graefestrasse 71, 10967
Tel *503 623 01*   **Closed** *Mon, Tue,*
lunch daily
Run by two enterprising New
Yorkers, this restaurant specializes
in cooking with locally grown
organic produce. Save room for
the ricotta cake with rhubarb.

Milo   €€
Jewish   **Map** 11 A3
Münstersche Strasse 6, 10709
Tel *492 053 60*   **Closed** *Sat*
Fine dining in this rabbi-
certificated kosher restaurant in
the Wilmersdor Lubawitsch
Chabad Jewish centre. Traditional
Jewish meat-based dishes,
salmon latkes and kosher sushi!

Mio   €€
Mediterranean
Samariterstrasse 36,
Friedrichshain, 10247
Tel *847 127 58*

Small neighbourhood bistro with
red-and-white check tablecloths
and candlelit dining. An eclectic
menu with healthy, flavoursome
food from all parts of the
Mediterranean.

Osmanya   €€
Turkish
Birkenstrasse 17, 10559
Tel *488 299 99*
A cut above the average, this
restaurant with opulent decor
offers excellent traditional
Ottoman cooking. Try the sea
bass fillet, cooked in a butter and
lime-flavoured sauce and served
on a bed of blanched celery. Live
music on weekends.

Restaurant Grunewaldturm   €€
German-International
Havelchaussee 61, 14193
Tel *417 200 02*
A not too formal restaurant in a
picturesque woodland setting.
The terrace and beer garden
offer sublime views.

Restaurant Vitruv   €€
German-
Mediterranean   **Map** 10 E1
Hotel Leonardo Royal, Otto-Braun-
Strasse 90, 10249
Tel *755 43 09 10*
Spacious hotel restaurant
near Alexanderplatz offering
classic German dishes and an

enterprising Mediterranean-
inspired menu with Asian touches.

Restaurant Z   €€
Greek-
Mediterranean   **Map** 15 A5
Friesenstrasse 12, 10965
Tel *692 27 16*
Friendly Greek taverna best
known for its lamb and fish
specialities, but also well-
suited to vegetarians. Greek
regional wines.

Schoenbrunn   €€
Austrian-
Mediterranean   **Map** 10 F1
Am Friedrichshain 8,
Friedrichshain 10407
Tel *453 05 65 10*
Enjoy a delicious Wiener schnitzel
on the sun terrace of this
restaurant-beer garden in
Volkspark Friedrichshain.

Zum Hax'nwirt   €€
Regional German   **Map** 11 B4
Hohenzollerndamm 185,
10713
Tel *822 51 33*   **Closed** *Sun &*
lunch daily
Hearty Bavarian home cooking,
mainly pork dishes, is the stock-
in-trade of this restaurant.
Chintzy dining room and a large,
leafy terrace.

Fortshaus Paulsborn   €€€
Traditional German
Hüttenweg 90, 14193
Tel *818 19 10*   **Closed** *Mon*
Set in a former hunting lodge
and picturesquely situated
near Grunewaldsee, Fortshaus
Paulsborn offers game
specialities, cakes and
delicious pastries.

Hartmann's   €€€
German   **Map** 16 D4
Fichtestrasse 31, 10967
Tel *612 010 03*
Stefan Hartmann's Michelin-
starred cellar restaurant is
perfect for a romantic dinner-à-
deux, Choose from the taster
menu or dine à la carte.
Judiciously selected wine list.

Horváth   €€€
Modern German   **Map** 16 E3
Paul Lincke Ufer 44a, 10999
Tel *612 899 92*   **Closed** *Mon*
The Austrian roots of the young
chef, Sebastian Frank, are
reflected in the sophisticated
regional German cuisine at this
Michelin-starred restaurant.

Restaurant Volt   €€€
Regional German   **Map** 16 F4
Paul-Lincke-Ufer 21, 10999
Tel *610 740 33*

Key to prices *see p232*

An original take on Brandenburg regional cooking from rising star chef Matthias Gleiss. Impressive setting in a 1920s electric power station.

Spindler & Klatt €€€
European-Asian **Map** 16 F1
Köpenicker Strasse 16-17, 10997
Tel *319 88 18 60*
Restaurant and nightclub overlooking the Spree. Seating indoors or on the pontoon terrace. The dance floor is in a converted warehouse building. Reservations advised.

Tugra €€€
Turkish **Map** 11 A2
Kurfürstendamm 96, 10709
Tel *323 40 27*
Smart Turkish restaurant at the far end of Ku'damm offering Ottoman recipes from the Sultan's Golden Book. Sample the saddle of lamb in pepper cream sauce, with dates wrapped in turkey ham.

Greater Berlin

Feine Dahme €
German-International
Gutenbergstraße 7, Kopenick, 12557
Tel *516486 47* **Closed** *Mon*
Views of Köpenick Old Town from this scenic spot at the confluence of the Spree and the Dahme rivers. Light meals, including breakfast and Sunday brunch, served on the sun terrace. Beer, wine and coffee also available.

Alexandrowka €€
Russian
Russische Kolonie Haus1, Puschkinallee, Potsdam, D14469
Tel *0331 200 64 78* **Closed** *Mon*

This two-storey log cabin with carved gables is located in Potsdam's delightful Russian Colony. Relax in the homely interior, complete with icon corner, while sampling beautifully prepared *zakuski* with beef stroganoff and chicken Kiev to follow.

Juliette €€
French
Jagerstr. 39, Potsdam, 14467
Tel *0331 270 17 91*
Savoir vivre in Potsdam – this elegant restaurant pleases with refined French cuisine and unobtrusive service.

Kid Creole €€
American
Bölschestrasse 10, Friedrichshagen, 12587
Tel *650 766 80*
Berlin meets New Orleans in this laid-back restaurant a short walk from Friedrichshagen S-bahn. Mellow candelit interior and mouthwatering Cajun food. The menu features everything from gumbo and catfish to *jambalaya* (Creole stew) and ribs.

Krongut Bornstedt €€
Traditional German
Ribbeckstrasse 6, Potsdam, 14469
Tel *0331 550 65 10*
Formerly crown property, these splendid UNESCO-protected buildings have been converted into cafés and restaurants. The beer hall serves rustic cuisine and an original *Büffelbier* (Buffalo Beer) from 1689.

Maison Charlotte €€
French **Map** 8 F3
Mittelstrasse 20, Potsdam, 14467
Tel *0331 280 54 50*
Refined bistro in Potsdam's Dutch Quarter with a charming

back garden. Savoury pancakes as well as French classics such as coq au vin.

Spree-Arche €€
Modern German
Müggelschlösschenweg, 12559 Friedrichshagen
Tel *0172 304 21 11*
A boatman ferries guests to a floating blockhouse on the Spree. Alfresco dining on the terrace overlooking the attractive Muggelsee. The fish specialities are delicious.

Strandlust Grünau €€
Modern German
Seddinpromenade 3A, 12527
Tel *675 86 26* **Closed** *Nov–Feb, Mon*
A scenic tram ride from Köpenick Town Hall brings guests directly to the Muggelsee and this lakeside restaurant with terrace. Fish specialities and local draught beers on offer.

Weisse Villa €€
Modern German
Josef-Nawrocki-Strasse 10, 12587
Tel *640 956 47*
Wonderful views of the Muggelsee from the terrace of a 130-year-old villa, once part of the Friedrichshagen brewery. Well worth the trip out of town.

Speckers Landhaus €€€
German-International
Jägerallee 13, Potsdam, 14469
Tel *0331 280 43 11* **Closed** *Sun & Mon*
Sophisticated German cooking in a restored country house dating from 1645. The menu includes rack of lamb with rosemary and Wiener schnitzel.

Outdoor seating on the pontoon terrace of Spindler & Klatt, located by the Spree

For more information on types of restaurants *see p227*

Light Meals and Snacks

There are many popular fast-food bars and restaurants in Berlin that serve the all-pervading burgers, French fries and pizzas, some of them run by well-known international chains. By way of contrast, many of the self-service places specialize in local foods. The city's cafés are ideal stopping places for a quick meal and always offer something on the menu that will fill you up. Even more convenient are the many bars on wheels or small kiosks – *Imbissbuden* – that serve the traditional Berlin *Currywurst (see p228)*.

There are also many restaurants offering Indian food, mainly along Grolmanstrasse. Nearby, in Wielandstrasse, the Italian **Briganti** deserves a special recommendation.

Berlin's Japanese restaurants tend to be of the more exclusive type but still offer excellent soups and sushi. The best are **Sushi Bar Ishin**, **Tao**, **FUKU Sushi** and **Musashi**.

Langano in Kreuzberg serves deliciously-spiced Ethiopian platters, and it is customary to eat with your hands. **Taquiera Ta'Cabron** offers Mexican street food such as tacos and burritos.

Imbissbuden and Snack Bars

The classic *Imbissbude* is a simple little kiosk selling drinks and a few light snacks, such as *Currywurst* or French fries *(Pommes)* served with mayonnaise or ketchup (or both). The former is a genuine Berlin speciality consisting of grilled, sliced sausage *(Bratwurst)*, topped with a spicy sauce, and served on a paper plate with a plastic fork. These kiosks are usually located in convenient sites near the S-Bahn or U-Bahn stations, or on busy streets and junctions. **Ku'damm 195** and **Konnopke** are considered the best places to experience traditional *Currywurst*, which is served with home-made spicy sauce instead of the now standard tomato ketchup sprinkled with curry powder and fiery paprika.

Other popular snacks sold on the streets include various grilled sausages, collectively referred to as *Bratwurst*. The most common types are frankfurters *(Wienerwurst)* and a thicker kind of sausage known as *Bockwurst*. These are heated in hot water. The German variation on the hamburger theme is called *Boulette*.

Unfortunately there are few places similar to the *Imbissbude* that offer food from other regions of Germany. One of the exceptions is **Weitzmann**, which is in an arcade under the S-Bahn railway bridge near Bellevue station. Short, thick noodles called *Spätzle* feature heavily on its typically southern German menu. **Spätzleexpress** also offers southern German dishes such as *Spätzle*, *Knödel* and *Maultaschen*.

Specialities from Around the World

Traditional Berlin specialities are facing stiff competition from further afield. Turkish restaurants serving excellent *Döner Kebab* are on every corner. Typically a kebab is a piece of warmed flat *pitta* bread stuffed with hot sliced meat, lettuce, cucumber and tomatoes, and covered with a thick, aromatic, yoghurt-based sauce. Obviously the best kebabs are made by the Turks living around Kreuzberg, but you can also have an excellent version of this dish in most of the other Berlin districts. The restaurants worth trying are **Hasir**, **Maroush** or indeed any of the places around Kottbuser Tor or Oranienstrasse.

Vegetarians should try *falafel*, a Middle Eastern speciality widely available in Berlin. Balls of chickpeas and coriander or parsley are rolled in breadcrumbs and deep fried, then served stuffed inside flat bread with salad and yoghurt sauce. The best places to try this excellent snack are around Winterfeldtplatz, for example **Habibi**, **Dada Falafel** and **Baharat Falafel**, or **Baraka** in the eastern part of the city.

Fragrant Asian dishes are offered by **Hamy Cafe** in Hasenheide, while those with a passion for Chinese food should eat at **Pagode** in Kreuzberg on Bergmannstrasse. If you wish to try Korean cuisine, then pay a visit to **Korea-Haus** on Danziger Strasse, which servers a good-value "all you can eat" Korean buffet. A visit to **Vietnam Imbiss** is a good opportunity to try out some Vietnamese specialities.

Light Snacks

Those with an appetite for more traditional snacks are catered for in the establishments around S- and U-Bahn stations and along the main streets offering fresh baguettes filled with ham or cheese.

For an instant solution to hunger pangs, try one of the bakeries that offer delicious freshly-baked croissants or excellent *Brezeln* (pretzels) covered with coarse salt. During lunchtime, the popular **Nordsee** chain of restaurants offers fish sandwiches to take away, as does the stylish **Let's Go Sylt**. Some sandwich bars offer mouth-watering quiches and tarts alongside baguettes and rolls.

If a traditional American-Jewish bagel bar is what you fancy, then **Bagels & Bialys** in Rosenthaler Strasse is the place to go, where the variety of fillings is quite staggering.

Some places also specialize in one particular kind of dish or food. For example **Soup-Kultur** and **Intersoup** serve only soup, but in a multitude of varieties – hot, cold, exotic, spicy or mild. Garlic lovers should visit **Knofel** in Prenzlauer Berg. Also worth mentioning are **Deli 31** and **Deli Street**.

Another way to ensure a quick and inexpensive fill-up are self-service pizzerias such as **Piccola Italia**. A great alternative are the lighter pizza breads at **La Focacceria** served with any topping you like.

Eating in Shopping Centres

One of the problems for the dedicated shopper is that eating can seriously cut down on shopping time. Fortunately, many snack bars in shopping centres have put the emphasis on fast service. Some, however, such as **KaDeWe** manage this in stylish surroundings. A visit to this enormous shop features on most tourists' list of things to do, and its self-service café is therefore very popular. Lunch at one of the tables with a view of Wittenbergplatz is a very pleasant adjunct to a Berlin shopping trip. **The Duke** is another good choice and is just around the corner from KaDeWe and Peek & Cloppenburg, off Taventzienstrasse. The stylish restaurant serves light German and American fare, making it a popular lunch spot.

Another equally busy venue is the self-service café situated in the basement of the chic **Galeries Lafayette** in Friedrichstrasse.

For those reluctant shoppers who put more emphasis on the food, there is an oasis of bars and cafés near Potsdamer Platz, in the **Arkaden** shopping centre. As well as a branch of Salomon Bagels, this centre provides a taste of the Orient in Asia Pavillon, while fans of potatoes should pay a visit to Pomme de Terre. Here, the humble potato becomes the star of the meal and is served in a myriad of guises and with just as many different fillings.

For short stops in Arkaden, both the dedicated and the reluctant shopper should visit the classic Wiener Café for coffee and cakes and Caffé e Gelato for delicious ice cream.

Eating in Museums

As a city offering a wealth of culture, many of Berlin's museums have established fascinating cafés and bistros. **Café im Zeughaus** at the Deutsches Historisches Museum offers a great breakfast with views of the river Spree, while **Café im Jüdischen Museum** is a café/restaurant serving Jewish specialities at the Jüdisches Museum. **Sarah Wiener im Hamburger Bahnhof**, in the modern art museum, has some great German cakes, and **Café Dix** at the Berlinische Galerie is one of the city's most enjoyable art cafés.

Cafés

Berlin is well served by cafés that provide a wide range of light snacks or cakes to suit everyone's budget and tastes. They are normally open from 9 or 10 in the morning until late at night. In the mornings they serve breakfast, either à la carte or as a buffet. After that the regular café menu comes into force, although breakfast items are often still available. Main meals on the menu might include several salads, several hearty soup-type stews (*Eintöpfe*) and a few simple hot dishes. Prices are quite reasonable, not greater than ten euros. Invariably, every café has a great choice of desserts, ice creams and cakes, as well as a range of alcoholic drinks.

Around the Technical University, **Café Hardenberg** is popular with students, and near Kantstrasse you can visit **Schwarzes Café**, which is open 24 hours a day. If you are on Savignyplatz you might want to try **Café Brel**. **Café am Neuen See** is situated near the lake in the Tiergarten Park. **Buchwald**, a patisserie in Hansaviertel, offers a wide range of *Baumkuchen* (so-called "tree cakes" that resemble tree stumps).

Kreuzberg's Oranienstrasse has an array of good cafés, including **Milch und Zucker** and **Pfeiffers**. You can also explore Graefestrasse, where you'll find the delightful **Café Matilda**.

Other renowned cafés include the charming **Café Wintergarten**, located in the Literaturhaus on Fasanenstrasse, and the Viennese-style **Café Einstein**. Here you can enjoy coffee made with beans fresh from their own roasting room. The original café, in Kurfürstenstrasse, has been joined by another branch in Mitte, on Unter den Linden, whose cakes are almost as refined as those at the **Caffeehaus am Roseneck** *(see p259)*. **St. Oberholz** in Mitte is popular with freelance workers who need wireless Internet access and good coffee.

While taking a walk around Checkpoint Charlie, you could drop in to **Sale e Tabacchi**, an excellent Italian restaurant.

There are many places that offer light lunches and coffee around Oranienburger Strasse and Alte and Neue Schönhauser Allees. In the evening they attract livelier crowds in search of decent music and good beer. You can stop by **Die Eins**, an atmospheric café.

An interesting evening can be spent investigating the options in Prenzlauer Berg. Join the in-crowd at **Anita Wronski**, a friendly café on two levels with menus in English and excellent people-watching from the tables outside. If you prefer somewhere cosy, try **Chagall**, with its welcoming open fire and Russian ballads. On hot days a good spot to enjoy the sun is on the terrace in **November** or at **Seeblick**, which is a good place to eat.

Other reliable cafés that are well worth looking out for include **Atlantic** and **Keyser Soze**.

Coffee Bars and Tea Rooms

There are not many coffee bars in Berlin, but they are easily spotted as they tend to be run by well-known coffee producers such as Eduscho or Tschibo.

Barcomi's is a real treat, an American-style coffee bar with its own roasting room and a large selection of coffees. If you need more sustenance than coffee and muffins, try **Barcomi's Deli** where you can build your own sandwiches.

If you want a good cup of tea, then you should go to **Tadschikische Teestube**, or **TTT (Tee, Tea, Thé)**, where the choice is quite amazing.

DIRECTORY

Imbissbuden and Snack Bars

Konnopke
Schönhauser Allee 44b
(U-Bahnhof Eberswalder Str).
Tel 442 77 65.
Open 10am–8pm Mon–Fri, noon–8pm Sat.

Ku'damm 195
Kurfürstendamm 195.
Map 11 B2.
Tel 881 89 42.
Open 11am–5am Mon–Thu, 11am–6am Fri & Sat, noon–5am Sun.

Spätzleexpress
Wiener Strasse 11, Kreuzberg. **Map** 16 F2.
Tel 69 53 44 63.
Open noon–10pm daily.

Weitzmann
Lüneburger Strasse 390.
Map 7 A3.
Tel 394 20 57.
Open noon–late Mon–Sat, noon–9pm Sun.

Specialities from Around the World

Baharat Falafel
Winterfeldstrasse 37.
Map 13 B3.
Tel 216 83 01.
Open 11am–2am daily.

Baraka
Lausitzer Platz 6.
Map 16 F2.
Tel 612 63 30.
Open noon–midnight Mon–Thu, noon–1am Fri, Sat & Sun.

Briganti
Wielandstrasse 15.
Map 11 B1.
Tel 323 53 62.
Open 11am–7pm Tue–Fri, 10am–4pm Sat.

Dada Falafel
Linienstrasse 132.
Map 8 F1.
Tel 27 59 69 27.
Open 10am–2am daily.

FUKU Sushi
Husemannstrasse 14.
Tel 44 04 90 77.
Open noon–11pm Mon–Fri, 4–11pm Sat & Sun.

Habibi
Goltzstrasse 24.
Map 13 A3.
Tel 215 33 32.
Open 11am–3am Sun–Thu, 11am–5am Fri & Sat.

Hamy Cafe
Hasenheide 10.
Map 16 E5.
Tel 61 62 59 59.

Hasir
Oranienburger Strasse 4.
Map 9 B2.
Tel 28 04 16 16.
Open 11:30am–1am daily.

Korea-Haus
Danziger Strasse 195.
Tel 423 34 41.
Open noon–midnight Tue–Sun.

Langano
Kohlfurter Strasse 44.
Map 16 D3.
Tel 6150 7103.
Open 4pm–midnight daily.

Maroush
Adalbertstrasse 93.
Map 16 E2.
Tel 69 53 61 71.
Open 11am–2am daily.

Musashi
Kottbusser Damm 102.
Map 16 E3.
Tel 693 20 42.
Open noon–10:30pm Mon–Sat, 2–10pm Sun.

Oshima Sushi Bar
Pariser Strasse 39–40.
Map 11 B2.
Tel 505 61 877.
Open noon–9pm Mon–Sat.

Pagode
Bergmannstrasse 88.
Map 15 A4.
Tel 691 26 40.
Open noon–11pm Mon–Thu, noon–midnight Fri–Sun.

Sushi Bar Ishin
Schlossstrasse 101.
Map 4 E4.
Tel 797 10 49.
Open 11am–8pm Mon–Sat.

Taqueria Ta'Cabron
Skalitzer Strasse 60.
Open 1–11pm Tue–Sun.

Tao
Wilmersdorferstrasse 94.
Map 11 A2.
Tel 88 77 38 87.
Open noon–11pm daily.

Vietnam Imbiss
Damaschkestrasse 30.
Tel 324 93 44. **Open** noon–9pm Mon–Sat.

Light Snacks

Bagels & Bialys
Rosenthaler Strasse 46–48. **Map** 9 B2.
Tel 283 65 46.
Open 8am–11pm Mon–Sat, 9am–10pm Sun.

Deli 31
Bleibtreustrasse 31.
Map 11 B2.
Tel 88 47 41 01.
Open 11am–9pm Mon–Sat.

Deli Street
Chauseestrasse 4.
Map 8 F1.
Tel 28 09 28 33.
Open 8:30am–4:30pm Mon–Thu, 8:30am–4pm Fri.

Intersoup
Schliemanstrasse 31.
Map 8 F1. **Tel** 23 27 30 45.
Open 5pm–midnight daily.

Knofel
Wichertstrasse 33.
Tel 447 67 17.
Open Nov–Apr: 6pm–late Mon–Thu, 2pm–late Fri, 1pm–late Sat & Sun; May–Oct: 6pm–late daily.

La Focacceria
Fehrbellinerstrasse 24.
Map 8 F1. **Tel** 44 03 27 71.
Open 11am–11pm daily.

Let's Go Sylt
Kurfürstendamm 212.
Map 11 C2.
Tel 88 68 28 00. **Open** 11am–midnight Mon–Sat, noon–midnight Sun.

Nordsee
Spandauer Strasse 4.
Map 9 C3, 16 F2.
Tel 24 26 881.
Open 10am–8pm daily.

Piccola Italia
Oranienburger Strasse 6.
Map 9 B2. **Tel** 283 58 43.
Open noon–1am daily.

Soup-Kultur
Kurfürstendamm 224.
Map 12 D1.
Tel 88 62 92 82. **Open** noon–6:30pm Mon–Sat.

Eating in Shopping Centres

Duke
Nurnbergerstrasse 50–55.
Map 12 A2.
Tel 68 31 54 00. **Open** 11:30am–11pm daily.

Galeries Lafayette
Französische Strasse 23.
Map 8 F4, 15 C3.
Tel 20 94 80.
Open 10am–8pm Mon–Sat.

KaDeWe
Tauentzienstrasse 21–24.
Map 12 E1. **Tel** 21 21 0.
Open 10am–8pm Mon–Thu, 10am–9pm Fri, 9:30am–8pm Sat.

Karstadt
Kurfürstendamm 231.
Map 12 D1. **Tel** 880 030.
Open 10am–8pm Mon–Sat.

Potsdamer Platz Arkaden
Alte Potsdamer Strasse 7.
Map 8 D5. **Open** 10am–9pm Mon–Sat.

Eating in Museums

Café Dix
Berlinische Galerie, Alte Jakobstrasse 128.
Map 9 C5.
Open 10am–7pm daily.

Café im Jüdischen Museum
Jüdisches Museum, Lindenstrasse 9–14.
Map 15 A2.
Open 10am–10pm Mon, 10am–8pm Tue–Sun.

Café im Zeughaus
Deutsches Historisches Museum, Unter den Linden 2. **Map** 9 A3. **Open** 10am–6pm daily.

Sarah Wiener im Hamburger Bahnhof
Invaliden Strasse 50–51.
Map 8 D1.
Tel 707 136 50.
Open 10am–6pm Tue–Fri, 11am–8pm Sat, 11am–6pm Sun.

Cafés

Anita Wronski
Knaackstrasse 26–28.
Tel 442 84 83.
Open 9am–late daily.

Atlantic
Bergmannstrasse 100.
Map 14 F4.
Tel 691 92 92.
Open 9:30am–1pm daily.

Buchwald
Bartningallee 29.
Map 6 F2. **Tel** 391 59 31.
Open 9am–6pm Mon–Sat, 10am–6pm Sun.

Café am Neuen See
Lichtensteinallee 1.
Map 6 F5. **Tel** 254 49 30.
Open 8am–late Mon–Fri, 9am–late Sat & Sun.

Café Brel
Savignyplatz 1.
Map 11 C1.
Tel 318 00 20.
Open 9am–1am daily.

Café Cinema
Rosenthaler Strasse 39.
Map 9 B2. **Tel** 280 64 15.
Open noon–2am daily.

Café Einstein
Kurfürstenstrasse 58.
Map 13 A2. **Tel** 261 50 96.
Open 8am–1am daily.

Unter den Linden 42.
Map 8 F3, 15 C3.
Tel 204 36 32.
Open 7am–10pm daily.

Café Hardenberg
Hardenbergstrasse 10.
Map 5 C5. **Tel** 312 26 44.
Open 9am–1am daily.

Café Lebensart
Unter den Linden 69–73.
Map 8 E3, 15 B3.
Tel 447 21 930.
Open 9am–10pm Sun–Thu, 9am–11pm Fri & Sat.

Café Matilda
Graefestrasse 12.
Map 16 D4.
Tel 81 79 72 88.
Open 9am–2am daily.

Café Morgenrot
Kanstanienallee 85.
Tel 44 31 78 44.
Open noon–1am Tue–Thu, 11am–3am Fri & Sat, 11am–midnight Sun.

Café Oliv
Münzstrasse 8.
Map 9 C2.
Tel 89 20 65 40.
Open 8:30am–7pm Mon–Fri, 9:30am–7pm Sat, 10am–6pm Sun.

Café Rix
Karl-Marx-Strasse 141.
Tel 686 9020.
Open 9am–midnight Mon–Thu, 9am–1am Fri & Sat, 10am–midnight Sun.

Café Ständige Vertretung
Schiffbauerdamm 8.
Tel 282 39 65.
Open 11am–late daily.

Café Wintergarten im Literaturhaus
Fasanenstrasse 23.
Map 12 D1.
Tel 882 54 14.
Open 9:30am–1am daily.

Caffeehaus am Roseneck
Hohenzollerndamm 92.
Tel 895 96 922.
Open 7:30am–10pm Mon–Fri, 8am–7pm Sat, 9am–7pm Sun.

Chagall
Kollwitzstrasse 2.
Tel 441 58 81.
Open 10am–2am daily.

Die Eins
Wilhelmstrasse 67A (eingang Reichstagsufer).
Map 8 E3.
Tel 22 48 98 88.
Open 9am–midnight Mon–Sat, 10am–midnight Sun.

Dolores
Rosa-Luxemburg-Strasse 7. **Map** 9 C2.
Tel 28 09 95 97.
Open 11:30am–10pm Mon–Sat, 1–10pm Sun.

Filmbühne am Steinplatz
Hardenbergstrasse 12.
Map 6 D5.
Tel 312 65 89.
Open 9am–midnight daily.

Gorky Park
Weinbergsweg 25.
Tel 44 87 286. **Open** 9:30am–1am daily.

Kaffeestube im Nikolaiviertel
Poststrasse 19. **Map** 9 C3.
Tel 24 63 06 41. **Open** 9am–midnight daily.

Keyser Soze
Tucholskystrasse 33.
Map 9 A1.
Tel 28 59 94 89.
Open 8am–3am daily.

Kleine Orangerie
Spandauer Damm 20.
Map 4 E3. **Tel** 322 20 21.
Open 9am–midnight daily.

Milch und Zucker
Oranienstrasse 37.
Map 16 D2.
Tel 61 67 14 97.
Open 7am–8pm Mon–Fri, 8am–8pm Sat & Sun.

November
Husemannstrasse 15.
Tel 442 84 25.
Open 10am–2am Mon–Fri, 9am–2am Sat & Sun.

Pfeiffers
Oranienstrasse 17.
Map 16 E2.
Tel 61 65 86 09.
Open 8:30am–late Mon–Fri, 9am–late Sat, 10am–late Sun.

St. Oberholz
Rosenthaler Strasse 72a.
Map 9 B1. **Tel** 214 61 311.
Open 8am–midnight Mon–Fri, 9am–midnight Sat & Sun.

Sale e Tabacchi
Rudi-Dutschkestrasse 23.
Tel 252 11 55. **Open** 10am–11:30pm daily.

San Remo
Falckensteinstrasse 46.
Tel 74 07 30 88.
Open noon–late daily.

Schwarzes Café
Kantstrasse 148.
Map 11 C1.
Tel 313 80 38.
Open 24 hours daily.

Seeblick
Rykestrasse 14.
Tel 442 92 26.
Open 10am–2am Mon–Fri, 10am–noon Sat & Sun.

Coffee Bars and Tea Rooms

Balzac Coffee
Knesebeckstrasse 1.
Map 5 C5.

Friedrichstrasse 125.
Map 15 C4, 6 F4.
Open 7:30am–7:30pm Mon–Fri, 8:30am–7:30pm Sat, 8:30am–6:30pm Sun

Barcomi's
Bergmannstrasse 21.
Map 15 A5.
Tel 694 81 38.
Open 8am–9pm Mon–Sat, 9am–9pm Sun.

Barcomi's Deli
Sophienstrasse 21 (second courtyard).
Map 9 B1.
Tel 28 59 83 63.
Open 9am–9pm Mon–Sat, 10am–9pm Sun.

Einstein Coffeeshop
Friedrichstrasse 166.
Map 8 F4.
Open 7am–8pm Mon–Fri, 7:30am–8pm Sat, 9am–6pm Sun.

Friedrichstrasse 185.
Map 8 F4.
Open 8am–8pm Mon–Sat, 9am–6:30pm Sun.

Savignyplatz 11.
Map 11 C1.
Open 8:30am–7pm Mon–Sat, 9am–6pm Sun.

Tadschikische Teestube
Am Festungsgraben 1.
Map 9 A3.
Tel 204 11 12.
Open 5pm–midnight Mon–Fri, 3pm–midnight Sat & Sun.

TTT – Tee, Tea, Thé
Goltzstrasse 2.
Map 13 A4.
Tel 21 75 22 40.
Open 9am–8pm Mon–Sat, 10am–8pm Sun (all year).

Bars and Wine Bars

Trying to make a clear distinction between wine bars, bars, pubs and *Bierstuben* or giving a precise definition for the word *Kneipe* is practically impossible. However, regardless of the nuances behind all these names, they do share some basic characteristics: they are places where drinking is the primary activity, although eating is sometimes possible; they are usually open from late afternoon or early evening but do not close till late at night or even till morning, if the atmosphere is lively.

Kneipen

In general terms, a *Kneipe* means a cosy sort of place which serves beer (although other drinks are available, too) and where you can have something to eat. The typical *Alberliner Kneipe* is a dark room with panelled oak walls, a big bar and buffet with snacks such as *Buletten* (made from pork), *Soleier* (pickled eggs), *Rollmöpse* (marinated herring) and a selection of cold meats, black pudding (blood sausage) and patés. This kind of traditional pub can still be found in the less affluent districts of Berlin – in Moabit, Kreuzberg and in Neukölln, for example, but they are not as common in the city centre. Among the most popular are **Zur Kneipe** and **Ranke 2**, as well as several *Kneipen* in Mitte around the Nikolaiviertel, including **Zum Nussbaum**.

Each *Kneipe* has its own character. More and more of them are choosing modern and inventive interiors, often specializing in less traditional kinds of food: Italian, French or Oriental. Whatever the blend, however, a relaxed atmosphere and a big choice of alcoholic beverages seem to be common features. Many *Kneipen* are evolving into a fashionable mix of *Kneipe*, bar, lounge and beer garden. One such is **Reingold** in Mitte. In Savignyplatz, you might want to visit **Dicke Wirtin**, where you can try a hearty *Eintopf* (a rich soup-type stew). The majority of these fashionable places are situated in Kreuzberg and in Prenzlauer Berg – especially around Kollwitzplatz, which is dotted with all sorts of bars

and pubs. At **Ankerklause** students and political activists come together to drink, dance and put the world to rights.

Biergarten

A *Biergarten* is an outdoor venue only open during the summer months, and usually located somewhere scenic, maybe in a park or by a lake. In addition to the usual food and drinks, it completes the outdoor experience with a barbecue. **Golgatha** and **Schleusenkrug** provide a much welcome breath of fresh air in the centre of Berlin; or if you are exploring Prenzlauer Berg, try the **Prater**. After enjoying the views in Tiergarten, the **Café am Neuen See** is a pleasant place to end the day.

A Berlin trend is the open-air beach bar situated on one of the city's waterways. A popular and attractive one is **Strandbar Mitte**.

Wine Bars

Berlin wine bars tend to have a Mediterranean feel to them. Interiors are often quite rustic in style, but there are exceptions. They open from early evening and stay open late. As for food, menus feature predominantly Italian, Spanish and French cuisine, while the bar serves a huge selection of wines by the glass, bottle or carafe. **Wiener Beisl**, a wine bar with an established reputation, features French food and wine. If you are visiting Prenzlauer Berg you might want to try **Weinstein** which offers French and Spanish food and wine.

By way of contrast, at **Lutter & Wegner** in Mitte you can match German-Austrian food with appropriate, native wines, or sample a selection of American snacks and cocktails at **Billy Wilder's**.

Bars

A Berlin bar is a good place to finish your evening, and the dedicated barfly is spoiled for choice. You should not count on food but you can drink till late, as most bars do not open until 8pm or later. Although there is no strict dress code, scruffy clothes are not really appropriate. The **Riva Bar**, one of the city's most elegant and hip bars, is tucked away under the S-Bahn viaduct, and serves some of the best cocktails in town. A Latin American atmosphere is created at **Roter Salon** by tango, salsa and all the fantastic dancers. You might step in to **Vox Bar** to try one of its huge range of cocktails in a pre-war movie setting. Don't forget to visit some of the hotel bars which are among the best late-night venues in the city. Two worthy of mention are **Harry's New York Bar** (the later the better), in the Hotel Esplanade and the **Newton Bar**.

Gay and Lesbian Bars

Berlin has a unique tradition of nightlife for homosexuals, dating back to the 1920s, when its cabarets and bars, especially around Nollendorfplatz, were the most outrageous in Europe. Today that hardcore legacy remains, but there are also bars to suit every taste. Some, like **Café Seidenfaden**, are for women only, while **Roses** is exclusively for men. Many, like **Die Busche**, are frequented by both gays and lesbians. For a more mixed ambiance, the friendly attitude of bars such as **Heile Welt** or **SO36** means they are popular with both gay and straight visitors alike.

DIRECTORY

Kneipen

Ankerklause
Maybachufer 1.
Map 16 E3.
Tel 693 56 49.

Dicke Wirtin
Carmerstrasse 9.
Map 5 C5.
Tel 312 49 52.

Diener Tattersall
Grolmanstrasse 47.
Map 11 C1.
Tel 881 53 29.

Gasthaus L.e.n.t.z
Stuttgarter Platz 20.
Tel 324 16 19.

Meilenstein
Oranienburger Strasse 7.
Map 9 B2.
Tel 282 89 95.

Ranke 2
Rankestrasse 2.
Map 12 E1.
Tel 885 543 26.

Reingold
Novalisstrasse 11.
Map 8 F1.
Tel 28 38 76 76.

Restaurant Zur Gerichtslaube
Poststrasse 28.
Map 9 C3.
Tel 241 56 97.

Slumberland
Goltzstrasse 24.
Map 13 A3.
Tel 216 53 49.

Zum Nussbaum
Am Nussbaum 3.
Map 9 C3.
Tel 242 30 95.

Zum Patzenhofer
Meinekestrasse 26.
Map 12 D1.
Tel 882 11 35.

Zur Kneipe
Rankestrasse 9.
Map 12 D2.
Tel 883 82 55.

Biergarten

Café am Neuen See
Lichtensteinallee 2.
Map 6 F5.
Tel 25 44 930.

Golgatha
Dudenstrasse 40, in Viktoriapark.
Map 14 E5.
Tel 78 52 453.

Prater
Kastanienallee 7–9.
Map 3 A5, 3 B3.
Tel 448 56 88.

Schleusenkrug
Müller-Breslau-Strasse at Tiergartenschleuse.
Map 6 E4.
Tel 313 99 09.

Strandbar Mitte
Am Monbijoupark.
Map 9 C1.
Tel 28 38 55 88.

Wine Bars

Billy Wilder's
Potsdamer Strasse 2.
Map 8 D5.
Tel 26 55 48 60.

Lutter & Wegner
Charlottenstrasse 56.
Map 9 A4.
Tel 202 95 40.

Weinstein
Lychener Strasse 33.
Tel 441 18 42.

Wiener Beisl
Kantstrasse 152.
Map 12 D1.
Tel 31 01 50 90.

Bars

Altes Europa
Gipsstrasse 11.
Map 9 B1.
Tel 28 09 38 40.

Ballhaus Berlin
Chausseestrasse 102.
Map 8 F1.
Tel 282 75 75.

Bar am Lützowplatz
Lützowplatz 7.
Map 13 A1.
Tel 262 68 07.

b-flat
Rosenthaler Strasse 13.
Map 9 B1.
Tel 283 31 23.

Gainsbourg – Bar Americain
Savignyplatz 5.
Map 11 B1, C1.
Tel 313 74 64.

Green Door
Winterfeldtstrasse 50.
Tel 215 25 15.

Haifischbar
Arndtstrasse 25.
Map 15 A5.
Tel 691 13 52.

Harry's New York Bar
Lützowufer 15 (in Hotel Esplanade).
Map 13 A1.
Tel 25 47 88 633.

Kumpelnest 3000
Lützowstrasse 23.
Map 13 B1.
Tel 26 16 918.

Newton Bar
Charlottenstrasse 57.
Map 9 A4.
Tel 20 29 540.

Riva Bar
Dircksenstrasse, S-Bahnbogen 142.
Map 9 C2.
Tel 24 72 26 88.

Roter Salon
Rosa-Luxemburg-Platz 2.
Map 9 C1.
Tel 41 71 75 12.

Times Bar (cigar bar)
Fasanenstrasse 9–10.
Map 12 D1.
Tel 31 10 30.

Trompete
Lützowplatz 9. **Map** 13 A1.
Tel 23 00 47/ 94.

Vox Bar at the Grand Hyatt
Marlene-Dietrich-Platz 2.
Map 8 D5.
Tel 030 2553 1772.

Zur Fetten Ecke
Schlesische Strasse 16.
Tel 44 65 16 99.

Gay and Lesbian Bars

Café Seidenfaden
Dircksenstrasse 47.
Map 9 C3.
Tel 283 27 83.

Die Busche
Warschauer Platz 18.
Tel 296 08 00.

Heile Welt
Motzstrasse 5.
Map 13 A2.
Tel 21 91 75 07.

Möbel Olfe
Reichenbergerstrasse 177.
Map 16 D2.
Tel 23 27 46 90.

Roses
Oranienstrasse 187.
Map 16 E2.
Tel 615 65 70.

SO36
Oranienstrasse 190.
Map 15 B1, 16 D1.
Tel 61 40 13 06.

The Sharon Stonewall Bar
Kleine Präsidentenstrasse 3.
Map 9 C1.
Tel 24 08 55 02.

SHOPPING IN BERLIN

With a shopping centre in every district, each selling a wide variety of merchandise, Berlin is a place where almost anything can be bought, so long as you know where to look. The most popular places are Kurfürstendamm and Friedrichstrasse, but the smaller shops in Prenzlauer Berg, Friedrichshain, Schöneberg and the Tiergarten are also worth a visit. Small boutiques selling flamboyant Berlin-style clothes crop up in unexpected courtyards, while the top fashion houses offer the latest in European elegance. Early on Saturday morning is often the best time to visit the city's various markets, the most popular of which – with their colourful stalls full of hats, bags and belts – can be found on Museum Island and at the Tiergarten. The Galeries Lafayette, KaDeWe and any of the city's numerous bookshops all make ideal venues for a pleasant afternoon's window shopping.

Inside the modern, multi-level Europa-Center *(see p154)*

Opening Hours

The majority of shops are open Monday to Friday from 10am to 8pm (10am to 6pm or 8pm on Saturday), but some department stores open as early as 9am. The larger stores may open until 10pm or midnight on Friday and Saturday.

Generally, there are no lunch breaks unless the shop is a one-person business. During the six weeks before Christmas, shops stay open until late on Saturdays. Most shops close on Sundays. If you are in need of groceries or food, try one of the main train stations. You'll find supermarkets open at Hauptbahnhof, Friedrichstrasse and Ostbahnhof.

Department Stores

Kaufhaus Des Westens, better known as **KaDeWe** at Wittenbergplatz *(see p159)*, is undoubtedly the biggest and the best department store in Germany. Only products of the highest quality are sold in these luxurious halls, where virtually everything you need is on sale – from unusual perfumes and elegant underwear to *haute couture*, all sold in a system of shops-within-shops. The food hall on the sixth floor is legendary for its restaurant overlooking Tauentzienstrasse.

Galeries Lafayette on Friedrichstrasse is nothing less than a slice of Paris placed in the heart of Berlin. Perfumes, domestic accessories and clothing attract an enormous clientele, many of whom also visit the food counter which offers a wide range of French specialities. An extraordinary glass cone rises through the middle of the store, reflecting the interiors of the shops.

Another very popular store is **Karstadt** on the Ku'damm. Although its range of goods is not as broad as the range at Galeries Lafayette, there is still

A typical street-side stall, brimming with souvenirs for visitors

an enormous choice and the top-floor restaurant offers excellent views over the city.

Shopping Centres

In addition to the two biggest shopping districts in town – the Ku'damm and Friedrichstrasse – shopping centres are constantly being built, usually conveniently situated

The spacious interior of the Hugendubel department store

Milano tie shop on Kurfürstendamm

DIRECTORY

Department Stores

Galeries Lafayette
Friedrichstrasse 76–78.
Map 9 A4. **Tel** 20 94 80.

KaDeWe
Tauentzienstrasse 21–24.
Map 12 F2. **Tel** 21 21 0.

Karstadt
Kurfürstendamm 231.
Map 12 D1. **Tel** 88 00 30.

Shopping Centres

Alexa
Grunerstrasse 20.
Map 10 D3. **Tel** 269 3400.

Das Schloss
Schlossstrasse 34.
Tel 66 69 120.

Potsdamer Platz Arkaden
Alte Potsdamer Strasse 7.
Map 8 E5. **Tel** 255 92 70.

Shopping Guide
🆆 berlin-shopper.com

close to S-Bahn stations. These massive three-level structures, resembling huge arcaded passageways, contain an enormous number of shops, ranging from supermarkets and chemists to bars, high-street fashion and bookshops. Like most of the shops in Berlin they stay open until 8pm during the week. One of the newest shopping centres is the **Potsdamer Platz Arkaden**. It is very popular both as a shopping mall and a meeting place. It is visited by thousands of tourists and Berliners every day.

Of a similar character, although smaller yet still upmarket, are the glitzy shopping mall **Das Schloss** and the budget-oriented Forum Steglitz, both on Schlossstrasse in the southern district of Steglitz. **Alexa** on Alexanderplatz is a huge shopping centre with some 180 stores spread over five levels, a large food court and extensive underground parking. Major international clothing retailers, bookshops, electronics outlets and toy shops are all represented.

Seasonal Sales

All shops in Berlin empty their racks and shelves in the sale, or *Schlussverkauf*, which takes

place twice a year. At the end of January, before the new year's collections are displayed in shop windows, you can buy winter clothes for as little as 50 per cent of their original price. During the summer sales (*Sommerschlussverkauf*), which take place at the end of July, you can find similarly-reduced summer outfits. Goods bought in a sale are officially non-returnable, but if you are really keen to take an item back, there is no harm in at least trying to negotiate with the shop assistant.

A number of shops sell a variety of articles marketed as "second season" items. These are always new articles, albeit stocked for the previous season, and they are offered at often generously reduced prices. You will also find that various shops specialize in top-brand jeans, selling them at much reduced rates owing to what are often very minor defects. These represent excellent value for money.

How to Pay

When it comes to paying for goods you may find that some small shops still insist on cash. In the centre of Berlin there should be a suitable cash machine not too far away (see p284). Larger shops and

department stores will also accept most major credit cards.

Shopping Guide

If you are planning to do some serious shopping in Berlin, and are worried about getting lost among the many possibilities, you may want to use the services of a "shopping guide". These are specialists who will tell you what is currently on offer in both the big department stores and in the smaller boutiques.

A shop-floor display in the lobby of KaDeWe *(see p159)*

Clothes and Accessories

There are many shopping centres in Berlin, and nearly every district has its own high street where residents do their shopping. If it's luxury, elegance and a wide variety of goods you are after, however, then head for the shops on Kurfürstendamm, Friedrichstrasse and Potsdamer Platz. This is where all the major fashion houses and perfume makers have their shops, right in the heart of the city. Alternatively, if you want to explore the smaller boutiques of some lesser-known designers, make your way to Hackescher Markt in the Mitte district, or to Prenzlauer Berg.

Women's Fashions

The most famous fashion houses are on the Ku'damm (Kurfürstendamm) and its side streets, particularly in the area around the quietly elegant Fasanenstrasse. Among the many famous names doing business here are **Yves Saint Laurent**, **Max Mara**, **Bogner**, **Louis Vuitton**, **Chanel** and **Gucci**. Simplicity is the order of the day in the **Designer Depot** shop, making it the ideal place to buy a straightforward dress with exquisite accessories. Gucci has two shops in the area, one in Fasanenstrasse and another in the fashionable Quartier 206 on Friedrichstrasse. The latter shares the street with many other fashion houses that specialize in women's clothes: **Evelin Brandt**, **Department Store Quartier 206**, **Strenesse**, **Strenesse Blue** and **ETRO**, to name a few. The city's first international fashion concept store, **The Corner Berlin**, offers a mix of rare designer clothes by stars such as Roland Mouret and John Galliano, accessories, beauty products and even art in a minimalist, ultra-stylish setting.

Men's Fashions

For the full range of the latest in fashion for men, on or near Kurfürstendamm is the place to go shopping, for this is where various retailers sell clothing straight from Europe's best-known fashion houses. **Patrick Hellmann** is certainly worth a visit with its wide choice of the best designer labels around. Clothes by Giorgio Armani, Helmut Lang, Christian Dior and Dolce e Gabbana can all be found here. Also very popular are **Anson's** and the more upmarket **Mientus**, which has a second outlet on Wilmersdorfer Strasse. **Peek & Cloppenburg**, Germany's second largest speciality store, sells its own budget labels as well as designer clothes by Boss, Armani and Joop. **Zegna** on Kurfürstendamm is a flagship store for men. This Italian company sells some of the finest-quality suits in Germany.

Children's Clothing

Shops selling children's clothes can generally satisfy any taste, depending on how much you are willing to spend. **I Pinco Pallino** offers *haute couture* for all ages. Alternatively, the Prenzlauer Berg district, which has the highest birth rate in the whole of Germany, is dotted with small children's boutiques offering both brand names and handmade clothes.

Young Designers

A number of galleries, studios and boutiques specialize in the so-called Berlin style, the collections on sale usually consisting of short-series items that are produced in strictly limited numbers. At one time it was possible to find shops like this across the whole of the city, but now they are concentrated mainly in the northern part of the Mitte area, where a unique fashion centre is firmly established. **NIX** offers timeless clothes made from heavy, dark fabrics and cut in classical fashion.

Among the other shops in Mitte, **Fishbelly** on Sophienstrasse is noted for its unique range of erotic underwear, designed by Jutta Teschner. **Made in Berlin**, on Neue Schönhauserstrasse, sells stylish vintage items. At **Molotow**, in Kreuzberg, the choice is more classical than the trendy name might suggest. Another very popular place to buy clothes is **Chapeaux**, in Charlottenburg, while **Lisa D** offers classic and elegant dresses by one of Berlin's top female designers. Young fashion hunters looking for the latest underground trends should head to **Apartment** and **Temporary Showroom**, both in the trendy fashion district Mitte.

Shoes and Accessories

One of the largest shoe shops in Berlin is **Schuhtick**, which has three branches in the city, though the highest quality can be found in the **Budapester Schuhe** chain. A good selection can also be found at the **Görtz** outlets around Kufürstendamm. The latest Italian designs are available at **Riccardo Cartillone**.

Penthesileia on Tucholsky-strasse offers an amusing range of handbags, which come in all kinds of shapes and sizes. If it's a hat you are after, then you need go no further than **Hut Up**, in the Heckmannhöfen. All kinds of headgear are available here, from typical Russian *shlapas* to party hats with Rastafarian dreadlocks.

Perfumes

All of the large department stores, including **KaDeWe** and **Galeries Lafayette**, offer a sizeable selection of the best-known perfumes, but there are also a number of specialist shops dotted around the city. The **Douglas** chain, which has numerous outlets, has a wide range of perfumes at very reasonable prices. **Quartier 206** has a good selection of the better-known perfumes, but if you are looking for something unusual, then **Harry Lehmann** is the place to visit. This unique store is a perfume-lover's

paradise, where Mr Lehmann himself continues an 80-year-long family tradition of mixing your very own perfume from a variety of 50 scents. He also stocks long-forgotten brands. The **Body Shop** group is

popular in Berlin. Natural perfumes of all kinds can be bought here, and its policy of no animal testing is popular with customers. It also encourages the return of its containers for recycling.

DIRECTORY

Women's Fashion

Bogner
Kurfürstendamm 42.
Map 11 C2.
Tel 88 71 77 80.

Chanel
Kurfürstendamm 188.
Map 11 C3.
Tel 885 14 24.

Department Store Quartier 206
Friedrichstrasse 71.
Map 8 F4.
Tel 20 94 68 00.

Designer Depot
Rochstrasse 2.
Map 9 C2.
Tel 28 04 67 00.

ETRO
Friedrichstrasse 71.
Map 8 F3.
Tel 20 94 61 20.

Evelin Brandt
Savignyplatz 6.
Map 11 C1.
Tel 313 80 80.

Gucci
Kurfürstendamm 190–192.
Map 11 C2.
Tel 885 12 03.
Friedrichstrasse 71.
Map 8 F3.
Tel 201 70 20.

Louis Vuitton
Friedrichstrasse 71.
Map 8 F4.
Tel 20 94 68 68.

Max Mara
Kurfürstendamm 178.
Map 12 D1.
Tel 885 25 45.

Strenesse & Strenesse Blue
Friedrichstrasse 71.
Map 8 F3.
Tel 20 94 60 30.

The Corner Berlin
Französische Strasse 40.
Map 9 A4.
Tel 20 67 09 40.

Yves Saint Laurent
Kurfürstendamm 52.
Map 11 A2.
Tel 883 39 18.

Men's Fashions

Anson's
Schlossstrasse 34.
Tel 79 09 60.

Mientus
Wilmersdorfer Strasse 73.
Map 4 F3, 5 A5, 11 A1.
Kurfürstendamm 52.
Map 11 A2.
Tel 323 90 77.

Patrick Hellmann
Kurfürstendamm 190–192.
Map 12 D2.
Tel 884 87 711.

Peek & Cloppenburg
Tauentzienstrasse 19.
Map 12 E1.
Tel 21 29 00.

Zegna
Kurfürstendamm 185.
Map 11 B2.
Tel 887 190 90.

Children's Clothing

H&M Kinder
Friedrichstrasse 78/80.
Map 8 F4.
Tel 200 739 88.

Pinco Pallino
Kurfürstendamm 46.
Map 12 D1.
Tel 881 28 63.

Young Designers

Apartment
Memhardtstrasse 8 10178.
Map 9 C2.
Tel 28 04 22 51.

Chapeaux
Bleibtreustrasse 51.
Map 11 B1.
Tel 312 09 13.

Fishbelly
Friedelstrasse 25.
Tel 28 04 51 80.

Lisa D
Hackesche Höfe,
Rosenthaler Strasse
40–41.
Map 9 B2.
Tel 28 29 061.

Made in Berlin
Neue Schönhauserstrasse 19.
Map 9 C2.
Tel 212 30 601.

Molotow
Gneisenaustrasse 112.
Map 15 A4.
Tel 693 08 18.

NIX
Oranienburger Strasse 32.
Map 9 A2.
Tel 281 80 44.

Temporary Showroom
Kastanienallee 36a.
Tel 662 04 564.

Shoes and Accessories

Budapester Schuhe
Kurfürstendamm 43 & 199.
Map 12 D1.
Tel 88 11 707.
Bleibtreustrasse 24.
Map 11 B1.
Tel 62 95 00.

Görtz
Kurfürstendamm 13-14.
Map 12 D1.
Tel 88 68 37 52.

Hut Up
Oranienburger Strasse 32.
Map 9 A2.
Tel 28 38 61 05.

Penthesileia
Tucholskystrasse 31.
Map 9 A2, 16 D1.
Tel 282 11 52.

Riccardo Cartillone
Savignyplatz 5.
Map 11 C1.
Tel 312 97 01.

Schuhtick
Savignyplatz 11.
Map 11 C1.
Tel 315 93 80.
Potsdamer Platz Arkaden,
Alte Potsdamer Strasse 7.
Map 8 D5.
Tel 25 29 33 58.

Perfumes

Body Shop
(in the main hall of
Zoologischer Garten
railway station).
Map 12 D1.
Tel 31 21 391.

Douglas
Kurfürstendamm 216.
Map 12 D1.
Tel 881 25 34.

Galeries Lafayette Parfümerie
Friedrichstrasse 76–78.
Map 8 F4.
Tel 20 94 80.

Harry Lehmann
Kantstrasse 106.
Map 11 A1.
Tel 324 35 82.

KaDeWe Parfümerie
Tauentzienstrasse 21–24.
Map 12 E1.
Tel 21 21 0.

Quartier 206
Friedrichstrasse 71.
Map 8 F3.
Tel 20 94 68 00.

Gifts and Souvenirs

Whether it is a piece of the Wall or a Prussian tin soldier, Berlin souvenirs are easy to come by. While most needs can be met on one of the main shopping thoroughfares, there are more exclusive options. If you are looking for something elegant, a piece of china made by Königliche Porzellan-Manufaktur Berlin *(see p137)* might be a good idea. Other good sources are the museum shops, notably the one in the Bauhaus Museum with its designer household objects. For a child, a teddy bear is always an option – after all, the bear is the city's emblem. For handmade jewellery or contemporary art, head for Berliner Kunstmarkt Unter den Linden on a Sunday. In December, find the most beautifully crafted gifts on the numerous Christmas markets all over the city, the one on Gendarmenmarkt being particularly worthwhile.

Books and Music

The best places to buy books on art are the shops at major museums, where you will also find a good selection of cards, posters and general souvenirs. The best of these are in **Hamburger Bahnhof** *(see p114–15)*, **Gemäldegalerie** *(see pp126–9)*, **Museum Berggruen** *(see p168)*, **Schloss Charlottenburg** *(see p164–5)* and **Altes Museum** *(see p77)*.

The **Bücherbogen** chain offers a huge choice of books and has several outlets in the city. Other good stores include **Autorenbuchhandlung** or, if you want to combine shopping for books and art appreciation, **Artificium** has a gallery attached.

For English-language books or papers, **Books in Berlin** and **Saint George's** are the places to go with their wide choice of both English and American literature. **Prinz Eisenherz** also has a good selection of gay literature. For second-hand books try **Another Country** in Kreuzberg, which also operates a book exchange system. **Do You Read Me?!** in Mitte and **Motto Bookshop** in Kreuzberg both sell a wide range of fascinating magazines, including rare, small-distribution independent press. In all of these shops the staff are usually very helpful.

Music lovers should head for **Artificium** in Schlossstrasse, **Cover Music** near the Ku'damm or, if it is classical music you are after, then **L & P Classics** has one of the finest selections. For something avant-garde don't miss **Gelbe Musik** on Schaperstrasse. If you happen to be short of funds there is always the option of flicking through the second-hand CDs on offer at the Sunday antique market on Strasse des 17 Juni *(see p256)*. The market is always crammed with souvenirs and is a great hunting-ground for collectors of old vinyl records.

Toys

You won't have to travel far to buy a typical Berlin teddy bear – you can find them in stores all over the city, especially the gift shops in the Nikolaiviertel. If you're after a wider variety of toys, then **KaDeWe** *(see p159)* is the place to go. Like all the major department stores, KaDeWe offers a whole range of toys for children of all ages, but its teddy bear section is second to none in Berlin. From the highly portable half-inch bear to the life-size two-metre model, every kind of bear you can imagine is on sale here, so you shouldn't be disappointed. Also, the store can arrange a delivery to your home, so if your child has always dreamed of having an enormous teddy bear, this is a perfect opportunity to fulfil the dream.

Small manufacturers still make old-style wooden toys, from doll's house furniture to traditional jigsaw puzzles, and these make excellent gifts to take home. **Heidi's Spielzeugladen** on Kantstrasse and **Original Erzgebirgskunst** on Sophienstrasse are the best places to go for souvenirs of this kind. Train lovers hoping to extend their tracks and build more depots and stations should visit **Michas Bahnhof** on Nürnberger Strasse, the city's top provider of model train set accessories. An amazing range of goods is available here, including model trains from the past 100 years. They also ship internationally.

As an old Prussian capital, Berlin is also a good place to find Germanic lead soldiers; the best place to look is **Berliner Zinnfiguren Kabinett**. While most of the soldiers available are designed for children, collecting them is a popular hobby among adults, and the rarities often fetch very high prices on the market.

Flowers

It is very easy to find a nice bouquet in Berlin. Flower shops stand on nearly every street corner and the majority of them are open for business on Sundays. **Blumen-Koch** in Wilmersdorf offers an amazing selection of beautiful and colourful plants and is famous for its bouquets of exotic flowers which are always arranged and wrapped with real artistry.

China and Ceramics

The history of European china started in Germany in 1708. The alchemist Böttger, while searching for the secret of making gold, discovered instead how to make Chinese-style porcelain. Berlin soon became a major producer. **KPM (Königliche Porzellan-Manufaktur Berlin)** *(see p137)* is still in operation, and its products will satisfy even the most choosy of porcelain collectors. Plenty of newly-made china is available, but if you are looking for something older, then an afternoon could be spent in some of the city's antique shops *(see pp256–7)*. Currently manufactured pieces can be bought in the KPM factory shop. Those who prefer Meissen porcelain will be able to find it in several shops along the Ku'damm.

While porcelain is expensive, an equally precious gift can be made of a ceramic dish or breakfast set, traditionally manufactured in Thuringia. With their characteristic blue and white patterns, a wide choice of exquisite Thuringian ceramics can be found in **Bürgel-Haus** on Friedrichstrasse.

Specialist Shops

If you are determined to find something unique, or even quirky, you might want to visit some of the interesting specialist shops – like **Knopf Paul**, which specializes in extraordinary buttons, or **Bären-Luftballons**, which offers a delightful variety of colourful and amusing balloons. There are also a number of shops which specialize in teas and tea-time accessories. **Tee Gschwendner** and **Berliner Teesalon** offer the best selection in this field.

Smart letter paper and good pens can be bought in **Papeterie**, but if you're still stuck for ideas, there's no harm in browsing through the specialist departments in **KaDeWe** *(see Toys)* where there's always something guaranteed to catch the eye. For gifts and clothing designed by local artists, visit **Aus Berlin** on Karl-Liebknecht-Strasse.

DIRECTORY

Books and Music

Another Country
Riemannstrasse 7.
Map 15 A4.
Tel 69 40 11 60.

Artificium
Rosenthaler Strasse 40/41.
Map 9 B1.
Tel 280 98 010.

Autorenbuch-handlung
Else-Urg-Bogen 599–600.
Map 5 C5.
Tel 313 01 51.

Books in Berlin
Goethestrasse 69.
Map 5 B5.
Tel 31 31 233.

Bücherbogen
Savignyplatz.
Map 11 C1.
Tel 31 86 95 11.

Cover Music
Kurfürstendamm 11.
Map 12 D1.
Tel 395 87 62.

Do You Read Me?!
Auguststrasse 28.
Map 9 A1.
Tel 69 54 96 95.

Gelbe Musik
Schaperstrasse 11.
Map 12 D2.
Tel 211 39 62.

Gemäldegalerie
Matthäikirchplatz 8.
Map 7 C5.
Tel 266 423 040.

Grober Unfug
Zossener Strasse 33.
Map 15 A3.
Tel 69 40 14 90.

Hamburger Bahnhof
Invalidenstrasse 50/51.
Map 8 D1.
Tel 266 42 42 42.

Hugendubel
Tauentzienstrasse 13.
Map 12 E1.
Tel (01801) 48 44 84.

Kulturkaufhaus Dussmann
Friedrichstrasse 90.
Map 8 F3.
Tel 202 51 111.

L & P Classics
Welserstrasse 28.
Map 11 C1.
Tel 88 04 30 43.

Lehmann's
Hardenbergstrasse 5.
Map 5 C4.
Tel 61 79 110.

Motto Bookshop
Skalitzer Strasse 68.
Tel 754 42 119.

Museum Berggruen
Schlossstrasse 1.
Map 4 E3.
Tel 266 42 42 42.

Prinz Eisenherz
Lietzenburger Strasse 9a.
Map 11 B2.
Tel 313 99 36.

Saint George's
Wörther Strasse 27,
Prenzlauer Berg.
Tel 81 79 83 33.

Toys

Berliner Zinnfiguren Kabinett
Knesebeckstrasse 88.
Map 5 C5.
Tel 315 70 00.

Heidi's Spielzeugladen
Kantstrasse 61.
Map 4 F5.
Tel 323 75 56.

Michas Bahnhof
Nürnberger Strasse 24.
Map 12 E2, 12 F2.
Tel 218 66 11.

Original Erzgebirgskunst
Sophienstrasse 9.
Map 9 B1.
Tel 282 67 54.

Flowers

Blumen Damerius
Potsdamer Platz Arkaden.
Tel 20 94 44 44.

Blumen-Koch
Westfälische Strasse 38.
Map 11 A4.
Tel 896 69 00.

China and Ceramics

Bürgel-Haus
Friedrichstrasse 154.
Map 8 F3.
Tel 20 45 26 95.

KPM
Wegelystrasse 1.
Tel 39 00 92 15.

Friedrichstrasse 158–164.
Map 8 F3.
Tel 204 55 835.

Specialist Shops

Aus Berlin
Karl-Liebknecht-Strasse 17.
Map 9 C3.
Tel 41 99 78 96.

Bären-Luftballons
Kurfürstenstrasse 31/32.
Map 11 C1.
Tel 26 97 50.

Berliner Teesalon
Invalidenstrasse 160.
Tel 28 04 06 60.

Knopf Paul
Zossener Strasse 10.
Map 15 A4.
Tel 692 12 12.

Papeterie
Uhlandstrasse 28.
Map 11 C2.
Tel 881 63 63.

Tee Gschwendner
Kurfürstendamm 217.
Map 12 D1.
Tel 881 91 81.

Antiques and Objets d'Art

The antique and art markets in Berlin are booming. New galleries are opening all the time, particularly in the eastern areas of town. Spandauer Vorstadt is full of antique shops and contemporary art galleries, but the northern part of Mitte (the area around East of the Centre) is the focus of the Berlin art market. Constantly raising their standards, the galleries attract numerous art dealers and collectors, while non-commercial exhibitions organized by art societies like NGbK, NBK and KunstWerke add to the creative atmosphere. As for the antique trade, a walk through any of the city's main thoroughfares should show that it is active in just about every district.

Auction Houses

Berlin's oldest and most prestigious auction houses are **Gerda Bassenge** and **Villa Grisebach**, both of which organize sales at the start of the year and in the autumn. Bassenge specializes in graphic art, and a month before each sale an auction of books and autographs is held. A photographic auction takes place a few days after the main sale of graphic art. The prices are usually higher at Grisebach which deals mainly in 19th-century paintings. Expressionists and modern classics often go under the hammer here. Another good auctioneer is **Kunst-Auktionen Leon Spik** on Ku'damm.

Galleries

If you are pressed for time, Spandauer Vorstadt in the northern part of Mitte might be the place to go. Since the fall of the Berlin Wall, some 30 galleries have been set up in the Linienstrasse, Auguststrasse, Sophienstrasse and Gipsstrasse areas. Among these are **Arndt** and **Eigen & Art**, both on Auguststrasse, **Contemporary Fine Arts**, **Carlier Gebauer**, **Max Hetzler**, **Mehdi Chouakri** and **Loock**. **Galerie & Buchladen Barbara Wien** and many other small galleries are on Linienstrasse. On so-called "open days" three or four times a year, all the galleries open at the same time to exhibit the new collections. One is always in early October, when the Art Forum Berlin fair is held, providing a chance to spot the changing trends in contemporary art. It can also be enjoyable to walk this district on a Friday evening, when many galleries have opening parties (Vernissages).

The galleries near Kurfürstendamm, such as **Rodendahl, Thöne und Westphal** offer high-quality art in a quieter atmosphere. Other galleries include **ATM Gallery, C/O Berlin** and **Michael Schultz,** as well as **Anselm Dreher, Barbara Weiss, Nature Morte** and **Galerie Stühler**. The latter offers a crossover of paintings, design and jewellery.

Antique Shops

Antique shops can be found in every district of Berlin. Near Kurfürstendamm and around Ludwigkirchplatz there are a number of high-class shops offering expensive *objets d'art*, from Chinese furniture in **Alte Asiatische Kunst** to Secession trinkets in **ART 1900**.

Furniture specialists can be found in Suarezstrasse in Charlottenburg, where original Thonets can be bought as well as modern steel items by well-known designers. For a slightly lower grade of antique, the best place to go is Bergmannstrasse in Kreuzberg. In its mildly Oriental atmosphere you can often find valuable pieces among masses of junk. **Das Zweite Büro** in Zossener Strasse specializes in trading old desks, cupboards and filing cabinets, which don't come cheap, but the quality of the merchandise is excellent. Standing opposite Das Zweite Büro is **Radio Art** with its extensive collection of old radios and record players. Some other interesting shops to try are **Bleibtreu Antik** and **Art Déco**. There's a real market atmosphere in the arcades of the S-Bahn railway bridge near Friedrichstrasse where a host of street traders sell all kinds of knick-knacks, from clothes and books to cutlery and domestic accessories.

Flea Markets

Many Berliners spend their Saturday and Sunday mornings at flea markets, and after a coffee go for a stroll in the Tiergarten or to a museum. Trödel- und Kunstmarkt, on Strasse des 17 Juni near Tiergarten S-Bahn station, is the most popular market in town. It is divided into two parts, and the antique section deals with books and magazines as well as pricey rarities. If you have the time and patience to sift through the enormous amount on offer, you are likely to find some great bargains. Arts and crafts trading takes place on the other side of Charlottenburger Brücke, and the goods on offer range from leather items and ceramics to colourful silk clothes and jewellery. Shops from all over Berlin are usually represented here.

From **Berliner Kunst- und Nostalgiemarkt an der Museumsinsel**, it is only a few steps to the museums. The stalls along Kupfergraben stand opposite the Pergamon- and Altes Museum, and art objects, books, records and other antiques are on display around the Zeughaus.

Young tourists and locals flock to the **Flohmarkt am Mauerpark**, occupying a stretch of land where the Berlin Wall once stood. This lively market offers antiques, curiosities, clothing, arts and crafts and home-made items every Sunday, and Saturdays in the summer. It's worth a visit just for the celebratory atmosphere with live music and street performers. Also worth a Sunday visit is the **Flohmarkt Boxhagener Platz** in Friedrichshain, one of the best small markets. For fabrics, as well as food, try the **Turkish Market** on Maybachufer in Neükolln each Tuesday and Friday.

The flea market operating in the car park near the Fehr-belliner Platz U-Bahn station opens at the weekends at 8am. You would do well to get there as early as possible as it is full of experienced collectors who only need a few minutes to spot something valuable. If you are after memorabilia from the former GDR, you should try the stalls around Potsdamer Platz and Leipziger Platz. However the quality and authenticity of what is on sale is often questionable.

The **Treptower Hallentrödel** market on Eichenstrasse offers everything under one roof, from old telephones and army boots to bathroom accessories and piles of very cheap books (5 for €2). The hall, a former bus depot, is worth visiting for its interesting architecture alone. Other flea markets to visit include **Antik & Trödelmarkt am Ostbahnhof**.

DIRECTORY

Auction Houses

Gerda Bassenge
Erdener Strasse 5a.
Tel 89 38 02 90.
Open 10am–6pm Mon–Thu, 10am–4pm Fri.

Kunst-Auktionen Leo Spik
Kurfürstendamm 66.
Map 12 D1.
Tel 883 61 70.

Villa Grisebach
Fasanenstrasse 25.
Map 12 D2.
Tel 885 91 50.

Galleries

Anselm Dreher
Pfalzburger Strasse 80.
Map 11 C2.
Tel 883 52 49.
Open 2–6pm Tue–Fri, 11am–2pm Sat.

Arndt
Potsdamerstrasse 96.
Map 13 C2.
Tel 20 61 38 70.
Open 11am–6pm Tue–Sat.

ATM Gallery
Eylauerstrasse 13.
Map 14 D5.
Tel 0176 34 64 222.
Open by appointment.

Barbara Weiss
Kohlfurterstrasse 41–43.
Map 16 D3.
Tel 262 42 84.
Open 11am–6pm Tue–Sat.

Carlier Gebauer
Markgrafenstrasse 67.
Map 9 A4.
Tel 24 00 86 30.
Open 11am–6pm Tue–Sat.

C/O Berlin
Oranienburger Strasse 35–36.
Map 9 A1.
Tel 28 44 41 60.

Contemporary Fine Arts

Am Kupfergraben 10.
Map 9 A2.
Tel 28 87 870.
Open 11am–6pm Tue–Fri, 11am–4pm Sat.

Eigen & Art
Auguststrasse 26.
Map 9 B1.
Tel 280 66 05.
Open 11am–6pm Tue–Sat.

Galerie Crystal Ball
Schönleinstrasse 7.
Map 16 E4.
Tel 600 52 828.
Open 3–8pm Tue, Fri & Sun.

Galerie Poll
Anna-Louisa-Karsch Strasse 9.
Tel 261 70 91.
Open 11am–6pm Tue–Fri, 11am–4pm Sat.

Galerie Stühler
Fasanenstrasse 69.
Map 12 D1.
Tel 881 76 33.

Galerie und Buchladen Barbara Wien
Schöneberger Ufer 65, 3rd floor.
Map 13 C1.
Tel 28 38 53 52.
Open 1–6pm Tue–Fri, noon–6pm Sat.

Loock
Invalidenstrasse 50–51.
Map 8 D1.
Tel 87 20 15.
Open 11am–6pm Tue–Sat.

Max Hetzler
Oudenarder Strasse 16–20.
Map 8 F5.
Tel 229 24 37.
Open 11am–6pm Tue–Sat.

Mehdi Chouakri
Schlegelstrasse 26.
Map 9 B1.
Tel 28 39 11 53.
Open 11am–6pm Tue–Sat.

Michael Schultz
Mommsenstrasse 34.
Tel 31 99 130.
Open 11am–7pm Tue–Fri, 10am–2pm Sat.

Nature Morte
3rd floor, Zimmerstrasse 90–91.
Map 8 F5.
Tel 030 206 548 77.
Open 11am–6pm Tue–Sat.

Rosendahl, Thöne und Westphal
Kurfürstendamm 213.
Map 11 C1.
Tel 882 76 82.
Open 10am–6pm Tue–Fri, 11am–3pm Sat.

Thomas Schulte
Charlottenstrasse 24.
Map 9 A3.
Tel 20 60 89 90.
Open noon–6pm Tue–Sat.

Antique Shops

Alte Asiatische Kunst
Fasanenstrasse 71.
Map 12 D1.
Tel 883 61 17.

ART 1900
Kurfürstendamm 53.
Map 11 B2.
Tel 01578 212 22 00.

Art Déco
Grolmanstrasse 51.
Map 5 C5.
Tel 31 50 62 05.

Bleibtreu Antik
Schlüterstrasse 54.
Map 11 B1.
Tel 883 52 12.

Das Zweite Büro
Zossener Strasse 6.
Map 15 A3.
Tel 693 07 59.
Open 10am–6pm Mon–Fri.

Lakeside Antiques
Neue Kantstrasse 14.
Map 4 E5.
Tel 25 45 99 30.

Radio Art
Zossener Strasse 2.
Map 15 A3.
Tel 693 94 35.
Open noon–6pm Thu & Fri, 10am–1pm Sat.

Flea Markets

Antik & Trödelmarkt am Ostbahnhof
Erich-Steinfurth-Strasse.
Open 10am–5pm Sun.

Berliner Kunst- und Nostalgiemarkt an der Museumsinsel
Museumsinsel & Kupfergraben.
Map 9 A2.
Open 11am–5pm Sat & Sun.

Flohmarkt am Mauerpark
Bernauer Strasse 63–64.
Open 7am–7pm Sun.

Flohmarkt Boxhagener Platz
Boxhagener Platz.
Open 10am–6pm Sun.

Treptower Hallentrödel
Puschkinallee.
Open 10am–5pm Sat & Sun.

Turkish Market
Maybachufer Neukölln.
Open 11am–6:30pm Tue & Fri.

Food Products

Food specialities from all over the world can be found in Berlin, a fact which is due partly to the city's own lack of traditional cuisine. Gone are the days when local fare was restricted to pork knuckle with cabbage, cutlets, *Currywurst* and potatoes. Today the side-streets and thoroughfares are teeming with the shops and restaurants of many nationalities – Italian, Greek, Turkish, Spanish and French, as well as Mexican, American, Japanese, Chinese and Thai. As befits any major European capital, the food is of the highest quality, and there are more and more shops providing organic products, from vegetables and wholemeal bread to various wines and beers.

Patisseries and Sweet Shops

Berliners certainly have a sweet tooth for there are plenty of patisseries and sweet shops all over the city, and a wide range of cakes is available. A typical speciality is a doughnut known simply as a *Berliner*, but the majority of places offer a whole range of cakes along with French pastries and fruits. **Buchwald** is renowned for producing some of the best cakes in town, mainly to take away, but there are also a number of patisseries, or *Konditoreien*. Among the best of these are **Caffeehaus am Roseneck** and **Caffeehaus Neu-Westend**.

Delicacies from Vienna can be bought in **Wiener Conditorei Caffeehaus**, while **Leysieffer** shops, with their exquisite chocolates and pralines, are a serious temptation for chocoholics. Visitors with a sweet tooth should also try the large stores: **KaDeWe's Feinschmecker Etage** and **Galeries Lafayette's Gourmet** departments both have a wonderful range of confectioneries.

Cheeses

The largest selection of cheeses in Berlin can be found at the Gourmet in Galeries Lafayette which has a particularly broad choice from France. KaDeWe's cheese department also offers a wide variety, while **Maître Philippe** sells only select cheeses from small producers. You won't find any fridges here but the whole shop is air conditioned and the aroma whets the appetite. A huge assortment of cheeses can also be found at **Vinaggio**. **Einhorn** specializes in international products, mainly sandwiches, pasta, meats and a wide variety of cheeses. **Salumeria** is also a must for cheese lovers.

Wines

Between them, **KaDeWe** and **Galeries Lafayette** have the biggest wine cellars, while smaller businesses usually specialize in wines from a particular region. **Der Rioja-Weinspezialist**, for example, sells only wines originating from northern Spain, while **La Vendemmia** specializes in Tuscan wines. A wide selection of German wines is available at **Viniculture**.

Meats, Cold Cuts and Fish

Berliners eat quite a lot of meat and meat products – the latter in particular are real German specialities. So if you are not vegetarian you should try something from the bewildering range of sausages and meat rolls. As well as the well-stocked departments in the big stores **KaDeWe** and **Galeries Lafayette**, small shops offer excellent quality products. **Neuland Fleischerei Bachhuber** is good. It specializes in chemical- and hormone-free meats, while a broad selection of fish (both fresh- and saltwater) and game is offered in **KaDeWe's** delicatessen. **Rogacki**

is another good fishmonger and **Kropp Delikatessen und Feinkost** is a well-stocked delicatessen where you can buy a variety of prepared meats.

Food Halls

The old 19th-century food halls are not as important today as they were before World War II, when they were the chief source of produce. The biggest of them all was on Alexanderplatz. The place used to teem with people 4 hours a day, but the hall wasn't rebuilt after sustaining damage during World War II. The GDR authorities had no use for such a large food hall, and with the advent of supermarkets, there was no need for it.

Today there are only four food halls in operation: **Arminiusmarkthalle** in Moabit, the **Marheineke Markthalle** in Kreuzberg, **Domäne Dahlem Hofladen** and **Markthalle Berlin-Tegel**. All of these are usually open all day six days per week – Monday to Saturday. Typically, Berliners use the food halls to pick up the one or two speciality items they can't find in the supermarkets. Shopping in these halls is a good opportunity to try traditional German *Currywurst*: the outlets in these food halls are regarded as the best in town.

Markets

Markets offer an additional way of shopping for food. They take place twice a week, and one of the best is the **Winterfeldtmarkt** which takes place on Wednesdays from 8am until 1pm and on Saturdays from 8am until 4pm. On Saturdays the opening hours are extended if the crowd is big, which it often is. You can buy everything from high-quality fruits, through vegetables and cheeses from all over the world to clothing and domestic accessories. Fast-food outlets offer *falafel* or grilled sausages, and the place is surrounded by bars and cafés full of clients and traders relaxing with a glass of beer. The atmosphere and range of goods on offer is truly international.

Türkisher Markt am Maybachufer is a big Turkish market which opens on Tuesdays and Fridays. It is popular with Turks living in Kreuzberg and Neukölln. The stalls offer all kinds of Turkish specialities. There are also markets in the city centre on Kollwitzplatz – the **Ökomarkt** and **Neuer Markt** on Thursdays

and Saturdays and the **Markt am Wittenbergplatz** on Thursdays. In fact, Thursday is the day when Wittenbergplatz is invaded by farmers from all over the region offering a variety of products. You won't find any exotic fruits at these, but if you have had enough of tasteless supermarket tomatoes and apples then

they should provide a good alternative. Depending on the season, you can buy pickled gherkins *(Salzgurken)* from the Spreewald, asparagus from the Beelitz region and delicious, sweet aromatic strawberries. **Domäne Dahlem Ökomarkt** offers a good selection of organic foods on Wednesdays and Saturdays.

DIRECTORY

Department Stores with Food Halls

Galeries Lafayette Gourmet
Friedrichstrasse 76–78.
Map 8 F4.
Tel 20 94 80.

KaDeWe's Feinschmecker Etage
Tauentzienstrasse 21–24.
Map 12 E2.
Tel 21 21 0.

Patisseries and Sweet Shops

Buchwald
Bartningallee 29.
Map 6 F3.
Tel 391 59 31.

Caffeehaus Am Roseneck
Hohenzollerndamm 92.
Tel 89 59 69 22.

Caffeehaus Neu-Westend
Reichstrasse 81.
Tel 364 106 11.

Fassbender & Rausch
Charlottenstrasse 60.
Map 9 A4.
Tel 20 45 84 430.

Kolbe & Stecher Bonbonmacherei
Heckmann Höfe,
Oranienburger Strasse 32.
Map 9 A1.
Tel 4405 52 43.

Leysieffer
Kurfürstendamm 218.
Map 12 D1.
Tel 885 74 80.

Leysieffer
Quartier 205,
Friedrichstr. 68.
Map 8 F4.
Tel 20 64 97 15.

Wiener Conditorei Caffeehaus
Hagenplatz 3.
Tel 89 72 93 60.

Cheeses

Einhorn
Wittenbergplatz 5–6.
Map 12 F2.
Tel 218 63 47.

Maître Philippe
Emser Strasse 42.
Map 11 B3, 11 C3.
Tel 88 68 36 10.

Salumeria
Windscheidstrasse 20.
Map 4 E5.
Tel 324 33 18.

Vinaggio
Monbijouplatz 2.
Map 9 B2.
Tel 257 60 831.

Wines

Der Rioja-Weinspezialist
Akazienstrasse 13.
Tel 782 25 78.

La Vendemmia
Akazienstrasse 20.
Tel 787 125 35.

Viniculture
Grolmanstrasse 44–45.
Tel 883 81 74.

Meats, Cold Cuts and Fish

Kropp Delikatessen und Feinkost
Karl-Marx-Strasse 82.
Map 16 F5.
Tel 623 1090.

Neuland Fleischerei Bachhuber
Güntzelstrasse 47.
Map 11 C4.
Tel 873 21 15.

Rogacki
Wilmersdorfer Strasse 145–146.
Map 4 F4.
Tel 343 82 50.

Food Halls

Arminiusmarkthalle
Arminiusstrasse 2–4.
Map 6 E1.
Open 7:30am–6pm Mon–Thu, 7:30am–7pm Fri, 7:30am–3pm Sat.

Domäne Dahlem Hofladen
Königin-Luise-Strasse 49, Dahlem.
Tel 66 63 00 23.

Marheineke Markthalle
Marheinekeplatz.
Map 15 A5.
Tel 6128 61 46.
Open 8am–8pm Mon–Fri, 8am–6pm Sat.

Markthalle Berlin-Tegel
Gorkistrasse 13–17.
Tel 43 43 849.
Open 8am–7pm Mon–Fri, 8am–4pm Sat.

Markets

Domäne Dahlem Ökomarkt
Königin-Luise-Strasse 49, Dahlem.
Tel 666 30023.
Open 8am–1pm Sat.

Markt am Wittenbergplatz
Wittenbergplatz.
Map 12 F2.
Open 10am–6pm Thu.

Neuer Markt am Kollwitzplatz
Prenzlauer Berg.
Open 9am–4pm Sat.

Ökomarkt am Kollwitzplatz
Prenzlauer Berg.
Open noon–7pm Thu.

Türkischer Markt am Maybachufer
Maybachufer.
Map 16 E3, 16 F4.
Open 11am–6:30pm Tue & Fri.

Winterfeldtmarkt
Winterfeldtplatz.
Map 13 A3.
Open 8am–1pm Wed, 8am–4pm Sat.

ENTERTAINMENT IN BERLIN

With so much on offer, from classical drama and cabaret to variety theatre and an eclectic nightclub scene, it is possible to indulge just about any taste in Berlin. During the summer months many bars and restaurants set up outdoor tables, and the area around Unter den Linden, the Kurfürstendamm, Kreuzberg and Prenzlauer Berg in particular, seems to turn into one large social arena. The city really comes into its own at night, when its clubs, all-night cafés and cocktail bars give you the chance to dance till dawn.

The city has many night-life centres, each with a slightly different character. Prenzlauer Berg is best for mainstream bars, cafés and clubs, while Friedrichshain has a bustling nightlife, and Kreuzberg and Schöneberg have a vibrant gay scene. The Mitte district (*see* East of the Centre) offers a true mixture, its opera house and classical theatre surrounded by lively and inexpensive bars. On a Sunday, a quiet trip down the river or along the canals offers a pleasant way to unwind.

The Berlin Philharmonic Orchestra

Practical Information

There are so many things going on in Berlin that it can be difficult to find what you're looking for. The Information Centre offers basic information (*see p278*), but for greater detail you can buy a copy of the listings magazines *Tip* or *Zitty* which offer the widest range of suggestions. Information on festivals, sports events, cinema programmes, theatre schedules, cabarets and concerts can be found on websites www.berlinonline.de and www.visitberlin.de.

But if you've only just arrived in town and haven't made it yet to an Internet café or a kiosk, the chances are the bar you're sitting in, or your hotel foyer, has leaflets on the wall to point you in the right direction. And there is no end of posters around town telling you what's on offer.

Guides

You won't be short of cultural guides in Berlin. The fortnightly listings magazines *Tip* and *Zitty*, which cover the widest choice of events, are issued on Wednesdays, while the daily newspaper *Berliner Morgenpost* has daily culture pages, as do the other major newspapers *Taz*, *Berliner Zeitung* and

Tagesspiegel. All of these can be bought at news kiosks.

For culture information in English, pick up a copy of the *Exberliner* magazine, which has feature stories and listings. It can be found at English-language bookshops, as well as a few cafés.

The monthly magazine *Kunst* (Art) is a dual-language guide to galleries and exhibitions. It also has an informative website (www.kunstmagazinberlin.de).

Tickets

Tickets can usually be bought two weeks before an event, and you can buy them directly at theatre box offices or make a telephone booking. Reserved tickets have to be picked up and paid for at least half an hour before a show. Students, pensioners and the disabled are entitled to a 50 per cent discount, but you will need to present appropriate

The Admiralspalast entertainment complex (*see p71*)

Berlin's Jazzfest features traditional jazz music *(see p268)*

documentation. You can also pre-book tickets at special outlets all over Berlin but they charge a 20 per cent commission. All the major theatres and concert halls have special wheelchair access, but the number of places for the disabled is limited; make it clear when buying a ticket that you need an appropriate place. Tickets to some theatres include a pass for public transport.

If a performance has sold out, you can always try to find tickets just before the show, for some of the pre-booked tickets may not have been collected. One agency which specializes in these last-minute purchases is called **Hekticket Theaterkassen**. You can buy tickets on the day, even an hour before a performance. If someone has already returned their ticket, you might be able to buy it at a 50 per cent discount.

Other agencies to contact for tickets are **Interklassik**, on Friedrichstrasse, and **Koka 36** on Oranienstrasse in Kreuzberg.

Information for the Disabled

In all the guides to theatres and concert halls the availability of wheelchair access is noted by a distinctive blue sign. The majority of the bigger theatres, halls and opera houses have special places for wheelchairs and seats reserved for people with walking difficulties. When

buying a ticket you must specify your need as the number of places is limited.

If you are disabled you should be able to commute without restriction on public transport, as the majority of U- and S-Bahn stations have lifts, and they are clearly marked on maps of the underground. Many buses now have special ramps and facilities for wheelchairs, but if you experience any difficulty members of the BVG staff will always help.

Public Transport at Night

The last U-Bahn trains run just before 1am, but buses and trams continue running every half an hour, making Berlin's night-time transport one of the

Ornate Elephant Gate at the Zoo Berlin *(see p154)*

most efficient in Germany. Bus and tram timetables are linked, and there are two major interchange points: one on Hardenbergplatz, near the Zoo railway station, and the other on Hackescher Markt. On Friday and Saturday nights you can also use all U-Bahn lines (except 4 and U55), which operate every 15 minutes throughout the night. Some S-Bahn lines also work at night over the weekend. Every ticket office and information point in town has brochures with details about night-time public transport.

Afternoon with the children in the Museumsdorf Düppel *(see p189)*

DIRECTORY

Ticket Agents

Hekticket Theaterkassen
Hardenbergstrasse 29d.
Map 12 D1.
Tel 230 99 30.

Karl Liebknechtstrasse 13.
Map 9 D2.
Tel 230 99 30.

Interklassik
in Dussmann Kulturkaufhaus,
Friedrichstrasse 90.
Map 8 F3.
Tel 20 16 60 93.

Koka 36
Oranienstrasse 29.
Map 16 E2.
Tel 61 10 13 13.
W koka36.de

Theatres

Thanks to Reinhardt and Brecht, Berlin became a landmark in the European theatre scene in the 1920s, and its success continues to this day. During the years of Nazi rule, many people working in the business were killed or forced to emigrate as the stage became a propaganda machine, but after World War II a revival spread through Berlin's theatres. At the heart of this revival were Bertolt Brecht and his Berliner Ensemble, and Peter Stein who ran the Schaubühne.

Modern History

Following the construction of the Berlin Wall, the number of venues doubled as each part of the divided city worked to build its own theatres. The Volksbühne in the East had its equivalent in the West called the Freie Volksbühne, and the eastern acting school, the Academy, was matched by a second Academy in the west.

The economic difficulties caused by the reunification of Germany forced a number of places to shut down, but the theatres of East Berlin managed to survive. In the west, the Freie Volksbühne and the Schiller-Theater (the largest stage in Germany) had to close, but the Volksbühne, under Frank Castorf, and the Deutsches Theater, led by Thomas Langhoff, continued to do well. Independent theatres have fared equally well in both parts of the city.

The theatre season runs from September to July, with its peak in May during Berliner Theatertreffen (Berlin Theatre Forum), when many other German theatre groups are invited to stage their plays. There are also a number of youth theatres which produce the work of young writers, and these follow the seasons of the major venues.

Repertoires are published in the listings magazines *Tip* and *Zitty*, and also displayed on yellow posters in U-Bahn stations and thoughout Berlin. Leaflets are available in many restaurants around the city.

Major Stages

The Deutsches Theater and its small hall Kammerspiele on Schumannstrasse is a top-class theatre and offers a varied repertoire of productions with very professional modern stagings. From the Greek classics to the modern classics and contemporary plays, the Deutches Theater has successfully staged them all. Tickets for these plays can be difficult to obtain, but it is worth persevering.

At Volksbühne you can see interesting performances of classical plays in modern settings, as well as adaptations of books or films or pieces written by young writers. Concerts, lectures and dance evenings are organized in the Red and Green Salon of the theatre, and with so much going on the Volksbühne now seems more of a cultural centre with a multimedia character than just a stage.

Although it was particularly important for German theatre in the 1970s and 80s, Schaubühne am Lehniner Platz is no longer as popular as it was, which is a shame, for production values don't get any higher than this. The close attention to detail – on everything from the sets and scenery to the choice of music and the editing of the printed programme – is extraordinary, and distinguishes it from the other theatres in town.

The Berliner Ensemble (or BE for short) has been managed by such influential dramatists as Bertolt Brecht from 1949 and then Heiner Müller in 1970. The spectacles created by these two are still performed today. The whole theatre is magnificent, and it has some superb architecture including the stage; after each performance you can meet the actors in the canteen in the courtyard. Another venue well worth visiting is Hebbel am Ufer, Hau Eins – an ambitious place with a programme that includes contemporary plays and modern dance.

Other major venues include the Maxim Gorki Theater and the Renaissance-Theater. The Schlosspark Theater is a former state theatre that is now a private enterprise with an interesting repertoire.

Small Stages and Alternative Theatre

There are a number of alternative theatres in Berlin, each enthusiastically playing the works of what are generally lesser known authors. Hebbel am Ufer, Hau Eins is devoted to avant-garde theatre and dance and is considered to be the city's best alternative stage. The smaller boulevard theatres, like Theater am Kurfürstendamm or Komödie am Kurfürsten-damm, offer different, lighter programmes.

Among other small theatres are Bat-Studiotheater and Kleines Theater. There are many other notable venues, including Theater 89, Heimathafen Neukölln and the Vagantenbühne.

To enjoy theatre in English, head to the English Theatre Berlin, which produces many of its own original productions, as well as classics and improvisational pieces.

Musicals, Reviews and Cabarets

There are four main musical theatres in Berlin, in addition to the many small venues which fit musicals into their repertoire. Friedrichstadtpalast and the historic Admiralspalast, both in the eastern part of the city, stage many of the new major shows as well as musicals and variety shows. A smaller stage at Friedrich-stadtpalast hosts cabaret. The Theater des Westens in Charlottenburg is more traditional, while the Theater

am Potsdamer Platz is a modern theatre set up in 1999.

As for cabaret, there are probably as many acts in Berlin today as there were in the 1920s, usually performed by small itinerant groups which rely on the hospitality of theatres for a venue. **Distel**, in Friedrichstrasse, continues its success from GDR times, and **Stachelschweine** celebrates its popularity in western Berlin.

There are many more venues for musicals, reviews and cabarets. Among these are **Bar jeder Vernunft**, **Chamäleon Variété**, **Shake! Das Zelt am Ostbahnhof**, **Scheinbar**, **Wintergarten Varieté** and **Die Wühlmäuse**.

Tickets

It is usually possible to pre-book tickets two weeks before a performance. You can buy them directly from the box office of the theatre or by telephone booking. There are also ticket vendors all over town, but they usually charge a per cent commission. Even if the theatre or concert has been sold out, there is still a chance of buying something just before the performance, provided that not all pre-booked tickets have been collected.

Hekticket Theaterkassen specializes in this kind of last-minute ticket. If you are lucky enough to pick up a ticket on the day of performance, you may find it has been returned and reduced to half its former price.

DIRECTORY

Major Stages

Berliner Ensemble
Bertold-Brecht-Platz 1.
Map 8 F2.
Tel 28 408 155.

Deutsches Theater
Schumannstrasse 13a.
Map 8 E2, 15 A1.
Tel 28 44 12 21.

Hebbel am Ufer

Hau Eins
Stresemanstrasse 29.

Hau Zwei
Hallesches Ufer 32.

Hau Drei
Tempelhofer Ufer 10.
Map 14 F2.
Tel 259 00 427.
🅦 hebel-am-ufer.de

Maxim Gorki Theater
Am Festungsgraben 2.
Map 9 A3.
Tel 20 22 11 15.

Renaissance-Theater
Knesebeckstrasse 100.
Map 5 C5.
Tel 312 42 02.

Schaubühne am Lehniner Platz
Kurfürstendamm 153.
Tel 89 00 23.

Schlosspark Theater
Schlossstrasse 48.
Map 4 E4.
Tel 789 566 71 00.

Volksbühne
Rosa-Luxemburg-Platz.
Map 10 D1.
Tel 30 24 065777.

Small Stages and Alternative Theatre

Bat-Studiotheater
Belforter Strasse 15.
Tel 755 41 77 77.
🅦 bat-berlin.de

English Theatre Berlin
Fidicinstrasse 40.
Map 14 F5.
Tel 693 56 92.
🅦 etberlin.de

Heimathafen Neukölln
Karl-Marx-Strasse 141.
Tel 56 82 13 33.

Kleines Theater
Südwestkorso 64.
Tel 821 20 21.
🅦 kleines-theater.de

Sophiensaele
Sophienstrasse 18.
Map 9 B1.
Tel 283 52 66.

Theater 89
Torstrasse 216.
Map 8 F1.
Tel 282 46 56.

Theater und Komödie am Kurfürstendamm
Kurfürstendamm 206/209. **Map** 11 C2.
Tel 88 59 11 88.

Vagantenbühne
Kantstrasse 12a.
Map 12 D1.
Tel 312 45 29.

Musicals, Reviews and Cabarets

Admiralspalast
Friedrichstrasse 101.
Map 8 F2.
Tel 47 99 74 99.

Bar jeder Vernunft
Schaperstrasse 24.
Map 12 D2.
Tel 883 15 82.

BKA Theater
Mehringdamm 34.
Map 14 F4.
Tel 202 20 07.

Chamäleon Varieté
Rosenthaler Strasse 40–41. **Map** 9 B2.
Tel 40 00 59 30.

Die Wühlmäuse
Pommernallee 2–4.
Map 3 B5.
Tel 30 67 30 11.

Distel
Friedrichstrasse 101.
Map 8 F2.
Tel 204 47 04.

Friedrichstadtpalast
Friedrichstrasse 107.
Map 8 F2.
Tel 23 26 23 26.

Kalkscheune
Johannisstrasse 2 (behind Friedrichstadtpalast).
Map 8 F2.
Tel 59 00 43 40.

Scheinbar
Monumentenstrasse 9.
Map 13 C5.
Tel 784 55 39.

Shake! Das Zelt am Ostbahnhof
Am Postbahnhof 1.
Tel 290 47 84 12.

Stachelschweine
Europa-Center,
Tauentzienstrasse 9–12.
Map 12 E1.
Tel 261 47 95.

Theater am Potsdamer Platz
Marlene-Dietrich-Platz 1.
Tel 25 92 90.

Theater des Westens
Kantstrasse 12.
Map 4 E5, 11 A1, 12 D1.
Tel (0180) 54 444.

Wintergarten Varieté
Potsdamer Strasse 96.
Map 13 C2.
Tel 58 84 33.

Tickets

Hekticket Theaterkassen
Hardenbergstrasse 29d.
Map 12 D1.
Tel 23 09 930.

Karl Liebknechtstrasse 13.
Map 9 D2.
Tel 230 99 30.

Cinema

Berlin has always been the capital of German cinema, and it is likely to remain so. In November 1895, exactly two months after the Lumière Brothers presented their first moving pictures in France, brothers Emil and Max Skladanowsky showed a series of short films to a spellbound German public. Wintergarten Varieté-theater was the place where you could go to see those famous pioneering films of kangaroos fighting, acrobats tumbling and children performing folk dances. By 1918 there were already some 251 cinemas with 82,796 seats available in Berlin, and by 1925 the number of people involved in the film industry had reached 47,600. The history of UFA (Universal Film AG), established in 1917, is intimately linked to that of Berlin, for the company has its two studios here.

Big Screens and Big Films

Many cinemas can be found around Breitscheidplatz, near the Ku'damm, Tauentzienstrasse and Alexanderplatz. After the fall of the Berlin Wall, many new multiplex cinemas were built, the biggest being the **CinemaxX Potsdamer Platz** and the **Cinestar Sony Center**. At the Cinestar, mainstream Anglo-American movies are dubbed, rather than subtitled, but you can also see films in their original language here. Next to the Cinestar, the CinemaxX is the city's largest multiplex, with a total of 19 screens. Here cinema-goers can see all the latest Hollywood and German blockbusters. The CinemaxX offers the best cinema technology, but it can get rather crowded on weekend nights.

Next door to CinemaxX is the **IMAX** cinema – the biggest screen in Germany. It can only show films that are shot with an Imax camera, but the spectacle is always breathtaking. Its huge curved screen is 27 m (89 ft) across and covers approximately 1,000 sq m (10,750 sq ft). It shows a range of films including natural history, travel and underwater features, as well as a selection of 3D films that require special viewing glasses.

Each February, Potsdamer Platz is taken over by the **Berlin International Film Festival**, or Berlinale. Hundreds of films are screened, and Berliners often queue for hours to get hold of the popular tickets. You can also buy tickets online at the festival's website.

Three other areas of Berlin are known as cinema centres: East of the City, in Friedrichshain and in Prenzlauer Berg. For those curious about the days of the GDR, the **Kino International** on Karl-Marx-Allee, built in 1963, is typical of cinemas built in the Communist era. It's pretty austere and only has 551 seats.

Studio Cinemas

There are plenty of small studio cinemas scattered across town, and it is in these that new independent films and retrospectives of particular actors and directors are shown. Cinemas like **Hackesche Höfe Kino** or **Central**, situated near Hackescher Markt, offer a pleasant break from the bustle of modern city life, and most have bars of their own. The café at Hackesche Höfe Kino offers light snacks as well as a wonderful fifth-floor view over the nearby neighbourhood.

The **Kino Arsenal**, on Potsdamer Platz, belongs to the Freunde der Deutschen Kinemathek (Friends of German Cinema), and is ideal for lovers of German film for this is where you can see all the national classics. The venue has a detailed monthly programme which includes four screenings per day, many of which come with a small introductory lecture. Copies of the programme are distributed in bars all over town.

If you're interested in original language movies, **Cinéma Paris** in Charlottenburg is the place to go for French films, while the **Odeon** in Schöneberg specializes in English and American films.

There are also many tiny neighbourhood cinemas and kino-bars, which have their own charm. Among the best are the **Tilsiter Lichtspiele** in Friedrichshain, and the **Lichtblick Kino** in Prenzlauer Berg, which plays *Casablanca* at midnight every Saturday.

Open-Air Cinema

Open-air cinemas start operating as soon as the weather allows. They can be found in parks and open spaces all across town. Some of the nicest are the **Freiluftkinos** Kreuzberg and Friedrichshain, as well as the **Openair** inside the Schloss Charlottenburg. All of these outdoor venues show a selection of current first-run films as well as the established classics. Screenings start when it starts to grow dark, around 9pm during summer.

Non-Commercial Films

Although most people tend to go to the cinema nowadays to see the latest blockbuster movie from Hollywood, it is still possible to track down some of the venues which show less popular films including documentaries and other non-commercial films.

The **Zeughauskino** specializes in non-commercial films. It co-ordinates its interesting and informative repertoire with exhibitions in the Deutsches Historisches Museum (the German Historical Museum), as well as showing its own series of documentaries.

Prices

Cinema tickets usually cost between €8–€11 and students and senior citizens don't always receive a discount. Many cinemas declare Tuesday or Wednesday as Cinema Day, when tickets are €1–€2 cheaper. Some cinemas also organize so-called "Blue

Mondays" when tickets are reduced to as little as €4.

In most cinemas there are usually three shows per evening, the first at 6pm, the last at around 10pm. Some cinemas accept telephone bookings, but you have to turn up to pay for your ticket at least half an hour before a show, otherwise it may go to somebody else. Most ticket offices don't take credit cards, so have cash in hand. Twenty minutes of commercials precede most screenings, although some venues use this time to show short films by up-and-coming directors.

The Film Business

If you're interested in the business of film production then you will want to visit Studio UFA in Babelsberg, Potsdam. A must for all cinema fans, the **Studiotour Babelsberg** allows you to see a live film crew working on a current production (see p207). You will also get a chance to see some classic film sets – some going back to the days of Marlene Dietrich – as well as samples of the latest technical wizardry.

A wide variety of books, in many different languages, about cinema and film can be found in **Bücherbogen** under the arcade of the S-Bahn railway bridge at Savignyplatz. Alternatively you can try **Bücherstube Marga Schoeller** at 33 Knesebeckstrasse, near Kurfüstendamm.

DIRECTORY

Big Screens and Big Films

CinemaxX Potsdamer Platz
Potsdamer Strasse 5.
Map 8 D5.
Tel (0180) 524 63 62 99.

Cinestar Sony Center
Potsdamer Strasse 4.
Map 8 D5.
Tel 26 06 64 00.

IMAX
Potsdamer Strasse 4.
Tel 26 06 64 00.

Kino International
Karl-Marx-Allee 33 (corner of Schillingstrasse).
Map 10 E3.
Tel 24 75 60 11.

Studio Cinemas

Central
Rosenthaler Strasse 39.
Map 9 B1.
Tel 28 59 99 73.

Cinéma Paris
Kurfürstendamm 211.
Map 11 A2, 12 D1.
Tel 881 31 19.

Hackesche Höfe Kino
Rosenthaler Strasse 40–41.
Map 11 C2.
Tel 283 46 03.

Kino Arsenal
Potsdamer Strasse 2/Sony Center.
Map 12 F2.
Tel 26 95 51 00.

Lichtblick Kino
Kanstanienallee 77.
Tel 44 05 81 79.

Odeon
Hauptstrasse 116.
Map 13 B5.
Tel 78 70 40 19.

Tilsiter Lichtspiele
Richard-Sorge-Strasse 25a. **Tel** 426 81 29.

Open-Air Cinema

Freiluftkino Friedrichshain
Volkspark Friedrichshain.
Map 10 F1.
Tel 29 36 16 28.

Freiluftkino Kreuzberg
Adalbertstrasse 73.
Map 16 E1.
Tel 29 36 16 28.

Openair Schloss Charlottenburg
Spandauer Damm 10.
Map 4 E2.
Tel (01805) 44 70.

Film Festivals

Berlin International Film Festival
Every February, Potsdamer Platz.
Tel 259 200.
W berlinale.de

The Film Business

Bücherbogen am Savignyplatz
Stadtbahnbogen 593.
Tel 31 86 95 11.

Studiotour Babelsberg
August-Bebel-Str. 26–53, Potsdam (entrance Grossbeerenstrasse).
Tel (0331) 721 21 31.

Non-Commercial Films

Zeughauskino
Unter den Linden 2.
Tel 20 30 47 70.

Famous Films About Berlin

Berlin Alexanderplatz
Germany 1931, directed by Phillip Jutzi, based on Alexander Döblin's book.

Berlin Alexanderplatz
GDR 1980, directed by Rainer Werner Fassbinder.

Berlin Calling
Germany 2008, directed by Hannes Stöhr.

Berlin, Chamissoplatz
GDR 1980, directed by Rudolf Thome.

Berlin, die Symphonie einer Grossstadt (Berlin, Symphony of a Great City)
Germany 1927, directed by Walter Ruttmann.

Berlin – Ecke Schönhauser
GDR 1957, directed by Gerhard Klein.

Berliner Ballade (Berlin Ballad)
American Occupied Zone 1948, directed by Robert Stemmle.

Cabaret
USA 1972, directed by Bob Fosse.

Coming Out
GDR 1988/1989, directed by Heiner Carow.

Das Leban der Anderen (The Lives of Others)
Germany 2006, directed by Florian Henckel von Donnersmarck.

Der Himmel über Berlin (Wings of Desire)
GDR/France 1987, directed by Wim Wenders.

Die Legende von Paul und Paula (The Legend of Paul and Paula)
GDR 1973, directed by Heiner Carow.

Eins, zwei, drei (One, two, three)
USA 1961, directed by Billy Wilder.

Goodbye Lenin!
Germany 2003, directed by Wolfgang Becker.

Kuhle Wampe
Germany 1932, directed by Slatan Dudow, script by Bertolt Brecht.

Menschen am Sonntag (Men on Sunday)
Germany 1930, directed by Robert Siodmak and Edgar G Ulmer.

Lola rennt (Run, Lola, Run)
Germany 1998, directed by Tom Tykwer.

Sonnenallee
Germany 1999, directed by Leander Haußmann.

Classical Music and Dance

Berlin has one of the world's finest orchestras (the Berlin Philharmonic Orchestra) and two of the most beautiful concert halls (the Philharmonie and the Konzerthaus). The Berlin Philharmonic is pre-eminent among the city's three symphonic orchestras, all of which perform regularly in Berlin. There are three major opera houses to choose from and a smaller one for lovers of the avant-garde. The opera houses have interesting ballet programmes built into their repertoires, performed largely by resident dance companies. Throughout the year, the city also attracts international ballet groups. Apart from regular concerts, the city offers many festivals, two of the most popular being *MaerzMusik* and the *Classic Open Air Festival* on Gendarmenmarkt. Smaller concerts are organized in the city's many churches, halls and palaces.

Concert Halls

The **Philharmonie** is one of Europe's grandest concert halls, with excellent acoustics. It houses the Berlin Philharmonic Orchestra, which was founded in 1882 and achieved great popularity under the conductor Herbert von Karajan. In 1989, the orchestra was taken over by Claudio Abbado, a worthy successor, and since 2002 it has been directed by Sir Simon Rattle, an acclaimed British conductor. Tickets for popular programmes quickly sell out. Chamber orchestras perform in the smaller **Kammermusiksaal** attached to the bigger hall.

With its elegant surroundings, **Konzerthaus Berlin**, formally known as the Schauspielhaus *(see p67)*, is one of the best places to listen to classical music. The building was restored after World War II and now contains a large concert hall and a smaller room for chamber music. Classical concerts are also held at the **Universität der Künste** and the **Staatsbibliothek** (State Library).

Many churches in Berlin also open their doors for concerts throughout the year. Berliner Dom in Mitte is a spectacular venue with an excellent concert programme. For a guide to all these events, look up the listings magazines *Tip* or *Zitty (see p260)*.

Opera and Classical Ballet

Among Berlin's three major opera houses, the **Staatsoper Unter den Linden** *(see p65)*, under the leadership of Daniel Barenboim, is a gem. However, this beautiful building is undergoing major restoration works until the end of 2014. In the meantime, performances take place at Schillertheater (Bismarckstrasse 110, Charlottenburg). The repertoire includes the traditional German classics, Italian opera, classical ballets and, to a lesser extent, contemporary pieces.

Komische Oper *(see p70)* is known for its broad range of lighter opera, for which you can nearly always find tickets. The ballet produced here is particularly innovative.

Opera productions at the **Deutsche Oper Berlin** are often modern and intriguing. The repertoire includes music ranging from major Italian operas and Mozart to Wagner and Saint Saëns.

The **Neuköllner Oper** in the Neukölln district is an innovative and productive stage.

Modern Dance

Modern dance productions are held in **Hebbel am Ufer** on Stresemannstrasse or Hallesches Ufer. In recent years, however, **Tanzfabrik** in Kreuzberg and **Sophiensaele** and **Radialsystem V** in Mitte have become equally dynamic centres of avant-garde dance, as has the International Choreographic Theater of Johann Kresnik in the Volksbühne *(see p263)*.

Contemporary Music

The Berlin organization **Initiative Neue Music Berlin e.V.** publishes a website with information about current performances of contemporary music. It always includes **BKA** near Mehringdamm with its weekly programme of **Unerhörte Musik**.

Festivals

The *Berliner Festwochen* festival has been divided into **Musikfest Berlin**, held throughout September, and **spielzeit-europa**, a theatre and dance festival stretching from October to December. Each festival promises a range of events and attracts famous orchestras and soloists from around the world.

Contemporary music festival **MaerzMusik**, held every March, sees numerous world premieres of newcomers and established composers alike.

The *Young Euro Classic* festival is a platform for the best young symphony orchestras from all over the world, who convene in Berlin's prestigious Konzerthaus every August.

Once a year for *Berlin Night of Theatres and Operas*, around 60 of the capital's stages, connected by shuttle buses, open late and offer short productions to touring visitors.

Berlin Klassiktage is an annual summer festival of classical music with evening concerts held in historic settings all over the city.

A real treat for music lovers is the wonderful *Classic Open Air Festival* featuring opera and concerts that is held every summer on an open stage on Gendarmenmarkt, which is built especially for the occasion. Another musical feast is the *Bach-Tage* festival in Potsdam, which takes place every year in September.

Open-Air Concerts

Classical open-air concerts are staged at **Waldbühne**, located in a beautiful leafy setting near the Olympiastadion. The venue seats 20,000 and once a year features the Berlin Philharmonic Orchestra. The atmosphere is relaxed and informal, with kids running around while parents eat and drink during the shows. After sunset, when the crowds light candles brought for the occasion, the atmosphere becomes magical.

Music in Palaces and Notable Buildings

During music festivals, recitals are often held in Berlin's beautiful historic buildings, and a concert in the Berliner Dom (see p79), the Orangerie in Schloss Charlottenburg (see p164–5) or Schloss Friedrichsfelde (see p182–3) can be an unforgettable and delightful experience.

Various

The **Musikinstrumenten Museum** offers entertaining concerts on selected Sunday mornings, and as a part of the Alte Musik Live scheme you can listen to the music of old masters played on their original instruments. A special booklet covering the museum's various musical events is available from all theatres, concert halls and music shops.

The Konzerthaus Berlin and Komische Oper have regular classical concerts, tours and demonstrations for children. Find a calendar of all classical music events in Berlin at the website www.klassik-in-berlin. de (English version is available).

The **Kulturkaufhaus Dussmann** shop offers the widest range of music in Berlin, with a stock of over 50,000 titles, and competent staff always ready to help you. Literary readings, lectures and other special cultural events are also staged at the store. **Gelbe Musik** is also more than a shop; it has a gallery specializing in contemporary music and co-ordinates many concerts and recitals.

DIRECTORY

Concert Halls

Konzerthaus Berlin
(Schauspielhaus)
Gendarmenmarkt 2.
Map 9 A4.
Tel 203 09 21 01/02.
ⓦ konzerthaus.de

Philharmonie & Kammermusiksaal
Herbert-von-Karajan-Strasse 1.
Map 8 D5.
Tel 25 48 89 99.

Staatsbibliothek
Potsdamer Strasse 33.
Tel 2660.

Universität der Künste
Hardenbergstrasse 33.
Map 6 E3.
Tel 31 85 23 74.

Opera and Ballet

Deutsche Oper Berlin
Bismarckstrasse 35.
Map 5 A4.
Tel 343 84 01.

Komische Oper
Behrenstrasse 55–57.
Map 8 F4.
Tel 47 99 74 00.

Neuköllner Oper
Karl-Marx-Strasse 131–133, Neukölln.
Map 16 F5.
Tel 688 90 777.

Staatsoper Unter den Linden
Unter den Linden 7.
Map 9 A3.
Tel 20 35 45 55.
(Until 2014: Bismarckstrasse 110.
Map 5 A4.)

Modern Dance

Hebbel am Ufer
Hau Eins
Stresemannstrasse 29.
Hau Zwei
Hallesches Ufer 32.
Map 14 F2.
Tel 259 00 427.
ⓦ hebbel-am-ufer.de

Radialsystem V
Holzmarktstrasse 33.
Map 10 F5.
Tel 288 788 50.

Sophiensaele
Sophienstrasse 18.
Map 9 B1.
Tel 283 52 66.

Tanzfabrik
Möckernstrasse 68.
Map 14 E4.
Tel 786 58 61.

Contemporary Music

Initiative Neue Musik Berlin e.V.
Klosterstrasse 68–70.
Map 10 D3.

Tel 242 45 34.
ⓦ inm-berlin.de

Unerhörte Musik (BKA)
Mehringdamm 34.
Map 14 F3.
Tel 202 20 07.

Festivals

MaerzMusik
Berliner Festspiele GmbH
Schaperstrasse 24.
Map 12 D2.
Tel 254 892 18.

Musikfest Berlin/spielzeiteuropa
Berliner Festspiele GmbH
Schaperstrasse 24.
Map 12 D2.
Tel 254 892 44.

Outdoor Concerts

Waldbühne
Glockenturmstrasse 1.
Tel (01805) 00 29 37.

Various

Gelbe Musik
Schaperstrasse 11.
Map 12 D2.
Tel 211 39 62.

Kulturkaufhaus Dussmann
Friedrichstrasse 90.
Tel 202 51 111.

Musikinstrumenten Museum
Tiergartenstrasse 1.
Map 8 D5.
Tel 25 48 11 78.

Tickets

Hekticket
Reduced and last-minute tickets only.
Tel 230 99 30.

Interklassik in Kulturkaufhaus Dussman
Friedrichstrasse 90.
Tel 201 660 93.

KaDeWe Theaterkassen
KaDeWe department store (6th floor),
Tauentzienstrasse 21.
Map 12 F2.
Tel 212 122 77.

Rock, Jazz and World Music

To music lovers Berlin can mean anything from techno to the Berlin Philharmonic Orchestra, for the city has a thriving and multi-faceted music industry. Between its classical and ultra-modern extremes the full spectrum of musical taste is catered for, from bar-room blues to rock'n'roll and international pop. Whether it's a major event by a world-famous band or a small-scale evening of jazz improvization, you needn't look far to find what you want. The biggest events take place in sports halls and stadiums, but most of the action can be found in discos, bars and the city's various clubs *(see pp270–71)*. There are also a number of cultural centres where you can stop by to listen to modern music. The best way to find something for yourself is to get hold of a copy of the listings magazines *Zitty* or *Tip*, and look out for flyers and leaflets in bars.

Big Concerts

Berlin is always high up on the list when major pop, rock or jazz bands go on tour. While people flock from all over the country to attend these events, there are a number of smaller events which attract an equally devoted audience. Since the closure of the huge Deutschlandhalle, the big events take place in **Max-Schmeling-Hall** and the Velodrom *(see p273)*. For the really big crowds, events are usually held at the **Olympiastadion** *(see p178)* which has seating for 100,000. The **Waldbühne** next door has a capacity of 20,000 and hosts both classical orchestras and rock bands. **Kindl-Bühne Wuhlheide** is another equally flexible venue. Concerts and plays are also organized at the popular **Arena** in Treptow – a very large music hall, dating from the 1920s, which used to be a local bus depot. The massive **O2 World** arena is located in Friedrichshain. It hosts many of the large touring pop concerts, as well as sport events and other productions. For detailed information about what's on and where, consult the websites berlinonline.de and berlin.de, or the listings magazines *Zitty* and *Tip*.

Other Musical Events

There are plenty of smaller venues in Berlin where concerts are held. Among them are **Lido** and the famous **SO36** in Kreuzberg. The future of this legendary venue is uncertain, due to the gentrification of the area. See it before it disappears.

Schöneberg was notorious in the 1980s for its punk rock scene, but while those days are now over, there are still plenty of exciting things on offer here today. One of the most popular places in town is **Tempodrom** (check listings magazines for up-to-the-minute details).

Columbia Halle, which is located near Columbiadamm, is a well-known location for medium-size events, and so is the **Astra Kulturhaus** on Revalerstrasse, which hosts a range of indie, rock, punk and pop artists. If you are looking for particularly atmospheric concerts, try the **Passionskirche**, a church in Kreuzberg. Another good location to check out is the large **Kulturbrauerei** complex in Prenzlauer Berg. This former brewery now houses dozens of venues, playing a mix of world, rock and electronic music.

Jazz

Jazz lovers from all over the world descend on Berlin for the **Jazzfest Berlin**, and its accompanying **Total Music Meeting**, both of which are held each year. The former is more traditional, but the latter is devoted to modern experimental music. "Jazz across the Border" takes place in July; it is a festival at which all kinds of

borders are crossed, not least those of musical inhibition.

As far as regular clubs are concerned, jazz is still very popular in Berlin, in spite of the pull of its perhaps better known electronic and techno discotheques. The **A Trane** and **b-flat** are classical jazz bars where you can listen to small bands just about every night of the week.

Another great venue is **Quasimodo** on Kantstrasse, which has a relaxed and intimate atmosphere. Its concerts only start after 10pm when performances at Theater des Westens have finished; the vibrations would otherwise disturb the neighbouring audience. The acoustics at Quasimodo are also excellent and many big names in jazz have performed on its stage. Another good venue for enjoying jazz is **Bilderbuch**, on Akazienstrasse.

Apart from the typical, classical jazz clubs, jazz can also be heard in many of the city's smaller bars, like **Kunstfabrik Schlot** on Kastanienallee. If it's a mixture of soul, rap and jazz you want to listen to then head for the **Junction Bar** in Kreuzberg. The **Badenscher Hof Jazzclub** on Badensche Strasse is another great place for jazz. It has a varied programme of mainstream jazz, modern jazz and blues.

World Music

As a broadly cosmopolitan city with an increasingly multi-national population, Berlin is home to a wide variety of music. Lovers of world music should visit Berlin in May, when the large and lively Karneval der Kulturen takes place. The main event is an exciting street parade through Kreuzberg featuring marching bands and dance troupes playing an extremely diverse array of music. The presence of music from all parts of the world is never that far away.

The **Haus der Kulturen der Welt** on John-Foster-Dulles-Allee is an institution set up by the Berlin Upper Chamber to support this cosmopolitanism, and its main aim is to make non-European cultures more accessible to Germany. As music is one of the best ways of bridging cross-cultural differences, the Haus der Kulturen der Welt organizes all kinds of concerts at its own **Café Global** – one of the best Saturday evening venues for listening to and dancing to music from all over the world. Details of the bands on offer can be found in a booklet which should be available in bookshops and restaurants around town.

A similar organization is the **Werkstatt der Kulturen** on Wissmannstrasse, which has been staging all kinds of cultural events for some years now.

These include regular concerts and music festivals. Between them, the Haus der Kulturen der Welt and the Werkstatt are the most reliable providers of world music in town, but you can also find a number of bars and clubs that specialize in the music of one particular nation. Details of these can be found in the listings magazines *Zitty* and *Tip*, and on flyers all over town.

Latin American discos are becoming ever more popular throughout Berlin – **Havanna** in Schöneberg is one of the city's most popular and largest.

Irish music is also well represented in the city, and all you have to do is visit a few pubs. Live music is played in **Wild at Heart** on almost every night of the week.

Tickets

The price of tickets for major pop concerts can be astronomical, particularly if you want to secure a good seat. At the other extreme, you should be able to get into smaller clubs for €5–€12, but again, if a famous person or band is playing you will have to pay a good deal more. Often you will find the ticket price includes a drink at the bar.

Tickets for major events are likely to sell out quickly and should be booked well in advance; there are numerous ticket offices in the busier parts of town (*see p261*).

If you just want to spend the night at a club you should have no trouble buying a ticket at the door.

DIRECTORY

Big Concerts

Arena
Eichenstrasse 4.
Tel 533 20 30.

Kindl-Bühne Wuhlheide
An der Wuhlheide 187.
Tel 85 75 810.

O2 World
Mühlenstrasse 14–30.
Tel 60 70 88 99.

Waldbühne
Glockenturmstrasse 1.
Tel (01805) 00 29 37.

Other Music Events

Astra Kulturhaus
Revalerstrasse 99.
Tel 20 05 67 67.

Columbia Halle and Columbia Club
Columbiadamm 13–21.
Tel 780 99 810.

Kulturbrauerei
Schönhauser Allee 36.
Tel 44 31 51 52.

Lido
Cuvrystrasse 7.
Map 8 E5.
Tel 695 66 840.

Meistersaal
Köthener Strasse 38.
Map 8 E5.
Tel 325 999 710.

Passionskirche
Marheineckeplatz 1–2.
Map 15 A5.
Tel 69 40 12 41.

SO36
Oranienstrasse 190.
Map 16 E2.
Tel 61 40 13 06.

Tempodrom
Am Anhalter Bahnhof, Möckernstrasse 10.
Map 14 E1.
Tel 0185 55 41 11.

Tipi am Kanzleramt
Grosse Querallee, Tiergarten.
Map 7 C3.
Tel 39 06 65 50.

UFA Fabrik
Victoriastrasse 10–18.
Tel 75 50 30.

Jazz

A Trane
Pestalozzistrasse 105.
Map 5 C5.
Tel 313 25 50.

Aufsturz
Oranienburger Strasse 67.
Map 9 A1.
Tel 280 474 07.

B-flat
Rosenthaler Strasse 13.
Map 9 B1.
Tel 283 31 23.

Badenscher Hof Jazzclub
Badensche Strasse 29.
Map 12 D5.
Tel 861 00 80.

Bilderbuch
Akazienstrasse 28.
Map 13 A5.
Tel 78 70 60 57.

Jazzfest Berlin
Schaperstrasse 24.
Map 12 D2.
Tel 25 48 90.

Junction Bar
Gneisenaustrasse 18.
Tel 694 66 02.

Kunstfabrik Schlot
Edisonhöfe,
Chausseestrasse 18.
Map 3 A4.
Tel 448 21 60.

Quasimodo
Kantstrasse 12a.
Tel 312 80 86.

Yorckschlösschen
Yorckstrasse 15.
Map 14 E4.
Tel 215 80 70.

World Music

Haus der Kulturen der Welt & Café Global
John-Foster-Dulles-Allee 10.
Map 7 C3.
Tel 39 78 70.

Havanna
Hauptstrasse 30.
Map 13 A5.
Tel 784 85 65.

Kulturbrauerei
Schönhauser Allee 36.
Tel 443 15 152.

Werkstatt der Kulturen
Wissmannstrasse 32.
Map 16 E5.
Tel 60 97 700.

Wild at Heart
Wiener Strasse 20 (Kreuzberg).
Tel 611 92 31.

Clubs

Berlin is considered the clubbing capital of Europe. Countless clubs with an atmosphere from trashy to classy attract visitors from all over the world. The years after the fall of the Wall provided a limitless supply of new locations, from old bank vaults to abandoned power stations, though some of these have closed to make way for more profit-oriented uses. Still, the city parties on and the endurance of Berlin's late-night scene is stunning. Parties rarely get going before midnight, and after-work and after-hours parties serve as a connection to the next night out. Few clubs specialize in a particular kind of music but rather reserve certain days of the week for different styles; find out what you are in for online, or through a number of free magazines and flyers distributed widely in bars.

Techno

Although the legendary Love Parade that used to lure over a million devotees into town has moved on, Berlin still considers itself to be the techno capital and looks on its clubs, with their striking locations, as cultural assets. **Berghain** is one of the world's biggest and most renowned techno clubs. Combined with its upstairs **Panorama Bar**, the former power station is a unique Saturday night cathedral of techno and house but is not always easy to get in due to its selective door policy. **Tresor**, Berlin's first techno club, moved from its old bank vaults to a post-industrial location in Mitte. The somewhat eerie place can absorb several thousand people and is open Wednesdays to Saturdays.

Watergate in Kreuzberg, is located right beside the beautiful Oberbaumbrücke bridge on the banks of the Spree and is favoured by techno, D&B, minimal and house DJs from all over the world. Both sound system and visual effects are spectacular at this temple of hedonism that also sports a floating outside terrace.

Also located on the banks of the Spree in Mitte is **Kater Holzig**. This multi-story complex is a continuation of Bar 25, the infamous afterparty club (now closed) and carries a similar exclusive door policy. One way around the surly door staff is to book a table at the club's restaurant.

On Thursdays, popular **Sage Club** in Mitte has mostly rock, less techno and house; it features live acts, DJs and theme nights. One of the dancefloors is adorned with a fire breathing dragon and instead of air conditioning, an outdoor pool provides welcome relief in the summer.

Discos

If it's a good old-fashioned disco you're looking for, with happy tunes and a little less of the techno, then **Sophienclub** is the place to go. It was famous even before the fall of the Wall and attracts a mixed crowd that is into classic and independent rock, soul, R&B, dance and pop. **FritzClub im Postbahnhof**, a multi-floor party and disco venue in two former mail cargo halls that accommodates up to 1,200 guests, is favoured by an under-25 student crowd that couldn't care less about dress codes. Also in Friedrichshain, **Matrix** is a booming club and disco, its vaulted brick catacombs bustling with a young crowd. **Narva Lounge** next door is a little more refined, with two dance floors, a cocktail bar and white leather booths. Ritzy **Adagio** at Potsdamer Platz is styled like a medieval castle and attracts a good mix of young and a little more mature party-goers. A stunning location with high ceilings, chandeliers and a dress code is **Goya**, favoured by thirty-somethings eager to dance.

Trendy and Alternative Clubs

Twelfth-floor **WeekEnd** at Alexanderplatz is a beautifully designed bar cum rooftop terrace club with a stunning view over downtown east Berlin. Resident and visiting DJs spin mostly hip-hop, electro, deep-house and funk. The most grown-up feature here is the prices.

For the quintessential Berlin experience, try retro-style **Kaffee Burger** where the legendary "Russendisko" was born. Parties, often featuring Russian bands and DJs, are wild; the interior is a mix of 1950s Germany and Soviet realism. **ADS**, near Ostbahnhof, has a programme spanning from techno raves to rock concerts to digital culture festivals, where experts in digital art, music and animation present their work to the public – culminating in a digital musica party. **K17** is a rather dark "goth", punk and electro club playing different music on each of its four floors.

Bohannon is an unpretentious but nicely styled soul and oldies club with two bars in Mitte. It is frequented by a friendly and open-minded thirty-something crowd. Also located near Hackescher Markt, **Flamingo** is a trendy nightclub and cocktail bar on the riverfront. **Felix Club Restaurant** at the backside of Adlon Hotel may be as posh as the location suggests – but the symbiosis of Italian cuisine and relaxed clubbing works for Berlin's fashionable and wealthy.

For a more underground experience, try the **Cassiopeia** in trendy Friedrichshain (good for electro, house, funk, ska, old school rap and reggae) that apart from dance floors, features an outdoor rock climbing tower. **SO36** in Kreuzberg is a classic and still worth a visit for a Karaoke or ballroom-dancing night, a punk or rock concert or one of the regular oriental gay parties.

The front part of **Oscar Wilde**, in the location of a popular 1920s dance hall on Friedrich-strasse, is an Irish pub, while the backroom has wild soul and hip-hop parties. There are also a couple of surviving old dance halls to go and waltz. Among the oldest is **Clärchens Ballhaus** in Mitte, shared by patrons of all ages dancing to an eclectic mix of German classics, chart hits and the Beatles.

Lounges

For those not sure whether they feel like dancing the night away, Berlin's lounges are good for a relaxed evening. In contrast to the clubs, they tend to be open every day. **PURO Sky Lounge** near the KaDeWe on Tauentzien is a very stylish rooftop club with great sunset views. Elegant **Solar** near Potsdamer Platz offers great views from the 17th floor. **40seconds** serves as a restaurant and bar before the DJs get going after 11pm. This exclusive penthouse venue also has incredible 360 degree views. **Spindler und Klatt** in Kreuzberg is a former grain warehouse now sporting lounge beds to sprawl on, one-stop dining and clubbing. In summer, the river-side terrace is a huge bonus.

Gay and Lesbian Clubs

Berlin has a very tolerant attitude to people with different sexual orientations. A big day for the whole city is the gigantic parade on Christopher Street Day, which takes place annually at the end of June. Berlin Pride Festival is celebrated for three weeks preceding the CSD. Berlin's gay community meets at countless bars, clubs and discos, many of them found around Nollendorfplatz in Schöneberg, or in gay-friendly clubs like **Berghain/Panorama Bar**. The city's most popular gay discos are **SchwuZ**, on Mehringdamm, and **Connection** on Fuggerstrasse. Many clubs usually frequented by straight people also have regular gay nights, such as Shade Inc at **Flamingo** on Wednesdays.

For lesbians the best club is Café Fatal at **SO36**. It admits gay men to a Sunday dance.

Special Interest

You want to check the dress/undress code before heading out to legendary **Kit-Kat Club**. On most nights, guests are requested to shed most of their clothes on entering this adult playground. The techno and trance club has plenty of room to dance but also to lie down and relax – which is practiced by clubbers of all sexual persuasions.

DIRECTORY

Techno

Berghain/ Panorama Bar
Am Wriezener Bahnhof 20 (Friedrichshain).
Tel 293 602 10.

Kater Holzig
Michaelkirchstrasse 26
Map 10 E5.
Tel 510 52 134.

Sage Club
Köpenicker Strasse 76–78.
Map 10 D5.
Tel 278 98 30.

Tresor
Köpenicker Strasse 70.
Map 10 E5.
Tel 629 08 750.

Watergate
Falckensteinstrasse 49 (Kreuzberg).
Tel 612 803 95.

Discos

Adagio
Marlene-Dietrich-Platz 1.
Map 8 D5.
Tel 258 98 90.

FritzClub im Postbahnhof
Strasse der Pariser Kommune 8.
Tel 698 12 80.

Goya
Nollendorfpl. 5.
Map 13 A2.
Tel 419 939 000.

Matrix
Warschauer Platz 18 (U/S Warschauer Strasse).
Tel 293 69 990.

Narva Lounge
Warschauer Platz 18.
Tel 293 69 990.

Sophienclub
Sophienstrasse 6.
Map 9 B1. **Tel** 306 42 440.

Trendy and Alternative

ADS
An der Schillingbrücke 33–34. **Map** 10 F5.
Tel 212 38 190.

Bohannon
Dircksenstrasse 40.
Map 9 C2.
Tel 695 05 287.

Cassiopeia
Revaler Strasse 99.
Tel 473 85 949.

Clärchens Ballhaus
Auguststrasse 24.
Map 9 A1.
Tel 282 92 95.

Felix Club Restaurant
Behrenstrasse 72.
Map 4 F3, 8 E4.
Tel 301 117 152.

K17
Pettenkoferstrasse 17.
Tel 42 08 93 00.

Kaffee Burger
Torstrasse 60.
Map 9 C1.
Tel 280 464 95.

Oscar Wilde
Friedrichstr. 112a.
Map 8 F1. **Tel** 282 81 66.

SO36
Oranienstrasse 190.
Map 16 E2.
Tel 614 013 06.

WeekEnd
Alexanderstrasse 5.
Map 10 D2.
Tel 246 31 676.

Lounges

40seconds
Potsdamer Strasse 58.
Map 13 C2.
Tel 890 642 20.

PURO Sky Lounge
Tauentzienstrasse 9–11.
Map 12 E1.
Tel 263 678 75.

Solar
Stresemannstrasse 76.
Map 14 E1.
Tel 0163 765 27 00.

Spindler und Klatt
Köpenicker Strasse 16 (Kreuzberg).
Tel 319 881 860.

Gay and Lesbian

Connection
Fuggerstrasse 33.
Map 12 F2.
Tel 218 14 32.

SchwuZ
Mehringdamm 61.
Map 14 F4.
Tel 629 08 80.

Shade Inc at Flamingo
Kleine Presidentenstrasse 158–9.
Tel 44 55 16 81.
SO36 (see Trendy & Alternative)

Special Interest

Kit-Kat Club
See Sage Club, Fri–Sun.

Sport and Recreation

Berlin is a sports-loving town, and every year the major sports events attract a growing number of fans and competitors. The Berlin Marathon, run in September, is now the third largest in the world, its 42-km (26-mile) distance tackled by runners and roller-skaters – able-bodied and disabled alike. The Bundesliga (German football league) cup final takes place in May in the Olympia Stadion. Crowds of each team's supporters converge on the city a few days before the game, and after the match they all join a huge party for the winners along the Ku'damm. The world tennis élite battle it out during the German Open championship every April.

Cycling

The flat terrain, numerous parks and countless special routes for cyclists – which reach a total of 850 km (530 miles) – make Berlin a cycle-friendly city. Outside rush hour you can take your bike on S- or U-Bahn trains, which provide easy access to the three most popular routes – along the Havel river, around the Grunewald forest and around the Müggelsee.

There are many places all over Berlin where you can rent a bike for €8–€15 per day *(see p293)*, provided you leave a deposit in cash. The best hotels and hostels in town also hire out their own bikes for guests. The route from the historic centre of Mitte to the Ku'damm via Tiergarten can be an unforgettable experience.

In January those lovers of two wheels meet during Berliner Sechs-Tage-Rennen in the **Velodrom** on Paul-Heyse-Strasse. You might have some problems buying a ticket as the event is very popular, so give them a call beforehand. For information concerning routes, events, tours or anything else you may need to know about cycling in Berlin, contact the **ADFC (Allgemeiner Deutscher Fahrrad-Club)**.

Golf

Just about every sporting discipline is catered for in Berlin, and golfing is no exception. The Golfer's Friend Driving Range golf club is located in the west of the city, on Cordesstrasse 3. It is open from 9am to 10pm on weekdays in summer, and from 10am on weekends. The hours are slightly shorter in spring, autumn and winter, and the range closes when it snows. A bucket of 30 balls costs €5. Golf Berlin-Mitte offers an indoor practice net.

There are two golf courses within Berlin: the **Golf und Landclub Berlin-Wannsee**, which has a large 18-hole course and a smaller one with 9 holes, and **Berliner Golfclub-Gatow** which only has an 18-hole course, plus a 6-hole practice course. There are more than 20 golf clubs around Berlin, most of which have excellent restaurants and are situated close to hotels.

Swimming Pools

Public swimming facilities in Berlin are extremely clean and you can always swim there safely. Some of the best places to try are on the Havel river and the city's lakes. Swimming on natural beaches is free, but there are no changing rooms or toilet facilities.

Berlin also has a number of artificial beaches which are all manned by lifeguards. The best known is the **Strandbad Wannsee**, which was built in the 1920s and remains very popular today. Other excellent spots can be found around Müggelsee.

One of the most beautiful swimming pool complexes is **Olympiastadion** *(see p184)*, which was a venue for the 1936 Berlin Olympic Games. A special pool for diving has a 10-m (33-ft) tower with a lift. Alternatively, you can simply sunbathe on the steps and admire the view.

The three most beautiful swimming pools are situated in Mitte, Neukölln and Wilmersdorf. **Stadtbad Mitte**, on Gartenstrasse, is a painstakingly restored building which dates from the 1930s. It has a 50-m (164-ft) pool designed for sporting events as well as recreational swimming. **Stadtbad Charlottenburg**, on the other hand, offers a smaller pool which is more appropriate for relaxation than serious swimming; it is also beautifully decorated with Secessionist paintings. But if it's a swim in luxurious surroundings you want, then take a dive at the **Stadtbad Neukölln**; the extraordinary decorative mosaics, frescos and marble-and-bronze ornamentation is enough to make you forget why you came here in the first place.

Two equally stunning experiences are guaranteed at the **Badeschiff Arena** on the river Spree in Treptow. In summer, the arena is a floating, open-air swimming pool on the river bank. In winter, it is transformed into a space-like, enclosed swimming hall. The **Tropical Islands** water and fun park, southeast of Berlin, is a huge, artificial paradise set in a vast construction hall once built for zeppelins.

Badminton, Squash and Tennis

You won't have to travel far in Berlin to find facilities to play badminton, squash or tennis, as numerous courts are scattered all over town, from local parks to sophisticated sports centres. It is customary to bring your own sports shoes, but rackets are almost always available to rent.

The entrance fee in most cases includes the use of a sauna, and at **Sportoase** there are 15 badminton courts in addition to 8 squash courts. **City Sports** offers an opportunity to play tennis on two courts, and also has squash and badminton courts. Other addresses can be found in the telephone directory

Other Sports

Every weekend in August, John-Foster-Dulles-Allee in Tiergarten is closed to traffic to become a genuine paradise for rollerblade and in-line skaters. If you fancy trying this yourself, there are plenty of shops in the area offering skates and safety equipment at reasonable rates.

If you fancy a boat trip, rowing boats are available for hire at many places along the banks of the lakes. In the Tiergarten you can rent them near Café am Neuen See and around Schlachtensee; the price is usually somewhere around €7–€10 per hour.

Fitness

There are always new gyms opening and others closing down in Berlin, so your best bet is to check the telephone directory for the most up-to-date listings. At many gyms you can buy a daily card, rather than becoming a member. But if your visit to Berlin is a long one, it may be worth joining. **Ars Vitalis** is the best independent fitness club and spa for men and women in Germany. **Fitness First** is one of the best options for women; it has five studios across the city and they are all large and well equipped. The main branch is directly beneath the TV tower in Alexanderplatz. A one-day ticket costs €19.

Spectator Sports

As a rule, Berlin's sports teams tend to be among the country's best, and rank highly in each of their respective leagues. Football matches of Hertha BSC take place in the Olympia Stadion and tickets are usually available at approximately €10–€36.

Alba Berlin is among the top basketball teams in Germany, and its matches in the **O2 World** can be attended by up to 8,500 fans. For international events it's best to pre-book tickets well in advance, and these can vary between €10 and €64, depending on the match. Berlin has a good hockey team, Eisbären Berlin, whose matches always sell out of tickets very quickly.

Horse Racing

Lovers of horse racing have two tracks to choose from in Berlin. **Trabrennbahn** in Mariendorf is open all year and the races held here are strictly commercial. **Galopprennbahn Hoppegarten**, on the other hand, has a more approachable feel.

Marathon

Marathon running isn't everyone's cup of tea, but when you see the enormous crowds gathered to run the **Berlin-Marathon** in August or September, you may well wish you were one of the pack.

The route is one of the fastest in the world, attracting top sponsors and athletes alike; the world record has been broken here several times. Thousands of viewers gather en route to cheer the runners, rollers and disabled athletes – the latter having their own group which starts before the others.

DIRECTORY

Cycling

ADFC
Brunnenstrasse 28.
Tel 448 47 24.

Velodrom
Paul-Heyse-Strasse 26.
Tel 44 30 45.

Golf

Berliner Golfclub-Gatow
Sparnecker Weg 100.
Tel 365 00 06.

Golf Berlin-Mitte
Markgrafenstrasse 58.
Tel 280 470 70.

Golf und Landclub Berlin-Wannsee
Golfweg 22.
Tel 806 70 60.

Golfer's Friend Driving Range
Cordesstrasse 3.
Tel 326 03 250.

Swimming Pools

Badeschiff Arena
Eichenstrasse 4.
Tel 01578 59 47 73.

Stadtbad Charlottenburg
Krumme Strasse 9.
Tel 34 38 38 60.

Stadtbad Mitte
Gartenstrasse 5.
Plan 7 A1.
Tel 308 80 90.

Stadtbad Neukölln
Ganghoferstrasse 3.
Tel 68 24 98 12.

Strandbad Wannsee
Wannseebadweg 25.
Tel 70 71 38 33.

Tropical Islands
Tropical Islands Allee 1,
15910 Krausnick.
Tel (035477) 605 050.

Badminton, Squash, Tennis

City Sports
Brandenburgische Strasse 53.
Tel 873 90 97.

Sport Factory
Warener Strasse 5.
Tel 563 85 85.

Sportoase
Stromstrasse 11–17.
Map 4 F1, 4 F2.
Tel 390 66 20.

Fitness

Ars Vitalis
Hauptstrasse 19.
Map 13 A5.
Tel 311 65 94 70.

Fitness First
Panoramastrasse 1a.
Map 9 C2.
Tel 279 0770.

Spectator Sports

O2 World
Mildred-Harnack-Strasse 14–30.
Tel 206 07 080.

Horse Racing

Galopprennbahn Hoppegarten
Goetheallee 1.
Tel (03342) 389 30.

Trabrennbahn Mariendorf
Mariendorfer Damm 222,
Tempelhof.
Tel 740 12 12.
Open race times vary.

Marathon

Berlin-Marathon
Hanns-Braun-Strasse/
Adlerplatz.
Tel 30 12 88 10.

CHILDREN'S BERLIN

When it comes to entertainment, people of all ages are catered for in Berlin, and children are no exception. There are numerous shops, theatres and cinemas to keep them occupied, not to mention circuses and zoological gardens. Additionally, there is the Deutsches Technikmuseum (German Museum of Technology), the Museumsdorf Düppel, or the Kinder- und Jugendmuseum, all of which encourage children to take part in the displays. Tickets for children under 14 are almost always reduced, and very young children are often admitted for free. Restaurants often have special areas for toddlers.

The Potsdam train, always a favourite among children

Information

Berlin is very welcoming to its younger visitors. Families with children are entitled to public transport discounts, and children can travel free or at a reduced rate, depending on their age. For detailed information on the discounts and opportunities for children, contact **Berlin Tourismus Marketing GmbH**. This organization offers several discount cards which entitle the holder to public transport use and entry to various museums and attractions. Some versions of these cards are valid for one adult and up to three children. Ask about the Berlin WelcomeCard and the CityTourCard *(see p279)*.

Zoological Gardens

One of Berlin's zoological gardens can be visited the moment you arrive in town, as it is located opposite the Zoo railway station. The **Zoo Berlin** offers extensive parkland and many animal enclosures, as well as an excellent aquarium with the biggest collection of aquatic fauna in the world.

The second zoo, **Tierpark Berlin** in Friedrichsfelde, isn't quite so convenient but it is much bigger and can still be reached by U-Bahn. Covering a wide area around Schloss Friedrichsfelde, the Tierpark is the largest park in Europe.

Apart from these zoological gardens, a lot of the parks in Berlin contain mini-zoos where many different kinds of animals can be seen. In a garden behind the Märkisches Museum, for example, you can see a family of bears.

As well as the more exotic animals, however, it is also possible to see the familiar favourites. Small children will love the **Kinderbauernhof Auf dem Görlitzer**, which has a collection of domestic animals. Here geese, pigs and rabbits run happily around the Görlitzer Park.

Museums

Generally speaking, Berlin's museums are well set up for children. Perhaps the most entertaining is the **Deutsches Technikmuseum** *(see p148)* where children can take part in all kinds of experiments. The **Ethnologisches Museum** *(see p185)* also prepares special exhibitions for children. On some days you can take part in a game with Mexican papier-mâché dolls, on others you can participate in a Japanese ceremonial bath. A visit to the **Museumsdorf Düppel** is an excellent way to show a child the workings of a medieval village. The Museum für Naturkunde *(see p113)* is another fun place for children, particularly the dinosaur sections and the dioramas of animals in their natural habitats. The **Kindermuseum Labyrinth** is another favourite.

Another great place to visit is the **Puppentheater-Museum**, which is always lively, and offers a chance for children to take part in minor performances.

Theatres

Established in 1969, **Grips Theater** is probably the most interesting theatre for children and teenagers. Its independent and ambitious programme attracts many spectators and one of its performances, *Linie 1*, was made into a film. Other venues worth trying are the **Theater an der Parkaue**,

Children admiring Neptune's Fountain by the Town Hall

A visit to the medieval village at Museumsdorf Düppel

Theater o.N., Zaubertheater Igor Jedlin and the **Puppentheater Berlin**. Another option is to go to one of the city's many circuses, all of which prepare their programmes with children in mind.

Sports

Ice-skating in winter and roller-skating in summer are popular in Berlin, and football and swimming are popular year-round. You can swim in rivers, lakes and swimming pools (Hotline **Berliner Bäderbetriebe** offers useful information). Each district has its own ice-skating rink, but the **Horst-Dohm-Eisstadion** is outstanding with its 400-m (1,312-ft) run and large ice-hockey rink. **FEZ Berlin** offers a special daily programme for kids.

Other Entertainment

Berlin is full of wonderfully equipped children's playgrounds. Each neighbourhood has at least one, usually complete with climbing frames, ping-pong tables and mini soccer courts.

An ascent of the Fernsehturm (television tower) at Alexanderplatz (see p95) is a great way to treat a child, perhaps for afternoon tea. You can buy cake and juice in the tower's rotating café. A lift in the Funkturm (radio tower) in the Messegelände (see p179) offers an excellent view of the city, from a slightly lower height.

Cabuwazi is a children's circus-training group that offers workshops and performances. It operates five permanent big-top tents, the main one being at Görlitzer Park in Kreuzberg. **The Story of Berlin** is a fun way for both parents and children to experience the history of Berlin in a thrilling multimedia exhibit. And the **Berliner Gruselkabinett** (Room of Fear) is enough to frighten anybody.

For an out-of-the-ordinary experience, you can't go wrong at either the **Zeiss-Großplanetarium** or the **Planetarium am Insulaner**, where fascinating shows allow you to explore the known universe and to have a good look at the stars.

DIRECTORY

Information

Berlin mit Kindern
🔳 berlin-with-children.com

Berlin Tourismus Marketing GmbH
Am Karlsbad 11.
Tel 25 00 25.
🔳 visitberlin.de

Zoological Gardens

Kinderbauernhof Auf dem Görlitzer
Wiener Strasse 59b.
Tel 611 74 24.

Tierpark Berlin
Am Tierpark 125, Lichtenberg.
Tel 51 53 10.

Zoo Berlin
Hardenbergplatz 8, Charlottenburg.
Tel 25 40 10.

Museums

Kindermuseum Labyrinth
Osloer Strasse 12.
Tel 800 93 11 50.
Open 1–6pm Fri & Sat, 11am–6pm Sun & hols.

Museumsdorf Düppel
Clauertstrasse 11.
Tel 862 11 80.
Open Apr–Oct: 3–7pm Thu, 10am–5pm Sun & holidays.

Puppentheater-Museum Berlin
Karl-Marx-Strasse 135.
Tel 687 81 32.
Open 9am–3:30pm Mon–Fri, 11am–4pm Sun.

Theatres

Grips Theater
Altonaer Strasse 22.
Tel 39 74 74 77.

Puppentheater Berlin

Gierkeplatz 2.
Tel 342 19 50.

Theater an der Parkaue
Parkaue 29.
Tel 55 77 520.

Theater o.N.
Kollwitzstrasse 53.
Tel 440 92 14.

Zaubertheater Igor Jedlin
Roscherstrasse 7.
Tel 323 37 77.

Sports

Berliner Bäderbetriebe
Tel (01803) 10 20 20.

FEZ Berlin
Strasse zum FEZ 2.
Tel 53 07 10.

Horst-Dohm-Eisstadion
Fritz-Wildung-Strasse 9.
Tel 897 32 734.

Other Entertainment

Berliner Gruselkabinett
Schöneberger Strasse 23a.
Map 14 E1.
Tel 26 55 55 46.

Cabuwazi Circus
Wiener Strasse 59H.
Tel 290 478 414.
🔳 cabuwazi.de

Planetarium am Insulaner
Munsterdamm 90.
Tel 790 09 30.

The Story of Berlin
Kurfürstendamm 207–208.
Map 11 A2.
Tel 88 72 01 00.

Zeiss-Großplanetarium
Prenzlauer Allee 80.
Tel 42 18 450.

SURVIVAL GUIDE

PRACTICAL INFORMATION

Berlin is a tourist-friendly city, so you shouldn't have too much difficulty getting around. Many Germans speak English and Berliners are usually welcoming to newcomers. Cash machines, telephones and parking meters all have clear instructions, and public transport is of the highest standard *(see pp292–3)*. For reduced fares on public transport, buy yourself a daily or weekly travel card, or a BerlinWelcomeCard which also gives you reduced access to many museums. There are plenty of information centres in the busiest areas of town and a number of different listings magazines and brochures are available. If you have Internet access, VisitBerlin.de is a good information source.

Visa and Customs

A valid passport is necessary for all visitors to Germany. Visas are not required for citizens of EU countries. A list, available from all German embassies, specifies other countries whose nationals do not need a visa for visits of less than 90 days. Non-EU citizens wishing to stay in Germany longer than three months will need a visa, available from German consulates. These must be obtained in advance. All visitors should check requirements before travelling.

On arrival in Germany, you will not be charged duty on personal articles. As in other European countries, no drugs or weapons may be brought across the border. The amount of cigarettes and alcohol allowed in or out of the country is restricted. Adults resident outside the EU can bring up to 200 cigarettes (50 cigars, or 250g of tobacco), one litre of spirits (or four litres of wine), and up to €430 worth of personal goods (including perfumes and electronic items). You may be asked to pay extra tax on items deemed to be worth more than your personal allowance.

Embassies and Consulates

Most large countries have embassies in Berlin. They are spread across different parts of the city, a result of the period when Germany was divided. Some of the newer embassies are wonderful examples of modern architecture, such as the Nordic countries' joint mission in Tiergarten, while some older embassies retain the design ethos of the divided period, such as the Czech Republic Embassy on Wilhelmstraße.

Tourist Information

There are many excellent tourist information centres in Berlin. The two biggest are at the **Neues Kranzler Eck** and the **Brandenburg Gate**, but others can be found at **Hauptbahnhof** and in the **ALEXA** shopping centre near Alexanderplatz. The **Potsdam Tourismus Service** office is in central Potsdam, on Brandenburger Strasse.

For up-to-the-minute news, turn to the Internet; **Visit Berlin. de**, which is managed by **Berlin Tourismus Marketing**, is a very reliable source of information for tourists.

Opening Hours

Offices in Berlin usually open from 9am to 6pm, with an hour's lunch break. Smaller shops open from 9:30 or 10am to 8pm, and on Saturdays most shops close at 4 or 5pm. Shops are closed on Sundays due to Germany's religious traditions. However, those in the main train stations remain open on Sundays; you can find supermarkets at Hauptbahnhof, Friedrichsstrasse and Ostbahnhof.

Trading rules are relaxed in the month before Christmas, when shops open every day and for longer hours. For typical bank opening hours, *see p284*.

SchauLUST Museen Berlin pass, for unlimited 3-day entry to museums

Museums and Historic Buildings

There are over 150 museums and galleries in Berlin, but exhibitions change and collections move continually. This guide covers the most important places, but plenty of information is also available on lesser-known museums and galleries. Tourist information offices can provide up-to-the-minute details.

A good information line is the **Info-Telefon der Staatlichen Museen zu Berlin** and its associated website, and there are also information centres devoted to the Pergamon-

Tourist information centre in Berlin

Sight-seeing boat tour along the Spree

museum and the Sanssouci complex in Potsdam. Contact the **Stiftung Preussiche Schlösser und Gärten Berlin-Brandenburg**, which is the authority in charge of most major gardens and castles in the region.

Museums and historic buildings are usually open 10am to 5pm (sometimes 6pm) Tuesday to Sunday. Some museums, however, close on another day instead of Monday, and many museums are open late on Thursdays, and often allow free entry during these hours.

For reduced entrance prices, you may want to get hold of the SchauLUST Museen Berlin pass, which allows three days' unlimited access to the major museums. This pass is sold at official tourist information centres. It can be used at all the national museums, including the whole Museum Island complex, the Kulturforum, Museen Dahlem and several additional institutions in Charlottenburg.

Other options for getting value for money are the Berlin Welcome Card (see www.VisitBerlin.de) and the **CityTourCard**, which both offer you public transport for three days, and discount entry to a long list of attractions. The conditions and attractions offered by both vary, so it's best to check which is most suitable for you.

Check event listings for the bi-annual Lange Nacht der Museen, held at the end of January and August, when many museums stay open until midnight, with special shuttle buses to transport visitors between them.

Guided Tours

There are many bus tours available in Berlin, each of which, in 3 or 4 hours, introduce you to the city's chief historic buildings. A single ticket usually allows you to get off at any stage and rejoin the tour at different stops. However, if you want to save some money, the double-decker public transport bus No. 100 follows a similar route *(see p295)*.

If you would rather go on foot, walking tours are also possible – these provide a more leisurely tour of the city, stopping at all the major landmarks and museums.

A variety of cycling tours, or tours by Segway (two-wheeled electronic vehicles), provide fun ways to see the sights.

There are many different companies offering tours; some ask you to pay in advance, wheras others offer "free" tours, but may request a tip at the end (the tour guides often earn very little for their work).

If you are in Potsdam *(see pp192–207)* you can ride a train around town, which starts outside the Kutscherhaus Inn in Sanssouci.

Guided bus tour offering an overview of Berlin and its environs

Social Customs and Etiquette

Older Germans are quite formal upon first meeting, and may introduce themselves with their surname and a stiff handshake. Younger Germans tend to be more casual.

As in most of Europe, smoking is technically illegal inside public buildings, cafés, restaurants, bars and nightclubs. However, there are many establishments in Berlin which circumvent these laws by naming themselves a *raucher kneipe* or smoking pub. It is quite common for people to smoke in public locations, and although this is increasingly discouraged, it is rarely punished.

Language

German is the official language, but many places have signs in English. Most staff and locals speak some English, but Berlin is a good place to try German *(see pp350–52)*, as the locals are used to hearing their language spoken in many accents.

A refurbished antique public convenience in Kreuzberg

Public Conveniences

There are plenty of public toilets in Berlin, but you can also use the facilities in museums, stores and cafés. In some places the convenience comes with a charge, usually 50 cents.

Men's toilets are marked by the word *"Herren"* or a triangle with the vertex pointing downwards; ladies', by the word *"Damen"* or *"Frauen"*, or a triangle with its vertex pointing upwards.

Travellers with Special Needs

Not all of Berlin's streets and shops have been altered to cater for the disabled, but the majority of theatres, galleries and other sights do have the required facilities, such as wheelchair access. Detailed information about accessibility can be obtained from **Mobidat Infoservice**. Two other organizations to consult are the **Berliner Behindertenverband** and **Der Landesbeauftragte für Menschen mit Behinderung**. Both of these organizations can be contacted if you need to hire a wheelchair, a special bus, or even someone to help assist for the day.

Gay and Lesbian Travellers

Berlin is a relaxed and tolerant city, and is home to one of the largest and most diversified gay communities in Europe. There are many vibrant gay scenes across the city, with numerous bars, cafés and clubs. Areas which are recommended are the district near Nollendorfplatz U-Bahn station in Schöneberg, around Mehringdamm and Oranienstrasse in Kreuzberg, as well as much of Prenzlauer Berg and Mitte. The magazine *Siegessaeule* is good for up-to-date information.

The Berlin Pride Festival is held at the end of June, and there are many other events and festivals held throughout the year. The **Schwules Museum** contains an exhibition about the development of gay rights and the gay community.

An ISIC card (International Student Identity card)

Travelling on a Budget

By European standards, Berlin is one of the cheapest cities and it is possible to get by with very little money. Travellers wishing to save can purchase a meal for a few euros at one of the many *volksküchen*, or "people's kitchens", which can be found in a number of former squat buildings in the eastern districts. For a full directory check www.tressfaktor.squat.net.de.

If eligible, before arriving in Berlin it is worth getting hold of an **ISIC** card (or International Student Identity Card). This entitles you to a 50 per cent reduction on some museum entrance fees and to occasional discounts on theatre, plane and rail tickets. Another discount card, **EURO<26**, is available for people up to the age of 30. These cards are only valid in Europe, but can provide many discounts.

Germany's excellent *mitfahrer*, or car-pooling systems, provide a free or cheap way to get between cities. The main one is www.mitfahrgelegenheit.de. Free accommodation-sharing schemes can be found at www.couchsurfing.com and www.hospitalityclub.org.

Time

Germany is in the Central-European time zone, which means that Berlin is 1 hour ahead of Greenwich Mean Time; 6 hours ahead of US Eastern Standard Time, and 11 hours behind Australian Eastern Standard Time. From late March to late October, clocks are set forward 1 hour.

Electrical Equipment

Most electrical sockets carry 220V, although in bathrooms the voltage may be slightly lower for safety reasons. Plugs are the standard continental type, with two round pins. Buy a European travel adaptor before you leave home.

A stall at Öko-markt in Kollwitzplatz – an organic market

Responsible Tourism

Germany is among the most ecologically aware countries in Europe, with many well-established systems in place to help reduce negative environmental impact. About 15 per cent of the country's energy comes from renewable sources, a percentage expected to increase. The Green Party is one of Berlin's major parties, and one of the strongest in Europe. There are often many independent demonstrations on environmental and political grounds.

Most Berliners are passionate cyclists, recyclers, and "bio" food consumers. Given the extent of environmental awareness, it's quite easy to participate in impact-reducing schemes whilst

Revellers at the Berlin Pride Festival

visiting Berlin. Recycling bins can be found at many public locations, such as train stations. It's possible to eat ecologically by visiting one of the many outdoor organic markets across the city (the **Öko-markt** in Kollwitzplatz on Thursdays is regarded as one of the best). Here you can be sure of the food's origin and buy locally sourced produce. Many restaurants also choose to serve organic food. To see green building practices in action in the city, visit

Potsdamer Platz, where many of the office buildings have grass roofs and water recycling schemes. The modern Reichstag building (see p138–9) is successfully powered by renewable energy.

There are a number of hotels in Berlin which claim to operate on ecological principles, using less harmful cleaning products, recycled and non-toxic furniture, or renewable electricity. Some accreditation schemes are available to help

guide guests opting for the green choice, for example **Green Key**. Check the green credentials of a hotel before booking – your query may encourage other hotels to adapt their practices.

Berlin is surrounded by nature reserves and there are many accommodation options located in forests with good connections to the city centre. Camping is possible, near Hauptbahnhof, for those wanting the greenest option.

DIRECTORY

Embassies

Australian Embassy
Wallstrasse 76–79.
Map 9 C4.
Tel 880 08 80.

British Embassy
Wilhelmstrasse 70.
Map 8 E4.
Tel 20 45 70.

Canadian Embassy
Leipziger Platz 17.
Map 8 E5.
Tel 20 31 20.

New Zealand Embassy
Friedrichstrasse 60.
Map 8 F2.
Tel 20 62 10.

South African Embassy
Tiergartenstrasse 18.
Tel 22 07 30.

US Embassy
Pariser Platz 2.
Map 8 E4. **Tel** 830 50.

Religious Services

American Church
Lutherkirche,
Bülowstrasse 71–72.
Tel 813 20 21.

Anglican Church
St Georg, Preussenallee 17–19.
Tel 304 12 80.
🔲 stgeorges.de

Huguenot
Französischer Dom,
Friedrichstadtkirche,
Gendarmenmarkt 5.
Map 9 A4.
Tel 206 49 922.

Jewish
Oranienburger Strasse 29.
Map 9 A1. **Tel** 88 02 80.

Muslim
Berliner Moschee,
Brienner Strasse 7–8.
Map 11 A5. **Tel** 87 357 03

Protestant
Berliner Dom,
Lustgarten.
Map 9 B3.
Tel 202 691 36.

Kaiser-Wilhelm-GedächtnisKirche,
Breitscheidplatz.
Map 12 E1.

Marienkirche,
Karl-Liebknecht-Strasse-8.
Map 9 C3.
Tel 242 44 67.

Roman Catholic
St-Hedwigs-Kathedrale,
Bebelplatz.
Map 9 A3.
Tel 20 348 10.

Tourist Information

Berlin Tourismus Marketing
Am Karlsbad 11.
Tel 25 00 25 (24-hour).
Fax 25 00 24 24.
🔲 visitberlin.de

Brandenburg Gate
Pariser Platz, southern building. **Map** 8 E3, 15 A3.
Open 9:30am–6pm daily.

Hauptbahnhof
Europaplatz 1, level 0,
northern entrance.
Map 8 D1.
Open 8am–10pm daily.

Neues Kranzler Eck
Kurfürstendamm 22.
Map 12 D1.
Open 10am–8pm Mon–Sat, 9:30am–6pm Sun.

Potsdam Tourismus Service
Brandenburger Strasse 3.
Tel (0331) 27 55 80.
Fax (0331) 275 58 29.
🔲 postdam tourismus.de

Museum Information

Berlin Welcome Card
🔲 berlin-welcomecard.de

CityTourCard
🔲 citytourcard.com

Info-Telefon der Staatlichen Museen zu Berlin
Tel 266 42 42 42.
🔲 smb.museum

Stiftung Preussische Schlösser und Gärten Berlin-Brandenburg
Tel (0331) 969 42 02.
🔲 spsg.de

Guided Tours

Segway Tours
Tel 240 479 91.
🔲 citysegwaytours.com/berlin

Travellers with Special Needs

Berliner Behindertenverband
Jägerstrasse 63d.
Tel 204 38 47.

Der Landesbeauftragte für Menschen mit Behinderung
Oranienstrasse 106.
Tel 90 28 29 17.

Mobidat Infoservice
Tel 747 771 125.
🔲 mobidat.net
🔲 wheelmap.org

Gay and Lesbian Travellers

Schwules Museum
Mehringdamm 61,
Kreuzberg.
Tel 69 59 90 50.
🔲 schwulesmuseum.de

Siegessäule
🔲 siegessaeule.de

Travelling on a Budget

EURO<26
🔲 euro26.org

ISIC
🔲 isiccard.com

Responsible Tourism

Green Key
🔲 green-key.org

Öko-markt
Kollwitzplatz, Prenzlauer Berg. **Open** mid-Mar–Dec: noon–7pm Thu; Jan–mid-Mar: noon–6pm Thu.

Personal Security and Health

Berlin is a relatively safe cosmopolitan city, with few serious security concerns. Crime isn't usually directed at tourists; the most serious incidents, such as car burnings (which the city has a reputation for), are usually targeted at rich residents living in formerly poor neighbourhoods. Nevertheless, as with all major European destinations, you should always be careful with your belongings, particularly during rush hours. If you do run into trouble, or need advice, you can always get help from the police.

Police officers in Berlin

Police (How to Report a Crime)

For serious crimes in progress, call the emergency police number, **110**. For all other crimes, you should call the non-emergency police number and ask to speak to an English-speaking officer. They will inform you of the address of the nearest police station and give you basic information about what to do next.

At the police station, you will be asked some questions and may have to sign a statement. The officer may ask for specific details, such as serial numbers or pictures of stolen items. If it is a more serious matter you may be asked to return to give evidence; smaller problems might be resolved in your absence.

If you are accused of a crime, you have the right to request that police contact your embassy (see p281), which should then provide basic assistance and may give you legal support or suggest a lawyer to represent you. You are

not obliged to answer any questions and any interviews that are conducted must be done in the presence of a translator.

What to be Aware of

Berlin, like most major cities, has a number of beggars who hassle tourists. It is common to be approached by women carrying cards written in English which request money. These people are often more of a nuisance than a threat. If you wish to help the homeless, it's more helpful to donate direct to a charity (www.berliner-stadtmission.de). Pickpockets can also be a problem.

Kottbusser Tor U-Bahn station is notorious for its drug pushers, so be careful there late at night. Like most big cities, few of the S- and U-Bahn stations are pleasant after dark, but they are often patrolled by guards – if you need help, you can approach them. Panic buttons on platforms can also be used in an emergency.

In an Emergency

The first number to call in an emergency is **112**, which connects you to the emergency call centre for medical, fire or police assistance. The police also operate a separate emergency number, 110.

If you spot a fire, phone the emergency number and ask for the **Fire Brigade**, or *Feuerwehr*, or use one of the emergency alarm buttons located in public areas.

Ambulances are operated by many different companies, but the emergency call centre will dispatch the nearest ambulance unit available. In less urgent circumstances you can request an ambulance or a doctor by calling the **Medical Services** number, which may take up to 2 hours to respond to a call.

On S- and U-Bahn platforms there are panic buttons that connect you to an operator who will call the appropriate emergency service.

A special Chemist Information number is available (see p283) offering information about chemists, which is helpful when searching for a pharmacist after hours. Another option is to contact your embassy, which should be able to inform you which doctors are able to speak your language. Other helplines include a **Poisons** emergencies service and a **Confidential Helpline for Women**.

Lost and Stolen Property

There is one central bureau for lost property in Berlin (the **Zentrales Fundbüro**) and this is where anything left in public is deposited. It is worth noting, however, that the BVG (Berliner Verkehrsbetriebe) has its own office (the **Fundbüro der BVG**) for items left on buses or trams or on the U-Bahn system. Some items left on S-Bahn trains may also be sent to the **Zentrales Fundbüro der Deutschen Bahn AG** in Wuppertal. Unfortunately, tourists are more frequently targeted by thieves than any other group, which is why all valuables should ideally be kept in a hotel safe. Thankfully, serious robberies are rare in Berlin, but pickpockets are active, particularly in crowds and on the U-Bahn system.

If you are unlucky enough to be the victim of street crime, you should report it to the police straight away. Remember to obtain a statement confirming what items were stolen – you

A public fire alarm

A German fire engine

German police van, a common sight

will need this when it comes to making any insurance claims.

If you are travelling by car, don't leave photographic equipment or luggage in open view, and try to use a secure car park or hotel garage whenever possible.

Pharmacies and Hospitals

It's never hard to find a pharmacy, or *Apotheke*. There is one on almost every city block, and they are marked by large distinctive signs bearing the letter "A".

Pharmacies are generally open from 8am to 6pm Monday to Saturday. At least one pharmacy in each district is open after hours and on Sundays and public holidays. The addresses are usually posted near the door of any pharmacy, or can be easily obtained by

Symbol for *Apotheke* (pharmacy)

calling the **Chemist Information** hotline. When visiting an after-hours pharmacy, you will be served through a window in the door and will have to wait outside while your prescription is provided. You may need a doctor's prescription to obtain certain pharmaceuticals and the pharmacist can inform you of the closest doctor's practice. Visitors who require prescribed medication should ensure they take enough to cover their stay, in case it is not available.

There are many so-called "*drogerie*" shops, such as the chain stores Rossmann and DM, which look like pharmacies but sell only cleaning and beauty products. Only *apothekes* are authorized to sell pharmaceutical products.

There are several major hospitals in Berlin, all equipped with casualty units. The most central hospital is **Charitie Mitte Campus** in Mitte. Call the emergency Medical Services number for information about your nearest hospital. When visiting a hospital or using an ambulance, you may be charged a €10 consultation fee even if you have health insurance.

Travel and Health Insurance

All EU nationals holding a European Health Insurance Card (EHIC) are entitled to use the German health service. Patients must pay for any treatments and then reclaim most of the cost from the health authorities. All tourists should have insurance for travel and personal possessions.

DIRECTORY

In an Emergency

Confidential Helpline for Women
Tel 615 42 43.

Fire Brigade and Ambulance
Tel 112.

Medical Services
Tel 31 00 31.

Poison Helpline
Tel 192 40.

Police
Tel 110 (Emergency).
Tel 4664 4664 (Non-Emergency).

Lost Property

Fundbüro der BVG
Potsdamer Strasse 180–182.
Tel 194 49.
Ⓦ bvg.de
Open 9am–6pm Mon–Thu,
9am–2pm Fri.

Zentrales Fundbüro
Platz der Luftbrücke 6.
Tel 90277 31 01.
Open 9am–2pm Fri–Wed,
1–6pm Thu.

Zentrales Fundbüro der Deutschen Bahn AG
Döppersberg 37, 42103 Wuppertal.
Tel 0900 190 599.

Pharmacies and Hospitals

Charitie Mitte Campus
Charitéplatz 1.
Tel 450 50.

Chemist Information
Tel 11 880.

An independent chemist in Berlin's city centre

Banking and Local Currency

Unlike in many other countries, it is quite hard to travel around in Germany without cash. Credit card use is not prevalent, although it has been steadily on the increase. Many retailers – including major supermarkets – still refuse credit cards or foreign bank cards, as do smaller shops, cafés and bars. However, ATMs are easy to find in most areas if you need to withdraw cash using a credit or debit card.

Banks and Bureaux de Change

Most visitors use debit cards for safety. Cash can be exchanged at banks and bureaux de change (Wechselstuben). The major banks, such as **Deutsche Bank** and **ReiseBank**, usually have similar rates of exchange, but some charge a commission; ask how much before commencing your transaction. Bank opening hours vary from branch to branch, but generally are as follows: 9am to 4pm (Monday, Wednesday, Friday) and 9am to 6pm (Tuesday and Thursday).

Bureaux de change are often located close to railway stations and airports. **Exchange AG** and Reisebank AG are among the most reliable places for exchanging cash or traveller's cheques. Others can be found downtown, around Joachimsthaler Strasse in the west and Friedrichstrasse in the east. You can also exchange cash at hotel reception desks, but rates are often poor. Given the high commission rates sometimes charged by banks and bureaux de change, the most economical way to get cash can be to withdraw from an ATM.

ATM – a convenient method for accessing cash while in Berlin

ATMs

ATMs are easy to find and use. Most are operated by banks and are accessible 24-hours a day, in well-serviced lobbies.

Most ATMs have multiple-language menu options and accept all major credit and debit card systems, including Maestro, Cirrus, VISA and MasterCard. Less commonly accepted are American Express, Diners Club and other cards. Check the machine for the corresponding logos.

Note that some ATMs are operated by private companies which charge large fees, and some banks may charge you extra for using an international terminal.

Always exercise caution while using ATMs; be aware of anyone standing close to you when using one and shield the numbered keypad when entering your PIN.

Debit and Credit Cards

You may find it difficult to get by using only a credit card. Cards are accepted in some hotels, shops and restaurants, but not all. A sign on the door should tell you if cards are accepted, and which brands they take – **VISA** and **MasterCard** are most frequently accepted, and sometimes **American Express** and **Diners Club** as well.

Some cafés and restaurants require a minimum purchase to use a credit card. If you are only ordering a snack, check that you have some cash in case your card is not accepted.

Many shops accept Electronic Cash cards, or EC cards, which are issued by German banks. Your regular bank debit card may be accepted in shops, but check before relying on this method of payment.

DIRECTORY

Banks and Bureaux de Change

Deutsche Bank
w deutsche-bank.de

Exchange AG
Friedrichstrasse 172.
Tel 20 45 57 21.

ReiseBank
w reisebank.de

Lost Cards and Cheques

American Express
Tel (069) 97 97 20 00.

Diners Club
Tel 07531 36 33 111.

MasterCard
Tel 0800 819 1040.

VISA
Tel 0800 811 8440.

One of the city's many banks where money can be exchanged

The Euro

The euro (€) is the common currency of the European Union. It went into general circulation on 1 January 2002, initially for 12 participating countries. Germany was one of those 12 countries, and the German mark was phased out in 2002. EU members using the euro as sole official currency are known as the Eurozone. Several EU members have opted out of joining this common currency.

Euro notes are identical throughout the Eurozone countries, each one including designs of fictional architectural structures. The coins, however, have one side identical (the value side), and one side with an image unique to each country. Both notes and coins are exchangeable in all participating euro countries.

Bank Notes

Euro bank notes have seven denominations. The €5 note (grey in colour) is the smallest, followed by the €10 note (pink), €20 note (blue), €50 note (orange), €100 note (green), €200 note (yellow) and €500 note (purple). All notes show the stars of the European Union.

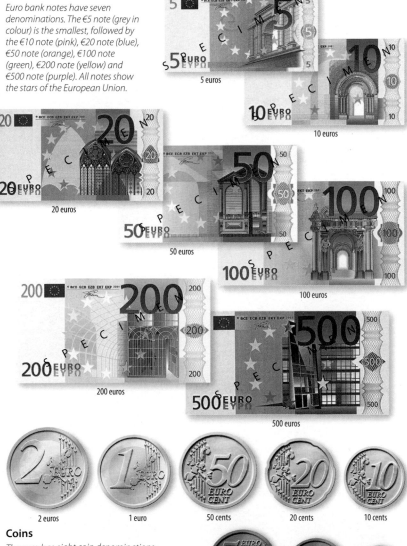

5 euros

10 euros

20 euros

50 euros

100 euros

200 euros

500 euros

2 euros

1 euro

50 cents

20 cents

10 cents

5 cents

2 cents

1 cent

Coins

The euro has eight coin denominations: €1 and €2; 50 cents, 20 cents, 10 cents, 5 cents, 2 cents and 1 cent. The €2 and €1 coins are both silver and gold in colour. The 50-, 20- and 10-cent coins are gold. The 5-, 2- and 1-cent coins are bronze.

Communications and Media

The postal and telecommunications networks and services in Germany are very efficient. Letters addressed within the country are usually delivered within 24 hours. Public telephones are becoming rare, though they can be found at railway stations and in some busy public areas. Mobile telephone coverage is excellent, and you can buy a cheap pre-paid SIM card to use during your visit. Internet facilities are widely available, with Internet cafes in many locations. News and information services are excellent in Germany. There is a plethora of good quality newspapers, magazines, and television and radio channels. For English-language news and information, the best place to turn is the Internet. The website VisitBerlin.de is a good information source and will keep you up-to-date with what is happening across the city.

A typical Deutsche Telekom public telephone booth in Berlin

International and Local Telephone Calls

Although the number of public phone booths is constantly being reduced, Deutsche Telekom still operates a network across Berlin and Germany. Some accept coins, but more common are phones that take credit cards as payment. It is also possible to buy a pre-paid telephone card from newspaper kiosks, post offices and tourist offices. A small number of telephone boxes for long-distance calls are operated by other companies. These normally accept coins and credit cards.

If you are staying in a hotel, making telephone calls from your room is usually the least economical option. For long-distance calls, the cheapest option is often to visit an Internet and telephone café.

Internet and telephone centres often sell international calling cards, which can be used from any phone. The quality and value of such cards varies greatly. It is worth requesting a receipt upon purchase in case your card is faulty.

Mobile Phones

If you are travelling with a mobile phone it can be a good idea to buy a local SIM card with a German telephone number. This can help reduce the costs of using public or hotel telephones to call local numbers. Having a

mobile is advisable in case of emergencies, for calling ahead to confirm bookings, or to find addresses. There are many companies offering cheap pre-paid SIM cards, for example **BASE**, which you can insert into your mobile telephone (check with your regular mobile service provider about possible restrictions that might prevent this). You can find SIM card packages on sale at most supermarkets and convenience stores.

To add credit, buy a credit voucher from the cashier. Sometimes you will be asked to enter your phone number into a point-of-sale machine at the cashier, or you may be given a voucher with instructions on entering a code into your handset.

To call local numbers using your mobile phone, you will have to enter the local area code, 030 for Berlin and 0331

for Potsdam. If using an international mobile phone, you may need to add the national calling code (+49), remove the first zero, then complete the number as listed.

The Internet and Email

Internet centres are common throughout Berlin, particularly in areas of high ethnic diversity, such as Kreuzberg and Neukölln. They can be an economical way to check your email, and many locations offer printing services as well. Most Internet centres ask you to pay at the end of your computer session. Rates can vary greatly, so it's best to check before using a terminal.

If you are travelling with a laptop or mobile device, you can connect to the Internet at many cafés and libraries. Most wireless networks are password-controlled, and an access code is required, although it is usually provided free of charge to the customer.

A bustling Internet café in Berlin

Important Numbers

- Germany country code 49.
- Berlin area code 030.
- Potsdam area code 0331.
- National directory inquiries 11 8 33.
- International directory inquiries 11 8 34.
- Emergency 112.

- To make an international call, dial 00 followed by the country code, area code and number, omitting the initial 0. Country codes: UK 44; Eire 353; Canada and US 1; Australia 61; South Africa 27; New Zealand 64.

German magazines on display at a street vendor stall

Postal Services

German post offices are easy to spot with their distinctive yellow **Deutsche Post** signs. Mailboxes, too, are an eye-catching yellow.

As in other European countries, you can send registered letters, parcels and money orders from post offices. They also offer stamps, telephone cards and the usual variety of postal stationery, as well as some banking services. If the office is closed, you can use automatic stamp and package machines, which have instructions in multiple languages.

When posting a letter, always check the labels on the mailbox. Some boxes are divided, with one side accepting mail for within Berlin only, and the other accepting everything else.

Opening times can vary widely, but most post offices in Berlin are usually open from 8am to 6pm on weekdays, and until 1pm on Saturdays. Those with extended hours, including Sundays, are at major railway stations and central areas, such as **Bahnhof Friedrichstrasse** in Georgenstrasse. Poste restante letters can be collected from a number of post offices, depending on the post code they are addressed to. For the central Friedrichstrasse post office, the post code is 10117, and for the Joachimstaler Strasse post office in West Berlin, use the post code 10623.

As well as the nationalized Deutsche Post, Germany also has a private mail network, known as **PIN Mail**, which offers competitive prices for domestic mail and package delivery services. You can find their distinctive green-coloured offices in various locations across the city, and their mailboxes can be found in some newsagents.

Newspapers and Magazines

Newspapers can be bought in shops all over Berlin, but mostly they are sold by the city's numerous street vendors. In the evenings you may also find them on sale in bars and cafés. The most popular titles are the *Berliner Zeitung*, *Der Tagesspiegel*, the *Berliner Morgenpost* and *BZ*. Foreign-language papers can be found all over the city, especially at airport and railway kiosks. Some of the major department stores also have a good range of newspapers and magazines.

The two best magazines devoted to cultural events are *Zitty* and *Tip*, which cover the major (as well as minor) concerts, exhibitions and lectures held throughout Berlin. The very latest news can also be obtained from tourist information centres and the Internet. For visitors, VisitBerlin. de is essential for keeping up-to-date with events.

Television and Radio

You will be spoilt for choice when it comes to television channels. Apart from the national ARD and ZDF there are many regional and private channels. Berlin has its very own channel, RBB, alongside national channels RTL, RTL2, SAT1 and PRO7. You can also pick up special interest channels, like DSF for sport and VIVA or MTV for music.

In addition to these there is even an option for Turkish programmes in Berlin, and thanks to cable and satellite television you can easily tune into foreign programmes in English, American, French and many other languages. In hotels, television channels mainly cover the news, music and sport. For radio news in English, tune into the BBC World Service (94.8 MHz) and NPR Berlin (104.1 MHz).

DIRECTORY

Mobile Phones

BASE
W base.de

Internet

Internet Café
Schönhauser Allee 188, Mitte.
Open 8–4am daily.

Postal Services

Deustche Post
W deutschepost.de

PIN Mail
W pin-ag.de

Post Office
Bahnhof Friedrichstrasse, Georgenstrasse 12.
Open 6am–10pm Mon–Fri, 8am–10pm Sat & Sun.

Information about collection times

Slot for non-local letters

Slot for local letters

Typical Berlin-style mailbox found on street corners

GETTING TO BERLIN

Berlin lies at the heart of Europe and has excellent rail and air links with the rest of the continent. Its airport receives regular flights from major European cities as well as North America, the Middle East and southeast Asia. Likewise Lufthansa, the German national carrier, and airberlin offer flights to destinations around the world. The efficient railway network is as good as anywhere in Europe, and takes you to the centre of Berlin. One of the cheapest ways to travel to the city is by international coach, although this is usually the slowest form of transport. If you are travelling by car, the *Autobahn* (motorway) leads to the Berliner Ring (Berlin Circular Road), from where a number of exits are signposted to the city centre.

Quick boarding with an electronic boarding pass for Lufthansa Airlines

Arriving by Air

Schönefeld and Tegel airports are Berlin's main airports until Berlin Brandenburg Airport opens in 2014. This new airport will significantly increase the city's capacity to receive inter-national flights, with airlines such as airberlin, Lufthansa, Condor, Air France and easyJet able to increase the frequency of existing flights and adding numerous new destinations to their schedules.

Berlin receives many flights from destinations throughout Europe, North America and Asia. The most frequent flights are by **Lufthansa** and **British Airways**, offering flight connections from all over Europe and beyond. From North America, **Delta** and **United** fly to Berlin from New York. **easyJet** offers daily connections from London Luton and Gatwick airports, and **Ryanair** flies from London Stansted three times daily. **airberlin** has direct flights from New York and Los Angeles and indirect connections from London Stansted and Gatwick.

Lufthansa's low-cost subsidiary **German Wings** offers indirect connections to London and North America.

Tickets and Fares

When planning your trip to Berlin, it is worth shopping around as prices can vary enormously. Some of the best deals are offered by inclusive tour operators such as **Tuifly** and **Thomas Cook**; see your local travel agent for details. Air fares are usually cheaper when booked well in advance, and discounts are available for children and students. Low-cost airlines, such as Ryanair and easyJet, can be booked via the Internet. A useful source of up-to-date information on schedules and fares to Berlin is www.opodo. com, a site operated by a consortium of European airlines including Lufthansa. Another helpful site is www. skyscanner.net. If you are willing to travel at short notice, you may be able to find a last-minute bargain.

Berlin Brandenburg Airport

Following ongoing delays, Berlin's new airport is currently expected to open in 2014. It will ultimately replace the closed Tempelhof and Berlin's two remaining airports, Tegel and Schönefeld, which has been rebuilt and expanded. It is informally named after the late Willy Brandt, the former West Berlin mayor and chancellor of West Germany.

Berlin Brandenburg will have an initial capacity of 27 million passengers a year, an increase of about 5 million passengers from the previous airports. The design of the terminal will leave room for expansion, meaning that up to 45 million passengers could eventually pass through annually. The airport code will be BER, marked on all tickets

The 31-m (100-ft) observation tower at Berlin Brandenburg Airport

Lufthansa aeroplane

and baggage tags. The airport features a striking observation tower, designed by Berlin architects Karin and Ramsi Kusus. Visitors can climb the tower for a view over the airfield, which will have its own motorway exit on the A113 and excellent railway services.

Transport from the Airport

Shönefield is located 20 km (12 miles) southeast of the city centre; and is easily accessible by rail and road. It is near to the new Berlin Brandenburg airport and has good and affordable public transport connections.

The fastest way to the centre of the city is to take one of the frequent Airport Express trains operated by Deutsche Bahn. The RE7 travels via Ostbahnhof to Alexanderplatz, Hauptbahnhof and Zoologischer Garten; the RB14 takes the same route but continues on to Charlottenburg and Spandau; and the RE9 travels via Südkreuz and Potsdamer Platz to Hauptbahnhof. Trains run every 15 minutes. A ticket costs €3, and can be purchased from ticket machines on the platform; the same ticket price applies for all forms of public transport – S-Bahn, U-Bahn and bus.

Another rail option is the local S-Bahn network, which is slower, with more stations. The S9 and the S45 trains both run from the airport every 10 minutes and connect with the city-wide S-Bahn system. It is also possible to connect to the U-Bahn

network by taking a bus. The X7 and X11 shuttle buses go to Rudow U-bahn station, from where the U7 line runs to the city centre.

Most public transport services run from 4am until midnight from Monday to Friday. After this time, a night bus service continues to operate. From the airport, you can take the N7 bus, which travels slowly to the central districts and connects to other bus lines. On Fridays and Saturdays, most public transport runs 24 hours across the city.

A convenient but more expensive option to get to the city centre is by taxi, which should cost between €30 and €40.

Tegel airport is located 5 miles (8 km) from the city centre and can be reached easily by bus or taxi, both of which stop in front of the main hall. A trip by bus to the city centre usually takes 25–30 minutes. Alternatively, Bus No. 128 links the airport with U-Bahn station Kurt-Schumacher-Platz on the U6 line, while Bus No. 109 links to Jakob-Kaiser-Platz station on the U7 line. If travelling by taxi, a trip to the centre costs between €20 and €30.

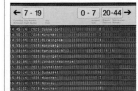
Destinations listings on the departures board

Former Airports

Airport aficionados may like to explore Berlin's now-closed terminals, especially the historic Flughafen Tempelhof (see p149). Built during the Third Reich, Tempelhof has since been transformed into a giant public park. At weekends the old airfield is full of kite-flyers, cyclists and urban gardeners. The old terminal is still in its original state, and is used for events and conferences. The future of the Tegel terminal is under debate; it may become a business centre or a university campus.

The engine of an ICE (Inter City Express) train

Arriving by Train

The standards of European public transport are generally very high, particularly in central Europe, so whichever rail link you take to Berlin your journey is bound to be comfortable. The city has excellent connections with most major German and European cities. There are direct services between Berlin and Zürich, Brussels, Prague, Amsterdam, Paris and Warsaw. Besides these lines, there are many con-venient international routes to choose from, via other German cities.

Deutsche Bahn, the national railway company, operates a famously efficient service that criss-crosses the country. The Regional Bahn (RB) and Regional Express (RE) trains operate routes around the greater Berlin and Potsdam area, while longer distances are served by Inter City (IC) and European City (EC) trains. For a luxurious experience, take an Inter City Express (ICE) service; these sleek trains are the most expensive mode of rail transport, but are also extremely fast and comfortable.

If you are thinking of staying in Germany for quite a while, and are keen to travel around a lot by train, one of the cheapest options is an **InterRail** card. This can be bought by persons of any age, from any European country (and a variety of neighbouring countries), and gives the traveller unlimited access to rail transport in a selection of European countries. Tickets can be bought online. North American visitors can enquire into **Eurail** cards, which are available through travel agents or online. The prices vary depending on your age and the number of countries you want to visit, and the duration of the pass; the younger the visitor, and the more limited number of countries you wish to visit, the cheaper the card.

At various times of the year, but especially in summer, there are often special deals offering discounted travel. Among these are weekend tickets and family tickets. It pays to visit the information desk and ask about

DB

Logo of Deutsche Bahn
(German Railways)

the different fares currently on offer. There are also discounts available by booking online, for travelling in groups and for those under 26 years of age.

Berlin's central railway station, **Hauptbahnhof**, opened in 2006 and is one of Europe's biggest rail traffic hubs. With its two soaring glass and steel office towers and a vast main hall, the station is a spectacular sight. The Hauptbahnhof is the main station for all Deutsche Bahn trains with German and international destinations or origins. Several S-Bahn routes (S3, S5, S7 and S75) link the station with the city. A short U-Bahn line, the U55, travels from here to the Bundestag and Brandenburger Tor, and there are plans to extend this line to meet the U5 at Alexanderplatz. The station also has a Deutsche Bahn Customer Centre, a tourist office, a lost and found bureau, shops, restaurants, rental car agencies, a bank, late- night services and a super-market that is open on Sundays.

The former West Berlin central railway station, the Bahnhof Zoo (now called Zoologischer Garten), has become a regional railway station, but with many U- and S-Bahn lines connecting here, it is still an important traffic hub in the western downtown area. The best place to obtain information about public transport is the BVG pavilion on Hardenbergplatz (see p295).

Some trains coming from destinations in the south or east arrive in Ostbahnhof, a conven-ient station where you can easily exchange money and send mail. Ostbahnhof is linked to other districts in Berlin via S-Bahn.

Remember that the ticket for your journey to Berlin is also valid on all S-Bahn connections to other stations, providing you use it immediately on arrival. For details of train times and destinations call the **Deutsche Bahn Information** line.

Covered platforms at the airy, modern Hauptbahnhof

Coach Travel

Wherever you can travel by train, the chances are you can also travel by coach (long-distance bus), and Germany is no exception. On international routes, the fast network of *Autobahnen* (motorways) enables coaches to nearly match the speed of trains. Some try to raise the level of comfort by showing videos and serving light refreshments, but coaches generally are less roomy and less comfortable than trains. It is often a question of cost; coach travel is nearly always cheaper than rail travel.

After you have visited Berlin, you may decide to take a coach trip to another German city or further afield. If so, the place to go is the **Zentral-Omnibus-Bahnhof**, situated near the Internationales Congress Centrum in the west of the city, best reached via the Messe Nord/ICC S-Bahn station. This is the city's largest long-distance bus station, and you will find connections to towns all over Germany, as well as links to other major European cities.

The main coach companies that stop in Berlin are **Eurolines**, **Berlin Linien Bus**, **Student Agency Bus** and **Ecolines**. Some coach companies, on overnight journeys, offer more comfortable sleeper seats for a small extra charge.

Typical road signs indicating the *Autobahn* and a district in Berlin

Travelling by Car

Berlin is surrounded by a circular *Autobahn* or motorway (the Berliner Ring), which is linked to *Autobahnen*, leading to Dresden, Nürnberg, Munich, Hannover, Hamburg and beyond. Numerous exits from the ring road are signposted into the city centre, but the road is so long that it is sometimes quicker to cut through town to

One of the many coach services available in Berlin

get to wherever you're going (although not during rush hour).

While driving around the city, keep an eye on your speed; the police are extremely vigilant at doing speed checks. Less-experienced drivers may feel a little uneasy on the *Autobahn* as German drivers tend to zoom along at speeds reaching 200 km/h (125 mph). Keep to the right, unless you are over-taking. Always remember to check your side- and rear-view mirrors before switching to a left-hand lane. If you want to overtake, make sure there's nobody coming up behind. The speed at which fast cars come up behind you can be surprising. On some stretches of the *Autobahn*, lower speed limits are imposed depending on weather and road conditions. For assistance on the road call ADAC Auto Assistance (*see p293*). If you are involved in an accident, call the police on 110.

Driving licences from all European countries are valid in Germany. Visitors from other countries need an international licence. You must also carry your passport and the standard documentation (including insurance certificate or "green card") if driving your own car. To rent a car you will need a credit card as well as a valid driver's licence. There are several places to rent vehicles around the city, including the major train stations and airports *(see p293)*.

As in most countries, German law is tough on drinking and driving. In the event of an accident, or being pulled over by the police, you may find yourself in serious trouble if alcohol is found in your blood-stream. It is better not to take the risk in the first place, and abstain from drinking.

GETTING AROUND BERLIN

Getting around Berlin is easy and enjoyable, thanks to the wonderfully efficient public transport system. It's also a great city to experience by bicycle or foot. Most of its main sights are located in the city centre and can easily be reached by cycling or walking. More peripheral areas can be reached by public transport. U- and S-Bahn trains systems are by far the quickest way to travel, but the trams and buses are also reliable. If you happen to get a double-decker, they are excellent for sightseeing. Drivers, however, may find that Berlin isn't the easiest of cities to drive in, largely because of the endless road works. Building sites are scattered all over the city, and the number of parking spaces is inadequate in central areas, so congestion is bad and driving should be avoided if possible.

Lights at a pedestrian crossing indicating when it's safe to cross

Green Travel

There is almost no reason to use a car in Berlin, as public transport is extensive and efficient, even to the outer reaches of the city. You can buy day-, week- or month-long passes to make your visit cost effective (see p294). For long distance trips, there are many fast train connections, as well as safe and effective *Mitfahrer* car-pooling schemes that stretch across Europe (www.mitfahrgelegenheit.de).

The best way to see Berlin is by bicycle. There are more than 600 km (372 miles) of dedicated bicycle lanes, and drivers give cyclists respect when sharing the road. It's easy to hire a bike for a day, a week, or even an hour through **DB Call-A-Bike**, the public cycling scheme operated by Deutsche Bahn (see p293).

There are several hundred *Umwelt Taxis* (Environmental Taxis) operating in Berlin. They carry a sign to indicate that they use *Erdgas*, or natural gas, which is slightly less polluting than other fossil fuels.

Other green travel systems include Segway tours (see p279) and Velo Taxi (see p293).

Walking

German drivers are generally careful and watch out for pedestrians, but vigilance is still needed. Cyclists travelling at speed can be dangerous as many cycle routes run along the pavements (sidewalks), only marked by a line or by a different colour (normally red). You can easily be hit, or at least scolded for being in the wrong lane.

When searching for a specific street address, keep in mind that street numbers sometimes increase along one side of the street and then turn around at the end and continue on the other side. Street signs on each corner include the numbers within that particular block.

Disabled visitors should contact **Mobidat Infoservice** or the **Berliner Behindertenverband** for advice on getting around, including wheelchair rental and other support services.

Driving

Driving around Berlin is not as straightforward as it is in some European capitals. Most of downtown Berlin (inside the S-Bahn ring) is a green zone, where only vehicles with an approved environmental badge are allowed. You can buy the badge online at www.umwelt-plakette.de. Most rental cars are covered.

Local drivers are mostly careful and don't break speed limits or enter junctions on yellow lights. You are allowed to turn right on a red light if a green arrow is also showing.

Petrol stations can be found right across the city. Some may require you to pay before your pump is activated.

You won't have a problem hiring a car in Berlin, as long as you show your passport and a valid driving licence; a credit card is the preferred method of payment. There are many hire

Stopping and parking prohibited from Monday to Friday

Parking permitted during working hours and at weekends only with a ticket

Parking Meter

Parking meters are used on most streets. You have to pay for parking depending on the parking zone; usually between 9am and 7pm on weekdays and 9am and 2pm on Saturdays. Check signs for information.

Information in different languages

Slot for inserting coins

Clock indicating date and time

Ticket is dispensed here

DIRECTORY

Walking

Berliner Behindertenverband Jägerstrasse 63d.
Tel 204 38 47.

Mobidat Infoservice
Tel 747 771 125.

Driving

ADAC Auto Assistance
Tel (01802) 22 22 22.
w adac.de

Avis
Tel (01805) 217702.
w avis.com

Europcar
Tel (01805) 8000.
w europcar.com

Hertz
Tel (01803) 33 535.
w hertz.com

Sixt
Tel (01805) 252 525.
w sixt.com

Parking

Berlin Police (towed vehicles)
Tel 4664 98 78 00.

Cycling

DB Call-a-Bike
Tel 07000 522 5522.

Fahrradstation
Dorotheenstrasse 30.
Tel 28 38 48 48. **Open** Mar–Oct: 8am–8pm Mon–Fri, 10am–6pm Sat; Nov–Feb: 10am–7pm Mon–Fri, 10am–3pm Sat.

Velo Taxi
Tel 2803 1609.
Open Apr–Oct. **w** velotaxi.com

companies, including **Avis**, **Europcar**, **Hertz** and **Sixt**, with offices at the airports, railway stations and in the city centre.

If you experience any trouble on the road, you should call **ADAC Auto Assistance**.

Parking

Finding a parking place won't always be easy, especially during lunchtime, but with a bit of luck you should be able to leave your car in the middle lane of the Ku'damm or near Alexanderplatz. There are also parking meters on nearly every street, and many car parks.

Parking your car illegally is not worth the risk; Berlin traffic wardens are constantly on the prowl, and as well as giving you a ticket, they can have your vehicle towed. If your vehicle is towed away, you must call the **Berlin Police**. It can cost up to €250 to locate your vehicle. For a cheaper solution, search nearby streets – cars are sometimes simply moved rather than impounded.

Cycling

Most of the main roads have designated cycling lanes and traffic lights at intersections. When using bicycle racks, make sure your bike is locked and don't leave it for too long.

You can take your bike on U- and S-Bahn trains and trams but must enter the carriage by the correct door and leave your bike

in the designated space. Bikes are prohibited on buses, except night buses, which can carry up to two at the driver's discretion. For all public transport an additional *Fahrrad* (bicycle) ticket is required.

Deutsche Bahn operates a fantastic public bicycle system. You can find ranks of their specially marked **DB Call-a-Bike** bicycles at train stations and major intersections. To rent one, register using the computer terminal found at each station by providing your credit card details. A one-off registration fee of €12 applies. The first 30 minutes are free, and then the cost is 8 cents a minute, up to a maximum of €15 a day or €60 a week.

You can also hire bikes at many cycling shops for similar or cheaper rates; one of the most reliable is **Fahrradstation**. Or take a ride in a **Velo Taxi**. You will be transported in an open-air coach on the back of a bike.

DB Call-a-Bike bicycles for rent

Buses, Trams and Taxis

Travelling by bus in Berlin is highly recommended. Buses are efficient, generally on time, and they travel useful routes – although some buses can get crowded during rush hour. Most of the major roads have special bus lanes so buses are punctual even when the main roads are congested. A double-decker bus is worth taking if you're new in town and want to have a good look round (see Useful Bus Routes map on the City Map). Trams are another particularly good option in the central and eastern parts of the city; like the buses and S-Bahn lines they are part of BVG and accept the same tickets.

BVG pavilion on Hardenbergplatz providing transport information

Tickets

The whole of Berlin is divided into three travel zones: A, B and C. Zone A covers the city centre, Zone B the outskirts of town and Zone C includes Potsdam and its environs. Travel between the zones is simple, with tickets available for each combination of zones.

The most expensive option is to travel by buying a single ticket, which is valid for 2 hours and valid on all forms of public transport, including S- and U-Bahn trains, with as many changes as you need. Travel is allowed in only one direction, so a second ticket is needed for the return journey. Short-trip (*Kurzstrecke*) tickets are cheaper, but can only be used for three stops on trains and six stops on buses or trams.

Tickets can be bought from ticket machines at U- or S-Bahn stations, on board trams, or from the bus driver. You must validate your ticket before you start your journey by inserting it in a red or yellow time-stamping machine found near the ticket machines, at platform entrances and on board buses. Children under 14 years old are entitled to a discount (*Ermässigungstarif*) and those under six can travel for free. The One-Day Ticket (*Tageskarte*) is valid from the moment it is validated until 3am the next morning. Weekly cards (*7-Tage-Karte*) are valid for seven days, and have the added benefit of allowing you to travel with one extra adult and up to three children for free after 8pm on weekdays, or all hours across the weekend.

Several tourist cards are available that combine public transport with discount entry to museums and attractions. The Berlin Welcome Card and the CityTourCard are both popular (*see p279*). For information about tickets and public transport in general, check the **BVG** website, visit a **BVG Pavilion** for all transport information, or check the **Ticket Information** line.

Berlin WelcomeCard ticket

Travelling By Bus

Bus stops are marked by signs bearing the letter H, for *haltestelle* or stop. All bus routes have a detailed time-table on display at each stop. Inner-city bus stops are equipped with digital screens indicating waiting times. Bus stops are often relocated due to road works. You can always find a replacement stop nearby.

Apart from its number, a bus will also have its destination on show; pay attention to this as some buses shorten their routes outside rush hour. It is not always necessary to flag down buses at stops, but it can help. Enter via the front door and buy a ticket from the driver. If you are transferring and already have a validated ticket, show this.

Approaching stop names are announced automatically and are displayed digitally. Press the "Halt" ("Stop") button to get off; most stops are made "on request" only (especially in the suburbs). To exit, you must press a button to open the doors.

A typical single decker bus

Types of Bus Service

There are several different bus services operating in Berlin, but all use the same ticket tariffs. Regular buses are marked by three-digit route codes and operate every 20 minutes between 5am and midnight. Important routes are serviced by Metro buses, marked by the letter M at the start of their route code. These operate 24 hours a day, and run every 10 to 20 minutes. Express buses, marked by the letter X, run every 5 to 20 minutes.

The night bus service begins operation after midnight and is a very reliable network. These buses are marked by the letter N and tickets can be bought direct from the driver. They operate every half-hour until about 4am, when the U-Bahn service resume

Routes 100 and 200

These special routes are served by double-deckers and include the most attractive parts of town. The buses operate between Bahnhof Zoo and Prenzlauer Berg, passing most of the city's interesting historic sights. For the price of a regular bus ticket, you can visit many of the locations as a more expensive tourist bus tour. The buses stop at Museum Island, Unter den Linden, Brandenburg Gate, the Reichstag, Potsdamer Platz, the Tiergarten and Kaiser-Wilhelm- Gedächtniskirche.

The BVG also operates a special historic bus tour called the Zille-Express, which makes a 50-minute circuit around the centre of Berlin, with commentary in German and English. The tour operates between April and October, departing from Brandenburg Gate every hour from 10:30am to 5pm. A trip costs €8 and is free for children under the age of ten.

Trams

Trams (*Strassenbahn*) operate in Mitte and the eastern parts of the city – a legacy from the city's division, when West Berlin tore up its once-extensive tram network. Despite servicing only

Modern tram operating in the former East Berlin quarter

Tram Stop

Every tram stop displays the appropriate tram numbers, timetables and maps. Buses sometimes also use the stops and are listed accordingly.

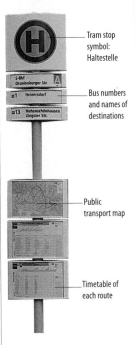

Tram stop symbol: Haltestelle

Bus numbers and names of destinations

Public transport map

Timetable of each route

one-third of the city, trams remain a great way to get around, particularly if you are travelling from Mitte to any part of Prenzlauer Berg. The M10 is also a convenient route, connecting Prenzlauer Berg to Friedrichshain.

Important routes are serviced by Metro trams, marked by the letter M at the front of their route code. These trams run every 10 or 20 minutes, 24 hours a day. Other trams operate between 5 or 6 am and midnight, arriving every 20 minutes.

The network runs a mix of modern wheelchair-friendly low-floor trams and old carriages with stairs; look for wheelchair symbols on timetables for guidance on which service is most suitable.

Tram tickets can also be used on buses, S- and U-Bahn trains. You can purchase tickets using machines (coin only) on board.

Taxis

Taxis are a comfortable but expensive way of getting around Berlin. All taxis are of the same cream colour and have a big TAXI sign on the roof. You can easily hail one on the street or arrange a cab by phone, through **Taxi Funk** or **Würfelfunk**. You can also get a taxi from a designated rank in popular locations, such as train stations.

The fare is calculated by a meter on the driver's dashboard. If you are travelling 2 km (1 mile) or less, you can request the *kurzstrecke* (short trip) for €4 – but only from taxis hailed in the street, and only if you inform the driver at the start of the trip.

A Berlin taxi with a yellow roof sign

Travelling by U-Bahn, S-Bahn and Regional Trains

While in theory Berlin has two separate train networks – the U-Bahn and S-Bahn systems – in practical terms there is not much difference between them, and commuters use the same tickets for both. Strictly speaking, the U-Bahn operates as a metro system, with most of its trains running underground, while the S-Bahn is a longer-distance commuter service. In practice, however, there is a great deal of overlap between the two systems, and many stations have both S- and U-Bahn platforms. The U-Bahn is owned by BVG and the S-Bahn by Deutsche Bahn.

Train arriving at a station on a U-Bahn platform

U-Bahn

The U-Bahn network is very dense, with numerous stations very close together. Don't be confused by the name – "underground" trains also run on elevated tracks above the street in some sections. During rush hours trains are very frequent, usually arriving every few minutes. There are ten U-Bahn lines in total. The service closes down between around 12.30am and 4am, and is replaced by night buses. On weekends, all lines are open 24 hours, except the two short-line services, the U4 and the U55.

S-Bahn

The S-Bahn is faster than the U-Bahn, with stations spaced further apart. Trains run every 10 or 20 minutes, or more frequently in peak hours. There are a total of 15 S-Bahn lines, all running well beyond the

confines of the city; four of them (S3, 5, 7 and 75) travel concurrently along the central line between Westkreuz and Ostkreuz. The Ring service (S41 and 42) is a convenient way to circle the city; it takes one hour to travel a complete circuit.

The S-Bahn has been plagued by problems due to cost-cutting over the years. If on your journey you face delays, it's worth noting you can use your ticket on the large red regional trains (RE and RB), which stop at most stations on the central line between Ostbahnhof and Zoologischer Garten.

Tickets

Tickets for S- and U-Bahn trains are the same as the tickets used on local buses and trams. The *Kurzstrecke* (short-trip) single ticket is also acceptable, although it is only valid for three stops. Vending machines

stand at the entrance to each station, selling single tickets, and one- and seven-day travelcards and other tickets. The red or yellow validation machines can be found next to the ticket machines, or near the entrance to each platform.

You may notice that there are no gates to stop free-riders trying their luck on the trains, but attempting to travel free of charge can be risky. Trains are patrolled by ticket inspectors who always work in plain clothes. They go on their rounds as soon as the train starts moving, and tend not to accept any excuses; fines for not having a ticket start at €40.

Signs and Trains

There's no mistaking a U-Bahn station, with its large rectangular sign and trademark white U on a blue background; similarly for S-Bahn stations, which have a round sign with a large white S on a green background. On metro maps each line is marked by a different colour and number.

The direction of the train is noted on the train and platform, which always give the final destination. When embarking, always check both the line number and the final destination of the train as it is very easy to confuse your direction. All stations have maps of the local area as well as maps of the entire metro system. Maps of the network are also on view in the train carriages.

Train doors do not open automatically; you must push a flashing button or pull a metal

An S-Bahn line 5 train heading out to Pichelsberg

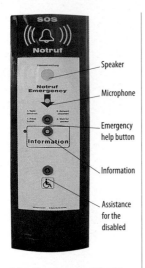

Information and emergency help point for the S-Bahn and U-Bahn

handle to open them. An alert sounds when doors are closing and the train conductor will announce "Zurück bleiben!" (remain back). During the journey the next station is announced inside the carriage and information is given on electronic screens.

Regional Trains

Operated by Deutsche Bahn (see p290), the Regional Bahn and Regional Express (RB & RE) trains service the wider Berlin-Brandenburg region and beyond. They are a great way to get to Potsdam (see pp192–207) or other smaller towns near Berlin.

Tickets can be bought at automatic machines on station platforms, or from ticket offices. If travelling at the weekend there are special offers available, including a five-person ticket that lasts all day. A normal U- and S-Bahn ticket can be used to ride these trains within Berlin – which is particularly useful when there are delays on the S-Bahn line.

Regional trains depart from only a small number of stations, including Hauptbahnhof, Friedrichstrasse, Alexanderplatz, Ostbahnhof, Zoologischer Garten and Gesundbrunnen.

USING THE U- AND S-BAHN

1 Find the station you want on a map and see which line runs there. Do not forget to make a note of the final destination of the line so you can be sure of travelling in the right direction

Map of U- and S-Bahn lines (see inside back cover)

2 Find the type of ticket you require on the touchscreen. After making your selection, the price is displayed and you can insert your coins, notes or credit cards.

Credit card

Bank notes

Tickets and change

3 A ticket from the machine looks different from one bought on a bus or tram, but it will always contain information about its type and price.

Weekly travel card and one-day travel card

4 After entering the station you must validate your ticket in one of the red or yellow stamping machines located on the platform.

Ticket

Colour-coded sign for various S-Bahn lines

5 Follow the signs to the appropriate platform and choose the correct side by checking the destinations of departing trains.

Information board indicating the destinations of departing trains

S 3	Westkreuz
S 5	Pichelsberg
S 7	Potsdam Stadt
S 9	Westkreuz
S 75	Pichelsberg

Sign indicating where to go for these U-Bahn lines

6 After leaving a train, proceed to the exit marked by the Ausgang sign. If there are several exits from the station additional signs will tell you the names of the streets outside.

A typical exit sign

Getting Around by Boat

The river routes of Berlin may not be as dense as those of Amsterdam or Venice, but the Spree and the Havel offer more than just a pleasure cruise in the sun. An extensive system of canals and lakes links the city centre with Potsdam, Spandau, Charlottenburg and the area of Müggelsee. All kinds of water transport are available, from rowing boats to catamarans and barges.

One of many tourist boats on the Spree river

Getting Around Berlin on the Water

One of the most relaxing ways to spend the afternoon in Berlin is to take a leisurely 3–4 hour journey by boat along the Spree river and the Landwehrkanal. There is no shortage of companies offering this kind of trip. Four of the most reliable are **Reederei Bruno Winkler**, **Stern und Kreisschiffahrt**, **Reederei Hartmut Triebler** and **Reederei Riedel**. Each has its own dock, but the routes they follow are similar. You can admire the historic buildings of Mitte as the boat passes by the Berliner Dom along Museum Island, before heading off to the government district and the Reichstag. You should have a good view of the Haus der Kulturen der Welt and the new city in Moabit shortly before entering the Landwehr-kanal. This runs alongside the Zoological Garden and new city buildings on Potsdamer Platz, and passes through Kreuzberg on its way to the junction with the Spree at Oberbaumbrücke.

Most of the boats available along this route have enclosed lower decks and open upper decks, with a bar serving snacks and drinks. All the sights are explained by a guide along the way; the commentary is usually in German, but some companies can arrange for an English speaker.

Public Ferries

In addition to the many privately operated cruises, there are also six public ferry lines that are integrated into the public transport system. These are marked by a stylized F and use the same tickets as trains and buses. Most of them provide cross-river connections in locations to the east where there are no bridges. However the F10 provides a particularly charming trip from Wannsee (near Potsdam) to the lakeside village of Alt-Kladow – a great budget option for those who don't want to pay a lot for a cruise.

Trips Along the Spree and Havel Rivers

If you want to try something a little more adventurous there are longer trips to choose from, some of which cover the western lakes as well as the city centre. A pleasant route takes you along the Spree, past the Mitte district, to Treptow, Charlottenburg and Spandau. From here you can carry on along the Havel river to the Grunewald and the Wannsee, then take a trip past Pfauen-insel to Potsdam. To do this, enquire at Stern und Kreis. Companies Reederei Bruno Winkler and Reederei Hartmut Triebler offer similar trips starting at Spandau and Charlottenburg.

Other options include a trip from Tegel port to Spandau and Wannsee, or a journey from Treptow to Köpenick. If you really want to, you can cover the whole of Berlin by boat, starting from Tegel in the north and finishing at Köpenick in the southeast, all within 5 or 6 hours.

Longer Journeys Around Berlin

For even longer tours, you may decide to take a whole day exploring the rivers, canals and lakes of Berlin. From Treptow you can take a boat to Woltersdorf which takes you

Boat moored along the river in the summer

One of the larger boats available on the Spree

through the charming lakeland area of Müggelsee. This region really is one of Berlin's greatest treasures and is ideal for anyone searching for a quiet place to relax. There are many man-made beaches to choose from, as well as summer gardens and cafés – and a large white fleet of ships to show you around Berlin. Müggelsee is best visited on a warm summer's day when you can easily spend a few hours on one of its beaches.

Reederei Riedel company logo

Another adventurous idea is to take a voyage along the Teltowkanal from Treptow to Potsdam. From here, **Weisse Flotte Potsdam** can take you not only to Wannsee and the other familiar routes around town, but also to Caputh, Werder and to many other sights to the south and west of Potsdam.

Boat Hire

It is possible to charter a small boat to use for several hours or longer. **Bootsverleih Spreepoint**, on the shores of Müggelsee in the east, hires motor-boats to those with the appropriate licences, or you can find a char-tered boat at the **Solar Boat Pavilion** in Köpenick. For a trip through the centre of the city, the **Spree Shuttle** offers private boat tours of the main sights.

Potsdam and its lakes and rivers teem with boat rental companies; check with the Potsdam Tourismus Information Centre (see p281) for contact details.

(see p281)

DIRECTORY

Boat Tours

Reederei Bruno Winkler
Mierendorffstrasse 16.
Tel 349 95 95.
w reedereiwinkler.de

Reederei Hartmut Triebler
Bratringweg 29.
Tel 37 15 10 52.

Reederei Riedel
Planufer 78.
Tel 693 46 46.
w reederei-riedel.de

Stern und Kreisschiffahrt
Puschkinallee 15.
Tel 536 36 00.
w sternundkreis.de

Weisse Flotte Potsdam
Lange Brücke 6.
Tel (0331) 275 92 10.

Boat Hire Companies

Bootsverleih Spreepoint
Müggelseedamm 70.
Tel 64 11 291.
w bootsverleih-spreepoint.de

Solar Boat Pavilion
Müggelheimer Strasse 10
Tel 01606 309 997.

Spree Shuttle
Lausitzer Strasse 36.
Tel 611 80 01.
w spree-shuttle.de

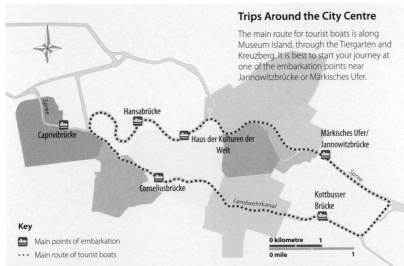

Trips Around the City Centre

The main route for tourist boats is along Museum Island, through the Tiergarten and Kreuzberg. It is best to start your journey at one of the embarkation points near Jannowitzbrücke or Märkisches Ufer.

Hansabrücke

Caprivibrücke

Haus der Kulturen der Welt

Märkisches Ufer/ Jannowitzbrücke

Corneliusbrücke

Landwehrkanal

Kottbusser Brücke

Key

🚢 Main points of embarkation

••• Main route of tourist boats

0 kilometre 1

0 mile 1

STREET FINDER

Map references given for historic buildings, hotels, restaurants, bars, shops and entertainment venues refer to the maps in this section of the guidebook only. A complete index of street names and all places of interest can be found on the following pages. The key map below shows the area of Berlin covered by the *Street Finder*. The maps include all the major

sightseeing areas, historic attractions, railway stations, bus stations and the suburban stations of the U-Bahn and S-Bahn, as well as the ferry embarkation points. The names of the streets and squares in the index and maps are given in German. The word Strasse (Str.) indicates a street, Platz a square, Brücke a bridge and Bahnhof a railway station.

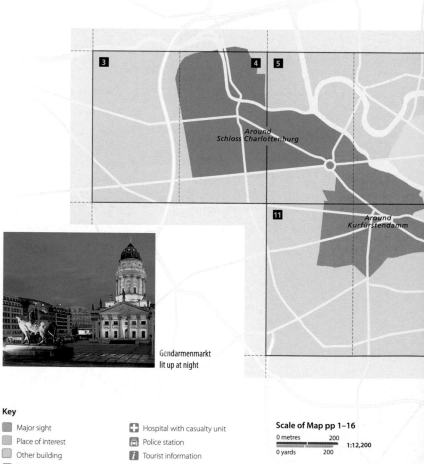

Gendarmenmarkt
lit up at night

Key

▪ Major sight	✚ Hospital with casualty unit
▪ Place of interest	🏠 Police station
▫ Other building	𝒊 Tourist information
Ⓢ S-Bahn station	✝ Church
Ⓤ U-Bahn station	✡ Synagogue
🚆 Railway station	═ Railway line
🚌 Bus station	Pedestrianized street
🚊 Tram stop	═ Autobahn (motorway)

Scale of Map pp 1–16

0 metres   200
0 yards   200   **1:12,200**

Palm house in the
Botanischer Garten

Rococo Chinesisches Haus in
Park Sanssouci, Potsdam

North of the Centre

Spree

East of
the Centre

Tiergarten

Around Unter
den Linden

Museum
Island

Kreuzberg

Modern business centre
of Potsdamer Platz

Street Finder Index

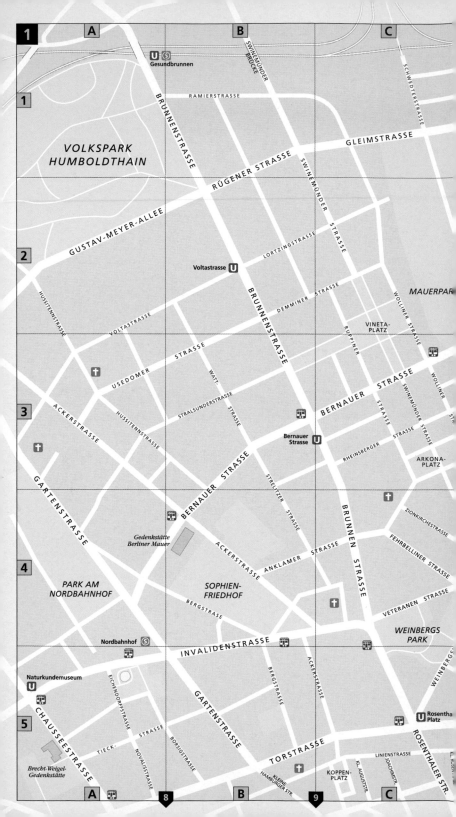

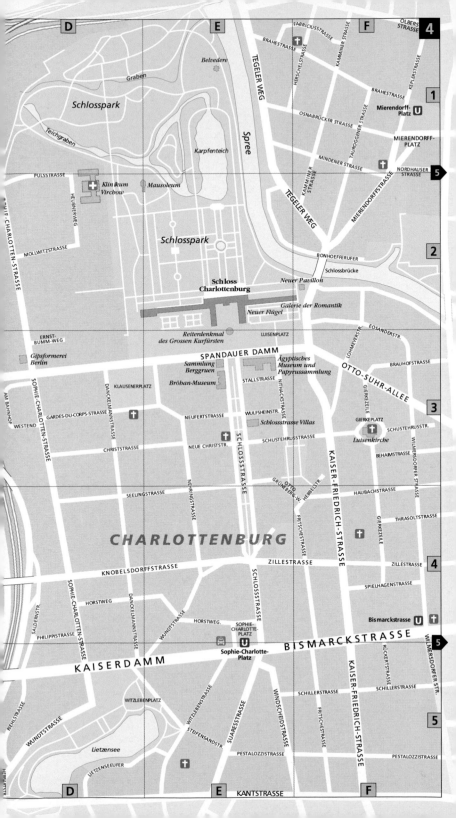

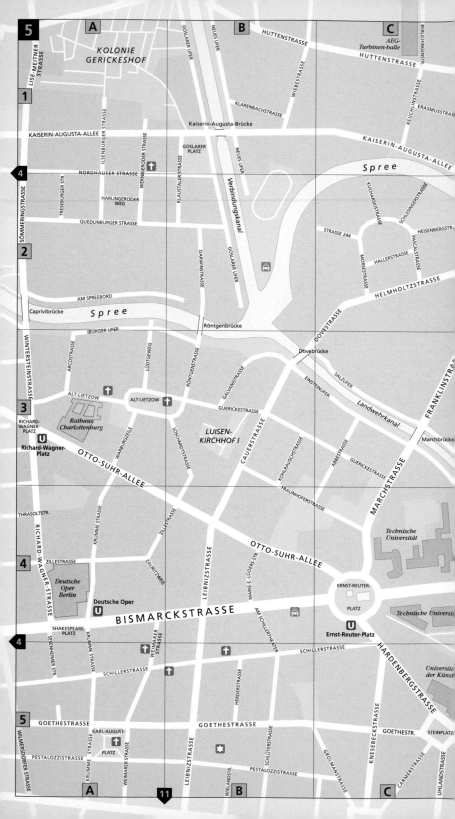

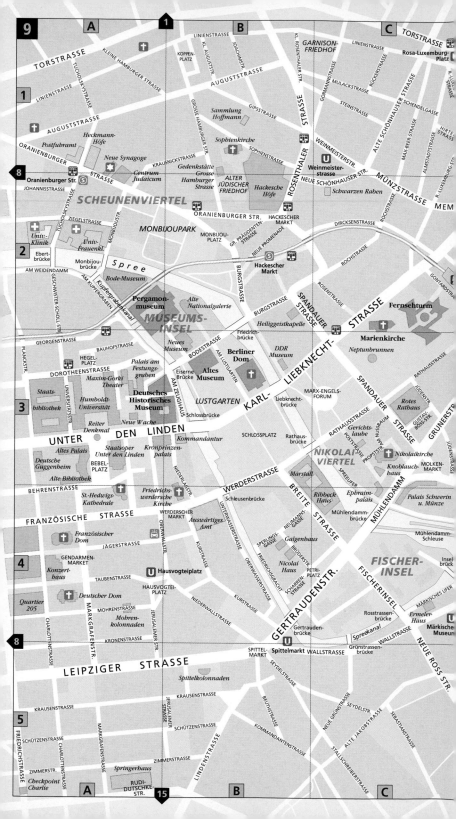

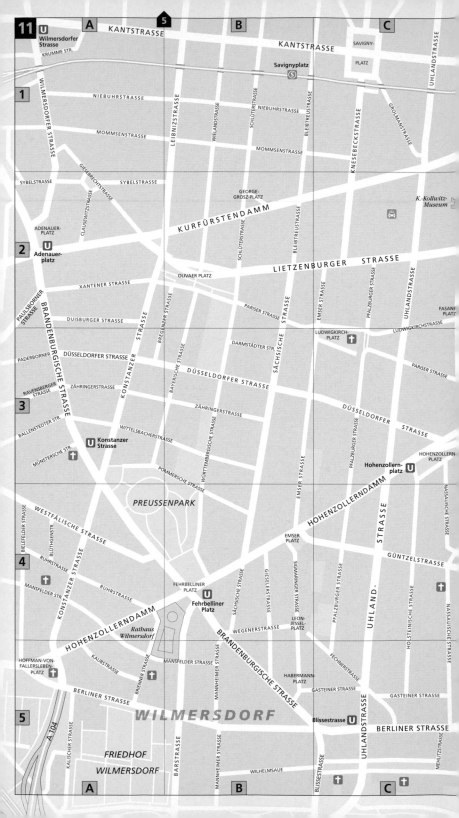

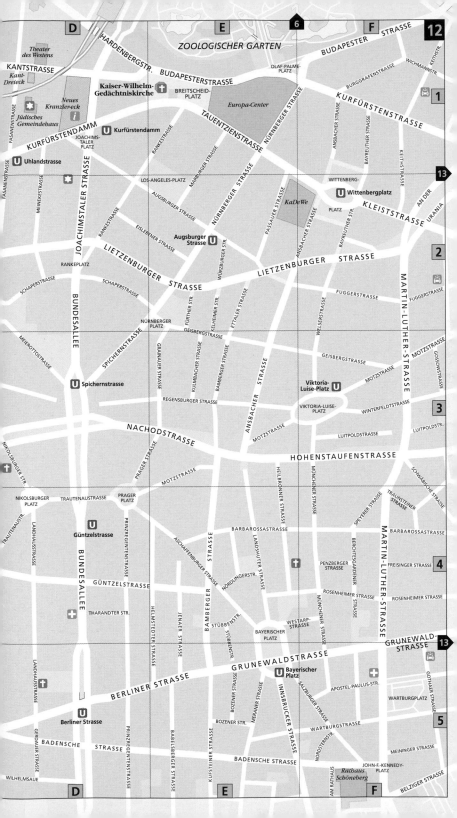

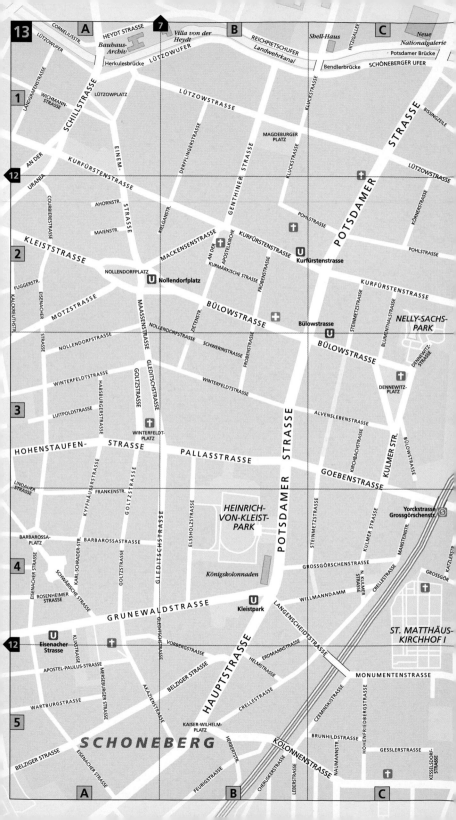

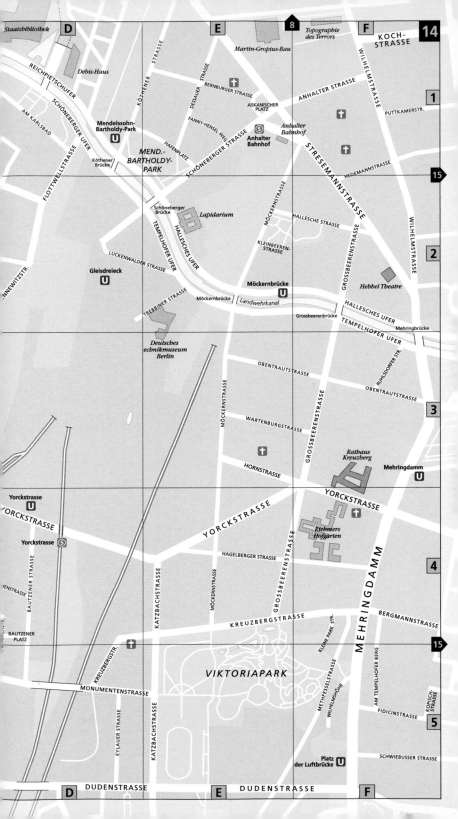

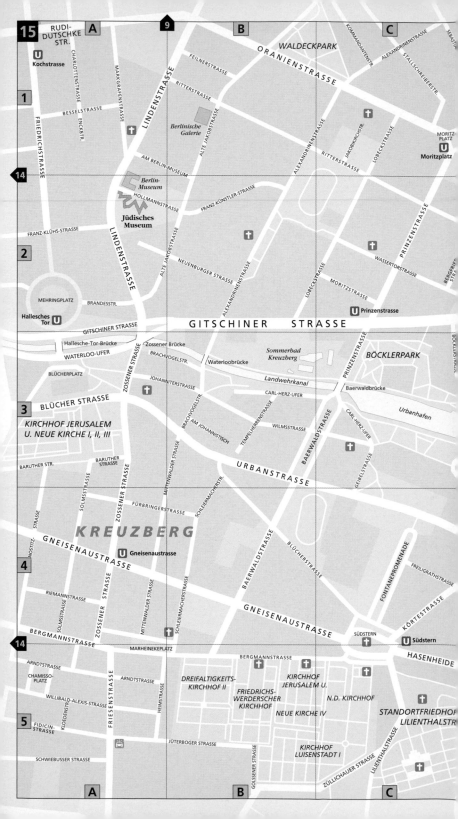

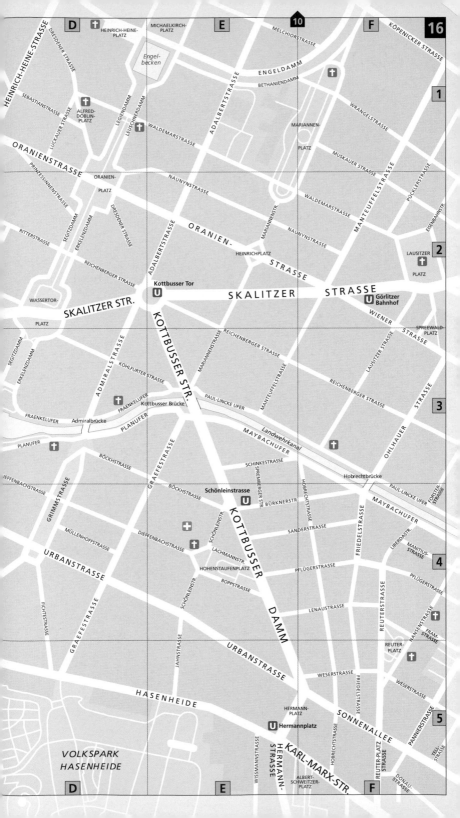

General Index

Acknowledgments

Dorling Kindersley would like to thank the following people whose contributions and assistance have made the preparation of this book possible.

Design and Editorial
Managing Art Editor Kate Poole
Editorial Director Vivien Crump
Art Director Gillian Allan
Consultant Gordon McLachlan
Factchecker Jürgen Scheunemann
Translators Magda Hannay, Anna Johnson, Ian Wisniewski
Proofreader Stewart Wild
Indexer Hilary Bird
Design and Editorial Assistance Namrata Adhwaryu, Asad Ali, Gillian Andrews, Brigitte Arora, Claire Baranowski, Marta Bescos Sanchez, Tessa Bindloss, Arwen Burnett, Divya Chowfin, Lucinda Cooke, Vidushi Duggal, Joel Dullroy, Nicola Erdpresser, Emer FitzGerald, Camilla Gersh, Mohammad Hassan, Kaberi Hazarika, Claudia Himmelreich, Jessica Hughes, Claire Jones, Priya Kukadia, Rakesh Kumar Pal, Maite Lantaron, Delphine Lawrance, Jude Ledger, Carly Madden, Franziska Marking, Kate Molan, Catherine Palmi, Rada Radojicic, Ellen Root, Simon Ryder, Sands Publishing Solutions, Azeem Siddiqui, Sadie Smith, Andrew Szudek, Maria Taari, Leah Tether, Helen Townsend, Conrad van Dyk, Ajay Verma, Deepika Verma, Hugo Wilkinson

DTP
Samantha Borland, Lee Redmond

Additional Illustrations
Paweł Pasternak

Additional Photography
Amir Akhtar, Francesca Bondy, Britta Jaschinski, Claire Jones, Catherine Marshall, Ian O'Leary, Jürgen Scheunemann

Additional Text
Joel Dullroy, Claudia Himmelreich, Jürgen Scheunemann

Special Assistance
Dorling Kindersley would like to thank the staff at the featured museums, shops, hotels, restaurants and other organizations in Berlin for their invaluable help. Special thanks go to the following for providing photographs and pictures: Heidrun Klein of the Bildarchiv Preussischer Kulturbesitz; Frau Betzker and Ingrid Jager of the Bröhan Museum; Margit Billeb of the Centrum Judaicum; Brucke-Museum; Deutsche Press Agency (DPA); Renate Forster of the Deutsches Technikmuseum Berlin; Andrei Holland-Moritz of Forschung- und Gedenkstätte Normannenstrasse (Stasi-Museum); Matthias Richter of Konzerthaus Berlin and the Berlin Symphony Orchestra; Georg Kolbe Museum; Carl Kamarz of Stiftung Preussische Schlösser und Gärten Berlin and the Berlin and Potsdam Palaces; Thomas Wellmann of the Museum of the City of Berlin; Hamburger Bahnhof; Annette Jäckel of DeragHotels for providing photographs of the interiors of DeragHotel Grosser Kurfürst; Reinhard Friedrich; Hans-Jürgen Dyck of Haus am Checkpoint Charlie; Gaby Hofmann of Komische Oper Berlin; Gesine Steiner of Museum für Naturkunde; Ute Grallert of Deutsches Historisches Museum; Elke Pfeil of the Brecht-Weigel-Museum; Ingrid Flindell of the Käthe-Kollwitz-Museum; Sylvia U Moller of Villa Kastania; Manuel Volsk of the Savoy Hotel; Sabine Rogge of the Grand Hotel Esplanade Berlin; Claude Borrmann of the Hotel Palace Berlin; Gerald Uhligow of the Einstein Café; Hotel Adlon; Hotel Brandenburger Hof and Restaurant Die Quadriga; Hotel Kempinski; Rockendorf's Restaurant; The Westin Grand Hotel.

Photography Permissions
Dorling Kindersley would like to thank the following for their kind permission to photograph at their establishments: Margaret Hilmer of the Berliner Dom; Kaiser-Wilhelm-Gedächtniskirche; Galeries Lafayette; KaDeWe; Frau Schneider of BVG (Berlin Underground System); Deutsche Bundes-bahn for allowing photography of the Zoo railway station; Dorotheenstädtischer Friedhof for allowing photographs of the tombs; Flughafen Schönefeld for allowing photography of the airfield; Annie Silbert of the Zoologischer Garten Berlin for allowing photography of the animals and attractions; Hilton Hotel; Carlos Beck of the Sorat Art'otel, Berlin; Manuel Volsk of the Savoy Hotel, Berlin; Sabine Rogge of the Grand Hotel Esplanade; Claude Borrmann of the Hotel Palace Berlin; Gerald Uhligow of the Einstein Café; the Olive restaurant; the Bamberger Reiter restaurant; Sklepo for allowing photography of its interiors and porcelain. Count Lehmann of Senatsverwaltung für Bauen, Wohnen und Verkehr for providing cartographic information as well as copyright for the use of maps; Ms Grazyna Kukowska of ZAIKS for her help in securing permission to reproduce works of art.

Picture Credits
a = above; b = below/bottom; c = centre; f = far; l = left; r = right; t = top. Works of art have been reproduced with the permission of the following copyright holders: Richtkräfte (1974-77) Joseph Beuys ©DACS, London 2011 114br; *Pariser Platz in Berlin* (1925–26) Oskar Kokoschka ©DACS, London 2011 69bl; *Mother and Child* Käthe Kollwitz ©DACS, London 2011 158c; *Girl on a Beach* Evadr Munch ©ADAGP, Paris and DACS, London 2011 121tc; *Head of the Faun* (1937) Pablo Picasso ©Sucession Picasso/DACS, London 2011 36tr, *Woman in a Hat* (1939) Pablo Picasso ©Sucession Picasso/DACS, London 2011 169tl; *First Time Painting* (1961) Robert Rauschenberg ©DACS, London/VAGA, NY 2011 114bl; *Farm in Daugart* (1910) Karl Schmidt-Rottluff ©DACS, London 2011 130tl; *Mao* (1973) Andy Warhol © Licensed by the Andy Warhol Foundation for the Visual Arts, Inc./ARS, NY and DACS, London 2011 114cr.

The publisher is grateful to the following individuals, companies and picture libraries for their permission to reproduce their photographs. The works of art have been reproduced with the consent of the copyright owners.

Admiralspalast: S. Greuner 260br; **Alamy Images:** Pat Behnke 54-5; Bildarchiv Monheim GmbH 187cl; David Crausby 283bl; Colstravel 2-3; Gavin Hellier 56; Imagebroker 160, 208, 216-7; JLImages 150; Leslie Garland Picture Library 138br; LOOK Die Bildagentur der Fotografen GmbH 10cra, 154tl; Eric Nathan 95cra; Joern Sackerman 11bl; Hartmut Schmidt 287tr; Peter Widmann 88; Woodystock 72; **Allstar:** cinetext 145tc; **AMJ Holding GmbH & Co. Kg:** Steffen Janicke 67br; **Austria restaurant:** 241bc; **Berger + Parkkinen Architekten Ziviltechnik GmbH:** 44br; **Berlin Brandenburg Airport:** Marion Schmieding/Alexander Obst 288br; **Berlin Tourismus Marketing GmbH:** 114cl, 280cr, 286br; visitBerlin.de 278crb; visitBerlin.de/adenis 279tl; visitBerlin.de/Koch 167br; visitBerlin.de/Koch 290bl; visitBerlin.de/Meise 278bl; **Berliner Dom:** 78br; **Berliner Festspiele:** Bianka Göbel 261tl; **Berliner Sparkasse:** 284bl; **Berliner Verkehrsbetriebe (BVG):** 294cb, 294cla, 297tr, 297c, 297cr, 297cra; **Berlinische Galerie:** *Stadtwandelverlag* (2004) © Florian Bulk and *Dreiheit* (1993) © Brigitte and Martin Matschinsky-Denninghoff 145br; **Bildarchiv Preussischer Kulturbesitz:** 24 all pics, 26cb, 26bl, 33cla, 33cl, 33cra, 34 all pics, 35tr, 36tr, 36br, 37ca, 37br, 69bl, 74cla, 82-3 all pics, 83-4 all pics, 87br, 118 all pics, 119cra, 122-3 all pics, 126-7 all pics, 128-9 all pics, 130tl, 185tr, 185crb, 200tc; Jorg P Anders 20cl, 30cl, 75ca, 121tc, 124c, 124br, 125crb, 125cb, 181bc; Margarete Busing 36c; Ingrid Geske- Heiden 34tl, 77cra; Klaus Goken 62t, 34crb, 80t; Dietmar Katz 45crb; Johannes Laurentius 77bl; Jürgen Liepe 34cra, 77cla, 168b; Jürgen Zimmermann 30tl; **Brandenburger Hof:** 224bc, Die Quadriga 238tl; **Bröhan-museum:** 169bl; **Centrum Judaicum:** 104tr; © **Charité - Universitätsmedizin Berlin:** 112ca; **Circus Hotel, Berlin:** 222br; Corbis: Atlandtide Phototravel 116; Christian Charisius 280bl; Sygma/Aneebicque Bernard 229tl; Blaine Harrington III 100, 192; Hemis/Rene Mattes 32; Jon Hicks 276-7; Hulton-Deutsche Collection 8-9; Andreas Schluter 166tl; Adam Woolfitt 228cla; Michael S. Yamashita 229c; **Michael Day:** 179cr; **Derag Livinghotel Henriette:** 223tc; **Deutsche Bahn AG:** 293br; **Deutsche Press Agency (Dpa):** 10bl, 50cla, 52cra, 52bl, 69tr, 149br, 155br, 201br; **Deutsches Historisches Museum:** (Zeughaus) 27clb, 27tr, 28-9, 29tr, 30tl, 30cb, 30br, 31tl, 35bl, 39tl, 60-1 all pics; **Deutsches Technikmuseum Berlin:** 34bl; **European Commission:** 285; **E.T.A. Hoffman:** 237bl; **Fernsehturm Sphere Restaurant:** 233tr; **Filmpark Babelsberg:** 207 cla/ crb/bl; **Fischers Fritz:** 232br; **Gedenkstätte Berlin Hohenschönhausen:** 174br; **Gedenkstatte und Museum Sachsenhausen:** 181cr; **Georg Kolbe Museum:** 178tc; **Getty Images:** David Bank 13br; Image Source 12tc;

Siegfried Layda 179bc; John Macdougall 282cla; Florian Seefried 115bl; **Guglehof, Berlin:** 234br; **Gullivers Bus GmbH:** 291tr; **Hamburger Bahnhof:** 114bl, 114br, 115cr; **Haus am Checkpoint Charlie:** 43br; **Haus der Wannsee-Konferenz:** 189tl; **Hotel Adlon:** 70tl; **Hotel Palace Berlin:** 221tr; **Imageworkshop Berlin:** Vincent Mosch 135br; **Jewish Museum Berlin:** 146tr, 147br; Deutsches Technikmuseum Berlin 147clb; Jens Ziehe, Berlin 146cl; Leo Baeck Institute, New York 146tr; **Kafers Dachgarten:** 236tr; **Käthe-kollwitz-museum:** 158b; **Kadewe:** 53b; **Komische Oper Monika Rittershaus:** 51br, 70br; **Konzerthaus Berlin:** 67tl; **Kurhaus Korsakow:** 239b; **Courtesy of Lufthansa AG:** 288cla, 289tl; **Max und Moritz:** 240tl; **Nhow Berlin:** 225tl; **Meyer Nils:** 30crb, 42tr; **Museum für Naturkunde:** 113br; **Pasternak, Berlin:** 235tr; **Philharmonie:** 119tl; **Popkomm:** 261bc; **Potsdam Museum:** Mathias Marx 206cl; **Presse- und Informationsamt des Landes Berlin:** BTM/Drewes 47bl; BTM/Koch 47cla, 133tl; G. Schneider 53cra; Landesarchive Berlin 133br; Meldepress/Ebner 130bc; **Partner fuer Berlin:** FTB-Werbefotografie 132cl, 147cr; **Radeberger Gruppe:** KG: 230cla, 230cr, 230bl, 230fcla; **Robert Harding Picture Library:** 31crb; **Rocco Forte Hotel de Rome:** 218br; **Rosa's Dance co.:** 261cr; **Courtesy the Company Sarah Wiener:** 114tr; **Photo Scala, Florence:** Volk Ding Zero (2009) © Georg Baselitz 115tc; **Schneider, Guenter:** 43tr; **Schirmer, Karsten:** 260cl; **Jürgen Scheunemann:** 51cra, 142tr, 143tl; **Spindler & Klatt:** 243b;**STA Travel Group:** 280tc; **Staatliche Museen zu Berlin-preussischa Kulturbesitz/kunstgewerbemuseum:** Irmgard Mues-Funke 125tl; **Stadtmuseum Berlin:** 20, 23tl, 23br, 25tr, 26t, 28cla, 59crb, 137tr; Hans-Joachim Bartsch, 21br, 22tl, 22bc, 29br, 87tr; Peter Straube 90bc, 92tr; **Stasimuseum/ASTAK e.V:** John Steer 175tr **Stiftung Preussische Schlösser und Gärten Berlin:** 18tr, 23c, 164cl, 164cb, 165 all, 194br, 196cla, 196br, 197tc, 197crb, 197br, 197bl, 202cl, 202br, 203cra, 203ca, 203bc, 203bl, 202br; **Superstock:** age fotostock 13tr, Blaine Harrington 190-1; imagebroker.net 12bl, Julie Woodhouse 170; **Tim Raue, Berlin:** 237tr; **View Pictures:** William Fife 45bl; **Villa Kastania:** 219bc; © visitberlin.de: 113; tl; Philip Koschel 107tr; **Restaurant Volt:** 242tl; **The Westin Grand:** 220br.

Front endpapers - **Alamy Images:** Gavin Hellier Rtl, imagebroker Lclb, JLImages Lbc, Peter Widmann Rtr, WoodyStock Rbr; **Corbis:** Atlandtide Phototravel Ltr, Blaine Harrington III Rtc.

Jacket Front and Spine – **4corners:** SIME/Luca Da Ros Map Cover – **4corners:** SIME/Luca Da Ros.

All other images © Dorling Kindersley. For further information see: www.dkimages.com

Special Editions of DK Travel Guides

DK Travel Guides can be purchased in bulk quantities at discounted prices for use in promotions or as premiums. We are also able to offer special editions and personalized jackets, corporate imprints, and excerpts from all of our books, tailored specifically to meet your own needs.

To find out more, please contact:
in the United States **SpecialSales@dk.com**
in the UK **travelspecialsales@uk.dk.com**
in Canada DK Special Sales at **general@ tourmaline.ca**
in Australia **business.development@pearson. com.au**

Phrase Book

In an Emergency

Where is the Telefon?	**Wo ist das tel-e-fone?**	*voh ist duss telephone?*
Help!	**Hilfe!**	*hilf-uh*
Please call a doctor	**Bitte rufen Sie einen Arzt**	*bitt-uh roof'n zee ine-en artst*
Please call the police	**Bitte rufen Sie die Polizei**	*bitt-uh roof'n zee dee poli-tsy*
Please call the fire brigade	**Bitte rufen Sie die Feuerwehr**	*bitt-uh roof'n zee dee foyer-vayr*
Stop!	**Halt!**	*hult*

Communication Essentials

Yes	**Ja**	*yah*
No	**Nein**	*nine*
Please	**Bitte**	*bitt-uh*
Thank you	**Danke**	*dunk-uh*
Excuse me	**Verzeihung**	*fair-tsy-hoong*
Hello (good day)	**Guten Tag**	*goot-en tahk*
Goodbye	**Auf Wiedersehen**	*owf-veed-er-zay-ern*
Good evening	**Guten Abend**	*goot'n ahb'nt*
Good night	**Gute Nacht**	*goot-uh nukht*
Until tomorrow	**Bis morgen**	*biss morg'n*
See you	**Tschüss**	*chooss*
What is that?	**Was ist das?**	*voss ist duss*
Why?	**Warum?**	*var-room*
Where?	**Wo?**	*voh*
When?	**Wann?**	*vunn*
today	**heute**	*hoyt-uh*
tomorrow	**morgen**	*morg'n*
month	**Monat**	*mohn-aht*
night	**Nacht**	*nukht*
afternoon	**Nachmittag**	*nahkh-mit-tahk*
morning	**Morgen**	*morg'n*
year	**Jahr**	*yar*
there	**dort**	*dort*
here	**hier**	*hear*
week	**Woche**	*vokh-uh*
yesterday	**gestern**	*gest'n*
evening	**Abend**	*ahb'nt*

Useful Phrases

How are you? (informal)	**Wie geht's?**	*vee gayts*
Fine, thanks	**Danke, es geht mir gut**	*dunk-uh, es gayt meer goot*
Until later	**Bis später**	*biss shpay-ter*
Where is/are?	**Wo ist/sind...?**	*voh ist/sind*
How far is it to...?	**Wie weit ist es...?**	*vee vite ist ess*
Do you speak English?	**Sprechen Sie Englisch?**	*shpresh'n zee eng-glish*
I don't understand	**Ich verstehe nicht**	*ish fair-shtay-uh nisht*
Could you speak more slowly?	**Könnten Sie langsamer sprechen?**	*kurnt-en zee lung-zam-er shpresh'n*

Useful Words

large	**gross**	*grohss*
small	**klein**	*kline*
hot	**heiss**	*hyce*
cold	**kalt**	*kult*
good	**gut**	*goot*
bad	**böse/schlecht**	*burss-uh/shlesht*
open	**geöffnet**	*g'urff-nett*
closed	**geschlossen**	*g'shloss'n*
left	**links**	*links*
right	**rechts**	*reshts*
straight ahead	**geradeaus**	*g'rah-der-owss*

Making a Telephone Call

I would like to make a phone call	**Ich möchte telefonieren**	*ish mer-shtuh tel-e-fon-eer'n*
I'll try again later	**Ich versuche es später noch einmal**	*ish fair-zookh-uh es shpay-ter nokh ine-mull*
Can I leave a message?	**Kann ich eine Nachricht hinterlassen?**	*kan ish ine-uh nakh-risht hint-er-lahss-en*
answer phone	**Anrufbeantworter**	*an-roof-be-ahnt-vort-er*
telephone card	**Telefonkarte**	*tel-e-fohn-kart-uh*
receiver	**Hörer**	*hur-er*
mobile	**Handy**	*han-dee*
engaged (busy)	**besetzt**	*b'zetst*
wrong number	**Falsche Verbindung**	*falsh-uh fair-bin-doong*

Sightseeing

library	**Bibliothek**	*bib-leo-tek*
entrance ticket	**Eintrittskarte**	*ine-tritz-kart-uh*
cemetery	**Friedhof**	*freed-hofe*
train station	**Bahnhof**	*barn-hofe*
gallery	**Galerie**	*gall-er-ree*
information	**Auskunft**	*owss-koonft*
church	**Kirche**	*keersh-uh*
garden	**Garten**	*gart'n*
palace/castle	**Palast/Schloss**	*pallast/shloss*
place (square)	**Platz**	*plats*
bus stop	**Haltestelle**	*hal-te-shtel-uh*
national holiday	**Nationalfeiertag**	*nats-yon-ahl-fire-tahk*
theatre	**Theater**	*tay-aht-er*
free admission	**Eintritt frei**	*ine-tritt fry*

Shopping

Do you have/ Is there...?	**Gibt es...?**	*geept ess*
How much does it cost?	**Was kostet das?**	*voss kost't duss?*
When do you open/ close?	**Wann öffnen Sie? schliessen Sie?**	*vunn off'n zee shlees'n zee*
this	**das**	*duss*
expensive	**teuer**	*toy-er*
cheap	**preiswert**	*price-vurt*
size	**Grösse**	*gruhs-uh*
number	**Nummer**	*noom-er*
colour	**Farbe**	*farb-uh*
brown	**braun**	*brown*
black	**schwarz**	*shvarts*
red	**rot**	*roht*
blue	**blau**	*blau*
green	**grün**	*groon*
yellow	**gelb**	*gelp*

Types of Shop

antique shop	**Antiquariat**	*antik-var-yat*
chemist (pharmacy)	**Apotheke**	*appo-tay-kuh*
bank	**Bank**	*bunk*
market	**Markt**	*markt*
travel agency	**Reisebüro**	*rye-zer-boo-roe*
department store	**Warenhaus**	*vahr'n-hows*
chemist's, drugstore	**Drogerie**	*droog-er-ree*
hairdresser	**Friseur**	*freezz-er*
newspaper kiosk	**Zeitungskiosk**	*tsytoongs-kee-osk*
bookshop	**Buchhandlung**	*bookh-hant-loong*

bakery	**Bäckerei**	beck-er-**eye**
post office	**Post**	posst
shop/store	**Geschäft/Laden**	gush-**eft/lard**'n
film processing shop	**Photogeschäft**	**fo**-to-gush-**eft**
self-service shop	**Selbstbedienungs- laden**	selpst-bed-**ee- nungs-lard**'n
shoe shop	**Schuhladen**	shoo-lard'n
clothes shop	**Kleiderladen, Boutique**	klyder-lard'n boo-**teek**-uh
food shop	**Lebensmittel- geschäft**	**lay**-bens-mittel- gush-eft
glass, porcelain	**Glas, Porzellan**	**glars, Port-sellahn**

Staying in a Hotel

Do you have any vacancies?	**Haben Sie noch Zimmer frei?**	harb'n zee nokh **tsimm**-er-fry
with twin beds?	**mit zwei Betten?**	mitt tsvy bett'n
with a double bed?	**mit einem Doppelbett?**	mitt ine'm **dopp**'l-bet
with a bath?	**mit Bad?**	mitt **bart**
with a shower?	**mit Dusche?**	mitt **doosh**-uh
I have a reservation	**Ich habe eine Reservierung**	ish **harb**-uh ine-uh rez-er-**veer**-oong
key	**Schlüssel**	shlooss'l
porter	**Pförtner**	**pfert**-ner

Eating Out

Do you have a table for...?	**Haben Sie einen Tisch für...?**	harb'n zee tish foor
I would like to reserve a table	**Ich möchte eine Reservierung machen**	ish **mer**-shtuh ine- uh rezer-**veer**- oong makh'n
I'm a vegetarian	**Ich bin Vegetarier**	ish bin vegg-er-**tah**- ree-er
Waiter!	**Herr Ober!**	hair oh-**bare**!
The bill (check), please	**Die Rechnung, bitte**	dee **resh**-noong bitt-uh
breakfast	**Frühstück**	**froo**-shtock
lunch	**Mittagessen**	**mit**-targ-ess'n
dinner	**Abendessen**	**arb**'nt-ess'n
bottle	**Flasche**	**flush**-uh
dish of the day	**Tagesgericht**	**tahg**-es-gur-isht
main dish	**Hauptgericht**	**howpt**-gur-isht
dessert	**Nachtisch**	**nahkh**-tish
cup	**Tasse**	**tass**-uh
wine list	**Weinkarte**	vine-kart-uh
tankard	**Krug**	khroog
glass	**Glas**	**glars**
spoon	**Löffel**	**lerff**'l
teaspoon	**Teelöffel**	tay-lerff'l
tip	**Trinkgeld**	**trink**-gelt
knife	**Messer**	**mess**-er
starter (appetizer)	**Vorspeise**	**for**-shpize-uh
the bill	**Rechnung**	**resh**-noong
plate	**Teller**	**tell**-er
fork	**Gabel**	**gahb**'l

Menu Decoder

Aal	**arl**	eel
Apfel	**upf**'l	apple
Apfelschorle	**upf**'l-shoorl-uh	apple juice with sparkling mineral water
Apfelsine	**upf**'l-seen-uh	orange
Aprikose	**upri-kawz**-uh	apricot
Artischocke	**arti-shokh**-uh-	artichoke
Aubergine (eggplant)	**or-ber-jeen**-uh	aubergine
Banane	**bar-narn**-uh	banana
Beefsteak	**beef-stayk**	steak
Bier	**beer**	beer

Bockwurst	**bokh**-voorst	a type of sausage
Bohnensuppe	burn-en-zoop-uh	bean soup
Branntwein	brant-vine	spirits
Bratkartoffeln	brat-kar-toff'ln	fried potatoes
Bratwurst	brat-voorst	fried sausage
Brötchen	bret-tchen	bread roll
Brot	brot	bread
Brühe	bruh-uh	broth
Butter	**boot**-ter	butter
Champignon	**shum**-pin-yong	mushroom
Currywurst	**kha**-ree-voorst	sausage with curry sauce
Dill	**dill**	dill
Ei	**eye**	egg
Eis	**ice**	ice/ ice cream
Ente	**ent**-uh	duck
Erdbeeren	ayrt-**beer**'n	strawberries
Fisch	**fish**	fish
Forelle	for-**ell**-uh	trout
Frikadelle	Frika-dayl-uh	rissole/hamburger
Gans	ganns	goose
Garnele	**gar**-nayl-uh	prawn/shrimp
gebraten	g'**braat**'n	fried
gegrillt	g'**grilt**	grilled
gekocht	g'**kokh**t	boiled
geräuchert	g'**rowk**-ert	smoked
Geflügel	g'**floog**'l	poultry
Gemüse	g'**mooz**-uh	vegetables
Grütze	**grurt**-ser	groats, gruel
Gulasch	**goo**-lush	goulash
Gurke	**goork**-uh	gherkin
Hammelbraten	hamm'l-**braat**'n	roast mutton
Hähnchen	haynsh'n	chicken
Hering	**hair**-ing	herring
Himbeeren	him-beer'n	raspberries
Honig	hoe-nikh	honey
Kaffee	kaf-**fay**	coffee
Kalbfleisch	kalp-flysh	veal
Kaninchen	ka-**neensh**'n	rabbit
Karpfen	**karpf**'n	carp
Kartoffelpüree	kar-toff'l-poor-ay	mashed potatoes
Käse	**kayz**-uh	cheese
Kaviar	**kar**-vee-ar	caviar
Knoblauch	k'**nob**-lowkh	garlic
Knödel	**k'nerd**'l	noodle
Kohl	**koal**	cabbage
Kopfsalat	**kopf**-zal-aat	lettuce
Krebs	**krayps**	crab
Kuchen	**kookh**'n	cake
Lachs	**lahkhs**	salmon
Leber	**lay**-ber	liver
mariniert	mari-neert	marinated
Marmelade	marmer-**lard**-uh	marmalade, jam
Meerrettich	may-re-tish	horseradish
Milch	**milsh**	milk
Mineralwasser	minn-er-**arl**-vuss-er	mineral water
Möhre	**mer**-uh	carrot
Nuss	**nooss**	nut
Öl	**erl**	oil
Olive	o-**leev**-uh	olive
Petersilie	payt-er-**zee**-li-uh	parsley
Pfeffer	**pfeff**-er	pepper
Pfirsich	**pfir**-zish	peach
Pflaumen	**pflow**-men	plum
Pommes frites	pomm-**fritt**	chips/ French fries
Quark	kvark	soft cheese
Radieschen	ra-**deesh**'n	radish
Rinderbraten	**rind**-er-brat'n	joint of beef
Rinderroulade	**rind**-er-roo-lard-uh	beef olive
Rindfleisch	**rint**-flysh	beef
Rippchen	**rip**-sh'n	cured pork rib
Rotkohl	roht-koal	red cabbage
Rüben	rhoob'n	turnip
Rührei	**rhoo**-er-eye	scrambled eggs
Saft	**zuft**	juice
Salat	zal-aat	salad

Salz	**zults**	*salt*
Salzkartoffeln	*zults-kar-toff'l*	*boiled potatoes*
Sauerkirschen	*zow-er-***keersh**'n	*cherries*
Sauerkraut	*zow-er-krowt*	*sauerkraut*
Sekt	**zekt**	*sparkling wine*
Senf	**zenf**	*mustard*
scharf	*sharf*	*spicy*
Schaschlik	*shash-lik*	*kebab*
Schlagsahne	*shlahgg-zarn-uh*	*whipped cream*
Schnittlauch	*shnit-lowhkh*	*chives*
Schnitzel	**shnitz**'l	*veal or pork cutlet*
Schweinefleisch	**shvine**-flysh	*pork*
Spargel	**shparg**'l	*asparagus*
Spiegelei	*shpeeg'l-eye*	*fried egg*
Spinat	*shpin-art*	*spinach*
Tee	**tay**	*tea*
Tomate	*tom-art-uh*	*tomato*
Wassermelone	*vuss-er-me-lohn-uh*	*watermelon*
Wein	**vine**	*wine*
Weintrauben	*vine-trowb'n*	*grapes*
Wiener Würstchen	*veen-er voorst-sh'n*	*frankfurter*
Zander	**tsan**-der	*pike-perch*
Zitrone	*tsi-trohn-uh*	*lemon*
Zucker	**tsook**-er	*sugar*
Zwieback	*tsvee-bak*	*rusk*
Zwiebel	**tsveeb**'l	*onion*

Numbers

0	**null**	**nool**
1	**eins**	**eye**'ns
2	**zwei**	**tsvy**
3	**drei**	**dry**
4	**vier**	**feer**
5	**fünf**	**foonf**
6	**sechs**	**zex**
7	**sieben**	**zeeb**'n
8	**acht**	**uhkht**
9	**neun**	**noyn**
10	**zehn**	**tsayn**
11	**elf**	**elf**
12	**zwölf**	**tserlf**
13	**dreizehn**	**dry**-tsayn
14	**vierzehn**	**feer**-tsayn
15	**fünfzehn**	**foonf**-tsayn
16	**sechzehn**	**zex**-tsayn
17	**siebzehn**	**zeep**-tsayn
18	**achtzehn**	**uhkht**-tsayn
19	**neunzehn**	**noyn**-tsayn
20	**zwanzig**	**tsvunn**-tsig
21	**einundzwanzig**	**ine**-oont-tsvunn-tsig
30	**dreissig**	**dry**-sig
40	**vierzig**	**feer**-sig
50	**fünfzig**	**foonf**-tsig
60	**sechzig**	**zex**-tsig
70	**siebzig**	**zeep**-tsig
80	**achtzig**	**uhkht**-tsig
90	**neunzig**	**noyn**-tsig
100	**hundert**	**hoond**'t
1000	**tausend**	**towz**'nt
1 000 000	**elne Million**	**ine**-uh **mill**-yon

Time

one minute	**eine Minute**	**ine**-uh min-**oot**-uh
one hour	**eine Stunde**	**ine**-uh **shtoond**-uh
half an hour	**eine halbe Stunde**	**ine**-uh hullb-uh **shtoond**-uh
Monday	**Montag**	**mohn**-targ
Tuesday	**Dienstag**	**deen**s-targ
Wednesday	**Mittwoch**	**mitt**-vokh
Thursday	**Donnerstag**	**donn**-ers-targ
Friday	**Freitag**	**fry**-targ
Saturday	**Samstag/**	**zum**s-targ
	Sonnabend	**zonn**-ah-bent
Sunday	**Sonntag**	**zon**-targ
January	**Januar**	**yan**-ooar
February	**Februar**	**fay**-brooar
March	**März**	**mairts**
April	**April**	*april*
May	**Mai**	**my**
June	**Juni**	**yoo**-ni
July	**Juli**	**yoo**-lee
August	**August**	*ow-***goost**
September	**September**	*zep-***tem**-ber
October	**Oktober**	*ok-toh-ber*
November	**November**	*no-***vem**-ber
December	**Dezember**	*day-***tsem**-ber
spring	**Frühling**	**froo**-ling
summer	**Sommer**	**zomm**-er
autumn (fall)	**Herbst**	**hairpst**
winter	**Winter**	**vint**-er

Berlin U-Bahn and S-Bahn

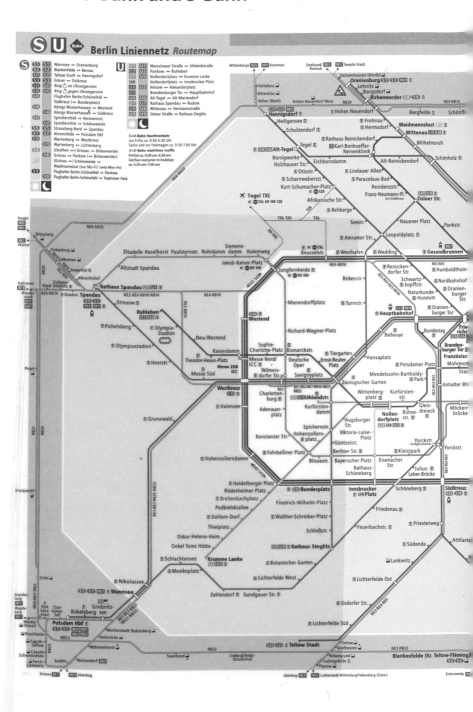